The Economic Aspect of the Abolition of the West Indian Slave Trade and Slavery

D1599108

WORLD SOCIAL CHANGE

Series Editor: Mark Selden

The Economic Aspect of the Abolition of the West Indian Slave Trade and Slavery

Eric Williams

Edited by Dale Tomich
With an Introduction by William Darity Jr.

A FERNAND BRAUDEL CENTER BOOK

ROWMAN & LITTLEFIELD
Lanham • Boulder • New York • London

Published by Rowman & Littlefield
An imprint of The Rowman & Littlefield Publishing Group, Inc.
4501 Forbes Boulevard, Suite 200, Lanham, Maryland 20706
www.rowman.com

6 Tinworth Street, London SE11 5AL, United Kingdom

British Library Cataloguing in Publication Information Available

The Library of Congress has cataloged the hardcover edition of this book as follows:

Williams, Eric Eustace, 1911-1981.
  The economic aspect of the abolition of the West Indian slave trade and slavery / Eric
Williams ; edited by Dale W. Tomich ; introduction by William Darity Jr.
     pages cm. — (World social change)
  Includes bibliographical references and index.
1. Industries--Great Britain—History. 2. Great Britain—Economic conditions. 3.
Slave trade—Great Britain. I. Tomich, Dale W., 1946- editor. II. Title.
  HC254.5.W5 2014
  382'.4409729—dc23
                                                              2013048228

ISBN 978-1-4422-3139-9 (cloth : alk. paper)
ISBN 978-1-5381-4708-5 (pbk. : alk. paper)
ISBN 978-1-4422-3140-5 (electronic)

∞™ The paper used in this publication meets the minimum requirements of
American National Standard for Information Sciences—Permanence of Paper
for Printed Library Materials, ANSI/NISO Z39.48-1992.

Contents

Bachelor's Degree: Oxford 1935

~

Preface

Dale Tomich

Distinguished West Indian historian and politician Eric Williams is perhaps best known for his *Capitalism and Slavery*, first published in 1944. The book's enduring importance lies in its comprehensive, systematic, and forceful effort to integrate the history of slavery and the history of capitalism into a unified analytical account. Williams boldly argued for the importance of slavery for the development of capitalism in Britain and for the role of industrial capitalism in creating the conditions for the abolition of the slave trade and slave emancipation. From within this framework, he counterposed economic motives and economic development to the prevailing humanitarian interpretation of British abolition. *Capitalism and Slavery* thus provides a critical account of colonialism, mercantilism, and capitalism articulated from a Caribbean perspective. *Capitalism and Slavery* remains a fundamental work of Caribbean and Atlantic history and is widely cited nearly seventy years after its publication. Beyond the study of history it has influenced international scholarship on questions of dependency, development, and the world-economy in a variety of disciplines. It is still a critical reference and continues to be the subject of scholarly controversy today.

In recent years, the controversy around *Capitalism and Slavery* has crystallized around what has come to be known as the "Williams debate." This debate has proven to be fertile ground for the new economic history. New economic historians have engaged in a broad examination of the economy of the slave trade and slavery and have interrogated the "Williams thesis" utilizing neoclassical economic theory, new techniques of analysis, and new sources of data made possible by the development of computer technology. They have produced impressive results, and their work has reshaped the study of slavery and economic history more generally. The consensus among the economic historians appears to be that Williams is incorrect. Slavery and the slave trade were profitable, and there was no economic impetus behind the abolition of the slave trade. Ironically, by invalidating the economic argument, they have resurrected the humanitarian argument and emphasize ideology and moral force as the factors behind the abolition of slavery. These results have engendered new controversy over the methods and techniques of the new economic history as well as the results that it has produced. The rejection of Williams's argument and analysis is contested, even from within the ranks of the economic historians and certainly from without.

It is against this background that the publication of *The Economic Aspect of the Abolition of the West Indian Slave Trade and Slavery* assumes renewed importance. The dissertation was defended at Oxford University in 1938. William Darity in his introduction as well as other Williams scholars have indicated the obstacles that Williams faced both in defending the dissertation and in getting it published. *Capitalism and Slavery* only came into print six years after the defense of the dissertation. For Williams, these were important years of intellectual and political development, influenced particularly by his experiences on the faculty at Howard University, further study of the entire Caribbean region, and by his voyage to Cuba, Haiti, the Dominican Republic, and Puerto Rico in 1940. When it finally appeared, *Capitalism and Slavery* was very different from the dissertation. This, of course, is not at all unusual, but in this instance, the dissertation arguably gains rather than loses significance in relation to the published work.

The Economic Aspect of the Abolition of the West Indian Slave Trade and Slavery brings three things—otherwise unavailable—to the contemporary reader. Firstly, its content is different from that of *Capitalism and Slavery*. It contains an extended analysis of slave emancipation and other questions that are not included in the later work. At the same time, none of the material concerning the role of slavery in the emergence of capitalism appears in the dissertation. Secondly, Williams's arguments are developed in greater detail and are more fully documented. The dissertation contains a wealth of information, insights, and hypotheses that will at once allow us to reinterpret *Capitalism and Slavery* and enrich current scholarship. Finally and perhaps most importantly, the dissertation gives us access to the workshop of a master historian as he comes to grips with the relation between slave abolition and emancipation, capitalist development, and imperial politics. Using the tools of his day, he asks questions and opens perspectives that are still pertinent and provocative. Indeed, his conceptual and theoretical preoccupations have become more pertinent with the passage of time.

The current "Williams debate," under pressure from the methodological assumptions and requirements of the new economic history, has subtly transmuted the terms of the discussion. Economics, politics, and ideology are increasingly separated from one another and treated as discrete and integral "factors." The "economy" is juxtaposed to "ideology" and "politics" while "capitalism," whatever we may wish to mean by it, is removed from consideration. Williams's subtle and complex argument is reduced to the question of whether or not slavery was "profitable." *The Economic Aspect of the Abolition of the West Indian Slave Trade and Slavery* allows us to recuperate Williams's efforts to construct an adequate conceptual framework for historical analysis. It forcefully reminds us that Williams understands capitalism as a complex historical relation embedded in and operating through specific political and social institutions and national and transnational geopolitical configurations. Consequently, he regards change not as the linear movement of discrete factors but as the outcome of the historically contingent and conjunctural relations and the shifting content of interrelated economic, political, and social processes. Williams is perhaps even more explicit in the dissertation than in the book that the condition for the crises of the British colonial system and British West Indian slavery were the American and Haitian revolutions and that the capitalist restructuring of economy and politics developed within the framework of transformations in Haiti, Cuba, Brazil, the United States, and the East Indies. He explores these issues more systematically and in greater detail in the dissertation than in the book.

As William Darity reminds us, *The Economic Aspect of the Abolition of the West Indian Slave Trade and Slavery* has remained an obscure document despite the prolonged and intense interest in the work of Eric Williams. It has been difficult to obtain. Those who have been able to gain access to it have read it through the optic of *Capitalism and Slavery* and mobilized it in the terms of the current debate. The dissertation does, indeed, present the same argument as the book as Darity insists, but it is a different work. The difference allows us to rethink questions that we have presumed to be resolved and to develop fresh questions, problems, and hypotheses. It offers the possibility of a much deeper renewal for issues that have lost none of their urgency.

The present text was prepared on the basis of two typed manuscript versions of the dissertation that are held at Eric Williams Memorial Collection Research Library, Archives and Museum, University of the West Indies, Trinidad and Tobago, West Indiana Collections and at the Green Library Special Collections, Florida International University, one of which had undergone more thorough copyediting. In the case of obvious misspellings or typographical errors, we have compared the two texts, and made corrections; we have also maintained, to the degree practical, much of the original formatting, but some idiosyncrasies (for instance, in abbreviations) remain. Otherwise, we left the text as it was accepted by Oxford University. In order to maintain the look and feel of the dissertation, we have retained the author's citation format. However, to facilitate publication, readability, and eventual citation the original typescript has been repaginated. We have also changed the footnote system by numbering the footnotes consecutively in each chapter. Finally, to assist the reader, we have added running heads and an index. Beyond those changes, we have endeavored to reproduce the text as it was presented for the dissertation defense.

I would like to thank Erica Williams Connell; this project would not have been possible without her generous support and encouragement. Kathleen Helenese-Paul and Maud Marie Sisnette (Eric Williams Memorial Collection Research Library, Archives and Museum, University of the West Indies, Trinidad and Tobago, West Indiana Collections) and Vicki Silvera and Chad Harris (Green Library Special Collections, Florida International University) photographed the original copies of the dissertation. Ina Brownridge and the staff of the Binghamton University Multimedia Information Technology Services put the photographs into a workable format. Amy Keough, Kelly Pueschel, and Becky Dunlop of Binghamton University's Fernand Braudel Center did a marvelous job transcribing the text. Richard E. Lee, director of the Fernand Braudel Center, was a steady source of support throughout.

The Economic Aspect of the Abolition of the West Indian Slave Trade and Slavery should have been published long ago, and we are honored to have a part in finally making it available to the public.

~

Introduction

From the Dissertation to Capitalism and Slavery: Did Williams's Abolition Thesis Change?

William Darity Jr.

"The idea that the slave trade was abolished despite the fact that it was profitable is a legend which would have surprised no one so much as the men who were chiefly responsible for the measure."

—Eric Williams

In the immediate aftermath of the riots that swept across Britain's urban centers in early August 2011, Prime Minister David Cameron indicted a "slow-motion moral collapse . . . in parts of our country" as the fundamental source of the disturbances. He contended that the rioting and looting arose out of: "Irresponsibility. Selfishness. Behaving as if your choices have no consequences. Children without fathers. Schools without discipline. Reward without effort. Crime without punishment. Rights without responsibilities. Communities without control" and constituted a "deep moral failure" across the polity. He pledged to "restore" the nation's "sense of morality" ("Cameron Blames" 2011).

Cameron's perspective invokes a mythical British Golden Age of "high morality." Precisely when that Golden Age occurred, from which the riots signaled a dramatic departure, is not transparent in the Prime Minister's remarks. Certainly the British imperial historians and their disciples have designated the parliamentary decision in 1807 to abolish the slave trade as a shining example of British national integrity, claiming that abolition was an act of humanitarian national self-sacrifice. Thus, Eric Williams's portrayal of abolition as a step taken far more out of perceived national self-interest in the context of mercantilist principles of statecraft and economic policy has constituted a sustained insult to the image of abolition as a moment of British ethical purity. Indeed, on the final page of the first part of his doctoral dissertation—the first part devoted to "The Abolition of the Slave Trade"—Williams made explicit that such a revision was exactly his intent: "By . . . giving all credit to humanity and none to sound policy a distorted view [of abolition] was presented which it is the purpose of this thesis to correct" (1938, 149). Williams's corrective was directed most forcefully at his own Oxford professor, Reginald Coupland, author of *The British Anti-Slavery Movement* (1933), who represented for Williams "a notable example" of "the deplorable tendency" among those "historians, writing a hundred years after, [who continued] to wrap the real interests in confusion" (1944, 211).

However, Coupland's position in Williams's academic career is complicated. Humberto Garcia-Muniz (2011) observes that Williams encountered great pressure to accommodate the humanitarian perspective in his dissertation from his thesis supervisor, Vincent Harlow. Garcia-Muniz also has discovered three letters written by Harlow to Williams that virtually demand that Williams capitulate to the imperial narrative. In a letter dated October 21, 1937, archived in Folder 005 in the Eric Williams Memorial Collection (hereafter EWMC) at the University of the West Indies at St. Augustine, Harlow wrote:

> You must endeavor, even though you yourself may be out of sympathy with it, to understand the tremendous dynamic force of the Evangelical Revival, which dominated the minds and thoughts of such a large section of the Nation during this period. It will require a great effort of imagination and sympathy on your part. It is not merely a question of accepting their sincerity but of *getting into their skins*. If you fail to do that, your economic facts, however true to themselves, will not be sound history, and of that account will not secure for you the D.Phil Degree. [emphasis in original]

Then in a letter dated November 15, 1937, Harlow directed Williams in the following manner (EWMC Folder 005):

> But do not forget, as I have frequently warned you, that a thesis which presents the economic aspect in isolation would be deemed by the Examiners as inadequate—and rightly so, for the economic factors must be set in their proper proportion and perspective in relation to other actuating motives if the thesis is to be true history. It will be an insufficient answer at your *Viva* [oral defense of the dissertation] if you point out that the title of your thesis is "the economic aspect" only. You are not called upon to do original research on

the humanitarian side, but you will be expected to have a sound appreciation of the character and the relative importance of that movement, and to have taken it into account in your Thesis. [emphasis in original]

Further, in a letter dated January 29, 1938, Harlow made explicit his preferred explanation for the British exit from maintenance of an enslaved population in the West Indies:

The slaves were emancipated primarily because the Nation was ashamed of a disgusting business. The idea that it might in the long run be an economic benefit was only dimly apprehended by a few; and I think that the evidence is conclusive that slavery would have been terminated even if the derivation of economic benefit had been an impossibility. Whether the Humanitarians could have got their way if the Nation as a whole had been convinced that the national economy would have been thereby seriously crippled is, of course, another matter.

Harlow, although leaving the door slightly ajar for the dominance of strategic/economic considerations in the last sentence above, appears to have been in complete sympathy with the humanitarian perspective. But Oxford thesis regulations at the time meant that the supervisor did not conduct the final oral examination. In all likelihood, Coupland was one of Williams's examiners, and, perhaps, Harlow's injunctions also were intended to prepare Williams for the types of questions he was sure to face at the *Viva*. Williams passed the examination in 1938 to earn the doctorate, so Coupland's presence as an examiner did not prove to be an insuperable obstacle. In addition, Garcia-Muniz also has uncovered evidence from both the EWMC and the Leathersellers Company archives that it was Coupland's favorable intercession in 1936 that helped procure a small grant to support Williams's graduate studies at Oxford from Sir Claud Hollis.

So why was Williams's rancor toward Coupland so much greater than it was toward Harlow or other voices in the humanitarian school? The answer may lie in the nature of their interpersonal interactions. If Coupland was paternalistic or patronizing toward the prideful Williams, that could have been the trigger for animus. Williams did note in his autobiography that after the dissertation was completed Coupland acknowledged that he had not given sufficient attention to the "economic factors" in his own work on British abolition (1969, 51).

The most sophisticated contemporary expression of the humanitarian viewpoint—indeed, the very perspective that Harlow seemed to be pushing Williams to accept—is found in the work of Seymour Drescher. His first major study on the subject was titled boldly *Econocide* to make transparent Drescher's claim that British abolition took place despite potential suicidal consequences for Britain's economy. Drescher's memorial lectures in honor of Roger Anstey, subsequently published as *Capitalism and Anti-Slavery* (1986) in an obvious backhanded homage to the title of Williams's *Capitalism and Slavery* (1944), extended his argument to explore the rise and swell of multiple ideological tides that culminated in a generalized popular assault on British involvement in the slave trade and the slave plantation system in the West Indies. In Drescher's work, it is the power of ideas and social action driven by those ideas that are the central agents of history; unlike Williams, he does not treat the emergence and tenacity of the ideas themselves as products of more fundamental factors. The distance between Drescher and Williams constitutes an epistemological gulf unlikely to be breached, regardless of the weight of evidence from the historical record.

That said, it is not coincidental that it was the late Roger Anstey who opened his critique of Williams's most famous work, *Capitalism and Slavery* (1944), with the following quotation attributed to the great imperial historian W. E. H. Lecky: "The unweary, unostentatious and inglorious crusade of England against slavery may probably be regarded as among the three or four perfectly virtuous pages comprised in the history of nations" (1968, 307). It is significant to note that Anstey—whose "use of the Lecky quotation [suggested] that there was, indeed, a long-standing claim in the British historiography of the abolition of the trade in Africans that British abolitionism was a relatively pristine affair" (Darity 1988, 29)—cites the second volume of the sixth edition of Lecky's *History of European Morals*, ostensibly published in 1884 (1968, 307n2).

Here a bit of a mystery unfolds, as I have previously recounted:

> No such edition actually exists dated 1884. Moreover, the quotation actually appeared in the first volume. The context is unclear as well. To which "crusade against slavery" is Lecky in fact referring? There is next to nothing on the Atlantic slave trade in Lecky's book. If anything he apparently was referring to the practice of slavery in Europe. The full title of Lecky's text is *A History of European Morals from Augustus to Charlemagne*, and obviously Charlemagne's reign preceded the era of the Atlantic slave trade. But most important, in another work where Lecky explicitly addressed the causes of the abolition of the Atlantic slave trade, his position was striking similar to Williams'! (Darity 1988, 29)

Nevertheless, Howard Temperley repeats this same quotation (albeit in mild paraphrase) in his review of David Brion Davis's *Inhuman Bondage* to make the same point—that British abolition was primarily the product of a humanitarian movement that transcended more parochial concerns about national self-interest:

> In his *History of European Morals from Augustus to Charlemagne* (1869), W. E. H. Lecky describes England's crusade against slavery as "among three or four perfectly virtuous acts recorded in the history of nations." Great powers do not as a rule behave selflessly. Not surprisingly, Lecky's comment has generally been regarded with skepticism. Now, knowing vastly more than he did about slavery and its abolition, Davis believes Lecky was basically right. Although the American abolition movement came later and assumed a somewhat different character, the same might equally well be said of it. Slaves had never liked being slaves, but the rise of a climate of opinion that objected to slavery on moral grounds was something new. There had been nothing like it in ancient or medieval times or in any other society of which we have record. The upsurge of popular support for abolition both in Britain and the northern USA was unprecedented. Perhaps, David Brion Davis hypothesizes, moral progress is possible (2006).

Apart from whether "moral progress is possible," the question raised in Eric Williams's *Capitalism and Slavery* is whether "moral progress" was the decisive factor shaping British abolition. Certainly Lecky's quotation, progressively transformed into a bromide for the humanitarian school, if interpreted accurately indicates that there had been an antislavery movement prior to British or American abolition of the trade in Africans—but it was a movement to end the enslavement (or "enserfment") of Europeans by other Europeans.

The "Williams debate," the controversy sparked by Eric Williams's *Capitalism and Slavery*, extends beyond the dispute over the causes of British abolition. Williams also advanced another hypothesis, a theory of British industrialization predicated on the centrality of the slave trade and slavery to the rise of the manufacturing sector in Britain in the late eighteenth century. Thus, Williams combined with some subtlety two arguments that might, at first blush, seem incompatible. First, he argued that the slave trade and slavery in the West Indies were the vital props that spurred the rise of British industry. Second, he argued that because the slave trade and slavery no longer were of economic and strategic importance to Britain, abolition became viable. For consistency, Williams had to demonstrate that there was a transition in the position of the West Indies plantations from critical sites for British mercantilism to locations of subordinate value. The mediating events that led to the diminution of the importance of the slave trade and, eventually, slavery in the British colonies were the American and Haitian

Revolutions. The Haitian Revolution proved to be the linchpin of Williams's argument about the non-humanitarian basis for abolition.

In addition, there is a third major hypothesis in *Capitalism and Slavery* (1944, 7–29), more briefly developed than the other two, that has been another source of contention. Williams explicitly argued that antiblack or anti-African racism was a consequence of the Atlantic slave trade rather than a cause. The African "pool" of forced laborers was not drawn upon because of a preexisting European animus toward Africans but because the African source promised the greatest profitability: "Here, then, is the origin of Negro slavery. The reason was economic, not racial; it had not to do with the color of the laborer, but the cheapness of the labor" (Williams 1944, 19). Williams encapsulated this third hypothesis in the following terse but powerful phrase: "Slavery was not born of racism; rather, racism was the consequence of slavery" (1944, 7).

In sum, *Capitalism and Slavery* is a provocative study of the impact of the slave trade and slavery on British economic development, the roots of British abolition of the slave trade, and the origins of antiblack racism. It is a project that integrates Caribbean history, the history of slavery in the Americas, the history of Africa and the slave trade, the history of the Atlantic economy, and the history of European economic growth.

However, the scope of Williams's doctoral dissertation, running at more than 400 typewritten pages, was limited to the single hypothesis concerning British abolition of the slave trade and eventually abolition of slavery or emancipation. The thesis was entitled "The Abolition of the West Indian Slave Trade and Slavery." While much fuller development is given to the causes of abolition of the slave trade than the causes of emancipation in *Capitalism and Slavery*, the dissertation devotes equal parts to each phase of the decline of direct British participation in Atlantic slavery. Indeed, the detailed examination of the conditions leading to emancipation in the dissertation is largely absent from *Capitalism and Slavery*.

Emancipation—albeit approximately thirty years after abolition—is a subsidiary event to abolition of the trade in *Capitalism and Slavery*. It is in the second half of the dissertation that Williams presents his analysis of emancipation, particularly chapter 11, "The Distressed Areas," and chapter 12, "The Industrialists and Emancipation," and where readers will find a lode of fascinating material that did not make its way into *Capitalism and Slavery*. Unlike his thesis supervisor, Vincent Harlow, Williams does not treat abolition of the slave trade and emancipation of the slaves as events linked by a singular chain of causation from the rise of the Evangelicalism in the late eighteenth century. For Williams, the factors leading to each are distinctive, requiring their respective sections of the dissertation. As will be suggested below, Williams also may have made a strategic decision in the construction of the two sections to enable him to placate his examiners' desires that he demonstrate, in Harlow's words, "a sound appreciation of the character and relative importance of [the humanitarian] movement."

Despite substantial differences in scope and detail, *Capitalism and Slavery* is often regarded as a "revised version" of Williams's doctoral dissertation (Martin 2008, 97). The dissertation, while playing an important role in the phase of the Williams debate over abolition of the trade, has not been published before now. It has maintained an existence in a sort of academic limbo, mobilized at the convenience of protagonists on both sides of the debate. The dissertation is also presumed to be the locus classicus of Williams's analysis of British abolition—an analysis that gives greatest weight to the pecuniary and strategic factors that lay at the heart of the Parliament's vote to end the legality of the slave trade in 1807.

Williams could not procure an academic post in Britain, nor could he find a British publisher who would commit to bringing his dissertation into print. Indeed, the late Walter Minchinton reports that Williams failed to place the work with six different publishers (1983). Instead, by mid-1939, he had become an assistant professor of social and political science at Howard University in Washington, DC, and, by 1944, finally published the "revised version" of the dissertation with the University of North Carolina (UNC) Press as the now famous study, *Capitalism and Slavery*. That was no easy task; in his introduction to the fiftieth anniversary edition of *Capitalism and Slavery*, Colin Palmer (1994, xi–xvii) chronicles the difficult path Williams had to take even to bring publication to fruition with UNC Press.

Subsequent to publication of *Capitalism and Slavery*, the dissertation effectively disappeared from public view. In fact, it has become a near spectral document invoked at opportune moments by those few scholars who have managed to access it from a handful of university repositories. Howard Temperley has suggested that the dissertation, despite its title, is more balanced, more temperate, and devoid of the economic determinism that he complains characterizes *Capitalism and Slavery* (1987; see also Drescher 1987, 183–84). Indeed, Temperley (1987) argues that the famous Williams abolition thesis really is absent from *The Economic Aspects of the West Indian Slave Trade and Slavery*. In short, for Temperley, *Capitalism and Slavery* constitutes a transgression from the more considered attention given to the strength of the humanitarian school's arguments in the dissertation. Indeed, for Temperley, the dissertation is more Temperley than Williams!

I demur. There is no significant difference between the abolition thesis presented in the dissertation and in *Capitalism and Slavery*; while the dissertation, unsurprisingly, is more subdued in tone and less colorful rhetorically—it is, after all, a *dissertation*—the substance of the analysis is identical:

> The dissertation [presents] an equally forceful statement of the main ideas of *Capitalism and Slavery*. Chapter 7 entitled "The Abolition of the Slave Trade" provides a detailed accounting of the economic factors in abolition—especially the split in the ranks of the anti-abolitionists due to rivalry between older British islands and newly conquered ones, the economic distress of the British West Indies, and the fall in the relative importance of the slave trade to London, Bristol, and even Liverpool [133–135]. At that stage Williams [137] writes, "It was absurd, with the great increase in industry and trade, to speak of abolition as likely to prove ruinous to the country or any one port." The early 19th century was not the world of mid-18th century when, Williams argued, the slave trade was vital to British economic growth. Williams concludes that "economics reinforced humanity" at the point when abolition was adopted: "Wilberforce's outlook was intensely religious, but Parliament was converted not by the truths of religion and the principles of humanity but by economics." (Darity 1988, 39–40n5)

Even here, Williams (1938, 151–53) cautions, the abolitionists' case in the latter part of the eighteenth century and the early nineteenth century was solely against the slave trade; they were vigilant in distancing themselves from a case for slave emancipation. In an apparent concession to the humanitarian school, perhaps in deference to Harlow's warning about the requirements for a successful *Viva*, Williams observes on page 151 of the thesis—with respect to emancipation (*not* abolition)—that: "It would be . . . a mistake to underestimate the humanitarian forces. The Government was subjected to the pressures of strong economic interests tending towards emancipation, but it would give a distorted view not to realize the powerful role played by the humanitarians, which in this particular question assumed the proportions of a national crusade."

On the question of slave emancipation, Williams apparently was willing to acknowledge a more significant role for the impact of a morally driven anti-slavery movement than he was willing to acknowledge with respect to abolition. But even emancipation, in the last instance, was a decision reached where material imperatives prevailed. The emergence of East India sugar as an alternative to slave-grown West Indian sugar, the growing numbers of slave rebellions in the West Indies, the ready access via trade to slave-grown produce (coffee from Brazil, sugar from Cuba, cotton from the United

States) in countries outside of the British empire, the rising industrialists' opposition to "monopolies" (including the monopoly in the sugar trade held by the West Indians), and the continued diminution in importance of the West Indies to British metropolitan economic growth, all made it easy by 1833 to take the "moral" high ground toward emancipation of slaves in the British colonies (Williams 1938, 274–337). Again, even with respect to the question of slave emancipation, in the thesis, the "economic factors" carried the decisive weight over the "moral factors."

The critical consistency between the dissertation and *Capitalism and Slavery* is over the treatment of William Pitt the Younger and Saint Domingue (present-day Haiti) in the context of Williams's analysis of abolition of the slave trade. Inspired by C. L. R. James's discussion of the British response to the Haitian slave revolt on pages 38–41 of James's *Black Jacobins* (1938), Williams is explicit about the influence in the annotated bibliography of *Capitalism and Slavery* (1944, 268), and he crafts a narrative in *Capitalism and Slavery* that argues that, had Pitt been successful in his efforts to capture Saint Domingue in the aftermath of the slave revolt, Britain's commitment to the slave trade would have continued indefinitely:

> Fearful that the idealism of the revolutionary movement would destroy the slave trade and slavery, the French planters of Saint Domingue in 1791 offered the island to England, and were soon followed by those of the Windward Islands. Pitt accepted the offer, when war broke out with France in 1793. Expedition after expedition was sent unsuccessfully to capture the precious colony, first from French, then from the Negroes. . . . Britain lost thousands of men and spent thousands of pounds in an attempt to capture Saint Domingue. She failed, but the world's sugar bowl was destroyed in the process and French colonial superiority smashed forever. . . . This is of more than academic interest. Pitt could not have had Saint Domingue and abolition as well. Without its 40,000 slave imports a year, Saint Domingue might as well have been at the bottom of the sea. (Williams 1944, 148–49)

David Geggus disagrees:

> Radicalism, damagingly linked to abolitionism, spread rapidly in Britain; the French monarchy was overthrown, the slave revolution in Saint Domingue remained unquelled. Suddenly, war with France became likely, and therefore a campaign for the West Indies. Henceforth, [Minister of War Henry] Dundas and [Prime Minister] Pitt, though he continued to speak for the cause in parliament, grew lukewarm in its support. The occupation of Saint Domingue, Williams argues, logically meant the end of Pitt's interest in abolition and proved the materialist nature of his motivation. This does not necessarily

follow. Pitt could indeed "have had Saint Domingue and abolition as well." The two might actually have complemented each other, both compensating amply for the decline in British production and ensuring that fewer Africans were enslaved. (1981, 293)

The resolution lies in whether Pitt and his cabinet intended, upon capturing Saint Domingue, to restore it to its productive heights as the world's most fertile sugar bowl or to destroy it altogether. If the former was the objective, Pitt could not have had both Saint Domingue and abolition. If the latter, he certainly could have had both, but his motives for abolition still would bear the taint of national self-interest rather than the purity of a humanitarian impulse.

Williams did argue that prior to abolition the British colonies in the West Indies were in economic decline, largely due to the shock created by the interruption of their customary trade networks by the American Revolution. The "decline thesis" has drawn particular fire from Drescher (1977, 1987) as a facet of his wider attack on Williams's abolition hypothesis. Drescher argues that the decline of the British West Indies was precipitated by abolition; prior to abolition of the slave trade, he contends, the islands were prosperous. Selwyn Carrington (2003), without pitching into the fight over the abolition debate, has provided a persuasive challenge to Drescher's case, arguing that the British West Indies were in economic distress before abolition, as has David Beck Ryden (2001).

But the case for *non-humanitarian* motives for British abolition can be sustained independently of whether the decline thesis is upheld or rejected. Suppose the primary objective of abolition was to gut the French colonies that had become ferocious competitors in the world market for raw sugar, particularly Saint Domingue. It was transparent that British slavers were a major source of slave labor for Saint Domingue and the rival French colonies. Even if the British colonies were not in decline, they certainly were being eclipsed competitively by the French sugar islands. Abolition might hurt the British West Indies, but the damage to the French colonies would be even greater, since they required much larger annual importations of slaves.

Alternatively, Britain could capture the French islands for herself and take one of two steps: drive them to ruin by denying them new imports directly or capture them and sustain their production by keeping the slave trade active. Neither of those options necessarily would be dictated by the economic performance or importance of the British sugar islands. Neither would the degree of prosperity of the British West Indies necessarily establish their relative importance for the British imperial project toward the end of the eighteenth century. It is not the decline or prosperity of the British West

Indies that lies at the heart of Eric Williams's abolition narrative; *it is the control and conquest of Saint Domingue that is the centerpiece of Eric Williams's abolition narrative.*

Moreover, whether or not Williams had gotten the story right, the question to be resolved here is whether this is the same story of abolition he tells in the dissertation. The answer is unequivocally yes. In fact, it is told in greater detail in the dissertation, particularly in chapter 6, entitled "The Significance of the West Indian Expeditions." Consider the following passages from the chapter that demonstrate the intimate parallel with the abolition thesis in *Capitalism and Slavery*:

> It is impossible to understand the great efforts made by Britain to acquire St. Domingo, the lives and money lost, unless one has grasped the essential point of the superiority of the French sugar islands. In the words of Professor Holland Rose, "when five or six valuable islands were to be had, to all appearances with little risk except from the slaves, ministers would have been craven in the extreme not to push on an enterprise which projected to benefit British commerce and cripple that of France." Would later historians, one wonders, have condemned the expeditions had they been successful? (Williams 1938, 113)

> The very structure of St. Domingo imperatively demanded the continuance of the slave trade. By 1789 St. Domingo needed 40,000 slaves a year. No offer of St. Domingo would have been made to Britain by French colonial planters, infuriated by the mere fear that the National Assembly would interfere with the basic structure of the colonial system, unless those planters were convinced that Britain would not herself do the same and would not abolish the slave trade. . . . Without the 40,000 slaves a year the great colony would have been useless to its owners. (Williams 1938, 114)

> It was this very necessity to continue slavery and with it the slave trade—for St. Domingo could not exist without it—which was the decisive political factor in the conflict. We have seen that the declaration abolishing slavery by the revolutionary commissioners in St. Domingo was a bid for black support against the aristocratic white planters supported by Britain. (Williams 1938, 116)

Intriguingly, Williams actually quotes Lecky, the architect of the vaunted "virtuous pages" quotation, to demonstrate Pitt's duplicitous support for abolition while seeking to capture Saint Domingue:

> The full extent of Pitt's defection from the cause can be seen from the discussions on the prohibition of the slave trade to the conquered French and British colonies. Lecky condemns Pitt strongly for this. "It was in the power of Pitt,"

he writes, "by an Order of Council to prevent it, but he refused to take this course. It was a political and commercial object to strengthen these new acquisitions, and as they had so long been prevented from supplying themselves with negroes, they were ready to take more than usual. The result was that, in consequence of the British conquests, and under the shelter of the British flag, the slave trade became more active than ever. . . . It was computed that under his administration the English slave trade more than doubled, and that the number of negroes imported annually in English ships rose from 25,000 to 57,000." (1938, 121)

Elsewhere in Lecky's *History of England in the Eighteenth Century*, he sustains his distinctly unflattering portrait of Pitt as the great obstructionist for abolition while mouthing his support for the cause (1918, 342–44). Had the expeditions been effective in capturing the French islands, especially Saint Domingue, Lecky himself suggests that abolition might have been postponed long beyond 1807. Nonetheless, they failed—beaten back by Haiti's ex-slaves and yellow fever; still Lecky finds himself in agreement with James Stephen that it was necessary for Pitt to die, prematurely, for abolition to become a reality. Apparently Lecky was more Williams than Temperley.

Indeed, without Pitt on the scene *and without Saint Domingue in British hands*, Williams concludes in the dissertation that "by 1807 the whole situation had undergone such a transformation that now it was not only the leaders, but even the dwarfs and pigmies, who favored abolition" (1938, 133).

In an exchange in January 2012 in the *New York Review of Books*, Barbara Solow concludes that "the insights Eric Williams displayed in *Capitalism and Slavery* are alive and well," while David Brion Davis maintains that the Williams abolition hypothesis "has been undermined by a vast mountain of empirical evidence and has been repudiated by the world's leading authorities on New World slavery, the transatlantic slave trade, and the British abolition movement." Apart from the question addressed above of whether Williams in the dissertation is the same Williams in *Capitalism and Slavery*, Solow and Davis are examining whether Williams did get the abolition story right. Solow says he did; Davis says he did not—based upon the weight of the findings of unnamed "leading authorities." The focus of their exchange hinges on the accuracy of the West Indian decline thesis.

But Eric Williams's abolition thesis rests on the implications of British efforts to reconquer Saint Domingue and bring it under the empire. It is the Haitian Revolution and the British response that subverts the argument that British abolition was primarily a matter of the successes of a movement motivated by humanitarian impulses. As Williams would have had it, both in the pages of his doctoral dissertation and in the pages of *Capitalism and Slavery*, humanitarianism was merely the glove cloaking the icy calculus of British imperialism.

Works Cited

"Cameron Blames UK Riots on 'Moral Collapse.'" 2011. CNN, August 15. http://news.blogs.cnn.com/2011/08/15/cameron-blames-uk-riots-on-moral-collapse.html (accessed June 25, 2012).

Carrington, Selwyn H. H. 2003. *The Sugar Industry and the Abolition of the Slave Trade, 1775–1810*. Gainesville: University of Florida Press.

Coupland, Reginald. 1964. *The British Anti-Slavery Movement*. (Orig. 1933.) New York: Barnes and Noble.

Darity, William, Jr. 1988. "The Williams Abolition Thesis before Williams." *Slavery and Abolition* 9 (1): 29–41.

Davis, David Brion. 2006. *Inhuman Bondage: The Rise and Fall of Slavery in the New World*. Oxford: Oxford University Press.

———. 2012. "The British and the Slave Trade: Reply to Barbara Solow." *New York Review of Books*, January 12. http://www.nybooks.com/articles/archives/2012/jan/12/british-slave-trade (accessed June 28, 2012).

Drescher, Seymour. 1977. *Econocide: British Slavery in the Era of Abolition*. Pittsburgh: University of Pittsburgh Press.

———. 1986. *Capitalism and Anti-Slavery: British Mobilization in Comparative Perspective*. London: Macmillan.

———. 1987. "Eric Williams: British Capitalism and British Slavery." *History and Theory* 26 (2): 180–96.

Garcia-Muniz, Humberto. 2011. "Eric Williams and C. L. R. James: Simbiosis intelectual y contrapunto ideologico," unpubl. ms.

Geggus, David. 1981. "The British Government and the Saint Domingue Slave Revolt, 1791–1793." *English Historical Review* 96 (379): 285–395.

James, C. L. R. 1938. *The Black Jacobins: Toussaint L'Ouverture and the San Domingo Revolution*. New York: Dial.

Lecky, W. E. H. 1911. *A History of European Morals from Augustus to Charlemagne*. 2 vols., 5th ed. London: Watts.

———. 1918. *A History of England in the Eighteenth Century*. Vol. 5. London: Longmans, Green.

Martin, Tony. 2008. "Williams, Eric." In *International Encyclopedia of the Social Sciences*, vol. 9, ed. William Darity Jr., 96–98. Detroit: Thomson Gale (Macmillan Reference).

Minchinton, Walter. 1983. "Williams and Drescher: Abolition and Emancipation." *Slavery and Abolition* 4 (2): 81–105.

Palmer, Colin. 1994. Introduction to *Capitalism and Slavery*, by Eric Williams, xi–xxii. Chapel Hill: University of North Carolina Press.

Ryden, David Beck. 2001. "Does Decline Make Sense? The West Indian Economy and the Abolition of the British Slave Trade." *Journal of Interdisciplinary History* 31 (3): 347–74.

Solow, Barbara L. 2012. "The British and the Slave Trade: Reply to David Brion Davis." *New York Review of Books*, January 12. http://www.nybooks.com/articles/archives/2012/jan/12/british-slave-trade (accessed June 28, 2012).

Temperley, Howard. 1997. "Eric Williams and British Abolition: The Birth of a New Orthodoxy." In *British Capitalism and Caribbean Slavery*, ed. Barbara L. Solow and Stanley Engerman. Cambridge: Cambridge University Press.

———. 2006. "The Abolition of Slavery." *Times Literary Supplement*, June 21. http://tls.timesonline.co.uk/article/0,,25340-2236229,00.html.

"UK Riots: David Cameron Promises to Restore 'Sense of Morality' as Police Get New Powers." 2011. *Daily Telegraph*, August 11. http://www.telegraph.co.uk/news/uknews/crime/8695318/UK-riots-police-get-new-powers.html.

Williams, Eric. 1938. "The Economic Aspect of the Abolition of West Indian Slave Trade and Slavery." PhD diss., Modern History, Oxford University.

———. 1966. *Inward Hunger: The Education of a Prime Minister*. Chicago: University of Chicago Press.

———. 1994. *Capitalism and Slavery*. (Orig. 1944.) Chapel Hill: University of North Carolina Press.

Archival Materials

Eric Williams Memorial Collection, University of the West Indies at St. Augustine.

THE ECONOMIC ASPECT

of the

ABOLITION of the

WEST INDIAN SLAVE TRADE AND SLAVERY

by

Eric Williams, B.A.

———————

Thesis submitted to the Board of
the Faculty of Modern History of
the University of Oxford for the
Degree of Doctor of Philosophy

———————

THE ECONOMIC ASPECT

of the

ABOLITION of the

WEST INDIAN SLAVE TRADE AND SLAVERY

by

Eric Williams, B.A.

———

Thesis submitted to the Board of
the Faculty of Modern History of
the University of Oxford for the
Degree of Doctor of Philosophy.

——— OXFORD, 1938.

Contents

Introduction

Many powerful writers in the past, for instance, Locke, Montesquieu and Rousseau, had brought their batteries to bear on the citadel of the slave trade and slavery, but their appeals were isolated and intellectual. Dr. Johnson might inveigh against the slave-driving American colonists, uttering "the loudest yelps for liberty,"[1] and propose toasts to the next insurrection in the West Indies. But the abolitionists were fighting against powerful vested interests with an economic stake in the maintenance of the slave trade and the perpetuation of slavery. These interests they had, if not to win over, at least to neutralise, by all the arguments in their power, humanitarian, religious or economic; and it too often happened, as we shall have ample occasion to see, that they were forced to accept the assistance of men who were actuated by the more sordid motives of gain and self-interest, and whose adhesion to the abolition campaign did much to sully the "bona fides" of the humanitarian group. These are the motives which this study proposes to treat.

The American rebellion was a factor of decisive importance in Caribbean history: for the British West Indies it was the "*fons et origo*" of a battalion of sorrows. It was the possession of North America which had ensured the inferiority of the foreign islands. The British West Indies found themselves after 1783 with no United States to depend upon, except by indirect means which

---

1. Compare, however, Franklin, writing from London in 1772 on the Somerset case—by which slaves were declared free in Great Britain and Ireland only—of "the hypocrisy of this country which encourages such a detestable commerce by laws for promoting the Guinea trade; while it piqued itself on its virtue, love of liberty, and the equity of its courts in setting free a single negro."

were bound to increase the price of their requirements.[2] The liberal free trade principle which regulated the relations between Britain and the United States was not extended to the British West Indies, despite the pleas of Pitt and Adam Smith.[3] As Chalmers bluntly said, "it cannot be surely inferred that 72,000 masters with 400,000 slaves form a community of sufficient bulk to whose gratifications the interest and even independence of the nation ought to be sacrificed."[4] The Americans, therefore, turned increasingly to the foreign islands, despite the strict mercantilism of the French, and before the French Revolution the contraband trade with them reached vast proportions. A sop was thrown to the British islands in the form of an extension of the free port system.[5] But the loss of America could not be tided over at all. In 1792–1793 American exports to the British West Indies were $1,855,307, while British exports for 1793 were £4,339,613; by 1795–1796 the American figures had almost trebled, being $5,446,559, while the British had declined by one half, to £2,176,433.[6]

American Independence revealed the inherent insignificance and insufficiency of the British islands, and is the key to the new orientations of British policy. Added to this, the withdrawal of the thirteen states considerably diminished the number of slaves in the Empire, and abolition was easier after 1783 than it would have been if the American colonies had not seceded. "Indeed," wrote Clarkson, "among the various events, that seem for some

---

2. B.T. 6/75. West Indies, 1786–1790. Gov. Lincoln of St. Vincent, Dec. 1, 1785—at the Dutch free port of St. Eustatius British planters bought American products at nearly 50 to 100 per cent dearer; "while the planter is compelled to give an exorbitant price for these necessary articles, the Americans find nearly the same demand as formerly, and consequently are only irritated, not injured, by the restrictions contained in the Proclamation." Prices in the West Indies went up as much as from 50 to 100 per cent on the very first publication of the Order in Council of July 1783, though they fell later. (*H. C. Bell: British Commercial Policy in the West Indies, 1783–1795.* English Historical Review, July, 1916, pages 437–438).

3. *Bell, op. cit.*, page 434. Adam Smith thought that "any interruptions or restraint of commerce would hurt our loyal much more than our revolted subjects." Strangely enough, whilst arguing against any "extraordinary either encouragement or discouragement . . . to the trade of any country more than to that of another . . . (as in every case a complete piece of dupery," he declared that he had little anxiety about what became of American commerce and visualized a trade with the neighbouring European nations infinitely more advantageous than that of so distant a country as America. *The Journal and Correspondence of William, Lord Auckland* (London, 1861), Vol. I, pages 64–65. Smith to Eden, Dec. 15, 1783. (Referred to hereafter as *Auckland Journal.*)

4. G. *Chalmers: Opinions on Interesting Subjects of public law and commercial policy; arising from American Independence* (London, 1784), page 60.

5. B.T. 6/103. Governor Orde from Dominica, Feb. 20, 1784. "The people look with uncommon anxiety for the arrival of a freeport act." Petitions from the various islands that the ports should be opened were so numerous that Lord Hawkesbury was "apprehensive that every port in our West India islands will apply to be made a free port from a sense of the great advantages to be derived therefrom." *Liverpool Papers*, Add. Mss. 38228, folio 324. Feb. 1793.

6. W. H. *Elkins: British Policy in its relation to the commerce and navigation of the U.S.A., 1794–1807.* (Oxford D. Phil. Thesis), page 96.

time to have been hastening on, and working together for the abolition of the slave trade, none appears to be of greater importance in this respect, than the revolution before mentioned.[7] As long as America was our own, there was no chance that a minister would have attended to the groans of the sons and daughters of Africa, however he might feel for their distress. From the same spot, which was once thus the means of creating an insuperable impediment to the relief of these unfortunate people, our affection, by a wonderful concatenation of events, has been taken off, and a prospect presented to our view, which shows it to be a *policy* to remove their pain."[8]

Up to 1783 the British Government publicly supported the slave trade. We may take three specific instances of the encouragement given to it. In December 1773 the Jamaica Assembly imposed a duty on every imported slave of ten shillings, increased by a further forty shillings in February 1774.[9] The Board of Trade, on the representation of the merchants of London, Bristol and Liverpool, condemned the law as unjustifiable, improper and prejudicial to British commerce, and, in reply to the objections of the agent for the island that Jamaica had an unquestionable right to judge of the ways and means of raising supplies for the public service, pointed out that legislative autonomy in the colonies did not extend to the imposition of duties upon British ships and goods or to the prejudice and obstruction of British commerce. But as the act was due to expire at the end of the year, the Board merely recommended that additional instructions should be issued to the Governor, charging him, upon pain of removal, not to assent on any pretence to any such act in the future. At the end of the year, however, to raise money to pay the troops and to minimise, moreover, the fear of servile rebellions—proved by experience to be caused in the main by old Negroes—, the Jamaica Legislature repeated its offence and passed an act imposing a duty of fifty shillings on every imported slave. The Governor was severely reprimanded for assenting to the act in direct contradiction to his instructions. He was blamed for failing in his duty to the merchants of Britain and for not stopping efforts made to "check and discourage a traffic which, however beneficial to the nation, is, with respect to the individuals who are engaged in it, attended with peculiar hazard and difficulty."[10]

---

7. i.e., the American revolution.

8. *T. Clarkson: Essay on the Impolicy of the African Slave Trade* (London, 1788), page 34. (Referred to hereafter as *Clarkson: Impolicy.*)

9. The whole duty, let it be noted, was to be returned in case of re-exportation.

10. H. of C. Sess. Pap., *Accounts & Papers,* 1795–1796. A. and P. 42, Series No. 100, Document 848, pages 1–21. *J. F. Barham: Observations on the Abolition of Negro Slavery* (London, 1823), page 26, emphasized that the first acts restricting the trade came from the colonies.

In 1774 and 1775 premature bills for abolition had been rejected offhand by Parliament. In 1783, the Quakers, who had already freed their slaves,[11] took advantage of a bill before the House of Commons, prohibiting the servants of the African Committee from engaging in the slave trade, to petition against the trade in general. Lord North complimented the Quakers on their humanity, but confessed that it would be almost impossible to abolish the slave trade, which had, in some measure, become necessary to almost every nation in Europe.[12]

Finally, the Governor of St. Vincent was instructed in October 1783 not to assent to any act imposing duties on Negroes imported or exported, provided the latter had not been in the island for the space of twelve months.[13] The instructions were repeated in June 1787 to the Governors of Grenada and Dominica as well as St. Vincent.[14]

Opponents of abolition always harped on this theme, the former sanctions given to the trade.[15] "In every variation," said Law, counsel for the defence before the House of Lords, "of our administration of public affairs, in every variation of parties, the policy, in respect to that trade, has been the same." Referring to the idea of abolition as "the conceits of enthusiasts and visionary people," he declared that the grievance seemed so intolerable and the wickedness so enormous that it may well have been thought that the men of the past, if they had the common sense and feelings and justice of men, would have revolted at it, as it was suggested that all reasonable and virtuous persons then ought to revolt.[16] The Duke of Clarence reminded the House of Lords in 1799 how Burke had written in the strongest terms against the impolicy of the peace of 1763, because Britain had neglected to supply not only the Spaniards but even the French with Negroes.[17] The Earl of Westmorland indignantly declared that the trade had been carried on for a number of years under the ablest ministers Britain had ever seen, who never thought of abolishing it;[18] while Hibbert, agent for Jamaica, fighting gamely at the last ditch, reminded the House that it ill became a member of the Parliament of a country which had pocketed the gains from the slave trade to stigmatise it as a crime.[19]

11. *Adam Smith: The Wealth of Nations* (London, 1796), Vol. III, page 89, is perhaps unfair in saying that "the late resolution of the Quakers in Pennsylvania to set at liberty all their negro slaves may satisfy us that their number cannot be very great."
12. *Parl. Hist.*, Vol. XXIII, pages 1026–1027. June 17, 1783. A petition from Bridgewater in 1785 was rejected.
13. C.O. 319/3, page 37. Instructions to Governors, 1783–1794.
14. Ibid., pages 125 and 234.
15. For the West Indian emphasis on the encouragement given by Britain to the slave trade, see Barham, *op. cit.*, page 26 and *Quarterly Review*, Vol. XXXII, 1825, page 507.
16. Add. Mss. 12433, folios 13 and 19. May 14, 1792.
17. *Parl. Hist.*, Vol. XXXIII, page 1094. July 5, 1799.
18. *Parl. Deb.*, Vol. VII, page 230. May 16, 1806.
19. Ibid., Vol. IX, page 127. March. 16, 1807.

In 1787, Pitt, in the presence of Grenville, urged Wilberforce to give notice of a motion on the slave trade, warning him that if time were lost, he might be forestalled.[20] By this time it was no longer possible for anyone to think, with Queen Elisabeth's naiveté, that the trade could be carried on without proving detrimental to the natives of Africa. As Ramsay put it, "that several worthy men have been concerned in this trade, and have without thought been guilty of barbarous oppression and multiplied murders in the course of it, is with real sorrow to be acknowledged. It can only be said, that they had never examined the nature of this commerce and went into it, and acted as others had done before them in it, as a thing of course, for which no account was to be given in this world or the next: but no man concerned in this trade can now pretend ignorance of the oppression and cruelty attending it."[21] With the humanitarianism and feelings of equality which were coming in with Rousseau, the Declaration of Independence, the Rights of Man and Methodism, a new attitude to the slave trade was manifested. In Clarkson's words, such a trade could have as its supporters only those who were influenced by interested motives.[22] This thesis will show the powerful searchlight brought to bear upon the slave trade, revealing all its economic disadvantages. It was seen to be a trade which "destroys our seamen annually by thousands, makes bankrupts of four out of five of those concerned in it, and is chiefly applied to the improvement of the French sugar colonies,"[23] and the West Indians, indebted to the enormous sum of 20 millions, could be challenged "on any principle to prove that any new system would involve them so deep as that on which they had hitherto proceeded."[24]

20. R. Coupland: Wilberforce (Oxford, 1923), page 93. Their selection was no doubt influenced, as Granville Sharp's was, by the consideration that "the respectability of his position as member of the largest county (Yorkshire), the great influence of his personal connexions, added to an amiable and unblemished character (would) secure every advantage to the cause." R. I. and S. Wilberforce: The Life of William Wilberforce (London, 1838), Vol. I, page 153. (Referred to hereafter as Life of Wilberforce.) It was this same canon of respectability which made French abolitionists like La Fayette regret the sponsorship of the cause in France by the brilliant but dissolute Mirabeau and made them prefer the virtuous La Rochefoucauld. T. Clarkson: History of the Rise, Progress and Accomplishment of the Abolition of the Slave Trade (London, 1839), page 394. (Referred to hereafter as Clarkson: History.)

21. J. Ramsay: A Ms. Vol. entirely in his own hand, mainly concerned with his activities towards the Abolition of the Slave Trade, 1787 (Rhodes House), folio 65. "An Address on the proposed bill for the Abolition of the Slave Trade." (Referred to hereafter as Ramsay: Ms. Vol.)

22. Clarkson: History, page 613.

23. Ramsay: Ms. Vol., folio 23. "Memorial on the supplying of the Navy with Seamen."

24. Parl. Hist., Vol. XXIX, page 260. Wilberforce, Apl. 18, 1791. A Report prepared by a Committee of the House of Assembly of Jamaica, Nov. 23, 1792, stated that in the course of twenty years, 177 estates had been sold for the payment of debts, 55 had been thrown up, and 92 were still in the hands of creditors, while 80,121 executions, amounting to £22,563,786 sterling, had been lodged in the office of the Provost Marshal.

PART I

THE ABOLITION
OF THE SLAVE TRADE

Instead of being very advantageous to Great Britain, this trade is the most destructive that can well be imagined to her interests.

—William Pitt, April 2, 1792.

CHAPTER ONE

The Impolicy of the Slave System

An American historian, speaking of John Wesley's attitude to the slave trade, says that Wesley "discusses the economic aspects of slave labour knowing, as did most of the men that came after him, that if he could prove the impolicy of the whole system, his battle would be half won. Statesmen might be unwilling to rid England of what was merely a moral crime, but would be ready to correct a mistake, following out Talleyrand's maxim 'a mistake is worse than a crime!'"[1] Those who could not be persuaded to abolish the inhuman traffic on the purer grounds of humanity and morality must be convinced, if that was the only language they could understand, that the trade was not merely degrading but unprofitable, and that the abolition would not be followed by the ruin which its opponents predicted.

At the very first meeting, May 22, 1787, of the Committee instituted for the purpose of abolishing the slave trade, it was resolved that the trade was both impolitic and unjust.[2] Clarkson, touring England in 1788 in his search for evidence, reported to the Abolition Committee the demands he had met with for his own pamphlet on "The Impolicy of the Slave Trade" and the great good it had already done, and suggested a third edition, giving permission for an unlimited number without any royalties to himself.[3] The

---

1. F. J. Klingberg: *The Anti-Slavery Movement in England* (Newhaven, 1926), pages 46–47.
2. *Proceedings of the Committee for Abolition of the Slave Trade. 1787–1819.* (Referred to hereafter as *Abolition Committee's Proceedings.*) Add. Mss. 21254, folio 2.
3. Ibid., Add. Mss. 21255, folio 62. Oct. 7, 1788. Clarkson was given £200 for the second edition. He sent a copy of the "Impolicy" to Lord Hawkesbury, flattering himself that it "will have its weight, but particularly with Your Lordship," because of Hawkesbury's interest in the navigation of Britain.

Committee's General Report of 1788 stated that "the voice of humanity calls loudly for the extinction of a traffic which no plea of policy or interest can justify in the eye of reason or conscience. Yet the Committee trust that on a candid and full examination, it will appear that policy and philanthropy are not at variance on this occasion, and that it is no less the interest of the nation than it is becoming the spirit of humanity which distinguishes its character to comply with the wishes of the people and prohibit the trade."[4] To the Committee the support given by many of the ablest, most talented and most distinguished statesmen of the day was sufficient proof of the policy as well as of the justice of the abolition, and that the abolition would not be ruinous to any part of the British dominions.[5] When, in 1795, Dundas retracted the assent he had given in 1792 to the date, 1796, chosen by the House of Commons for the "gradual" abolition he had successfully proposed, the Committee lugubriously reported that "it is indeed to be lamented that men should be so infatuated and so blind to their true interests, which are ever consistent with justice and benevolence."[6]

This idea of "philanthropy plus five per cent" is well illustrated by James Ramsay. After his examination by the Privy Council for Trade, deputed in February 1788 to examine the whole question of the slave trade, Ramsay wrote to Lord Hawkesbury expressing his fears that his evidence had not altogether met with approbation. "I shall never gain my own forgiveness," he added, "if through any impropriety in my management, I have injured a cause, which I am persuaded is not more the cause of humanity than it is of the soundest policy."[7]

To what extent the "impolicy" of the slave trade was used as an argument in the abolition campaign, we can see from the abolitionists themselves. It must be reiterated that it was imperative for the abolitionists to try to win over hostile forces thinking fundamentally in terms of economics. Pitt, a most zealous advocate of abolition in the early days of the campaign, told the House of Commons that after the results of the investigation before the Privy Council they could proceed to a decision founded on principles of humanity, justice and sound policy,[8] and he confessed later that he himself was persuaded of the policy as well as the humanity of the measure.[9] In his

---

This, Clarkson assured him, "you will find peculiarly to suffer by the prosecution of the Slave Trade." (*Liverpool Papers*, Add. Mss, 38416, folio 94. May 29, 1788.)

4. Ibid., Add. Mss. 21255, folio 50 (v). Aug. 12, 1788.
5. Ibid., Add. Mss. 21256, folio 20. April 26, 1791. See Appendix One for the "Influential Men."
6. Ibid., Add. Mss. 21256, folio 94(v). June 25, 1795.
7. B.T. 6/12. Minutes of the African Questions. See Appendix Two for the authenticity of Ramsay's facts.
8. *Parl. Hist.*, Vol. XXVII, page 496. May 9, 1788.
9. Ibid., Vol. XXVIII, page 72. May 12, 1789.

"inspired speech" of April 2, 1792, he declared his conviction that the immediate abolition was "the first, the principal, the most indispensable act of policy, of duty, and of justice, that the legislature of this country has to take,"[10] and he admitted how heavily he felt the infamy, and how clearly he saw the impolicy, of the trade.[11]

Wilberforce, too, leaned on this argument. In 1791 he expressed the hope that the slave trade would be found to be contrary to every principle of religion, morality, and sound policy,[12] and, a year later, that time and reflection had convinced the House that the trade was as injurious to their interests as it was disgraceful to their feelings.[13] The rank and file in the abolitionist camp put their feet in the tracks of their leaders, and neither wandered nor stumbled: the policy of the measure, declared Mr. Milbank, was as great as its justice was undeniable.[14]

Let us follow the arguments of the abolitionists more closely, and in this connection consider them according to the lines of the rough draft of Clarkson's "Impolicy" presented to the Abolition Committee[15]—the possibility of keeping up the stock of slaves in the British Islands without further importations; the mortality amongst the seamen engaged in the trade; the foreign slave trade, which was "replete with the most pernicious consequences to the British nation"; the declining profits of the slave trade—and in addition the attempt by foreign powers to build up their own slave trade and the expensiveness of slave labour.

(a) Imports Unnecessary for the British West Indies

The abolitionists attempted to make out that the British West Indian Islands had reached the state where cultivation could be carried on without the aid of fresh importations from Africa. Replying to a resolution of the West Indian Planters and Merchants, the Abolition Committee declared in 1789 that there was no reason to be alarmed at the abolition under the delusive fear that a decline in the cultivation of the sugar colonies would be the consequence,[16] and tried to neutralise the powerful combination of interest excited against them by assuring the West Indian planter that his true interest lay rather in natural increase than in purchase, for the slaves trained in

10. Ibid., Vol. XXIX, page 1151.
11. Ibid., page 1279. April 27, 1792.
12. Ibid., page 250. April 18, 1791.
13. Ibid., page 1055. April 2, 1792.
14. Ibid., page 1104.
15. *Abolition Committee's Proceedings*, Add. Mss. 21254, folios 3 (v)–5. May 24, 1787.
16. Ibid., Add. Mss. 21255, folio 100(v). April 14, 1789.

the habits of labour were, by the unanimous testimony of all parties, much superior in value to new recruits from Africa. To the West Indian merchant it was represented that the evidence given of the success of many plantations in supporting their numbers by births justified the hope that a similar success would be achieved on all estates except those which by reason of their situation were peculiarly unhealthy.[17] Dr. Dickson was more outspoken: "The suspension and diminution of the American trade obliged the planters to be at some pains in raising provisions; the abolition of the African trade will oblige them to raise negroes."[18]

In the debate of 1791 Pitt made this topic the object of his particular attention, for, as this appeared to be the chief objection in the minds of many members, he trusted that, if he removed this argument as groundless, there would be no ground for resisting Wilberforce's motion.[19] Pitt confined his statistics chiefly to Jamaica, which contained more than half the slaves in all the British West Indies. Arguing from the answers to queries submitted to the islands by the Privy Council, he showed that there had been a gradual diminution in the death rate in Jamaica, until in 1788 the excess of deaths over births was only 1 in 100. These figures included a heavy recent mortality, due to the sudden suspension of the provision trade as a result of American Independence, and to a peculiar calamity which had claimed 15,000 victims—evils not likely to recur, especially since the islands had taken to growing their own provisions. These figures, too, included the mortality among the newly-imported Negroes, universally acknowledged to be higher, in consequence of the process so aptly described as the "seasoning"—Pitt later estimated this mortality at one-half—, than the mortality among the creole or "seasoned" Negroes. In fact, this mortality of itself would account for almost the whole of that one per cent. Consequently, it was this very mortality, occasioned by the slave trade, which was used to justify the continuance of the trade, and the improvements which more prudent management and a spirit of benevolence must naturally furnish, and the new ameliorating regulations which the Jamaica Legislature claimed that it was introducing seemed to show the possibility of keeping up the slave population without imports.

Proceeding to the other islands, Pitt showed there was no decrease in Barbados which might occasion alarm; on the contrary the slaves there seemed to increase.[20] In St. Kitts the decrease was but ¾ per cent; in Antigua, but

---

17. Ibid., Add. Mss. 21256, folios 4(v)-5. July 20, 1790.
18. W. *Dickson: Letters on Slavery* (London, 1789), page 148. Clarkson and Dickson were jocosely described by Pitt as Wilberforce's "White Negroes."
19. *Parl. Hist.*, Vol. XXIX, pages 336–341. April 19, 1791.
20. *Report of the Committee of Privy Council for Trade and Plantations, 1789.* (Referred to hereafter as *Report, 1789.*) Papers received since the date of the Report. Gov. Parry, Aug. 18, 1788—births: 353 males, 343 females; 604 deaths.

for a particular calamity, the decrease would have been trifling; and in Dominica Governor Orde had reported an increase of births over deaths.[21] Was there, therefore, asked Pitt, any serious ground of alarm from the measure of an entire and immediate abolition? His arguments, he assured the House later, were taken from authentic documents, and were the clear, simple and obvious result of a careful examination which he had made of the subject.[22] The West Indians quoted an act of 1750, the preamble of which stated the advantageousness of the trade as necessary for supplying the British West Indies with a sufficient number of Negroes at reasonable rates. Pitt retorted that, "instead of being very advantageous to Great Britain, this trade is the most destructive that can well be imagined to her interests."[23] Pitt's statistics, it was emphasized, to which no attempt had been made to give an answer, irrefutably proved that the abolition of the slave trade would be not only effectual, but safe, and even beneficial to the planter.[24]

After Pitt, Wilberforce. As early as November 1787 Wilberforce was writing to William Eden, confidential British envoy in Paris, that there was no doubt of the old plantations being able to keep up their stock by propagation, provided ill-treatment did not prevent the operation and effect of the great law of nature.[25] Soon after he wrote: "But we have other, must I say better grounds, on which to rest our cause than those of humanity. . . . In all estates brôt [sic] into actual cultivation the stock of negroes may be more than kept up by generation, without any fresh purchases, as is proved to me beyond all question." Abolition, therefore, instead of injuring the planters, would "confer on them the most essential benefit, by laying them under an obligation to relieve themselves from what is at present their most burthensome expense."[26] Again in the same year he repeated his argument that he had had conclusive proof of estates in various islands and different situations being able to keep up their population by generation.[27]

---

21. *Report, 1789.* Part V: Gov. Orde, "In this island I believe I may venture to say that now our numbers rather increase than decrease, it arises principally from superior feeding, occasioned by quantity of spare land, and from our good and great supply of water."

22. *Parl. Hist.,* Vol. XXIX, page 1136. April 2, 1792.

23. Ibid., page 1147.

24. Ibid., page 1099. Mr. Montagu.

25. *Auckland Papers,* Add. Mss. 34427, folio 50. Nov. 7, 1787. Eden, later Lord Auckland, had negotiated the commercial treaty with France, and was then trying to persuade the French to abolish the slave trade.

26. Ibid., folio 123. Nov. 23, 1787.

27. Ibid., folio 184(v). Dec. 7, 1787. In this letter Wilberforce drew a distinction which the abolitionists for a long time insisted upon (see below, Part II, Chapter 8) between Abolition and Emancipation. "With respect to the practicability of cultivating the plantations without importing or using slaves: observe that the former of these two points is the only one which it is essential for us to establish."

In the House of Commons Wilberforce was equally insistent on this point. He too took Jamaica as a fair specimen of the islands, and showed that from 1698 to 1730 the decrease in Jamaica in the slave population was 3½ per cent; from 1730 to 1755 it was 2½ per cent; from 1755 to 1768, 1¾ per cent; and from 1768 to 1788 it was not more than one per cent at the utmost. From this, and other considerations, he felt himself warranted in asserting that the slaves in Jamaica were actually increasing. This gradual reduction in the death rate was parallel with the improvement in the treatment of the slaves, and he pointed to the astonishing increase of the slaves in the unfavourable climate of North America.[28]

According to the British Ambassador in Paris, the French, at this period of the attempted joint abolition by France and Britain, agreed that the West Indian islands would not necessarily be ruined by the abolition of the slave trade, as the numbers of the slaves could be kept up by propagation.[29] Rev. Isham Baggs, who was very familiar with Barbados, gave to the Privy Council his firm opinion, based on intimate knowledge of the Africans at home and in the colonies, that the planters could do without fresh supplies if they chose, and that the slave trade was totally unnecessary.[30] Sir George Young, who was acquainted with both the French and British islands, but particularly with Jamaica, asserted that the population would not only be kept up, but would increase, if polygamy were forbidden, and the women confined to domestic work only and carefully attended to in a state of pregnancy.[31] Rev. Nicholls, a native of Barbados, imputed the heavy mortality of the slaves to the hard work the women were compelled to do and to the insufficient time allowed them to take care of their children.[32]

The anti-abolitionists retorted that it was impossible for the West Indian islands to maintain themselves without imports, despite the much-vaunted humanity of the planters, of which they adduced such evidence as the Jamaica Consolidated Act of 1787. They gave as reasons for this inability the disproportion of the sexes, due, they alleged, to the polygamy of the male slaves and the promiscuousness of the females. Other reasons were at various times advanced—the preference of the comelier female slaves for white men who

---

28. *Parl. Hist.*, Vol. XXIX, page 260. Wilberforce might have pointed out that North America then grew no sugar, and, if he referred to the U.S.A., very little cotton.

29. *Liverpool Papers*, Add. Mss. 38224, folio 140(v), Lord Dorset to Lord Hawkesbury, May 21, 1789—"M. de Montmorin's ideas as well as those of M. Necker seem to coincide (respecting the slave trade) with those already broached in the House of Commons, viz: that a total abolition of that traffick would not be a detriment to the European settlements in the West India islands, as the propagation of the Africans (if well treated) might answer every purpose."

30. *Report, 1789*, Part III. Further Evidence received by the Committee.

31. Ibid., Part III.

32. Ibid., Part III.

rewarded such connexions with freedom; the diseases spread through whole plantations by sailors and seamen;[33] the rigid caste distinction which slavery implied, and which encouraged freed female slaves to prefer cohabitation with whites rather than marriage, thereby retarding their natural increase; the las-civious abuse of authority by whites over the unprotected women.[34]

All these factors must have contributed to the disproportion of the sexes, but the main reason was undoubtedly that in a system of slave labour physical strength was the most important criterion in the labour gang on the estate and consequently in the cargoes of the slave traders. The Guinea captains brought a greater number of males than females from Africa, because that enabled them to sell at a better average.[35] The general proportion was two-thirds male and one-third female. Ramsay told his examiners that the dispro-portion of the sexes was due to inhumanity and avarice. "A few years present labour, without charging himself with the maintenance of unproductive old age, or the interruption of pregnancy or nursing in the other sex, has made the planter generally prefer males to females, the ready prepared supply of the slave market to the slow recruits of generation."[36] The planters openly asserted that it was cheaper to work the slave to death and replace him by purchase than to keep up the population by breeding.[37]

Were the Abolition Committee wrong in their conviction that investigation would make the inhumanity and impolicy of the traffic more evident?[38] Did Ramsay err in writing that a parliamentary inquiry "would open such scenes of oppression, cruelty and such schemes of wretched policy, as, even without a blow, must have its effect on the opinions and practice of the public?"[39]

There is one other point, which we have already adverted to in one of Pitt's speeches, namely, that of the heavier mortality among the newly im-ported slaves. The creole slaves were as a result twice as valuable as the newly imported slaves:[40] These new Negroes, in the words of the Jamaica agents,

33. Ibid., Part III. Messrs. Hutchinson, Burton and Dr. Adair, from Antigua.
34. Ibid., Papers received since the date of the Report. A Barbados Planter's reply to queries of Gov. Parry.
35. Ibid., Part III. Messrs. Bruce, Gillon and Fraser of Dominica.
36. Ibid., Part III.
37. Ibid., Part III. See Ramsay, "That the slaves are purchased, not for the purposes of population, but of being worked down I shall readily admit . . . but I deny that it ever answers the purposes of avarice."
38. *Abolition Committee's Proceedings*, Add. Mss. 21256, folio 7(v). July 20, 1790.
39. *Ramsay: Ms. Vol.*, folios l (v)–2. To Dean Tucker.
40. *Report, 1789*, Part III. In Barbados the proportion was given as two to one. Lieut. Gen. Mathew of Grenada said there was little difference between the creole and the imported slave "pro-vided the imported is become seasoned," and estimated the value of the new Negro at one-half or two-thirds that of the seasoned Negro. The Dominica representatives valued the healthy imported Negro at £76 sterling, the seasoned one at £120.

were necessarily inferior in value, because "they enter into a new climate, and perhaps change of diet; are unfit for immediate labour; unacquainted with tools or implements of work, or the manner of performing it; have everything to learn, and earn nothing."[41]

Mr. Law, arguing before the House of Lords in 1792 on behalf of the West Indian planters, complained that, just at the moment when it would have been convenient for the planter to turn his uncultivated lands to the culture of the cane and give up the exhausted soils, "he is told that he must cultivate it no longer, or at least cultivate it at an expense and under difficulties which it would be impossible for him to undergo."[42] It was precisely this new cultivation the abolitionists wished to restrain.[43]

Pitt had already proved to what extent the mortality among the newly imported slaves was mainly responsible for what excess of deaths over births there still was in the islands. As early as 1788 he had written to Wilberforce stressing the importance of ascertaining whether a large proportion of the annual imports of slaves was not devoted to bringing new land into cultivation. This was certainly the case as far as Dominica, St. Vincent and Grenada—the islands ceded by France in 1763—were concerned. The abolition of the slave trade would therefore "only prevent *further* improvements which *would have taken place*, and not break in upon the advantages at present subsisting."[44] Wilberforce advised the planters, that if they had more ground than was cultivated, they might employ it to greater advantage in cotton and cinnamon than in canes,[45] and drew a contrast between "the slow, perhaps, but sure progress of cultivation, carried on in the natural way, and the attempt to force improvements which, however flattering the prospect might appear at the outset, soon produced a load of debts and inextricable embarrassments."[46] Even Dundas, who was in reality the friend of the West Indians, admitted that the desire to increase the cultivation of the West Indian Islands was no good cause for continuing so unjust a traffic as the slave trade.[47] Governor Orde, writing of Dominica, described the situation of all the West Indian islands. He declared that Dominica must materially suffer from the abolition, more perhaps than any other colony, because the island was so little cleared; "for although I have no doubt that the number

---

41. Ibid., Part III. Messrs. Fuller, Long and Chisholme.
42. Add. Mss. 12433, folio 39. May 14, 1792.
43. It is possible that, in view of the superiority of French St. Domingo (see chapter 2), the question of overproduction, so much to the fore in 1807, was also in the minds of the abolitionists.
44. *Life of Wilberforce*, Vol. I, pages 162–163.
45. *Parl. Hist.*, Vol. XXIX, page 1072. April 2, 1792.
46. Ibid., pages 259–260. April 18, 1791.
47. Ibid., page 1218. Stated by Pitt, April 18, 1792.

of slaves we now have may be kept up without any additional importation, yet I much fear the increase cannot be such as will enable us much to extend the agriculture of the country."[48] In other words, imports were unnecessary to maintain the existing population.

The West Indians were fighting tooth and nail. But when it is remembered that Mr. Long, the historian of Jamaica, had urged that the cessation of imports would diminish the fear of slave risings, the new Negroes being the most intractable, the most likely to rebel against a life which seemed to some a veritable paradise for them as compared with their life in Africa;[49] when it is remembered that after St. Domingo had gone up in flames the fear of a servile war hung like a sword of Damocles over the heads of the planters in the British islands, we can see that the prosecution had a strong case.

(b) Mortality among the Seamen Engaged in the African Trade

One great argument of defenders of the slave trade was that it was the chief nursery of British seamen, which, with the fisheries and the coasting trade, contributed to British supremacy on the seas. Whatever the truth of this assertion in the days when the slave trade was an object of national importance and its utility not yet questioned, it was quite different when the campaign for abolition began.

It was to Clarkson's magnificent researches that the abolitionists were indebted for the revelation of the true facts. Bearding the lion in his den, Clarkson at much personal risk roamed the docks of Liverpool, Bristol and London, questioned seamen, examined muster rolls and collected evidence which was a terrific indictment of the effects of the slave trade, not now upon the blacks but upon the whites.

That able abolitionist, Ramsay, also enlarged on this point. The loss of seamen on the voyage was, in his opinion, so generally understood and acknowledged as to preclude the necessity of any particular inquiry.[50] His indignation at the squandering of the lives of the seamen, as a result of pushing "to a most indiscreet length" a trade which was most precarious and in general unprofitable, knew no bounds.[51] From personal experience he could say that the trade was not a nursery for seamen: "it forms not but destroys seamen. And this destruction of seamen is a strong argument for the abolition of

---

48. B.T. 1/5. June 13, 1792.
49. *Parl. Deb.*, Vol. VIII, page 669. Earl St. Vincent, Feb. 2, 1807.
50. *Ramsay: Ms. Vol.*, folio 7. "Observations on the condition in which African slaves are imported into the West Indies."
51. Ibid., folio 23. "Memorial on the supplying of the Navy with seamen."

it." He quoted Clarkson's figures that the annual losses amounted to at least 2,000 men, and that the proportion of deaths in the African trade to those in the Newfoundland trade was as 200 to 10, and agreed that ill-treatment and the disorders attendant on the trade permanently crippled almost all of those who engaged in it. "If, therefore," he concluded, "we have any regard to the lives of seamen, we ought to abandon a branch of trade which dissipates the men in so unprofitable a manner."[52]

Wilberforce, in a letter to Eden, condemned the slave trade as the grave rather than the nursery of seamen, and estimated the annual losses as one-fourth of the sailors engaged in it.[53] From the Liverpool and Bristol muster rolls he showed the House that on 350 slave vessels, with 12,263 seamen, there were 2,643 deaths in 12 months, whereas of 462 ships engaged in the West Indian trade, with 7,640 seamen on board, there were only 118 deaths in seven months.[54] Despite the good regulations Britain had lost over eleven per cent of her sailors in the trade.[55]

William Smith, exposing to the House of Commons what he called the numerous fallacies and mis-statements of the anti-abolitionists, easily disposed of the argument that the slave trade was responsible for introducing many "landsmen" to the mercantile marine and as a consequence to the Navy. The proportion of landsmen, from the Bristol muster rolls, little exceeded one-twelfth; in Liverpool it was only one-sixteenth.[56] According to Lord Howick, the losses among seamen in the African slave trade as compared with the West Indian trade were eight to one, and the slave trade was unique in the readiness with which men deserted it on their arrival in the West Indies for the King's ships.[57]

The Abolition Committee, replying to resolutions of the West Indian Planters and Merchants in 1789, condemned the slave trade as a national injury, in that the mortality occasioned by it was more than double that of all the other branches of commerce in the kingdom.[58] And the venerable John Newton argued that the "truly alarming" loss in the African trade, if a

---

52. Ibid., folio 64. "An Address on the proposed bill for the Abolition of the Slave Trade."
53. *Auckland Papers*, Add. Mss. 34427, folio 123. Nov. 23, 1787. Wilberforce also pointed out that the mortality amongst the French seamen was greater, because, their ships being larger, they were obliged to wait longer on the coast for cargoes. Ibid., folio 50. Nov. 7, 1787.
54. *Parl. Hist.*, Vol. XXIX, page 270. April 18, 1791.
55. Ibid., page 1069. April 2, 1792. Clarkson computed that five-sixths of those who sailed for Africa died.
56. Ibid., page 322. April 18, 1791.
57. *Parl. Deb.*, Vol. VIII, pages 948–949. Feb. 23, 1807.
58. *Abolition Committee's Proceedings*. Add. Mss. 21255, folio 100(v). April 14, 1789.

rapid loss of seamen deserved the attention of a maritime people, was surely of political importance.[59]

In the face of these glaring facts, which no attempt was made to refute, opponents indulged only in lame excuses. Bordering almost on the facetious, Law, before the House of Lords, excused the heavy mortality on the ground that it was not as large as the loss in the transportation of British convicts.[60] He referred to slaves only, but the Middle Passage affected whites as well, largely because of the unlimited power of the Captains, those proud men, dressed in a little brief authority, whom Fox compared to Roman Caesars. Alderman Watson argued that the West Indian trade was intimately connected with the Newfoundland fisheries, and that abolition of the slave trade would not only annihilate the marine by cutting off a great source of seamen, but would destroy the Newfoundland fisheries, "which the slaves in the West Indies supported, by consuming that part of the fish that was fit for no other consumption";[61] and Mr. Grosvenor acknowledged that "it was not an amiable trade, but neither was the trade of a butcher an amiable trade, and yet a mutton chop was, nevertheless, a good thing."[62]

(c) The Foreign Slave Trade

The importance of the slave trade to Britain in former times lay not only in supplying Negro slaves to her own colonies in the West Indies—without whom, in the words of Dr. Hochstetter, cultivation would have been analogous to a factory today without steam engines or coal—, but also in supplying the needs of foreign powers. One has only to think of the Asiento, and Chatham's boast that his conquests in Africa during the Seven Years' War had placed almost the whole of the foreign supply in British hands, to realise the justice of this statement. By 1788 the old order had changed.

The great resurgence of the British slave trade after the American war was directed mainly to the supplying of the foreign colonies. Britain, in Ramsay's words, had become the "honourable slave carriers" of her rivals,[63] and the British planters, in opposing abolition, were only contending for French and Spanish interests.[64] He attributed to this British supply for the last twenty-five years that great improvement of the French colonies which had contributed to their formidable sea power in the American war. He asked pertinently

---

59. J. Newton: Thoughts on the African Slave Trade (Liverpool, 1792), page 8.
60. Add. Mss. 12433, folio 28(v). May 14, 1792.
61. Parl. Hist., Vol. XXIX, page 343. April 18, 1791.
62. Ibid., page 281.
63. Ramsay: Ms.Vol., folio 23 (v). "Memorial on the supplying of the Navy with seamen."
64. Ibid., folio 67(v). For the "Morning Chronicle."

"whether a branch of trade, confessedly of some importance, but confined to two or three ports, ought at the expense of every human feeling to be put in competition with our future naval superiority; or, if it must be preserved, whether it should not be confined to the demands of our own colonies."[65] In one of the numerous anonymous pamphlets which swamped England during the whole period of this long, large-scale agitation, one writer, in defence of the slave trade and even of the foreign slave trade, estimated that of the 40,500 slaves exported from Africa by British merchants, one-eighth was lost by death, of the remainder one-eighth sold in the British islands, and the rest sold to the French and Spaniards, to the great profit of the slave merchants.[66]

One must be chary of accepting unquestionably what these contemporary pamphleteers have to say. But official documents bear striking testimony to the general truth of their statements. Among the Board of Trade papers there is a curious document entitled "Committee's Answers to Queries on the Free Ports in the West Indies."[67] According to this paper, the utility of Free Ports in the West Indies arose from the importation of various enumerated articles, above all of slaves, a trade which "from the present encouragement given by the Court of France . . . is of the utmost value to this nation, as the slaves are purchased on the coast with British manufactures and East India goods, and employs a very large proportion of our shipping." Dominica was selected as the most conveniently situated island in the West Indies for a free port, because of its position among the foreign islands, its proximity to the Spanish Main, and its abundance of good water and all the other refreshments necessary for a cargo of slaves. As regards the competition of the French planters tending to enhance the price of slaves, the Committee remarked that the British planters had the first choice, but their inability to pay cash and the long credits they asked for made it essential for the merchant to sell to foreigners for immediate returns.

The best evidence of the extent of the British slave trade to the foreign islands is afforded by the merchants themselves engaged in it. The Privy Council was told that what the French were suffering from was chiefly lack of capital. The inducements to British subjects to take up the trade were the bounty of 40 livres per ton; the premium of 160 livres per head on slaves imported into the French Windward Islands and of 230 livres per head on

---

65. J. Ramsay: *An Inquiry into the effects of putting a stop to the African Slave Trade* (London, 1784), page 21. (Referred to hereafter as *Ramsay: Inquiry*.)

66. *An Address to the Inhabitants in general of Great Britain and Ireland* (Liverpool, 1788), page 27.

67. B.T. 6/75. West Indies, 1786–1790. This is probably the Committee of the Privy Council for Trade itself.

those imported into the south side of St. Domingo, then being developed;[68] and thirdly, the high prices paid for Negroes in the French colonies, from 30 to 50 per cent higher than in the British islands. Of two cargoes of slaves sold in 1787, one in St. Domingo, the other in Jamaica, the first fetched £66 sterling per head on an average, the second £42. From this great encouragement the merchants prophesied that soon one-half of the British trade would be carried on by the sale of slaves to the French on the African coast, where the prices offered were nearly equal to those obtainable in the British islands, and they estimated that of the annual British export of 40,000 slaves, only one-third was wanted for the supply of the British islands: the other two-thirds were disposed of to foreigners.[69]

Corroboration can be sought from the answers given to the Privy Council by the Islands and their agents in London. Governor Parry of Barbados agreed that large numbers were exported to other countries, where a higher price could be procured, though he could not give the exact proportion, and he thought that even this additional supply was not equal to the foreign demand.[70] In Dominica about five-eighths of the imports in the four years preceding 1788 had been sold to the French, one-fourth to the Spaniards, and a few to the Dutch, and it was estimated that three-fourths of the Negroes the French had purchased had been furnished by British traders on the African coast and in the West Indies.[71] From Grenada came the same tale. According to Governor Mathew, of 11,000 slaves sold since the peace, half had been sold to foreigners, and the island legislature agreed that, since St. George had been made a free port, the French had purchased a considerable number of slaves from British traders.[72] In 1786 the merchants of Kingston had expressed in a memorial their conviction that "the export of negroes from hence to the neighbouring islands is a trade of great benefit to this island, and consequently to the mother country."[73] The Jamaica Agents examined by the Privy Council spoke to the same effect, though they hinted

---

68. C.O. 137/88. Proclamation of May 1789. Foreign ships were not allowed to land Negroes in other parts of St. Domingo.

69. *Report, 1789*, Part VI. Messrs. Baillie, King, Camden and Hubbert.

70. Ibid. Papers received since the date of the Report. Governor Parry's Further Answers, Aug. 18, 1788.

71. Ibid., Part V. Mr. Robinson. Governor Orde confirmed this: "About one-sixth part of the negroes, salted provisions and dry goods are used in this island, the rest are illicitly introduced into the foreign ones." B.T. 6/41: Dominica, 1772–1790. Sept. 1, 1787.

72. *Report, 1789*, Part V. Governor Mathew thought the French paid less for these slaves, "as wholesale dealers and less nice in choice."

73. B.T. 6/75. West Indies, 1786–1790. May 29, 1786.

that the sale of Negroes to the French by the British on the Guinea coast was decreasing, owing to the more extended connections the French had made.[74]

The actual figures speak no less eloquently. The imports into and exports from Dominica and Jamaica during the years 1784–1788 were as follows:—[75]

Table 1.1.   Dominica

Year	Imports	Exports	Approximate Percentage
1784	4,998	1,925	38.5
1785	6,254	3,328	53.2
1786	8,407	5,927	70.5
1787	5,709	2,852	50.0
1788	2,185	1,749	80.1
Total	27,553	15,781	57.3

Table 1.2.   Jamaica

		Exports		
Year	Imports	Estimate[a] I	Estimate[b] II	Approximate Percentage[c]
1784	15,468	4,465	4,635	28.9
1785	11,046	4,589	4,667	41.5
1786	5,645	3,643	3,764	64.6
1787	5,682	1,780	2,158	31.3
Total	37,841	14,477	15,224	38.3

a. Ibid. Two tables used in conjunction.
b. Add. Mss. 12435, folio 37(v). Jamaica Statistics.
c. Based on the lower figures. Neither set of figures is reliable for Jamaica, because of the clandestine exports to St. Domingo—*Report 1789.* Part VI.

In St. Christopher the imports for the years 1778–1788 amounted to 2,784, the exports to 1,769—percentage 63.5. In Antigua the figures varied, the export being as high as 56 per cent in 1778 (177 out of 345) and 50 per cent in 1783 (593 out of 1,164), to as low as 14 per cent in 1785 (136 out of 952).[76] Of 44,712 slaves imported into Grenada between 1784 and 1792, no less than 31,210—nearly 70 per cent—were re-exported, and, referring to

74. *Report, 1789*, Part V.
75. Ibid., Part IV.
76. *Report, 1789*. Papers received since the date of the Report.

the benefits conferred on Grenada by the Free Port Act, the Governor stated that "the supplying of the foreign colonies with slaves is another branch of this commerce, nearly equal in value to the rest."[77]

One more set of statistics may be given. They were used by Dundas in his speech in the House of Commons on April 23, 1792.[78]

Table 1.3.

Island	1789		1790		1791	
	Imports	Exports	Imports	Exports	Imports	Exports
Antigua	311	140				
Barbados	444	399	126	72	382	100
Grenada	6,490	3,040	3,900	3,142	9,283	6,000
Jamaica	9,808	2,030	14,063	1,970	15,000	3,082
St. Kitts	67	332				
St. Vincent	938	58	1,552	611	2,863	1,346

Using Dundas's figures, for Barbados we get an export for the three years of 60 per cent—571 out of 952; for Jamaica, about 18 per cent—7,082 out of 38,871; for Grenada, over 60 per cent—12,182 out of 19,673; for St. Vincent, nearly 40 per cent—2,015 out of 5,353. The Dominica figures from the Chatham Papers give the huge export of 6,137 out of 7,906—no less than 77.2 per cent.[79]

Can one wonder that Dundas, opposing Wilberforce's motion of 1792, on the ground that abolition should be "gradual, that is, that time should be allowed to the planters to purchase sufficient supplies so that they should be well stocked when abolition took place,"[80] can one wonder that Dundas,

77. *Liverpool Papers*, Add. Mss. 38228, folios 327 and 331. Mathew to Hawkesbury, Feb. 1793.

78. *Parl. Hist.*, Vol. XXIX, page 1210. There are some figures in the Chatham Papers, G.D. 8/351: West Indies, Miscellaneous Papers, 1778–1801. In the main they are the same as those of Dundas, though the Jamaica figures are:—

Table 1.4.

Year	Imports	Exports
1789	9,691	2,575
1790	14,069	1,970
1791	15,293	2,915

79. Chatham Papers, G.D. 8/351.

80. Compare *Ramsay: Inquiry*, pages 32–33. "Suppose a statute enacted that the present slave trade should cease after a period of three or six years, every planter would immediately set himself seriously to stock his plantation and to give such orders for the treatment of his slaves as would favour their health and population. This in the meantime would divert our slave trade from the improvement of the French colonies to that of our own."

so determined an enemy of abolition, moved the immediate abolition of the foreign slave trade, which, according to him, amounted in 1791 to 34,000 out of 74,000 imported?[81] The Abolition Committee wrote of the unsuccessful foreign slave trade bill that no plea of necessity, however it might be urged as far as abolition for the British islands was concerned, could be adduced in opposition.[82] A thing so disgusting, morally, as the slave trade could receive little support when it was seen, in its economic aspect, to be primarily responsible for the superiority of Britain's colonial rivals.

The key to this aspect of the British slave trade is to be found in the French demand for slaves. The period from 1784 is marked by the great development of hitherto uncultivated lands in French St. Domingo. French St. Domingo was the most fertile island in the West Indies and will be discussed in the following chapter. For the present it is sufficient to state that the French islands needed a vast number of slaves, far more than the British islands. One reason for this was, French writers suggest, the sub-tropical climate of St. Domingo,[83] in which the slaves died more rapidly than they did in the British islands. More important, however, was the fact that the slaves in St. Domingo were needed for bringing new lands into cultivation, and what the mortality among imported Negroes, particularly for new cultivation, was, we have already seen from the arguments of Wilberforce and Pitt.

The attempt to stop the foreign slave trade suffered, as everything else connected with abolition, from the reaction which set in as a result of the French war. Wilberforce's bill for the abolition of the foreign slave trade in 1794 met with no more success than Dundas's. Pitt, with a lack of enthusiasm which compares unfavourably with his zeal in 1792, argued that the foreign slave trade had actually ceased of itself, and that the motion was not so much to abolish it as to prevent its revival.[84] The foreign colonies were now nearly all British, and Pitt was probably thinking of the prevention of the foreign slave trade, if and when the colonies were restored at the end of the war.

Wilberforce's bill—and this is significant of developments which were to arise with the turn of the century—was supported by some of the West Indian planters. Already, when the question of abolition had first been mooted in England, an anonymous planter had, while defending the slave trade as absolutely necessary to the British colonies, advocated the abolition of the

---

81. *Parl. Hist.*, Vol. XXIX, page 1206. April 23, 1792.
82. *Abolition Committee's Proceedings*, Add. Mss. 21256, folio 86. Aug. 20, 1793.
83. *Cahiers de la Révolution Française*, No. III (Paris, 1935), page 40. *Gaston-Martin: La Doctrine Coloniale de la France en 1789.* (Referred to hereafter as *Gaston-Martin*.)
84. *Parl. Hist.*, Vol. XXX, page 1444. Feb. 7, 1794.

foreign slave trade as "prejudicial to the real interest of the nation."[85] One influential planter wrote to Wilberforce describing his bill as "a compromise which ought to attach every West Indian to you and induce them to support you in every future plan you may propose."[86] The majority of the West Indians, however, preferred to regard the continuance of the foreign slave trade as essential from its magnitude to the existence of the general trade.[87]

When the bill was sent up to the House of Lords, who were conducting an inquiry into the trade, Lord Abingdon distinguished himself as a defender of the constitution. It was an "indecent" bill. The Lower House had no right to dictate to them; "in the rejection of this bill, this will not be the first time that this country and this constitution have been saved by this House, from the rash and intemperate measures of the other."[88] It was a sure instinct which made the Jamaica Assembly state categorically in 1792: "The safety of the West Indies not only depends on the slave trade not being abolished, but on a speedy declaration of the House of Lords that they will not suffer the trade to be abolished."[89] It was significant that Dundas, in reply to Wilberforce's private appeal on behalf of the foreign slave trade bill, admitted that it was only the belief that the bill would not pass the House of Lords which reconciled him to silence,[90] and he declared openly in the House in 1795, when the question of abolishing the entire slave trade in 1796, as had been agreed in 1792, was being discussed, that he had "entertained a hope that in another place the impolicy of such a measure would be apparent, and that means would be taken to render the resolution of the Commons ineffectual."[91]

Wilberforce was not wrong when he wrote to Rev. Newton, so late as June 1804, "I fear the House of Lords!"[92] In the House of Lords there were many stalwart champions of the slave trade. The Earl of Westmorland did not hesitate to remind his peers that it was to the existence of the slave trade that they owed their seats in it,[93] and he took pride in the consideration that the slave merchants and the colonists would see that their interests were as

---

85. *Considerations on the Emancipation of Negroes and on the Abolition of the Slave Trade*, (London, 1788), pages 29–30. The author estimated that only half the imports were necessary for the British Islands.

86. *Life of Wilberforce*, Vol. II, page 49.

87. Ibid.

88. *Parl. Hist.*, Vol. XXXI, page 469. May 2, 1794.

89. C.O. 137/91. Petition of Committee of House of Assembly on the Sugar and Slave Trade, Dec. 5, 1792.

90. *Life of Wilberforce*, Vol. II, pages 49–50.

91. *Parl. Hist.*, Vol. XXXI, page 1338. Feb. 26, 1795.

92. *Life of Wilberforce*. Vol. III, page 120.

93. *Parl. Deb.*, Vol. IX, page 170. March 23, 1807.

much attended to as if they were directly represented in that House.[94] The royal Duke of Clarence, the recipient of a service of plate as the poor but honourable testimony of the gratitude of the people of Jamaica,[95] who was generally considered as representing the ideas of the Royal Family,[96] attacked Wilberforce in 1793 as either a fanatic or a hypocrite.[97] Hawkesbury, president of the Privy Council for Trade, was himself possessed of West Indian estates.[98] Tracts in defence of the slave trade were dedicated to him,[99] and he was rewarded with the freedom of the city of Liverpool for his great attention to the commercial interests of the country at large, and more particularly in gratitude for the essential services rendered to Liverpool by his great exertion in Parliament in support of the slave trade.[100] When elevated to the dignity of an earl of the kingdom, Hawkesbury took the title of Earl of Liverpool and accepted the Corporation's offer to quarter its arms with his own.[101] In such an assembly it was not surprising that the dictates of policy or even of morality made little headway, and that the idea of abolition was considered a "damned and cursed doctrine, held only by hypocrites,"[102] which first originated among "atheists, enthusiasts, jacobins, and such descriptions of persons."[103]

(d) Foreign Encroachments on the British Slave Trade

A point to be considered in connection with the re-export of slaves from the British to the foreign colonies is the danger to which even this branch of

---

94. Ibid., Vol. II, page 929. July 3, 1804.

95. G. W. Bridges: The Annals of Jamaica (London, 1828), Vol. II, page 263 (footnote).

96. Vide Life of Wilberforce, Vol. III, page 34—"It was truly humiliating to see, in the House of Lords, four of the Royal Family come down to vote against the poor, helpless, friendless slaves." Wilberforce to Muncaster, July 6, 1804. George III, who at one time had whispered jestingly to Wilberforce at a levée: "How go on your black clients, Mr. Wilberforce?" afterwards was a determined opponent of abolition. Ibid., Vol. I, page 343.

97. Parl. Hist., Vol. XXX, page 659. April 11, 1793.

98. Report of the Proceedings of the Committee of Sugar Refiners (London, 1792), page 34.

99. A Merchant to his friend on the Continent; Letters Concerning the Slave Trade (Liverpool, n.d.). To Lord Hawkesbury, "as a patron to the trade of this country in general, and a favorer of that, the subject of these letters."

100. Liverpool Papers, Add. Mss. 38223, folios 170 and 175. Sept. 7 and 12, 1788. See also Hawkesbury's letter to Lord Rodney, agreeing to use the proxy entrusted to him by the latter, promising to "make the best use of it in defending the island of Jamaica and the other West India islands which his Lordship so gloriously defended against a foreign enemy on the memorable 12th April," and expressing his sorrow that only a severe fit of the gout prevented Rodney from "attending Parliament and affording his personal support to those who are in so much want of it"—Add. Mss. 38227, folio 202, Jan. 1792.

101. Ibid., Add. Mss. 38231, folio 59. Thomas Naylor, Mayor, to Hawkesbury, July 10, 1796; folio 60, Minutes of the Common Council, July 6, 1796; folio 64, Hawkesbury to Naylor, July 16, 1796.

102. Earl St. Vincent. Cit. Klingberg, page 127.

103. Parl. Deb., Vol. VIII, page 230. Earl of Westmorland, May 16, 1806.

the slave trade—quite apart from its economic implications which we have already traced—was likely in the future to be exposed.

One of the most important gains which resulted to France from her assistance to the American colonists was an increase of her possessions in Africa, an increase which, nevertheless, seemed to some Frenchmen inadequate.[104] Britain was forced to restore the Isle of Goree in the state in which it was before its capture during the war, and to cede certain forts in the River Senegal, while France guaranteed to Britain Fort James in the Gambia. As for the rest of the African coast, it was resolved, in almost Bismarckian language, that the subjects of both countries should continue to resort there according to custom.[105]

The French followed hard on the heels of the British both as slave traders and sugar growers. The British traders complained bitterly of the encroachments of France in Africa. In 1786, and again in 1787, the African Committee petitioned the Marquis of Carmarthen, pointing out violations by France of the Versailles Treaty and the imminent danger to the British African settlements if effective measures were not taken for their protection, and expressing the hope that in any political discussions which might take place every possible care would be taken to preserve British rights and possessions upon the coast of Africa.[106] The Committee in a memorial to the Lords of the Committee of Privy Council stressed the efforts to share that very valuable commerce made by other nations, particularly the French, who seemed to be dissatisfied with a mere share and to desire a monopoly, either by supplanting the British with the natives or by encroaching upon the British spheres of influence. In direct violation of the Versailles Treaty, and "contrary to all right and justice," the French had been effecting settlements in the Sierra Leone river, with a view to monopolising the very valuable trade of that part of Africa, and had always backed their usurpations by a display of naval force. Even the Americans, according to the memorial, were suffered without molestation to carry on a very extensive trade upon the Gold Coast with rum only, manufactured in America, to the great detriment of the West Indian distilleries.[107]

The French were so energetic in their exertions to encourage this trade by their own subjects that they had created a powerful competition in Africa, which the British merchant could not well resist, and the trade, the African

---

104. Gaston-Martin, *op. cit.*, page 13.

105. F.O. 93/33(2). Definitive Treaty of Peace signed at Versailles—Articles 9, 10, 12. The Bismarckian phrase is "selon l'usage qui a eu lieu jusqu'au présent."

106. F.O. 27/26. Oct. 3, 1787.

107. B.T. 6/8. Sept. 29, 1786. How clearly did the men of that day realise the interdependence of the slave and West Indian trades!

merchants confessed dolefully, was in a rather languid state.[108] It was reported that more French ships of war were expected on the coast, to the great danger of the British settlements. "It appears very plain to us," it was said ironically, "if the French compleat their intended works on the coast, it will save those gentlemen that are inimical to the Slave Trade a vast deal of trouble as a few years hence there will be an effectual stop put to our *Slave Trade here.*"[109]

We have already referred to the inducements held out by the French Government to foreigners as well as to French subjects to engage in the African trade and supply the French islands,[110] whose need was so great that Louis XVI was persuaded to distinguish those planters who treated their slaves with lenity and humanity, a measure which was expected to yield excellent results.[111] When the question of abolition was first agitated in Great Britain, very good offers were made to British traders to set up in France. The French had no need of ships or seamen, what they lacked was capital, and the type of goods—"Guinées"—necessary for purposes of barter. Mr. Taylor, a Manchester merchant, told the Privy Council of the surprise manifested by certain French African merchants from Bordeaux, Nantes and Havre on a visit to Britain, at the quality and cheapness of those goods and the speed with which they were furnished, and he had been assured by them that he or any other manufacturer who set up in Rouen on the same scale would be given every encouragement by them and no doubt by the French Government.[112]

Stephen Fuller, agent for Jamaica, after a visit to Havre, reported to Lord Sydney the efforts the French were making in order to monopolise the African trade. It was an open secret that the French had felt for some time the inconvenience of buying their slaves from British merchants, and "finding that this country was disposed to bind their African trade in shackles, they determined to liberate theirs, and wisely to take the advantage of our absurdities. . . . Surely this is too great a sacrifice to the whimsical absurdities of a set of fanatics, who have ingrossed not only all the religion and piety of their countrymen, but their feelings into the bargain."[113]

---

108. B.T. 6/12. Minutes of the African Questions, Feb.19, 1788.

109. F.O. 27/32. March 31, 1789. Extracts of the letter were ordered by the Privy Council to be sent to Lord Dorset, British Ambassador in Paris, July 7, 1789.

110. These bounties etc. cost the French Government, 1785–1788, 2,340,000 livres annually: A. M. Arnould: *De La Balance Du Commerce et des rélations commerciales extérieures de la France, dans toutes les parties du globe, particulièrement à la fin du règne de Louis XIV, et au moment de la Révolution* (Paris, 1791), Vol. I, page 303.

111. F.O. 27/27. March 20, 1788.

112. *Report, 1789.* Part VI, Mr. Taylor, "though he is a friend his country," felt bound, because of his large family, to accept the offer, if abolition should take place.

113. C.O. 137/87. Aug. 24, 1788.

The great argument of the anti-abolitionists, amply justified in the course of time, was that if the British abandoned the slave trade the French would take it up. But there is no question that abolition by Britain would have been a serious blow to the French colonies. The French slave trade could not have been increased overnight; it would have taken years for France to overcome the deficiency in capital, and to supply through her own subjects that vast number of slaves for which she depended upon British traders and the British islands. But on the other hand, the sudden advances recently made by the French in Africa meant that, were the slave trade to continue, the time would come—in the future, no doubt, but come it would—when the British slave trade, confined even in 1790 mainly to the foreign islands, would, through the economic nationalism of foreign powers, fall to the ground, to the detriment of British shipping interests.

For side by side with the attempt of France to build up her own slave trade went the attempts of Holland and Spain. The Dutch Government, while they agreed with the claim of the colonists that "the chief, the only means of prosperity, the pivot on which all turns . . . consists in the importation of negroes at a cheapened price: this is the barometer of cultivation in the colonies," nevertheless refused to depart from "the fundamental truth" that the slave trade should be carried on by the inhabitants, forbade the importation of Negroes by foreigners, and began to devise ways and means—premiums, pensions and reduction of duties—of inducing the Dutch merchants to engage in the trade to an extent sufficient for the supply of the colonies.[114]

On the first news, too, of the question of abolition in Britain, the Spanish Government, whose former efforts to build up its own slave trade had all failed,[115] and who, suffering as it did from a lack of experienced Spaniards to carry on the trade, had been forced to depend on British ships with an outfit of British manufactures, now began to make desperate efforts to take up the trade itself. A contract which Mr. Dawson of Liverpool was on the point of signing for the delivery of at least 3,000 slaves a year to the Spanish colonies was at once stopped, and the leading Spanish House in Cadiz began to make efforts to get the trade into its own hands, with the intention of carrying it on by means of British seamen but in Spanish ships flying Spanish colours. Mr. Dawson himself was invited to go to Spain to carry on his trade from there, and Spanish agents were sent to Manchester and to Liverpool to inspect the goods and ships used in the trade and to make extensive enquiries. Spain,

---

114. *Report, 1789*, Part VI, Holland. Information from H. M.'s Ambassadors, Ministers and Consuls, concerning the treatment of slaves in the foreign islands.

115. Ibid., Spain. "They have not, nor have had, for many years, a single Spanish bottom trading immediately to the coast of Africa."

too, began to give preferences to her own merchants and to encourage the manufacture of goods in Spain for the prosecution of the slave trade, and a Royal order of 1788 forbade foreigners to enter unauthorised ports in the colonies and decreed premiums of four dollars, to be paid from the royal treasury, to each Spaniard for every slave of good quality introduced in Spanish ships into the Spanish colonies.[116]

This foreign competition boded ill for the future to the British merchants, the only class who benefited by the re-export of slaves to the rivals of the British colonies, and for whom, therefore, abolition was not, commercially, advantageous. So, providing the means by which foreign colonies could compete with its own, and putting an effective stop to their development, for some years at least, by abolishing the slave trade—these were the sober economic alternatives which faced the British Government.

(e) Decline in the Profits of the Slave Trade

It was again owing mainly to Clarkson's untiring researches that the legend of the vast wealth of the West Indians and the enormous profits accruing from the slave trade was exposed. Lord Shelburne had said in 1778 that "there was scarcely ten miles together throughout the country where the house and estate of a rich West Indian were not to be seen,"[117] and the Duke of Clarence was later to defend the West Indians on the ground that the great schools of Eton, Westminster, Harrow and Winchester were full of the sons of West Indians.[118] But West Indian cultivation and the slave trade were a lottery, in which the fortunate few acquired great profits,[119] the unfortunate many suffered heavy losses.

The eighteenth century is remarkable in British commercial history for the rapid rise of the town of Liverpool. Clarkson, combating the popular view, contended that its rise was due to a variety of causes, among which were the salt trade, the prodigious increase of the population of Lancashire, and the very rapid and great extension of the manufactures of Manchester.[120] How correct Clarkson's explanation is for the period of the Industrial Revolution every student of history knows, but it is certain that the initial

116. Ibid.
117. Note Pitt, 1798: "In proposing the income tax of 1798 (he) calculated that, of the incomes enjoyed in Great Britain, those derived from the West Indies very much surpassed those from Ireland, and from all the rest of the world outside the British Isles." Cit. *Klingberg*, page 89 (footnote).
118. *Parl. Hist.*, Vol. XXXIV, page 1102. July 5, 1799.
119. Commonly said to exceed 30 per cent.
120. *Clarkson: Impolicy*, pages 123–125.

greatness of Liverpool, as that of Nantes in France,[121] was the result of the slave trade. "Beyond a doubt," says Ramsay Muir in his history of Liverpool, "it was the slave trade which raised Liverpool from a struggling port to one of the richest and most prosperous trading centres of the world."[122]

In the seventeenth century London and Bristol monopolized the slave trade, but when in 1708 the first slave trader left Liverpool for the African coast, her geographical position soon made her a formidable rival. The account of the wealth to be obtained operated "like electricity"[123] and by 1784 she had outstripped her competitors, to such an extent that it was said that the city was built on the bones of African slaves, that several of the principal streets had been marked out by the chains, and the walls of the houses cemented by the blood, of Africans[124] and one street was nicknamed "Negro Row."[125] It was no moral scruple which restrained Liverpool from stooping to conquer in the race for commercial greatness and from participating in a trade in which every seaport of Europe was engaged from Gottenburg to Cadiz. "No more scruple was then felt as to the lawfulness of the slave trade than as to the lawfulness of the trade in black cattle."[126] A Liverpool historian contemporary with the discussion of the abolition of the slave trade stated that the African trade had increased in 1764 to such an extent that more than one-fourth of Liverpool's shipping sailed for Africa, and she had more than one-half of the African trade of the whole kingdom.[127] The American War suspended the slave trade,[128] but the resurgence of the trade after the war led to renewed prosperity, and for its amazing popularity we have the verdict of our contemporary historians: "Almost every man in Liverpool is a merchant, and he who cannot send a bale will send a band-box . . . almost every order of people is interested in a Guinea cargo, it is to this influenza that (there are) so many small ships," and in a footnote he added, "it is well known that many of the small vessels that import about 100 slaves are fitted out by attornies, drapers, ropers, grocers, tallow-chandlers, barbers, taylors, etc. Some have 1/8th, some 1/15th, some 1/32nd."[129]

121. For an excellent account see *Gaston-Martin: Nantes, l'Ère des Négriers, 1714–1774* (Paris, 1931).

122. Cit. *Klingberg*, pages 78–79.

123. *J. Corry: The History of Lancashire* (London, 1825), Vol. II, page 689.

124. Ibid., page 690.

125. *H. Smithers: Liverpool, its Commerce, Statistics and Institutions* (Liverpool, 1825), page 105.

126. *T. Baines: History of the Commerce and the Town of Liverpool.* (Liverpool 1852), page 694.

127. *J. Wallace: A General and Descriptive History of the Ancient and Present State of the Town of Liverpool . . . together with a circumstantial account of the true causes of its extensive African trade* (Liverpool, 1795), page 217.

128. *Baines, op. cit.,* page 717.

129. *Wallace, op. cit.,* pages 229–230.

But when the subject of abolition came up, many hitherto unknown and unpleasant facts were brought to light. Lord Sheffield might resent the fact that boroughs and towns of as little weight as Old Sarum were prevailed on to address against the continuance of the slave trade, to join in the popular cry, and take upon themselves to decide the fate of Bristol and of Liverpool.[130] But despite the danger of giving evidence against the trade,[131] many writers were at hand to prove that the unanimity of the Liverpool inhabitants to support the slave trade was a myth and that the halcyon days of prosperity for the slave trade were over.

According to Liverpool's eighteenth century historian, about ten capital houses had almost a monopoly of Liverpool's African trade and made large profits, but "the remainder by reason of their various subdivisions can contribute little to the increase of a fortune, although the returns may sometimes timely arrive to prop a tottering credit."[132] Another Liverpool writer, William Roscoe, estimated that of thirty mercantile houses, which had carried on nearly the whole of the trade since 1773, twelve had actually gone bankrupt, many others were supposed to have sustained considerable losses, and those known to have made profits out of it were few in number. The only exception to this was the masters of the slave ships, to whom the trade had been uniformly advantageous, their profits arising chiefly from a commission on the purchase.[133]

---

130. *Lord Sheffield: Observations on the Project for Abolishing the Slave Trade* (London, 1790), page 57.

131. Mr. Gotwold, invited to attend the Privy Council to give information on the innocent point of the methods used by the missionaries in converting the Negroes and of the success of their efforts, wrote in reply that "he was going out of town and wished not to interfere publickly in the business of the slave trade" (B.T. 6/12. Minutes of the African Questions, June 18, 1788). Much to Clarkson's surprise, a Mr. Norris, who had vehemently denounced the trade and even outlined a plan for encouraging a legitimate commerce with Africa, later differed from Clarkson, and turned out to be one of Liverpool's chief delegates who gave evidence on the necessity of continuing the slave trade (*Clarkson: History*, pages 275–276), Mr. Hercules Ross wrote to Wilberforce that his testimony before the House of Commons had gained him plentiful abuse and the grossest insult and the loss of all his West Indian connexions (*Life of Wilberforce*, Vol. I, pages 354–355). Capt. Hall craved his friendship on behalf of a virtuous family of eight, deprived of his assistance through the loss of his employment because of his testimony about the slaves (Ibid.). Glasgow petitioners had to address the box containing their petitions to other persons, that its contents might be unsuspected (Ibid.). James Adair, entreating Lord Hawkesbury to intercede with Dundas on behalf of the author of a plan to preserve the health and lives of the troops in the West Indies, wrote: "Were Mr. Dundas to know that your Lordship did not disapprove of my conduct respecting the long agitated business of the slave trade that gentleman might perhaps be more favourable to my application in favour of a deserving young man." (*Liverpool Papers*, Add. Mss. 38230, folio 76. Oct. 25, 1794).

132. *Wallace, op. cit.*, page 231.

133. W. Roscoe: *A General View of the African Slave Trade demonstrating its Injustice and Impolicy* (London, 1788), pages 23–24. This tract was sympathetically reviewed by Arthur Young: *Annals of Agriculture*, Vol. IX, 1788, page 181.

Other authors support the contention of the Liverpool writers. In answer to a usual objection that the West Indian trade was most profitable to Britain, Ramsay asked: "why is every sugar factor trying all he can to shake off his connections with the sugar planters, or to confine them entirely to the sale of his sugars and the shipping of his stores? Can any planter now borrow money on his West Indian property, either to improve it or pay off pressing demands? Has there not been more bankruptcies among capital houses connected with the sugar colonies, than in any other branch of trade? Nay, it will be found that the slave trader himself complains of the tardiness of the planters' payments."[134] The African Committee, though vested with extraordinary powers, failed twice. According to Clarkson, the London merchants, from 1763 to 1778, avoided all connection with those of Liverpool from the conviction that the trade had been prosecuted at the loss £700,000 and had led to many bankruptcies.[135] While Clarkson, we note, spoke only of the period ending in 1778, in the last four years of which Britain was at war with the American colonists, still we see to what extent public confidence had been shaken in a trade till then considered one of the plums of commerce.

The profits of the slave trader were considerably curtailed by reason of the sad plight of the majority of the West Indian proprietors. We have already seen how the re-export of slaves to the foreign islands was justified by the fact that the foreign planters paid in cash, while the British planters needed long credits. According to Roscoe, these long credits were another heavy deduction from the profits of the slave merchant, as well as a very important condition to his risk. It was not infrequent for these bills to be drawn at even three years' date, and even then it was usual for them to be returned to the West Indies for want of payment.[136]

In addition to this it could be said that, for all practical purposes, Liverpool by 1788 was the sole port still interested in the continuance of the slave traffic. Clarkson computed that London and Bristol only possessed forty vessels employed in the trade; "to suppose, therefore, that any kind of distress could be felt by the total secession of these, or any kind of stagnation take place, would be to expose myself to derision: for I might as well suppose, that if forty drops of water were to be taken from a bucket, they would be missed."[137]

In the House of Commons these arguments were repeated. Wilberforce, following Clarkson, rejected the view that it was the slave trade which had

---

134. J. Ramsay: *Objections to the Abolition of the Slave Trade with answers* (London, 1788), page 42.
135. *Clarkson: Impolicy*, page 29.
136. *Roscoe, op. cit.*, page 23.
137. *Clarkson: Impolicy*, page 123.

brought Liverpool greatness, because it formed only one-thirtieth part of her export trade, and was a losing trade on the whole. In Bristol, the trade was a still smaller proportion of the total commerce.[138] A few individuals profited by the traffic, but to state it as a great source of national wealth was ridiculous.[139]

One other argument was easily refuted, that the slave trade was the means of exporting a vast quantity of British manufactures to Africa. These cheap cotton and East India goods, trinkets, instruments of torture, bad rum from the West Indies, and firearms—"for the purposes, doubtless," gibed William Smith, "of maintaining peace and encouraging civilization among its various tribes"[140]—, all this trade amounted on an average, according to the reliable evidence of Mr. Irving of the Custom House, to about £400,000 a year.[141] William Smith put the average figure at £500,000, and said it had never risen to more than £900,000;[142] according to Clarkson it was £800,000 in 1786. Ramsay was, therefore, amply justified in saying that this trade was "not of that consequence which may not be made to yield to weighty considerations"; and in view of "the shuffling way, at which a Jew pedlar would blush," in which it was carried on, the damaged goods, false measures and frauds on the unsuspecting Africans, "we should take shame as a people that such a trade should find among us a single advocate."[143]

Taking all these facts into consideration, it is difficult not to agree with Wilberforce that the superior capital, ingenuity, industry and integrity of the British manufacturer would command new markets for the produce of his industry, if the slave trade was abolished.[144] If Britain was not ruined by the secession of the American colonies, it was absurd to think that she was entirely dependent for her wealth and importance upon the slave trade, or that, as was said later of the bill for the abolition of the foreign slave trade, the consequence of abolition would be that the manufacturers of Manchester, Stockport and Paisley would be going about naked and starving.[145] Bristol soon petitioned against the slave trade. Dr. Currie wrote to Wilberforce in

---

138. *Parl. Hist,*. Vol. XXIX, pages 271–272. April 18, 1791.
139. Ibid., page 1065. April 2, 1792.
140. Ibid., page 320. April 18, 1791. Of 7,700,000 tons of gunpowder exported from Britain in one year, half went to Africa. To the credit of the abolitionists it must be said that they admitted that it was the European demand for slaves which produced the slave trade, the consequent distracted state of Africa and the destruction of what "civilization" Africa formerly knew. See Pitt's speeches, April 19, 1791 and April 2, 1792.
141. Ibid., page 272. Quoted by Wilberforce, April 18, 1791.
142. Ibid., pages 319–320. April 18, 1791.
143. *Ramsay: Ms Vol.*, folio 63(v). "An Address on the proposed bill for the Abolition of the Slave Trade."
144. *Parl. Hist.*, Vol. XXIX, page 273. April 18, 1791.
145. *Parl. Deb.*, Vol. VI, page 917. Mr. Rose, April 25, 1806.

1792 that Liverpool would never again petition on the subject[146] and one of the foremost defenders of the trade in 1790, General Tarleton, lost his seat at the next election. The City of London returned to its "liberal traditions," and though the Mayor and Aldermen were strong enough to stifle a petition of the Common Council, the Liverymen at a meeting, with many groans and hisses, carried a motion in favour of abolition, which was presented to the House just as Wilberforce rose to make his motion in 1792.[147]

(f) The Expensiveness of Slave Labour

Such was the impolicy of the slave system. But these arguments must be seen against the background of the general economic movement of the time. The West Indians were attacked not only on the specific points at issue but on another, the full significance of which would only be appreciated in years to come, the expensiveness of slave labour as compared with free. That slave labour was in itself a reactionary form of production, both from the point of view of the productivity of labour and the full development of the capitalist market, was a lesson which the bourgeoisie were to learn fully before the end of the nineteenth century. In certain places the paucity of labour required and the fertility of the soil—usually combined—enabled slave cultivation still to be carried on at a profit; but on the whole, at the beginning of the Industrial Revolution, the bourgeoisie established the principle of the superiority of free labour over slave.

Telling blows against the slave system were struck by the two foremost champions of the rising middle class, Arthur Young and Adam Smith. "I have reason to believe," wrote Young, "the culture of sugar by slaves is the dearest species of labour in the world."[148] He, unlike other writers, preferred to deal rather with the impolicy and expense of the system than with the ill-treatment and cruelties attendant upon it. The product raised by slaves was absolutely contemptible in comparison with that of free labour in England, and he could think of no system of free labour which would not be cheaper than that of African slaves. It was slavery alone that induced the planters to prefer "the most preposterous modes of tillage that are known in the world . . . the overseers of plantations like the dominion of slaves better than that of cattle"; and he roundly condemned the system of slave labour as the least productive of any that was known, probably, in the world.[149]

146. *Life of Wilberforce*, Vol. I, pages 344–345.

147. *Coupland: Wilberforce* (Oxford, 1923), page 157; and *The British Anti-Slavery Movement* (London, 1933), page 95.

148. *Young, op. cit.*, Vol. IX, 1788, pages 92–93. "On the abolition of slavery in the West Indies."

149. Ibid., pages 88–89 and 94; and Vol. X, 1788, page 344. "West Indian Agriculture."

Adam Smith was no less vehement in his attack on slave labour and on monopolies in general—the West Indian colonies then enjoyed the greatest monopoly. "It appears," he wrote, "from the experience of all ages and nations, I believe, that the work done by free men comes cheaper than that performed by slaves."[150] He regarded the whole system as most uneconomical and held that it was only the superior profits from sugar and tobacco plantations which could afford the expense of slave cultivation[151]—when sugar profits decreased, the system, therefore, lost its only justification. Inventions were not to be expected from slaves, but from freemen only, and therefore more labour was needed to perform a certain quantity of work when done by slaves than when done by freemen.[152] Universal experience demonstrated conclusively that "work done by slaves, though it appears to cost only their maintenance, is in the end the dearest of any. A person who can acquire no property can have no other interest than to eat as much, and to labour as little as possible."[153]

One might possibly exaggerate the importance of the well-known story of Pitt's compliment to Adam Smith at a dinner party, "we are all your scholars," but Pitt's own speeches show that he had indeed sat at the feet of his Gamaliel. Smith, we know, was introduced by Dundas, in the spring of 1787, to Pitt and Wilberforce, and they met frequently.[154] Pitt proved a good disciple. Speaking in 1791 he argued eloquently in favour of free labour, asserted that "wherever there was the incentive of honour, credit and fair profit, there industry would be," and showed the danger of degrading the slaves into mere machines, for then they would become "more unprofitable, and every day more disadvantageous, than any other instrument of labour whatsoever."[155] Again in 1792 when we hear of the superior productivity of the labour of man over that of a mere brute, it is Adam Smith, with Pitt as mouthpiece, who speaks,[156] and in the same speech Pitt, using arguments of the colonial legislatures, proved that the productive labour of the colonies would, if the Negroes worked as free labourers instead of slaves, be literally doubled.[157] Lapse of years did nothing to lessen the disciple's faith in the

150. *Smith, op. cit.*, Vol. I, page 123. For a similar and interesting view of a Portuguese planter see *Report, 1789*, Part VI.

151. *Smith, op. cit.*, Vol. III, page 89.

152. Ibid., Vol. IV, page 37.

153. Ibid., Vol. III, page 88.

154. *R. I. and S. Wilberforce: The Correspondence of William Wilberforce* (London, 1840), Vol. I, page 40, footnote. (Referred to hereafter as *Wilberforce: Correspondence*.)

155. *Parl. Hist.*, Vol. XXIX, page 340. April 19, 1791.

156. Ibid., page 1139. April 2, 1792. "If you restore to this degraded race the true feelings of men; If you take them out from among the order of brutes, and place them on a level with the rest of the human species, they will work with that energy which is natural to men, and their labour will be productive, in a thousand ways, above what it has yet been; as the labour of a man is always more productive than that of a mere brute."

157. Ibid., page 1140.

master; in 1804, we hear an echo of the *Wealth of Nations*, that the principles of general philosophy proved that the system of restraint was as unprofitable as it was odious, and that the labour of a man who was conscious of freedom was much more valuable than that of one who felt he was a slave.[158]

The best commentary on Pitt's interest in this aspect of the question of abolition was supplied by one of his trusted friends, and an abolitionist, Grenville. Speaking in 1806, Grenville, in a comparison of slave labour with free, described Pitt's calculations in this respect as luminous and convincing. One of the incontrovertible results of these was that the expense of procuring the slaves, of transporting them, and of maintaining them afterwards, when compared with the value of the labour actually performed, was not nearly so profitable as the labour of free men brought to work in the first instance.[159] The master was dead: able disciples continued to popularize his teachings.

(g) Summary

By those connected with the colonies slavery was regarded as vital to their very existence. The West Indian islands, as the African merchants emphasized in a petition of 1788, would probably have been uncultivated and useless but for the African Negroes.[160] It was not surprising, therefore, that the colonists should have been alarmed at the idea of abolition. Stephen Fuller wrote to Lord Hawkesbury urging that the Colonial Governors should be instructed to put into execution the act against assemblies of 1760. The slaves, he affirmed, would be well informed of what was transpiring in Britain, and he asked "whether it is most probable that they will wait with patience for a tardy event, or whether they will not strike whilst the iron is hot, and by a sudden blow finish the business in the most expeditious and effectual manner, without giving their zealous friends here any further trouble."[161]

As early as 1788 the Governor of Jamaica reported the great alarm occasioned in all ranks of people there;[162] "they conceive the prosperity or ruin of the island to depend upon the issue of a question in which their all is involved," and he condemned the apparent misrepresentations upon which the agitation for abolition seemed to be founded.[163] The Jamaica Assembly resolved in 1789 that "the slave trade being the great source of every West Indian improvement, its abolition must inevitably diminish the value of all such securities," and that it would lead to the ruin of many mortgagees and annuitants. They

158. *Parl. Deb.* Vol. II, page 550. June 7, 1804.
159. Ibid., Vol. VII, page 804. June 24, 1806.
160. B.T. 6/12. Feb. 19, 1788.
161. *Liverpool Papers*, Add. Mss. 38416, folio 6. Jan. 29, 1788.
162. C.O. 137/87. April 22, 1788.
163. Ibid. Dec. 9, 1788.

demanded, if the worst came to the worst, the compensation to which they were undoubtedly entitled, quoting as precedents the compensation made to the African Committee in 1752 and to the slave merchants on the passing of Dolben's Act in 1788 regulating the transport of slaves.[164] Major-General Williamson, sent to Jamaica in 1790, wrote to Dundas: "I cannot help expressing my earnest wish that the Abolition Bill should not pass the House of Lords, as it is impossible to say what the consequences here may be."[165] The Council of Barbados expected from its agent in London his forcible opposition to the pernicious plan of abolition which, if successful, must effectively ruin the island. The Antigua Assembly expressed the hope that, "if it is now thought proper, from motives of more refined humanity," to abolish the slave trade, they would be entitled to the justice of Parliament and reasonable compensation.[166]

Bridges, the Jamaica annalist, ascribed the agitation for abolition to unworthy and interested motives.[167] But the colonists as a body could not be expected to understand those weighty economic considerations which had emerged from the discussion of the question, still less the revulsion of feeling which was sweeping over Britain as the true facts came to light. Population statistics of the British West Indies, the extent to which Britain herself was responsible for that amazing development of the foreign islands, particularly the French, which was one of the chief objects of inquiry with the Privy Council,[168] the mortality among British seamen and the pecuniary losses among the majority of British Merchants engaged in the trade: all these considerations contributed to the general idea of the impolicy of the slave trade which was summed up so well by Ramsay: "we may confidently conclude that the African trade is more confined in its utility than is generally imagined and that of late years it has contributed more to the aggrandisement of our rivals than of our national wealth."[169]

---

164. C.O. 137/88. Oct. 20, 1789. Report, Resolutions and Remonstrance of the Hon. the Council and Assembly of Jamaica at a Joint Committee on the subject of the Slave Trade.

165. C.O. 137/91. Dec. 2, 1792.

166. *Report, 1789*, Part III. Feb. 27, 1788.

167. *Bridges, op. cit.*, Vol. II, pages 195–196. "It might be true, but it would be ungenerous, to attribute to party feeling or to political principle what at first assumed the appearance of that spirit of freedom and liberty which characterises our native land: and we may rather ascribe to unworthy motives the interference of those who embraced the opportunity to impose upon the popular credulity, and raise their fortune by preaching the crusade which now commenced against the sugar colonies."

168. *Report, 1789*, Part V.

169. *Ramsay: Inquiry*, page 24. Clarkson dotted the i's and crossed the t's of Ramsay's statement. "The slave trade, considered abstractedly by itself, is *of no emolument to the nation*; it is *unprofitable, on the whole, to individuals*; and it is the *grave of our seamen*, destroying more of them in one year than all the other trades of Great Britain, when put together, destroy in two." *Impolicy*, page 136.

CHAPTER TWO

The Superiority
of the French West Indies

"While the English stood first in the Slave Trade," writes Klingberg, "the French led all others in their genius for using slave labour."[1] The superiority of the French islands in the West Indies was for their British rivals the chief among the many ills which flew out of the Pandora's box which was the American revolution.

All writers of the time admitted without hesitation this cardinal fact of the superiority of the French islands and the superiority of French colonial genius. "Nothing," wrote Chalmers on the morrow of the American secession, "has ever appeared more striking or unaccountable than the difference between the British West Indies and the French."[2] Ramsay warned his countrymen that if they continued to encourage the slave trade for the supply of the French colonies, such was the extensiveness and fertility of those islands and such the frugality of their planters, that, despite the enormous bounty paid in Britain, "in less than 20 years . . . they will worm us out of every foreign market for sugar."[3] The abolitionist historian emphasized the greater extent and more advantageous disposition of territory, and the superior natural resources of the French islands.[4]

---

1. *Klingberg, op. cit.,* page 14.
2. *Chalmers, op. cit.,* page 138.
3. *Ramsay: Inquiry,* pages 23–24.
4. H. Brougham: *The Colonial Policy of the European Powers* (Edinburgh, 1803), Vol. I, page 520. Brougham estimated that the average fertility of St. Domingo was above three times greater than that of Jamaica, Ibid., page 521.

So striking was the disparity between the British and French islands that it became an object of particular inquiry with the Privy Council of 1788 to find out why the French planters could send their sugars to the European market so much cheaper than the British. The abolitionists very early directed their attention to this point. Ramsay alleged the residence of the planters,[5] the fresher and more luxuriant soil, and the comparative independence of foreign supplies of food as the reasons why the French could produce sugar at two-thirds of its usual price in the British colonies: the French price he reckoned at 16/- per cwt. the British at 25/-[6] and he observed that these cheaper French sugars had long been finding their way into the British colonies.[7] Clarkson, too, admitted that the French, from a variety of reasons, were able to under-sell their British rivals in the European markets, and indicated the danger to British naval supremacy from the fact that this larger produce demanded an increased number of ships which, carrying double the number of seamen as compared with British ships, constituted a menace to Britain, all the more as the French depended solely upon their American possessions for recruits for the navy.[8] The careful investigation of the Privy Council proved that the difference of price arose from the superior quality of the land in St. Domingo and that the same number of Negroes yielded considerably more on the French than on the British plantations.[9]

If we allow for some undoubtedly pardonable exaggeration on the part of the British planters giving evidence before the Privy Council we can nevertheless see the extent of French superiority. "The lands of St. Domingo," testified the Jamaica agents, "are beyond all controversy far more productive, and cultivated by much fewer hands in proportion than those of Jamaica." They estimated that the French sugar which cost 36/4, cost in Jamaica 45/-, that the average yield of a property in St. Domingo was two and a half hogsheads of muscovado sugar, whereas in Jamaica it did not much exceed half a hogshead, and in the most productive parish, St. James, did not amount in a favourable year to three-quarters of a hogshead. A property sold in St. Domingo for upwards of £25,000, would probably not have fetched in Jamaica more than £6,000 or £7,000 at the utmost. St. Domingo furnished three-quarters of all the sugar grown in the French colonies, Jamaica only

---

5. There was no West Indian interest in France comparable to the formidable body in Britain. The planter's residence was universally conceded to be advantageous, because it did not leave the slaves at the mercy of an overseer whose position depended upon the output of sugar. The Council and Assembly of Montserrat advanced another reason, "the great benefit the offals of his table are to his poor and sick negroes." *Report*, 1789. Part III.

6. *Ramsay: Inquiry*, pages 22–23.

7. *Ramsay: Objections*, page 22.

8. *Clarkson: Impolicy*, page 81.

9. *Brougham, op. cit.*, Vol. I, page 522.

one-half of that grown in the British, and they reckoned, undoubtedly an exaggeration, that the average produce of cane lands in St. Domingo was five and a quarter times the produce in Jamaica. They quoted a well-known French planter, Hilliard d'Auberteuil, as proof that this disparity was attested by French as well as British planters, doubted the power of the British planters to compete with the French, and declared that they could no longer continue to "retain in the European market that ascendancy which, we now fear, is irretrievably lost to Britain." The agents of the other islands expatiated with equal fervour on the superior advantages of the French islands, and agreed that the French could undersell them from 10 to 20 per cent cheaper, the Governor of Grenada even putting the percentage as high as from 20 to 25 per cent.[10]

The greater fertility of soil in French St. Domingo was a striking contrast to the variability of the soil in the British colonies. In Antigua the yield varied from three hogsheads to half a hogshead per acre; in Nevis the average was somewhat more than one hogshead per acre; in Grenada some plantations produced three hogsheads per acre while others did not produce one; and in Dominica the amount varied from three to five hogsheads per acre to scarcely half a hogshead on plantations within a very short distance.[11]

Contemporary writers complained of the amount of British colonial debts and asserted that in this respect of the sums owed to the mother country the French colonies were superior. Money which might be better expended on British internal development was being squandered on unprofitable colonies whose utility was now being questioned.[12] But these writers were quite wrong in insisting, like Adam Smith, that the capital which went to improve the French colonies, particularly the great colony of St. Domingo, was raised almost entirely from the produce of the soil and industry of the colonists, whereas improvements in the British colonies were the result of capital sent out from Britain.[13] It was only the greater opportunities for borrowing

---

10. For all this testimony see *Report, 1789*. Part V. d'Auberteuil boasted that "in Jamaica, Grenada, etc., the price of sugars is always 15 or 20 per cent higher than at St. Domingo."

11. *Report, 1789*, Part III.

12. Adam Smith regretted the readiness with which societies of merchants in London and other trading towns bought waste land in the sugar colonies, which they expected to improve and cultivate by means of agents, despite the distance and uncertain returns. *Op. cit.*, Vol. 1, page 245. Arthur Young thought that even one-half of the capital invested in the colonies would, if invested in domestic industry, produce a greater amount of national prosperity and a greater public revenue, and employ more shipping and more seamen. *Op. cit.*, Vol. IX, 1788, pages 95–96. Ramsay did not doubt that "we should have been a happier, wealthier nation had we attended to agriculture and manufactures, without possessing a foot of land out of Great Britain and Ireland." Ms.Vol., folio 64. "An address on the proposed bill for the abolition of the Slave Trade."

13. *Smith, op. cit.*, Vol IV, pages 396–397. Chalmers compared the British planter, bred in the lap of luxury, with his French competitor, reared in the school of misfortune, and therefore forced to be

capital which made the British planter "not satisfied with the slow and frugal process of the French planter," and induced him to proceed "in a more rapid and expensive mode in the improvement of his property and his produce."[14] According to Brougham, even during the most flourishing periods of the French colonies, their cultivation depended on a much more extensive system of credit than in the British islands, the result of the encouragement to speculation held out by the extent of the fertile lands in the French colonies. He estimated the French planters' debts before the Revolution at the value of two whole years' produce of the islands, and we are informed that in the French islands such premiums were paid for ready money that in the purchase of slaves an abatement of twenty per cent was not at all uncommon for cash.[15] Bordeaux invested one hundred million livres in St. Domingo in the five years after the American war. The French merchant held the colonist as the usurer held his debtor. Colonial debts were estimated at twenty millions in 1774, and at three hundred, and even five hundred, millions in 1789.[16]

Adam Smith, despite his dislike of colonies in general, considered the French colonies far superior to the British, and the specific point he selected for mention was the good management of their slaves by the French.[17] We have already referred to the heavier mortality of the French slaves, due either to the more brutal treatment of the French masters, or to the climate, or more probably, as has been hazarded in another place, because French imports were generally used immediately for taking new lands into cultivation before they were properly "seasoned." In general it is difficult to agree with Adam Smith, though he was speaking of the greater protection the underdog gets in an arbitrary government. The Code Noir was always an ideal, it was never translated into reality. There was no fundamental difference between the French and the British slave owner: in both cases it is not individuals we have to deal with but the hard inescapable logic of economic necessity.

---

careful and to proceed gradually. "The French planters found capital in their resources; the British found capitals in England." *Op. cit.*, page 138. He estimated West Indian debts to Britain at fifty million and warned the nation that "it ought to be constantly remembered that the frugality of the French, from the peer to the peasant, will ultimately degrade the greatness of Britain." Ibid., pages 139 and 117.

14. *Report, 1789*, Part V. Lt. Gen. Mathew of Grenada. See Mr. Laing of Dominica (ibid): "a Frenchman skims his coppers with a perforated calabash; an Englishman with a copper skimmer. The former strains his liquor through a basket; the latter through a fine wire strainer. The latter feeds his mules with oats and other grain; the former with the skum of his coppers."

15. *Brougham, op. cit.*, Vol. I, pages 515–516.

16. *L. Deschamps: Les Colonies pendant la Révolution* (Paris, 1898); page 25.

17. *Smith, op. cit.*, Vol. IV, page 395. Compare Wilberforce to Eden: "To our shame we use them more barbarously than any other European nation." *Auckland Papers*, Add.Mss. 34427, folio 122(v). Nov. 23, 1787.

But bearing this in mind, the French treatment of their slaves was in one important respect superior to the British. The French never had a North America to depend on; "*l'exclusif*" in France was as severe as mercantilism in Britain—any French statesman might have uttered Chatham's famous *mot* which forbade the colonies to manufacture even a horseshoe[18]—, but the French marine was unable to keep pace with colonial demands, and the Seven Years' War had shown the danger of famine. As a result the colonists were forced to aim, as far as was possible, at economic self-sufficiency and to grow those provisions and provide that food for their Negroes which their British rivals obtained from America. The British by this were enabled to devote their attention more and more to the growth of the staple crops, especially sugar. "Sugar, sugar," lamented Ramsay, "is the incessant cry of luxury and of debt. . . . Hence the annual expence of plantations within less than thirty years has been more than doubled. Hence the sending of two or three extra casks of sugar to market has been attended with an expence of hundreds of pounds in provisions to slaves, in oats to horses, and in keeping up the stock of slaves and cattle, worn out before their time by indiscreet extraordinary efforts and a scanty allowance." The superior fertility of St. Christopher, in his view, had the most baneful effects. It enabled the proprietors to live in Britain, "where, insensible of the sufferings of their slaves, they think and dream of nothing but sugar; to which in consequence, every spot of land is condemned."[19] No wonder the Governor of the Bahamas could write, to the Privy Council, "we grow no sugar and I hope never will."[20] The French islands, St. Domingo in particular, apart from growing their own food, grew not only sugar, but coffee, cotton and indigo in large quantities.

It is clear that the French slaves were not treated better than their unfortunate brethren in the British islands. Manumissions, admittedly, were more numerous in the French Islands: in 1788 the proportion of free Mulattoes to slaves was in the British islands only 1 in 42, as compared with 1 in 19 in the French, though the number of British slaves was only two-thirds that of the French.[21] This can be accounted for by the different attitude of the French planters to the Negroes, and the greater wealth of St. Domingo, where Mulattoes were known who were quite rich. But no attention to food, provision

18. *Gaston-Martin*, *op. cit.*, page 27.

19. *J. Ramsay: Essay on the Treatment and Conversion of African Slaves in the British Colonies* (London, 1784), page 80 (footnote).

20. *Report, 1789*, Part III.

21. *A. Moreau de Jonnès: Recherches Statistiques sur l'Esclavage Colonial* (Paris, 1842), pages 42–43. "On voit que les colons anglais avaient affranchi beaucoup moins d'esclaves que les colons français. Au bout d'un siècle et demi, la proportion était d'un sur trente-six, au lieu d'un sur seize. C'était la moitié moins proportionnellement à leur nombre."

grounds, clothing and observance of rest days for the slaves, could alter this single fact of the heavy mortality from the new cultivation, as Wilberforce early recognised.[22] The Jamaica agents stated the annual diminution in the French islands, by the confession of the French planters themselves, as one-fifth of the whole number of slaves, whereas in the British islands it was only one-fortieth, and the French reckoned that one-third of all their imported Negroes died within three years from the time of importation.[23]

But despite the greater need of slaves and the higher prices paid for them,[24] the French advantages were so great that their profits far exceeded those of their British rivals, and it was those profits and the increase in sugar prices during the 1780's which permitted them to develop new plantations in St. Domingo, less fertile than the rest. The Committee of the Council of Jamaica estimated the average profits at four per cent. Governor Parry thought that the profit in Barbados did not exceed six per cent, and doubted if it was as high. For Montserrat the Council and Assembly gave three per cent as the net income, while its agent put the Jamaica figure at three and a half per cent, St. Kitts at six per cent perhaps on the most fertile lands, and Grenada, Antigua and other islands at five per cent. Governor Mathew of Grenada gave the maximum profit at six per cent, while on the majority of plantations it was only four percent, leading as a result to the wholesale abandonment of plantations.[25] One Barbados planter even went so far as to say that the general distress in the island was encouraging a transfer from sugar to cotton.[26] Rev. Ramsay doubted whether the majority of the small plantations paid the interest due upon them, and asserted that even those which supplied their owners with the most splendid revenues would not bear closer examination.[27] A planter resident in Britain confirmed that the instances were few where the planter obtained eight per cent upon his capital, the usual return being but five or six per cent.[28] In the consensus of opinion a fair profit upon the capital of a sugar plantation in the British islands was reckoned at not less than ten per cent.[29]

---

22. *Auckland Papers*, Add.Mss. 34427, folios 49(v)–50. To Eden, Nov. 7, 1787.

23. *Report, 1789*, Part V. The merchants of Roseau computed that the French plantations required five per cent to keep up the numbers of the slaves, whereas the British required only about three per cent.

24. Ibid. Mr. Robinson of Dominica: "his capital is greater in slaves, about 10 per cent more than the English planter, because he pays more for imported slaves, about 15 per cent."

25. Ibid., Part III.

26. Ibid. Papers received since the date of the Report.

27. Ibid., Part III. Further Evidence received by the Committee.

28. *Considerations on the Emancipation of Negroes and on the Abolition of the Slave Trade*, page 4.

29. *H. of C. Sess. Pap. Report on the Commercial State of the West India Colonies*. Reports II, Series III, page 4. July 24, 1807.

If we turn to the French islands, particularly St. Domingo, we see just the opposite. The Jamaica agents quoted M. d'Auberteuil's estimate that one-third of the plantations in St. Domingo yielded a profit of twelve per cent, and the others eight per cent, and declared that these profits were much more than double what was gained by the planters in Jamaica, where the average was only four per cent.[30] The condition of the British West Indies was truly parlous.

All the factors outlined above contributed to make French St. Domingo in 1789 the cynosure of all eyes, "the gem of the West Indies."[31] With a population of over 30,000 whites, nearly 25,000 free Negroes, and over 480,000 slaves, it contained some 800 sugar plantations, over 3,000 coffee, nearly 800 cotton and 2,950 indigo.[32] "In 1789," writes Stoddard, "San Domingo had attained a height of prosperity not surpassed in the history of European colonies. The greatest part of its soil was covered by plantations on a gigantic scale which supplied half Europe with sugar, coffee and cotton."[33] The exports from St. Domingo in 1788 totalled 70,227,709 lbs. of clayed sugar, 93,177,512 lbs. of raw sugar, 68,151,181 lbs. of coffee, 6,286,126 lbs. of cotton, and 930,016 lbs of indigo.[34] "Santo Domingo," commented Leroy-Beaulieu, "became the greatest sugar producer in the world. Its exports rose from 11,000 *livres tournois* in 1711 to 193 million in 1788 or nearly £8 million sterling; it was almost double the actual exportation from Jamaica, calculated in money, and it was more than double calculated in quantity, its commerce employed 1,000 ships and 15,000 French sailors."[35] The exports of sugar, coffee and cotton were valued in 1789 at more than one-third than those of all the British West Indies combined.[36] "All the English sugar colonies," boasted d'Auberteuil, "were not equal French St. Domingo."[37] The importation into France from all the French colonies of colonial products in 1789 was estimated at £10,935,000;[38] the value of the produce from St. Domingo, Guadeloupe and Martinique was, according to Mr. Irving of the Custom House, over eleven million pounds in 1790.[39]

30. *Report, 1789*, Part V.
31. *T. L. Stoddard: The French Revolution in San Domingo* (New York, 1914), page 6.
32. *Liverpool Papers*, Add.Mss. 38349, folio 364. Written after 1789. The figures of *Moreau de Jonnès*, *op. cit.*, page 27, for 1788 are: Whites 27,787; free coloured 21,810, slaves 405,828. *Stoddard*, *op. cit.*, page 9, agrees with this.
33. *Stoddard*, *op. cit.*, pages 14–15.
34. *Liverpool Papers*, Add. Mss. 38349, folio 395.
35. Cit. *Klingberg*, pages 13–14.
36. Ibid., page 103.
37. *Chatham Papers*, G.D. 8/349.
38. *Liverpool Papers*, Add. Mss. 38349, folio 355. Written after 1789.
39. *Chatham Papers*, G.D. 8/351.

The French dominated the sugar market of Europe because of their lower costs of production. French colonial products re-exported abroad rose from 15 millions at the end of the reign of Louis XIV to 152 millions at the outbreak of the revolution.[40] Jaurès quotes the speech of one Ducos, the deputy for Bordeaux, in the Legislative Assembly, in which he explained the French domination of the sugar market by the higher standard of living in Britain, which made the use of sugar more general and considerable than in France. Such was French influence, the deputy continued, over her neighbours that prices in the various markets of the North followed the fluctuations of the French market, for the simple reason that France retained only one-eighth of her sugar imports for domestic consumption, the remainder being purchased by agents for foreign countries.[41] In 1807 the Jamaica agent, Hibbert, estimated that at the outbreak of the Revolution, when France had attained the zenith of her colonial prosperity, of 80 million livres exported to the Baltic, 55 were in colonial produce; of 424 millions exported to Europe, the Levant and continental America, 152 were in colonial produce. It was "by it, and by it alone, that she turned the balance of the trade with all the world to a favourable result."[42]

The amazing development of St. Domingo took place during the years immediately preceding the Revolution. According to Arnould, French imports from the colonies increased from 16,700,000 livres at the end of the reign of Louis XIV to 185 millions on the eve of the Revolution, and French exports to the colonies from 9 millions to 77,900,000 livres during the same period, although in the intervening years France had lost Canada and Grenada.[43] This development was much more rapid than anything of the same kind in the history of colonization. In the period of ten years the Negro population and total produce of St. Domingo had almost doubled.[44] Comparing the import and export figures of the British and French islands, Brougham put the French colonial exports at £8,300,000, which employed 164,081 tons of shipping, navigated by 33,400 men, and the imports at £4,100,000; and the British exports at £5,200,000, which employed 148,176 tons of shipping, navigated by 13,936 seamen, and he valued the British imports at £1,900,000. "Such," he concluded, "was the decided superiority of the French over the British colonies before the Revolution. The proportion

---

40. *Arnould, op. cit.* Vol. I, page 263. "The consumption of coffee and sugar, the produce of the French islands, for which Amsterdam and Hamburg are the *entrepôts*, is considerable in Germany, Switzerland, Denmark, Sweden and Russia." Ibid., Vol. I, page 331.
41. *J. Jaurès: Histoire Socialiste de la Révolution Française.* (Paris, 1927), Vol. III, pages 295–296.
42. *Parl. Deb.*, Vol. IX, pages 90–91. March 12, 1807.
43. *Arnould, op. cit.*, Vol. I, page 326.
44. *Brougham, op. cit.*, Vol. I, page 522.

which the French colony trade bore to the whole French trade was greater than that which the British colony trade bore to the whole British trade. . . . In every view the French American colonies were much more essential to the mother country than the English."[45]

M. de Curt, a planter from the French Windward Islands, reminded the National Assembly of France in 1789 that the colonies were "the principal and almost the only market for the sale of French manufactures as well as the principal support of the maritime power of France."[46] Barnave, the inveterate opponent in the Assembly of the idealism which threatened by its implications the entire social fabric of the colonial system, pointed out that French navigation was entirely the result of her colonial possessions; for France, unlike Britain, had no coasting trade, and could not compare with Britain in the importance of her fisheries, the immensity of her trade with India or with the Baltic. "To relinquish her colonies is therefore to relinquish the naval power of France: in which case the English power will acquire an unrivalled ascendancy in the ocean."[47]

Such was the essential difference in 1789 between the British and French islands. The French colonies, vastly superior to the British, were indispensable to France. The British colonies, comparatively insignificant and unprofitable, seemed in the eyes of many to be a burden to the mother country. The system of mutual monopoly, which was what mercantilism meant, seemed to be operating to the benefit more of the colonies than of the mother country. Between the West Indies of 1789 and the West Indies of 1774 there was the wide chasm of the American Revolution. France could point to tangible results from her intervention on the side of the American colonists. Her greatest gain was the altered situation in the Caribbean.

---

45. Ibid., Vol. I, pages 539–540.
46. *Chatham Papers*, G.D. 8/334.
47. Ibid.

CHAPTER THREE

East India Sugar

The loss of the American colonies shifted the Centre of gravity from West to East, from the Caribbean Sea to the Indian Ocean. The Treaty of Versailles was followed in quick succession by the India Bills of Fox and Pitt, and there is evidence to show that as early as 1783 Pitt took an abnormally great interest in the British dominions in the East.[1]

It has already been emphasized that since the American War the rapid strides and development made by the French colonists had resulted in their complete ascendancy in the European market. How to recover this lost supremacy was the problem that confronted British statesmen in the last decade of the century. The key to the question of the introduction of East India sugar lies not so much in the high prices which prevailed from 1789 and reached their peak in 1792 and 1793—these high prices only encouraged the idea of a substitute—but in the export market.

The question of East India sugar, of sugar grown by freemen, was intimately connected, by abolitionists themselves, with the abolition movement. "The great question in the cultivation of sugar at present," wrote Arthur Young,

---

1. *Chatham Papers*, G.D. 8/102. Pitt, probably to the Governor of the East India Company, Nov. 25, 1783—"It has occurred to me to be a very material part of the Company's case, to show that the bill-holders are willing to allow the company all convenient time before they call for payment. I have in general understood that they are inclined to do so; but it would add a great weight if a public declaration could be obtained from them *as a body* to that effect. For that purpose it might be desirable to convene a public meeting of them; tho' such a measure ought not undoubtedly to be proposed without a certainty of success, I could not forbear suggesting this to your consideration. I must beg the favour of you, however, not to mention the idea *as from me*, and to excuse the liberty I take in troubling you."

"is that of employing free hands or slaves. Those who have been the warmest advocates for the abolition insist that the culture could be effected by free men; as sugar is raised much cheaper in Bengal by free hands than in the West Indies by slaves, the opinion seems not to be without weight."[2] The sugar which in the British islands cost 25/- per cwt. and in the French 16/- per cwt. could be raised in the East Indies, according to Ramsay, for 3/4d. per cwt.,[3] according to Dickson for 2/6d. per cwt.,[4] due to the single fact of free labour. A Mr. Botham, giving evidence before the Privy Council as to the mode of cultivating the sugar cane in the East Indies, declared that "slavery necessarily required a degree of cruelty," advised the West Indian planter in his own interest to "give more labour to beast and less to man," and handed in a paper to prove that sugar of a superior quality and lower price could be raised in the East Indies, merely because a sugar plantation in the East Indies was cultivated with one-third less human labour than a similar plantation in the West Indies.[5]

"It is a remarkable fact," we read in a tract written in 1827, "that the first few chests of indigo, the produce of free labour in the East, arrived in England in 1787, just about the time when the first efforts were making for the abolition of the slave trade."[6] In dealing with the question of the new importance of the East Indies, we must think not of sugar only, but of cotton and indigo. St. Domingo was pre-eminent in all three, the British Islands deficient; the East was to be called into existence to redress the balance of the West.

Bengal cotton, it was asserted, was the finest in the world: "the qualities most in esteem are the East India and Pernambuco cottons, which are used for our finest fabrics." One of the observations relative to the resources of the East India Company for productive remittance was that "the article of fine cotton wool claims a pre-eminence over everything else." If the raw wool, it was stated, was imported from India it would greatly injure and perhaps ruin most of the West Indian colonies.[7]

The Company was equally alive to the value of indigo. The Committee of Warehouses reported in 1788 that, while it was not likely to prove of any commercial benefit because of the high price, they conceived it to be an object worthy of every attention from a political point of view. It would increase the value of the Company's territories in Bengal by creating an export

---

2. *Arthur Young, op. cit.*, Vol. XVII, 1792, page 523: "Abolition of the Slave Trade."
3. *J. Ramsay: Inquiry*, pages 22–23. See also *Objections*, page 22.
4. *Dickson, op. cit.*, page 28.
5. *Report*, 1789, Part III. Further Evidence received by the Committee.
6. *Short Review of the Slave Trade and Slavery* (Birmingham, 1827), page 103.
7. B.T. 6/227. E.I. Accounts, 1778–1793.

commerce of great potentialities, and would benefit Great Britain by supplying her manufacturers with an article so essential to them, for which large
sums were annually paid to foreigners. The Committee recommended for
the future an opening of the trade to individuals, as a measure most likely to
create that competition which would bring the article to its greatest possible
state of perfection as well as reduce the cost of production to the minimum.[8]

If the coincidence of the arrival of indigo from the East Indies with the
question of abolition seemed remarkable, still more remarkable was the
coincidence with regard to the introduction of East India sugar. As early as
March 1787 one writer pointed out the wealth which might accrue to the
Company and to individuals from due encouragement to the cultivation of
sugar in Bengal. Under "the fostering care and protection" of Lord Cornwallis, "what advantages might not be expected, even to the utter ruin of the
Dutch trade in this article."[9]

In April 1789 a Committee of the East India Company represented to the
Court of Directors that the introduction of sugar be undertaken.[10] Despite
the low prices of that year and preceding years, and the small possibilities
of profit due to the high freight, the Court of Directors transmitted instructions to the Government of Bengal that a quantity of sugar should be sent to
England on trial. In March 1791, the first shipment from India of 97 cwt. arrived. As sugar was not to be found in the list of articles which comprised the
Company's usual importations, the duty levied was not that on West Indian
sugar but an *ad valorem* one, at the high rate of £37.16.3d. per cwt. on the
gross sale price, as on any manufactured article. An application to the Lords
Commissioners of the Treasury that East India sugar should be liable to the
same duty and drawback as if imported from the West Indies proved unsuccessful. Despite this setback, however, the sugar was profitably disposed of.

The Company at once sought the opinion of experts as to the quality of
their sugars. Mr. Travers, of the refining firm of Bracebridge and Travers, in
a private letter to the Deputy Chairman, remarked that it was different from
any sugar that had ever passed his pans and that it did not granulate like
West Indian sugar, but added more encouragingly that it deserved the serious
attention of the Directors, and that under able management it might amply

8. Ibid.
9. *Sugar: Various Mss.* (in my possession). Mr. Alexander Adamson to Mr. John Ferguson, Bombay, March 25, 1787.
10. *East India Sugar. Papers respecting the Culture and Manufacture of Sugar* (London, 1822), Appendix I, page 3. (Referred to hereafter as *East India Sugar.*) The Company, unwilling to act themselves as planters and manufacturers, engaged in 1791 to purchase all the sugar grown by a Lt. John
Paterson in North Eastern India during a period of twelve years.

reward those who should seriously set about its cultivation.[11] The firm's official report held out still greater hopes. The refineries were usually idle for four months in the year from want of sugar for refining. Consequently Bengal sugar would be always acceptable in the London market, even in its present state, but they were inclined to think that its quality might be greatly improved by better management and that it would certainly be found to deserve the Company's attention and encouragement.[12]

At this period there came the St. Domingo insurrection, the unrest in all the French colonies and the threatened failure of the French sugar crop[13] on which the European market depended. "That trade, with all its valuable appendages, which the French supplanted us in half a century back, and have preserved till almost the hour in which he was speaking, seemed to extend itself towards us and court our embrace."[14] Prices began to rise rapidly. From a maximum of 60/- in September 1788, the price rose to 86/- in September 1792 and 90/- in April 1793. The sugar refiners in their petition to Parliament in 1792 blamed the evils of the West Indian monopoly and the extraordinary bounty on the exportation of refined sugar as the causes of the excessive prices, pointed to "the decay of their once flourishing manufactory," and prayed for the admission of foreign sugars in British ships at a preferential tariff in favour of the West Indies, and the admission of East India sugar at the same duties and with the same privileges as sugar from the British West Indies.[15]

The high prices of sugar were beginning to cause universal distress. In Paris the peace of the city was threatened, masses assembled before grocers' shops and insisted upon a reduction of the price, and a Mr. La Borde, a banker possessed of a large stock of sugar from his own estate in St. Domingo, judged it necessary for his personal safety to quit the kingdom.[16] In Britain the sugar refiners were made the scapegoat and blamed unjustly for the high prices.[17] In January 1792 a committee was appointed at a public meeting to consider means of reducing the price of sugar. The Committee pointed out

---

11. *East India Sugar*, Appendix I, page 5. April 19, 1791.

12. Ibid. May 9, 1791.

13. We have the authority of Jaurès that in 1792, despite the gravity of the colonial disorders, the sugar crops were not affected. *Op. cit.*, Vol. III, page 299.

14. *Debate on the expediency of cultivating sugar in the territories of the East India Company*, East India House, 1793 (referred to hereafter as *East India House Debate*, 1793). India Office Tract, 393 (3). Mr. Randle Jackson, page 6.

15. *Report of the Proceedings of the Committee of Sugar Refiners*, pages 3, 8, 15.

16. F.O. 27/38. Earl Gower, Jan. 27, 1792.

17. *Report of the Proceedings of the Committee of Sugar Refiners*, page 18 (footnote). "At some fires which lately happened at sugar houses (the lower orders of people) exclaimed with horrid imprecations against the firemen and others for giving assistance in saving the property."

that a diminution of the consumption of tea was an inevitable consequence of the disuse of sugar. They had no intention of course of casting any disrespectful reflections on the West Indian interest, but they emphasized the increase of the cultivation of sugar in India in the last three years, and recommended, firstly, a suspension of drawback and bounty—originally intended as an encouragement to the West Indies in case of overproduction, which did not then exist; and secondly, an equalisation of the duties on East and West Indian sugar as "an act of Justice."[18]

This public demand for East India sugar was based on the grandiose claims of the Company itself. Sugar, reported the Committee of Warehouses in February 1792, was a natural product of Bengal, and was capable of being produced to any extent for which a demand could be found. From various considerations, as well as from the fact that the Company had been publicly appealed to to assist in effecting a reduction of the price by encouraging imports from India,[19] they thought a most favorable opportunity had presented itself for making a vigorous effort to secure to the Bengal provinces a participation in the sugar trade.[20] There was one difficulty—the duty was so high that it operated almost as a prohibition.

The demand for East India sugar is a question which is important for an understanding of the abolition movement. The threat to the West Indian islands from East India competition really became formidable only in the 1820's, but the danger in 1793 was not to be despised. The ruin of St. Domingo seemed to many to be the moment to strike for the repossession of the invaluable though long lost foreign trade, for it was useless to talk of encouraging West Indian cultivation by bounties or drawbacks unless Government could "communicate elasticity to the soil of our Islands." If Britain, Randle Jackson argued, did not step in to engross the Indian sugar trade, the Americans would forestall her, for it was vain to attempt to suppress the spirit of cultivation which was abroad—"lay it in Bengal, it would spring up in Benares; check it in Benares it would be found in the country of the Mahrattas; root it out there with fire and sword, the hills and the valleys in the Mysore dominions would laugh us to scorn, and pour forth the abundance of their produce into the bosom of Europe."[21]

---

18. *Liverpool Papers*, Add. Mss. 38227, folio 217. Chairman to Hawkesbury, Jan, 23, 1792; folios 219–222. Chairman to Pitt, Jan. 12, 1792.

19. In a letter from Jackson Barwis, chairman of the Committee, set up at the public meeting, Dec. 28, 1791.

20. *East India Sugar*, Appendix I, page 7. One writer declared that sugar was so common in India that the natives "eat it with their victuals, drink it in their beverages, and smoke it with their tobacco." *Strictures and Occasional Observations upon the system of British Commerce with the East Indies.* (London, 1792), page 43. India Office Tract 130(1).

21. *East India House Debate*, 1793, pages 9, 11, 12.

Mr. Jackson's views secured great support from "plain merchants" like Mr. Twining; from Alderman le Mesurier, refusing to "subscribe to the West Indies having been of much consequence to this country"; from Mr. Thornton denying the existence of any compact in favour of a West Indian monopoly; from a noble lord, Kinnaird, "one who always thought that emulative commerce was best"; and Jackson's resolutions, for the equalization of the duties for the benefit of the public and the revenue, were carried by a large majority.[22]

There were not wanting men to encourage the Directors of the East India Company. One William Fitz-Maurice, who had lived in Jamaica for sixteen years, and was therefore, in his own opinion, a competent judge of the soil fit for sugar, wrote lyrically to the Court of Directors on the fertility of the Indian soil, which was such that it did not require the labour of one-fourth of its inhabitants, and the abundance of cheap native labour. The British West Indies were inadequate for the supply of Great Britain and Ireland,[23] but, almost prophetically, he warned the Directors not to be led away by the popularity of East India sugar when West Indian crops had failed, and at the time of "the rage for abolishing the slave trade." With a return to normal conditions East India sugar would be little in demand because of its inferior quality and its lack of saccharine content, and he warned the Directors that it was important to guard against two evils, the failure of the trade generally through the imperfect quality of the sugar, and the great loss sustained by the ignorance of the natives in clarification and boiling.[24] Fitz-Maurice, whose services had been rejected by Lt. Paterson after he had been engaged to superintend the latter's sugar manufactories in Bengal, wrote to Dundas from Calcutta informing him that he was engaged on a Practical Treatise on the culture of sugar and indigo. Cornwallis and the Government in India had subscribed and he hoped Dundas would head the list of subscribers at home. He begged Dundas to appoint him Inspector of Sugars to the Company at Bengal, he had written to Wilberforce, with whom he was acquainted, to use his influence with Dundas in this direction, and he assured the latter that from his experience he could promote the interests of the Company.[25]

It was claimed that, with proper management, India could supply the whole of Europe with sugar cheaper than any other country in the world,

22. Ibid., pages 24–27.
23. It might seem that the surplus for export invalidated Fitz-Maurice's contention. But it was not a genuine surplus and it existed only because of the bounty and drawback. The refiners had, we have seen, demanded the importation of foreign sugar.
24. *Sugar: Various Mss.* Jan. 29, 1793.
25. Ibid. March 26, 1793.

"without slavery or oppression of any kind whatever."[26] But for the attention paid in the past to those West Indian colonies by Britain and France, another writer complained, "slavery might have been confined to the malefactor or at least the national reproach of inflicting it on the innocent have rested with the possessors of the mines of Mexico and Peru." The West Indies were roundly trounced as "an eternal sponge on the capitals of this country, both national and commercial"; without their insatiable calls for money . . . no cultivation of their sterile rocks (would) have been forced, at such an enormous and unnecessary expence." Britain was now "ripe for an abolition of monopolies," a general hardship could not be inflicted on the community at large for the sake of affording a partial and unreasonable benefit to a small number of its members. The British Islands, moreover, could not hope to compete with the French and Spanish, for all together they were not as large as either Cuba or St. Domingo, much less any one province of South America.[27]

These arguments show the claims that were being made by interested publicists of the East as a substitute for the departed glory from the West,[28] and as a means of recovering a valuable branch of trade now almost wholly in French hands. By this it must not be inferred that the introduction of East India sugar was unopposed. It was, and very strongly, by that formidable phalanx of planters and merchants, in Parliament and the Cabinet, dreaded by one of the advocates of equalization of the duties, "of whose support in emergency every administration in turn has experienced the value,"[29] and even in the ranks of the East Indians themselves there was division. It was pointed out how absurd it was of the Directors to declare that they did not intend to become the rivals of the West Indians. It was futile to talk, if the duties were equalized, of East and West Indians being "the right and left hands of the country."[30] East or West Indies: there could be no alternative. The West could not compete with the East if the duties were equalized. According to the hopes of the Directors, the East Indies would become not merely the competitors but rather the successors of the West Indians.[31] India, too,

26. *Strictures and Occasional Observations*, pages 37–38.

27. *The Right in the West India Merchants to a Double Monopoly of the Sugar-Market of Great Britain, and the expedience of all monopolies, examined* (London, n.d.), pages 18–19, 74–75, 17, 53, 50–51, 26–27.

28. *East India House Debate, 1793*, page 14. Randle Jackson: "It seemed as if Providence when it took from us America would not leave its favourite people without an ample substitute, or who should say that Providence had not taken from us one member, more seriously to impress us with the value of another."

29. *The Right in the West India Merchants*, pages 59–60.

30. *East India House Debate, 1793*, page 12. Mr. Randle Jackson.

31. *Three letters addressed to a friend in India by a Proprietor. Principally on the subject of importing Bengal Sugars into England* (London, 1793), pages 67–68.

Mr. Dallas argued, had other resources; the West Indians had none, and the losses sustained by the West Indian planters in recent years made sympathy with them imperative.[32] But the laws of economics preclude any sympathy with systems which have outlived their usefulness. What case there was for the West Indies can be seen from Dallas's argument that, "at this very moment they were the pillar of our commerce and possessions, which all Europe looked on with envy, all was to be forgotten, all to be sacrificed to ideal prosperity, new fangled systems and false philosophy."[33] Could that convince British statesmen in view of the Privy Council's Report?

On behalf of the West Indians it was emphasized that despite the high duty the East Indian imports sold at no inconsiderable profit. The possibility in the future of reducing the enormous freight by more than one-half and of diminishing the cost of production would enable the Company to reap still greater profits. Consequently a modification of the duties was all that was needed.[34] In days, too, when the axiom of the balance of trade had not been definitely laid to rest, it was important that the cost of East India sugars was paid for in bullion, whereas West Indian sugars were paid for mostly in British merchandise, and a great part of the income of West Indian proprietors was spent in Britain.[35] Lord Hawkesbury, staunch champion of the West Indian interest, objected to the alteration of an existing law "in favour of a monopolising company" as injurious to the planters and contrary to the general interests of the kingdom, and recommended that a monopolising company should be forbidden to carry on any trade which was not included in the rights granted by the original charter.[36]

The East India Company, in their struggle with the West Indian interest, were aided by the determination of the abolitionists to refrain from the use of West Indian sugar and rum—what Cochin calls "une sorte de croisade pieuse et niaise."[37] The high-water mark of this self-abnegation was reached by William Allen, staunch Quaker, "the Spitalfields genius," who was not to taste sugar for forty-three years, when slavery was abolished.[38] The average person was probably influenced more by economics than by morality in his decision

32. *East India House Debate, 1793*, page 19. "Was it not equally true that for years following almost every commercial house connected with them had materially suffered?"

33. Ibid., pages 21–22.

34. *Chatham Papers*, G.D. 8/355. Miscellaneous Papers, East India Company: Observations of Mr. Henchman. How, it was asked, could a duty be considered to operate as a prohibition when articles imported, subject to that duty, yielded a profit of from 24 to 48 per cent? *Three Letters addressed to a Friend in India*, page 17.

35. D. Macpherson: *The History of the European Commerce with India* (London, 1812), page 389.

36. *Liverpool Papers*, Add. Mss. 38409, folios 151 and 155. Written probably in 1789.

37. A. Cochin: *L'Abolition de l'Esclavage* (Paris, 1861), Introduction, pages XIV–XV.

38. R. M. Jones: *The Later Periods of Quakerism* (London, 1921), Vol. I, pages 335–336.

to boycott West Indian sugar. "Many abstain," reported the Directors of the East India Company, "from eating sugar on account of the price."[39]

This determination to abstain from the use of West Indian sugar was greatly encouraged by a pamphlet by William Fox. To purchase the commodity, he asserted, was to participate in the crime, for in every pound of sugar one might be considered as consuming two ounces of human flesh. He called for a boycott of West Indian sugar until the slave trade was abolished, and the West Indians had begun "as speedy and effectual a subversion of slavery in their islands as the circumstances and situation of the slaves will permit," or until it was possible to obtain sugar in some other way unconnected with slavery, and unpolluted with blood.[40]

Fox's pamphlet helped the cause enormously, though the anti-abolitionists did not lack publicists who could justly laugh at the inconsistency of those people who in the frenzy for abolition had rejected sugar but continued to drink chocolate, coffee and rum, and use tobacco.[41] It was estimated that no fewer than three hundred thousand persons had abandoned the use of sugar, and it was also reported that the sugar revenue had fallen off £200,000 in one quarter.[42]

The Abolition Committee as a whole, after some hesitation—a natural hesitation, too, in view of the possibilities involved—itself recommended the measure. In 1795 they recommended that during the continuance of the slave trade, a decided preference should be given to East India sugar, as well as to all other substitutes for the produce of the West Indies.[43]

The last word rested with Wilberforce. Gisborne asked his opinion,[44] and so did Newton, who reported that Mr. Thornton and Sir Charles Middleton, ardent abolitionists, had advocated such a boycott, but he thought it premature and wished to have the sanction of Wilberforce's name.[45] Wilberforce was at first inclined to consent, but after careful consideration he decided

39. Quoted in *The Right in the West India Merchants to a Double Monopoly*, page 10 (footnote).

40. *Address to the people of Great Britain on the propriety of abstaining from West India Sugar and Rum* (London, 1791).

41. *Fugitive Thoughts on the African Slave Trade* (Liverpool, 1792), pages 48–49. This argument was to enjoy great vogue in later years.

42. K. Farrer (ed.): *Correspondence of Josiah Wedgwood* (London, 1906), pages 183–186. Wedgwood, urged by Clarkson to order 1,000 copies of Fox's pamphlet, ordered 2,000, and recommended a wooden cut of a Negro kneeling, with the motto "Am I not a man and a brother?" on the title page (Ibid., page 187). Quoted also by E. L. Griggs: *Thomas Clarkson, the Friend of Slaves* (London, 1936), page 69.

43. *Abolition Committee's Proceedings*, Add. Mss. 21256, folio 95. June 26, 1795. The Committee had previously recommended it on July 4, 1793 (Ibid., folio 82), but had suspended proceedings for this purpose on August 13, 1793 (Ibid., folio 84).

44. *Life of Wilberforce*, Vol. I, pages 338–339.

45. *Wilberforce, Correspondence*, Vol. 1, page 114. Dec. 13, 1794.

that it should be suspended until, if necessary, it might be adopted with effect by general concurrence. It was not without a struggle, however, that the
more violent of his followers obeyed his temperate counsels.[46]

The key to the introduction of East India sugar is to be found in the
export market. Pitt and Dundas strongly favoured attempting the capture of
continental markets with East India sugar.[47] Why did the project fail?

"Pitt's proposal," according to Ragatz, "to supply European consumers
with East Indian sugar largely came to naught in consequence of the high ad
valorem charge imposed upon its initial entry into home markets."[48] It would
appear that Pitt, eager to secure the export trade for Britain, had decided,
in view of the outcry raised by the West Indian interest, not to equalize the
duties,[49] which would enable the East India Company to compete in the
home market with the West Indian planters, but to allow the Company to
secure almost the whole of the high ad valorem duty by re-exportation. The
East India Company, however, were unsuccessful in their appeal in 1795 for
the necessary alteration in the oath to be taken on re-exportation, by which
the bounty payable was limited to sugar the growth of the British West Indies, and by which East India sugar was consequently confined to the home
market or could be re-exported only in a raw state.[50]

But the chief reason why the East India sugar trade lost its importance
was that by 1793 other and better means of securing the export trade were at
hand, in the shape of the French islands themselves. Lord Hawkesbury had
from the outset opposed the introduction of East India sugar on the ground
that it was impracticable and diverted attention from a better scheme, that
of permitting the importation of all foreign sugar in British ships, for re-
exportation in a raw or refined state, to supply the European markets. "The
commerce and shipping of France will be more diminished, and the commerce and shipping of Great Britain more augmented, than by any single
measure that has been pursued for the last century."[51] Hawkesbury showed,
from various points of view, how very important the trade of the French
colonies in the West Indies was to the general interests of France, to prove
how greatly France would suffer were she to be deprived of any considerable
part of that trade. In view of the insurrections in the French colonies, he
gave it as his opinion that it was in the power of Great Britain, "by a few very
simple regulations of which France can have no right to complain, to deprive

---

46. *Life of Wilberforce*, Vol. I, page 339.
47. L. J. Ragatz: *The Fall of the Planter Class in the British Caribbean* (New York, 1927), page 211.
48. Ibid., *op. cit.*, pages 213–214.
49. *Liverpool Papers*, Add. Mss. 38227, folios 282(v)–283. Long to Hawkesbury, March 10, 1792.
50. B.T. 1/12. June 19, 1795.
51. *Liverpool Papers*. Add. Mss. 38409, folios 147–148. Written probably in 1789.

her (France) for ever of a still further portion of the trade with her colonies, and to restore to Great Britain that ascendancy in the trade of sugar which she enjoyed from 1660 to 1713, but which she lost soon after the Treaty of Utrecht, and which France then obtained from her."[52]

But this is not to say that the propaganda in favour of East India sugar did not cause some mischief. How effective it was we can see from the bitter complaints of Mr. Hibbert in 1807. Far from the St. Domingo insurrection being a boon to the British planters, as was often averred, he declared that it had contributed to their distresses, for the shortage it had occasioned was primarily responsible for that considerable advance in the price of sugar which had encouraged the demand for East India sugar. While the annual consumption of East India sugar was, in 1807, only 50,000 to 60,000 cwt., being kept down by the very low prices of colonial produce, as far as the principle was concerned, its admission could not be justified.[53]

This attempt to secure sugar from India has received its full significance from French historians. After the Treaty of Versailles, says Saintoyant, the British Government, with Pitt at its head, adopted a policy which was to cripple the colonial and national power of France in revenge for French support to the rebellious American colonists. The superiority of the French islands depended entirely on slavery. Great Britain, in order to recapture the European market, resolved to turn for sugar to the East where there was an indigenous population accustomed to manual labour, but whose labour was free.[54] Gaston-Martin endorses this view, and points out that abolition would have been a blow also at the revolted colonies, the southern states of which equally depended on slave labour.[55]

In a speech prepared for the opening of the General Anti-Slavery Convention in 1840, Clarkson, the Grand Old Man of the Abolition Movement, illustrated the importance of introducing East India sugar in 1790 no less than in 1840. The extirpation of slavery from the whole world could be effected only by the introduction of the produce of free tropical labour in the European markets, which would undersell slave-grown products. "If you can do this, your victory is sure." Part of his speech Clarkson judged it wise to omit, but it was published later at his own request. In this unexpurgated version, he stated that the East India Company could achieve his aim "by means that are perfectly *moral and pacific, according to your own principles,* namely,

52. Ibid., Add. Mss. 38349, folio 393. Written probably after 1791.

53. *Parl. Deb.,* Vol. IX, pages 94–95. March 12, 1807.

54. J. *Saintoyant: La Colonisation Française pendant la Révolution 1789–1799* (Paris, 1932), Vol. I, pages 323–324.

55. *Gaston-Martin, op. cit.,* page 39.

by the cultivation of the earth and by the employment of *free labour.*" The East India Company had three advantages; land in their possession twenty times more than equal to the supply of all Europe with tropical produce; tens of millions of free labourers; and, most important of all, those labourers were paid only from a penny to three halfpence per day. "What slavery," asked Clarkson, "can stand against these prices?"[56]

---

56. *Clarkson Papers*, Add. Mss. 41267A, folios 178–179.

CHAPTER FOUR

The Attempt to Secure
an International Abolition

In considering the attempt to secure the abolition of the slave trade by other countries, particularly by France, it is important to bear in mind this background of economic facts—the state of the population in the British colonies, the greater advantages of the French and the comparative insignificance of the British islands as a consequence of the American Revolution. In the words of a West Indian planter wise in his generation, "were other European states to concur in the measure and to pass similar plans for the abolition of the slave trade, which would leave us all in the same relative situation we now are, perhaps nothing could be more salutary."[1]

Even before the Privy Council investigation which was to prove abundantly, for those who needed proof, the cardinal fact of French colonial superiority, Pitt and Wilberforce were alive to the necessity of a French abolition, "the idea," as Pitt expressed it, "of the two nations agreeing to discontinue the villainous traffic carried on in Africa."[2]

This would remove one of the strongest arguments against the abolition in Britain—that France would take up the trade. Wilberforce, while admitting the greater necessity of the trade to France on account of the cultivation of new lands, believed for many reasons that she would agree to the abolition,[3] though he confessed he knew enough of the French to make him a little diffident in trusting their assurances. "It may be material," he wrote to Eden, "to

---

1. *Considerations on the Emancipation of Negroes and on the Abolition of the Slave Trade*, pages 11–12.
2. *Auckland Journal*, Vol. I, pages 266–267. Pitt to Eden, Nov. 2, 1787.
3. Ibid., Vol. I, page 239. Oct. 20, 1787.

draw this declaration from them before the matter comes into full discussion on many accounts which I am persuaded it is unnecessary to suggest to you."[4]

This note of secrecy, of diplomatic bargaining behind the scenes, recurs frequently, and can no doubt be adequately explained by the desire to get the matter well under weigh and if possible settled before the West Indian interest had brought their powerful guns into play. "I am labouring," wrote Wilberforce, "to keep a number of people quiet in London and elsewhere, who are extremely humane and extremely imprudent." He admitted that great tact was necessary, but Eden's diplomatic skill and the character of the French consoled him: "I think you know those French fellows well and can mould and shape them to your purpose; you really too have good stuff to work with for they are a good natured and ambitious people."[5]

National character may vary, but a sober appraisement of economic interests is an attribute peculiar to no one race or nation. The French seemed, to Wilberforce, to relax in that zeal and alacrity by which alone one could hope for their making the considerable sacrifice of interest demanded, as abolition for France would mean either an end to bringing new lands in cultivation in St. Domingo, or at least proceeding more slowly. Eden was to use the formation of the "Amis des Noirs" as an argument for expedition; the Spanish Government was to be applied to, and Sir James Harris had been instructed "to sound his way in Holland." As regards Britain, there could be no doubt of success—"the evident, the glaring justice of the proposition itself, Mr. Pitt's support, and the temper of the House, the disposition of which I know rather better than I wish'd at so early a period thro' the indiscreet threat of some vy worthy people who have been rather too chattering and communicative."[6]

Wilberforce's exhortations and advice were reinforced by a private communication from Pitt himself. "The more I reflect on it," he wrote to Eden, "the more anxious and impatient I am that the business should be brought as speedily as possible to a point; that if the real difficulties of it can be overcome, it may not suffer from the prejudices and interested objections which will multiply during the discussion." Eden was to keep the memorandum which he intended to transmit secret for the present, and, if there was any chance of success in France, he was to make his plans to include Spain as well.[7]

Eden, however, was not very optimistic. French economic necessities were not to be the dupe of French vanity or French ambition. "I am never

4. *Auckland Papers*, Add. Mss. 34427, folios 49–50. Nov. 7, 1787.
5. Ibid., folios 124–125. Nov. 23, 1787.
6. Ibid., folios 183–184(v). Dec. 7, 1787.
7. *Chatham Papers*, G.D. 8/102. Dec. 7, 1787.

sanguine," he wrote to Wilberforce, "as to the success of any proposition, however just and right, which must militate against a large host of private interests." In case, he continued, the whole point could not be carried, he desired Wilberforce to discuss with Pitt whether it would not be essentially useful to make a sort of provisional convention with France and Spain, reprobating the slave trade in the strongest terms, and continuing it solely on the ground of necessity, "under a mutual stipulation to prepare measures for abolishing it, without any convulsion to commerce and private property."[8] Eden evidently did not understand the strength of public feeling in Britain on the subject. Pitt and Wilberforce refused. They were having the abolition, the whole abolition and nothing but the abolition. "The flame which is kindled," replied Wilberforce, "will die away and the public attention be attracted to some new object."[9] Pitt pointed out the inconveniences and difficulties in the way of a temporary suspension, and added that "if the principle of humanity and justice, on which the whole rests, is in any degree compromised, the cause is in a manner given up."[10]

The French were afraid that it would be found impossible in Britain to abolish the slave trade. This fear Wilberforce dismissed as unfounded. A liberal subscription at Manchester, "deeply interested in the African trade"; a society instituted for abolition and a liberal subscription at Birmingham; the sudden increase of the Quaker Society in London; "an universal disposition in our favour in the House of Commons"—all these factors enabled him to assure Eden that there was no doubt of success. As proceedings in the House of Commons might be materially affected by the answer given by Montmorin, "you will have the goodness to keep him with a hot fire and as soon as possible communicate to Mr. Pitt or myself the result of our renewed attack."[11]

The waiting game continued. Montmorin's language on the universal abolition was full of earnestness, but it would encounter great difficulties from those interested in the islands.[12] His indecision later became a decided negative. There were great doubts in France whether abolition would not produce utter and sudden ruin to the French islands: "it was one of those subjects upon which the *interests* of men and their *sentiments* were so much at variance that it was difficult to learn what was practicable."[13]

---

8. *Life of Wilberforce*, Vol. I, page 157. Dec. 19, 1787.
9. *Auckland Papers*, Add. Mss. 34427, folio 367. Jan. 5, 1788.
10. *Auckland Journal*, Vol. I, page 304. Jan. 7, 1788.
11. *Auckland Papers*, Add. Mss. 34427, folios 401–402(v). Jan. 1788.
12. F.O. 27/27. Eden to Marquis of Carmarthen, Jan. 17, 1788.
13. *Life of Wilberforce*, Vol. I, page 158. Eden is reporting Montmorin.

Pitt, however, still did not give up hope. The summer might be employed in treating with foreign powers to advantage. He was determined to "set about it with the utmost activity, and with good hopes of success, tho' founded as yet on rather general grounds than any positive information,"[14] and he thought that one good result of the new constitution in France would be that "our chance for settling something about the Slave Trade" would be improved.[15]

But there never was any real hope that the Government of the Ancien Régime would abolish the slave trade. Louis XVI was personally an abolitionist, but the policy of the monarchy, as French writers have always pointed out, was linked with that of the bourgeoisie in the seaport towns who were interested in the slave trade and the colonies. The British Ambassador in Paris, Lord Dorset, himself an opponent of abolition,[16] realised this and wrote to Lord Hawkesbury that the flattering references to British humanitarianism "seem'd only meant to compliment us and to keep us quiet and in good humour; and I have reason to believe the intention of the Government is at present to do nothing respecting that business but to wait and take advantage of any *faux-pas* we may make."[17]

The failure to secure abolition by France must be read with the parallel failure in Holland. Sir James Harris had endeavoured to persuade certain influential men to co-operate in "the humane measure" Wilberforce and Grenville were sponsoring in Britain, but he confessed to Grenville that the principles of humanity were not likely to make much impression on the Dutch merchants and that it would be difficult to obtain their acquiescence.[18] M. de Lynden, one of the men approached, was content with compliments: it was a laudable design, all the more so if it could be effected, as was thought, without detriment to the cultivation in the West Indies.[19] When Harris wrote later promising to seize any opening which might present itself, or to do anything which Grenville might suggest as likely to contribute towards the success of the undertaking,[20] the futility of all further approaches was evident.

---

14. A. M. *Wilberforce: The Private Papers of William Wilberforce* (London, 1897), page 20. June 28, 1788. (Referred to hereafter as *Wilberforce, Private Papers.*)

15. *The Manuscripts of J. B. Fortescue Esq., preserved at Dropmore.* Historical Manuscripts Commission, 13th Report, Appendix, Part III; 14th Report, Appendix, Part IV. (London etc. 1892–1927), Vol. I, page 353. Pitt to Grenville, Aug. 29, 1788. (Referred to hereafter as *Dropmore Papers.*)

16. *Liverpool Papers,* Add. Mss. 38224, folio 178. Dorset to Hawkesbury. May 28, 1789, "I sincerely hope Mr. Pitt will be beat upon the slave trade bill."

17. Ibid., folio 118. May 7, 1789. See also folio 140. May 21, 1789.

18. *Dropmore Papers,* Vol. III, pages 442–443. Jan. 4, 1788. It must be pointed out that none of the considerations of the "impolicy" of the trade find any expression in the political démarches of the time.

19. Ibid., Vol. III, page 444. Feb. 1788.

20. Ibid., Vol. III, page 446. March 4, 1788.

It had proved impossible to influence the French Government; the French idealists remained. Already in 1787 Wilberforce had considered the advisability of going over to Paris, and he wrote to Eden that he was prepared to do so cheerfully.[21] He invited Grenville to join him on his expedition, but Grenville, after consulting Pitt, replied that no useful purpose would be gained by their going over, that they could do no more than Eden was doing, and appearing over-solicitous "might give rise to a suspicion that what we are proposing is not so perfectly fair and equal as we would wish it to be believed." He advised Wilberforce to remain at home and attend to his health rather than endanger it and the cause by a troublesome and fruitless journey to Paris.[22]

Again in 1789 Wilberforce toyed with the idea of a trip to France. This time it fell to Addington to dissuade him, and soon after he arranged for Clarkson to take his place.[23] Clarkson was greatly impressed with the idealism of the French: "I should not be surprised if the French were to do themselves the honour of voting away the diabolical traffic in a single night." As late as June 1790 Clarkson's enthusiasm was as buoyant as ever, and he was convinced that the slave trade would, in the course of a few months, fall in France.[24] His confidence was not shared by some of his supporters in London. Samuel Hoare, Quaker business man, Treasurer of the Abolition Committee, had "seen too much of the silent and powerful operations of self-interest, either real or imaginary, to believe that the first impulse of patriotism and justice will counter-balance its influence." The work would be more gradual, but there was ground for optimism.[25]

Clarkson's instructions particularly warned him to resist every tendency to the idea of a joint abolition by both countries. He once wrote to Wilberforce that Mirabeau was about to request the latter's personal assurance of Pitt's sentiments, an assurance which he intended to use as proof that Britain would follow France and not take advantage of the French abolition, and with which he undertook to abolish the slave trade within three weeks. But the British Government would not and could not bind itself.

---

21. *Auckland Journal*, Vol. I, page 239. Oct. 20, 1787.
22. *Life of Wilberforce*, Vol. I, pages 155–156. Dec. 18, 1787.
23. Ibid., Vol. I, page 228. July 7, 1789.
24. Ibid., Vol. I, pages 229–230.
25. Ibid., Vol. I, page 231. Clarkson's impetuous and enthusiastic zeal had already earned for him a serious reprimand from Hoare: "I hope the zeal and animation with which thou hast taken up the cause will be accompanied with temper and moderation, which alone can insure its success." *Abolition Committee's Proceedings*, Add. Mss. 21254, folios 12–12(v). Hoare's letter, July 26, 1787, was approved by the Committee on August 7. The occasion was Clarkson's request to the Abolition Committee to take a Mr. Fawconbridge with him to Liverpool in his search for evidence, and allow him £10 for the assistance already received from him.

Clarkson was employed in "stirring up the slumbering energies of the *Amis des Noirs*."[26] Wilberforce had already written to Eden for information about the French Society—"what are its objects, and is it respectable from the rank, character and number of its members?"[27] French historians have for over a century been unanimous as to the aim which Britain had in mind. While the Abolition Committee declined Brissot's offer of pecuniary aid from France,[28] Gaston-Martin, the well-known French historian of the slave trade and the Caribbean colonies, accuses Britain of aiming by propaganda to free the slaves, "in the name no doubt of humanity, but also to ruin French commerce,"[29] and concludes that in this philanthropic propaganda there were economic motives which explain the liberality with which Britain put funds at the disposal of the French abolitionists, and the way in which the country was swamped with translations of Clarkson's works.[30] Saintoyant says that the Amis des Noirs counted British members; it was popularly said that they received subsidies from Britain to incite the French colonies to revolt, but the fact remains unproved.[31] He also states that Ogé, one of the leaders of the Mulatto insurrection in St. Domingo, was sent by the Amis des Noirs to their "friends" in Britain from whom he received money and letters of credit, equipped with which he sailed to the United States, where he procured arms and ammunition. It was, therefore, Paris politicians, subsidised by a British group in league with the head of the British Government, which produced the first conflict in St. Domingo between whites and Mulattoes.[32]

This question of British abolitionist propaganda is confirmed by the Clarkson papers, drawn on by Clarkson's latest biographer. Clarkson was dependent on Wilberforce for the directions and supplies required by the cause. "Money now becomes absolutely necessary"; "in my last letter to you,

---

26. *Life of Wilberforce*, Vol. I, page 228.

27. *Auckland Papers*, Add. Mss. 34427, folio 367(v). Jan. 5, 1788. Comparing the French and British abolitionists, a French historian writes: "Tandis que le groupe anglais se savait subordonné à la politique de son gouvernement, le groupe français se réclamait de principes abstraits récemment érigés en axiomes et méprisant les intérêts engagés, nationaux et privés." He also suggests that the French society collectively had no fixed aim: only an inner circle of the more influential members knew the real objectives. *Saintoyant, op. cit.*, Vol. I, pages 323–324, and Vol. II, page 77.

28. *Abolition Committee's Proceedings*. Add. Mss. 21254, folio 13(v). Aug. 27, 1787.

29. *Gaston-Martin, op. cit.*, page 25.

30. Ibid., page 39. "Je ne connais pas une bibliothèque de Chambre de Commerce qui n'ait encore en archives cinq à six exemplaires du livre *sur les Désavantages Politiques de la Traite des Nègres*."

31. *Saintoyant, op. cit.*, Vol. I, page 45 (footnote).

32. Ibid., Vol. II, page 77 and footnote. Saintoyant gives Bryan Edwards and Pamphile de Lacroix as his authorities. But all that Bryan Edwards says is that the Amis des Noirs, finding it difficult to send arms and ammunition to the Mulattoes in St. Domingo without arousing the suspicions of the Government and the colonial planters in Paris, recommended Ogé "to make a circuitous voyage for that purpose. Accordingly, being furnished with money and letters of credit, Ogé embarked for New England in the month of July 1790." B. *Edwards: An Historical Survey of the French Colony in the Island of St. Domingo* (London, 1797), page 42.

I said it had been determined to draw on your account for £120 to advance the business here, etc. etc. More will not be wanted at present. The greatest part of the £56 has been spent and I hope and believe very judiciously."[33] Griggs records that for several months Clarkson "wrote regularly to Brissot, telling of the progress of affairs, offering advice, and helping with the financial concerns of *Les Amis des Noirs*—Brissot frequently asked for money." Brissot once wrote of "a bill drawn by me on you for livres d'or; be so kind as to pay them to him," and in another letter he declared that "the assistance which you and your friends will give to the Society shall be very acceptable for promoting the sacred object we are contending for; the soonest the best, because the publications are going on very briskly."[34]

But any well-informed person, who kept his eye on the French situation, would have seen that the Amis des Noirs, despite their programme, never meant to touch the thorny question of the slave trade. A short digression into the state of French politics will illustrate this. A fortnight after the Declaration of the Rights of Man, the National Assembly dodged the question of equal rights for the Mulattoes, who were men of education and property. In March 1790 a decree concerning St. Domingo gave the vote to all persons of twenty-five possessing certain qualifications. The Abbé Grégoire inquired whether the coloured people were included. The National Assembly refused to discuss the question, and in the view of the British Ambassador "the prudence and moderation which the National Assembly has discovered in the affair of the colonies are subjects of general applause here at present altho' many are persuaded and especially the planters here, that the remedy comes too late and that the islands are in fact lost to this country."[35]

The Assembly never meant to abolish the slave trade. Eventually, in May 1791, after a four days' session, it arrived at an ingenious compromise: political and social rights were granted to Mulattoes born of free parents only— about 400 in all in St. Domingo. This decree was revoked in September, on the day before the dissolution of the Constituent Assembly. It was only in April 1792, when the white planters had begun to turn to Britain, that the Assembly, for reasons which were undoubtedly partly political, conceded full rights to the Mulattoes. But, let it be noted, to the Mulattoes only; in the great debates of the Legislative Assembly the famous men, Brissot, Guadet, Verniaud, spoke for the men of colour. No one touched the question of the

<hr>

33. *Life of Wilberforce*, Vol. I, page 228.
34. *Griggs, op. cit.*, page 58.
35. F.O. 27/34. Lord Robert Stephen FitzGerald to Duke of Leeds, March 12, 1790. See also Ibid., April 2, 1790. "The temper and moderation," wrote FitzGerald, "which has been shown throughout this important affair may, possibly, be the means of preserving to this country those islands which the public were at one time tempted to believe aimed at total independence."

slave trade, much less of slavery. Brissot was quite willing to avail himself of Clarkson's assistance, but while Clarkson was thinking of abolition, the Amis des Noirs spoke only for the men of colour. Ogé distinctly stated that he was opposed to abolition.

Speakers who dared to mention the word "slavery" were shouted down. For instance when in 1791 Moreau de Saint Méry proposed that the words "persons not free" should be altered to "slaves," Robespierre cried out indignantly: "From the moment when in one of your decrees you pronounce the word slave, you will have pronounced your own dishonour." The servitude of the slaves was to be maintained, though the Assembly refused to allow the "brutal and literal consecration of the word slavery."[36] The Assembly, not wishing to put itself in the position of opposing the measure, merely fenced. The warning of Deputy Merlet, that although an abolition bill had passed the House of Commons it had not passed the House of Lords,[37] did not fall on stony ground. It was only when the Negroes in St. Domingo had already won their freedom, only when the hostility of the white planters to the Revolution made the fear of a British invasion certain, and the need of weaning the Negroes from their royalism imperative, that the revolutionary commissioners in St. Domingo turned to the blacks and decreed the abolition of slavery. In France itself it was only at the peak of the Revolution, when all property was struck at short of private property, when idealistic fervour was reinforced by weighty political considerations, that the commissioners' decree received legislative sanction. Cochin has reminded us "the first laws in Europe which struck at slavery came from France, they were the work of the Revolution."[38] These laws only recognised a *fait accompli*.

---

36. *Jaurès, op. cit.*, Vol. II, page 223.
37. *Saintoyant, op. cit.*, Vol. I, page 324. "The House of Commons might make manifestations, knowing that the Lords would arrest the effects of them." Dundas himself had said as much.
38. *Cochin, op. cit.*, Vol. I, page 7.

CHAPTER FIVE

The West Indian Expeditions

The West Indian Expeditions, which were intended to, and which did, for some time, bring all or most of the French Caribbean colonies under British rule, are of outstanding significance for a proper understanding of the abolition movement, though, so far as I am aware, this significance has never been traced by any British historian.[1]

It is important to bear in mind the course of events in France itself. On July 14, 1789, the Bastille was taken; on August 4, out of the ruins caused by that orgy of destruction, with which all feudal rights were overthrown, the Declaration of the Rights of Man was born, in theory committing the National Assembly to principles which condemned the very bases of colonial society.[2] On August 10, at that early date, the Marquis of Buckingham wrote to his brother Grenville that he had been assured by a very intelligent Irishman that the deputies of St. Lucia, Tobago and St. Domingo were already beginning to talk of revolting to Britain.[3] A few days later the British Ambassador in Paris hastened to notify his Government of the rumoured determination of the National Assembly to discuss a motion to abolish the slave trade and emancipate the Negroes, for from the alarm already aroused among the St. Domingo planters resident in Paris, there was "reason to expect that

---

1. J. W. *Fortescue: History of the British Army*, Vol. IV, Part I (London, 1915), confines himself solely to the military aspect of the Expeditions.
2. We have already seen how the National Assembly dodged these implications.
3. *Dropmore Papers*, Vol. I, page 490. Aug. 10, 1789.

some most material alteration in the Government of the French West Indies may be the result of such a decision."[4]

In May 1790, when there were differences with Spain over Nootka Sound, Grenville called the attention of the Governor of Jamaica "in the strongest and most particular manner" to the importance of procuring and transmitting "continued and active intelligence" with respect to the French and Spanish islands, emphasizing that the disorder in the former seemed to "afford a peculiar facility for acquiring such intelligence."[5] Effingham promised to send what authentic information he could procure of St. Domingo;[6] Governor Orde of Dominica sent messengers to Martinique, ostensibly on some trifling business, in reality to gain information,[7] and he admitted that had there been a war, the disorder in the French islands would have made them an easy prey.[8]

About the same time Gilbert Francklyn, a West Indian planter in close touch with Lord Hawkesbury,[9] was arguing that the French colonies had as much right to secede as Avignon to refuse obedience to its lawful sovereign.[10] By 1791 the unrest in the French colonies was so great that there was hardly one colony which was not in a state of insurrection.[11] The reason was that the royalist planters feared that the men who were undermining the monarchical system would also tamper with the very foundations of colonial society. The Decree of March 1790, which left it to the colonial assemblies to decide the question whether the Mulattoes were to be included in the franchise for those over twenty-five, though it represented a triumph for the conservatives, really begged the question of the colonies. But until the spring of 1791 the National Assembly avoided the two thorny questions of slavery and the colour line.

On the very eve, however, of the decree of May 15, 1791, which declared equality with whites for Mulattoes born of free parents, Earl Gower reported from Paris that the French colonists were talking of "throwing themselves into the arms of England."[12] The decree meant the virtual secession of the

4. F.O. 27/33A. Fitzgerald to Duke of Leeds, Aug. 20, 1789.

5. C.O. 137/88. May 6, 1790, secret.

6. Ibid. June 13, 1790.

7. C.O. 71/20. March 27, 1791.

8. C.O. 71/18. Dec. 13, 1790.

9. As a relief, no doubt, from his literary labours in refuting the arguments for abolition with the aid of scriptural references and in upholding the claims of the West Indian planters to the exclusive possession of the British market against their new competitors from the East, he seemed to have filled the part, and filled it well, of Lord Hawkesbury's special if unofficial informant behind the scenes.

10. *Liverpool Papers*, Add. Mss. 38225, folio 263. July 2, 1790.

11. F.O. 27/36, Gower to Grenville, Feb. 4, 1791.

12. Ibid. May 13, 1791.

French colonies, and Gower informed Grenville that a delegate from Paris and commissioners from St. Domingo were being sent over to Britain.[13] The colonists had crossed the Rubicon.

From Dominica, too, came news of talk of independence. Gilbert Francklyn informed Lord Hawkesbury—if Lord Hawkesbury needed the information—that proposals in St. Domingo to hoist the British colours and to send deputies to Britain had been loudly applauded, and wrote of an offer made to Pitt in the previous year.[14]

The first definite offer of St. Domingo to Britain came from a quarter the respectability of which could not be impugned. The writer was de Cadusey, President of the Assembly. Necessity justified a step which would normally be treason. For obvious reasons the offer could not be "official." All St. Domingo was ready to take an oath of allegiance to Britain, in return for two concessions only—the guarantee of St. Domingo's internal régime (the significance of this we shall see later) and permission to trade with the United States similar to that granted to Jamaica. In the name of policy as well as of humanity he begged Pitt to accept an offer, which was—the language almost suggests Rousseau—"the expression of the general will."[15]

The offer was not accepted at the time, as Britain still adhered to her strict neutrality. After all, the situation in France was not yet irremediable, the King had recently signed the Civil Constitution of the Clergy, the Legislative Assembly had just met, and France still seemed to be travelling—rather uncertainly, perhaps, and somewhat strangely—the road of constitutional monarchy. In fact, it might even be said that reaction was triumphant: Marat and Danton had to flee for their lives. The offer was put away in cold storage but was not forgotten. Any doubts of the sentiments of the St. Domingo planters were removed by the assurance of Major General Williamson,[16] sent to Jamaica in 1790 in preparation for all eventualities[17] (Spain was the enemy then), and the appearance of M. Charmilly, probably the official emissary from the St. Domingo Assembly, with his "proposition of a very serious nature respecting St. Domingo to administration."[18]

In 1792 events moved rapidly. In April Austria declared war on France, followed by Prussia in July. On August 10—the key date in the French Revolution which turned all Europe against France—the Tuileries was invaded by the

---

13. Ibid. Aug. 26, 1791.

14. *Liverpool Papers*, Add. Mss. 38227, folio 43. Sept. 9, 1791; also folio 50. Sept. 14, 1791.

15. *Chatham Papers*, G.D. 8/349. West Indian Islands: Papers relating to Jamaica and St. Domingo.

16. C.O. 137/89. To Dundas, Sept. 10, 1791.

17. C.O. 137/88. Grenville to Effingham, May 22, 1790.

18. *Liverpool Papers*, Add. Mss. 38227, folios 140 and 141. Francklyn to Hawkesbury, Nov. 15 and 17, 1791.

masses and Louis XVI was suspended. On August 17 the British Ambassador was recalled from Paris, though the British Government declared its determination to remain strictly neutral in respect to the internal government of France.[19]

At this period the French Windward Islands appeared on the scene. The deputy for Guadeloupe declared the determination of the inhabitants to "consider themselves no longer as a French colony if the present system of government in France continue." M. de Curt begged to be considered in all respects as an Englishman, assured Hawkesbury that St. Domingo would follow the lead of the Windward Islands,[20] and formally asked for protection "in the name of humanity and English loyalty."[21] Pitt wished to know the sources of de Curt's important account of the French colonies, though he did not want to take so formal a step as examining him by the Cabinet,[22] and Hawkesbury wrote to de Curt asking for an account of the produce of the Windward Islands.[23]

By the end of the year the relations between Britain and France had become strained and war to many seemed inevitable. Already in 1791 one anonymous writer in Jamaica had voiced the opinion of many people that St. Domingo would be "a noble compensation" for the loss of America.[24] A more important memorial couched in a similar strain was sent to Pitt by Lt. Colonel James Chalmers, dilating on "the vast, vast importance of French St. Domingo." St. Domingo would give Britain a monopoly of sugar, indigo, cotton and coffee: "this island, for ages, would give such aid and force to industry as would be most happily felt in every part of the kingdom," and the safety of Jamaica would be ensured. Chalmers concluded by recommending an alliance, offensive and defensive, between Britain and Spain. "Such friendship for ages might preclude France and America from the New World, and effectually secure the invaluable possessions of Spain."[25]

Until the outbreak of hostilities the British Government consistently maintained its attitude of neutrality.[26] The French West Indies were not

19. F.O. 27/39. Dundas to Gower, Aug. 17, 1792.
20. F.O. 27/40. Dec. 18, 1792.
21. *Liverpool Papers*, Add. Mss. 38228, folio 197. Jan. 3, 1793.
22. Ibid., Add. Mss. 38192, folio 93. Pitt to Hawkesbury, Dec. 17, 1792.
23. Ibid., Add. Mss. 38228, folio 237. Jan. 26, 1793.
24. Ibid., Add. Mss. 38227, folio 5. Aug. 7, 1791.
25. *Chatham Papers*, G.D. 8/334. Miscellaneous Papers relating to France, 1784–1795.
26. In 1790 the Governor of Dominica was warned against interfering in the internal concerns of the French islands (C.O. 71/20. Oct. 1790). The assistance given to an armed French brig from Martinique, driven for wood and water to Dominica, was, however, approved (Ibid. Nov. 18, 1790). Grenville, while insisting on "the most perfect impartiality towards all parties in those islands" (Ibid. Dec. 16, 1790), even went so far as to forbid any reprisals against "irregularities" which at other times might be worthy of notice (Ibid. April 16, 1791).

considered to be worth "one year of that invaluable tranquility which we are now enjoying."[27]

The difficulties which faced the whites in St. Domingo early forced them to apply to Jamaica for assistance. On two occasions Governor Effingham reported that he had supplied the St. Domingo planters with muskets and ammunition at their request, though he had naturally refused the appeal for troops as well.[28] Grenville subsequently expressed his approval of Effingham's action,[29] and the British Ambassador in Paris, ordered to communicate to the French ministers the approval of this assistance, welcomed the opportunity "of giving a proof of British generosity as there are not wanting men who industriously propagate a notion that the English have by underhand means fomented the dissensions in the French colonies."[30]

By January 1793, however, Dundas was writing secretly to Williamson to introduce four St. Domingo planters who had applied to Britain for aid. This aid, Dundas explicitly stated, could not then be given, in accordance with the British attitude of neutrality, but in the event of hostilities, which was highly probable, it would certainly be a part of the plan of operations to take over the French islands. Until further orders Williamson was to take no part in their plans, though he could converse with them in preparation for any eventuality which might "remove that restraint which is necessarily imposed upon your conduct by the continuance of peace."[31] In a later secret letter Charmilly was introduced, Williamson was to transmit regularly and carefully, without arousing suspicion, any information he received from him, and to avoid as much as possible the appearance of any particular intercourse with him.[32]

The outbreak of war in February was immediately followed by the acceptance of the offers of the French Windward Islands, and by Charmilly's proposition to Williamson, pledging Britain to defend St. Domingo until the end of the war. Article 4 of these "Capitulations" stated that the Mulattoes in St. Domingo were to have the privileges enjoyed by their fellow Mulattoes in the British islands; by Article 5 it was agreed that the laws relative to property and all civil rights should be those which had existed in St. Domingo before the French Revolution; and by Article 12 St. Domingo was allowed to import from the United States, in *American* vessels, livestock, grain and wood of all kinds.[33]

27. *Dropmore Papers*, Vol. II, page 181. Grenville to Gower, Aug. 3, 1791, private.
28. C.O. 137/89. Sept. 7 and 17, 1791.
29. Ibid. Nov. 11, 1791.
30. F.O. 27/37. Nov. 4, 1791.
31. C.O. 137/91. Jan. 12, 1793.
32. Ibid. Apl. 4, 1793.
33. Ibid., Feb. 25, 1793.

The leading statesmen were unanimous in their approval of the West Indian expedition. In the opinion of the Marquis of Buckingham the expedition was a lottery, but the bare possibility of success justified the attempt.[34] Dundas thought that the West Indies were "certainly the first point to make certain."[35] Pitt viewed cheerfully the fact that the expedition would retard the sending of twenty ships to the Mediterranean,[36] and was opposed to delay. The position in Flanders only called for additional exertions to safeguard Britain.[37] Delays began to make Dundas anxious and "very nearly out of temper."[38] Charged with the conduct of the war, he must have feared accusations of incapacity from his contemporaries more than from the Fortescues of later years.[39] Grenville was equally opposed to postponement of the expedition. Postponement would give "an impression of alarm which would operate against us," and there was no serious danger of invasion.[40] The incessant delays drove Buckingham to bitter sarcasm, and he grudged the force "most bitterly at Cowes."[41] Even as late as 1796, when the tide of initial successes had turned against Britain, Pitt still considered that St. Domingo ought to be made the first object of attack.[42] In fact, it would be no exaggeration to say that there was only one person in authority who opposed the expedition. Lord Auckland thought that the first and great object ought to be to destroy

---

34. *Dropmore Papers*, Vol. II, page 405. To Grenville, July 17, 1793.
35. Ibid. Vol. II, pages 407–408. To Grenville, July 1793.
36. Ibid., Vol. II, pages 402–403. To Grenville, June–July, 1793.
37. Ibid., Vol. II, page 443. To Grenville, Oct. 11, 1793.
38. Ibid., Vol. II, page 444. To Grenville, Oct. 12, 1793.
39. Fortescue was criticising the Pitt-Dundas policy of West Indian conquest in relation to the struggle in Europe from the point of view of military strategy. But it is incomprehensible that he should conclude that the French planters who, faced with the probable loss of their possessions and even their lives, besieged the British Ministry were "simply selfish, avaricious adventurers" (*Op. cit.*, page 78). "With Grenville," he continues, "who was as high bred as he was high principled and as courteous as he was austere, their arts were powerless; and they therefore turned to Dundas, whose hatred of the Revolution was extravagant and whose vanity, it must be feared, was less proof against the subtleties of French flattery" (Pages 78–79). The influence of noble ideas and elevated sentiments in history cannot be denied, but they flourish best in an economic atmosphere which is congenial to them. Fortescue was, to say the very least, quite deceived by Grenville. Grenville, on January 14, 1791, wrote to Hawkesbury—"This man is unfortunately for our purpose, by what I hear of him, rather of a questionable character, but you will know that the utility of things of this sort very often stands on very different grounds from that of the honesty of the persons employed in them" (*Liverpool Papers*, Add. Mss. 38226, folio 42). What have breeding and principles to do with the ramifications of policy or the exigencies of war? The actual explanation is very simple. When the refugees approached Grenville, Britain still maintained her neutrality. When Dundas replaced Grenville, hostilities were inevitable. Dundas signed the St. Domingo Capitulations after the war had broken out. Grenville would have done the same. The Government of Britain at this period, as Fortescue himself admits (page 70), lay in the hands of three men, Pitt, Dundas and Grenville. The responsibility must be collective. Pitt and Grenville were no less eager than Dundas to acquire the French colonies.
40. *Dropmore Papers*, Vol. II, page 464. To Auckland, Nov. 11, 1793.
41. Ibid., Vol. II, page 501. To Grenville, Jan. 31, 1794.
42. Ibid., Vol. III, pages 166–167. To Grenville, Jan. 3, 1796.

the Convention. It was not the mortality of the troops in the West Indies he was thinking of; it was merely that he was convinced that the French West Indies would be secured by success in Europe.[43] The French colonies were to be conquered on the fields of Flanders.

It was left to the discretion of the commander-in-chief to decide the order and course of his operations.[44] Britain meant to conquer all the French possessions, though she was by no means blind to the peculiar value and importance of St. Domingo. Williamson repeatedly assured Dundas of the readiness of the French inhabitants to change their Government, of the dislike felt for the Spaniards, and of the certain welcome which would await the British.[45] Dundas could go ahead merrily with few qualms. In June he authorised Williamson to advance to Charmilly a sum not exceeding £5,000, to be repaid out of the revenues of the colony.[46]

At the outset everything went smoothly in Britain's favour, and there was nothing but successes, surrenders, hoisting of the British colours and oaths of allegiance. The zenith of British successes was marked by the appointment of Williamson in September, 1794, as Governor of such parts of St. Domingo as were in their possession.[47]

But now Britain's difficulties began in real earnest. It was easier to conquer than to retain the conquests. By the autumn of 1794 yellow fever, the white man's most dreaded enemy in the West Indies, had begun its campaign and the British soldiers were dying like rotten sheep.[48] A revolt in St. Domingo headed by the Mulatto Rigaud resulted in the loss of Léogane and Tiburon, and at least 12,000 Englishmen were buried in the West Indies in 1794. The year 1795 proved even worse. It produced serious Negro revolts in St. Vincent and Grenada, which did not prevent Dundas, however, from taking over the Dutch colonies when Holland joined France. The year 1795 was "perhaps the most discreditable in the records of the British Army."[49] Britain

43. Ibid., Vol. II, page 454. To Grenville, Nov. 7, 1793.

44. C.O. 137/91. Dundas to Williamson, Nov. 8, 1793.

45. Ibid. March 9, and July 13, 1793; and C.O., 137/92. Nov. 26, 1793. An anonymous writer from St. Eustatous averred that the French islands would "unanimously accept the benefits of the British constitution as a blessing." *Liverpool Papers*, Add. Mss. 38228, folio 233. Jan. 24, 1793. The master of *L'Aimable*, a brig bound from St. Domingo to Bordeaux but captured and taken to Liverpool after the outbreak of hostilities, confirmed that "the planters to a man wished to see an English fleet coming to the island but dare not express themselves," and that they would be certain to flock to the British standard if it was displayed in St. Domingo. *Chatham Papers*, G.D. 8/349.

46. C.O. 137/91. June 4, 1793.

47. C.O. 137/93. Sept. 5, 1794.

48. *Fortescue, op. cit.*, page 344.

49. Ibid., page 454.

was finding that her effort to destroy the power of France was resulting in the practical destruction of the British Army.[50]

The cession of Spanish St. Domingo to France by the Treaty of Basle induced Britain to make greater efforts and to concentrate on St. Domingo. The result was an appalling mortality among the European troops.[51] Fortescue's estimate of the losses in the West Indian campaigns for the years 1794 to 1796 is the huge total of "80,000 soldiers lost to the service, including 40,000 actually dead, the latter number exceeding the total losses of Wellington's army from death, discharges, desertion and all causes from the beginning to the end of the Peninsular War."[52] The expense of St. Domingo was equally great. From £300,000 in 1794 it had risen to close upon £800,000 in 1795, more than 2 million pounds in 1796, and £700,000 in January 1797 alone.[53] In Dundas's own words, "it clearly exceeds all the bounds of expense we had resolved upon, and what the country either can or will bear."[54]

It was with this background in mind that by 1796 the British Cabinet was prepared for the evacuation of the whole of St. Domingo, except the Mole St. Nicholas. In 1798 Maitland, after much hesitation on the part of the Cabinet, took the initiative into his own hands. At first he decided on evacuating the whole island except the Mole and Jeremie, to afford protection to Jamaica,[55] but by August he confessed to Balcarres that he thought "the thing to be done most for the interests of Great Britain is to give the whole up,"[56] and a few days later he had decided irrevocably on entire evacuation.[57]

Fortescue has told us what Maitland's game was. He was laying a snare for France, into which Napoleon promptly fell. "Napoleon, falling into the pit that Maitland had digged for him, emulated and outdid the folly of Pitt and Dundas."[58] If Britain could not retain the world's finest colony, she could prevent France from recovering it and thereby regaining that colonial ascendancy which had formed part of the economic background of the abolition movement. For this reason Maitland signed his convention with Toussaint, by which Toussaint gave his pledge not to attack Jamaica and Britain promised to refrain from interference in the internal affairs of St. Domingo, and to permit the entry into certain ports of St. Domingo agreed upon of a quantity of provisions without risk of capture by British ships.

50. Ibid., page 385.
51. Ibid., pages 473–474.
52. Ibid., page 496.
53. Ibid., page 456.
54. *Dropmore Papers*, Vol. III, pages 390–391. To Grenville, Nov. 8, 1791.
55. C.O. 137/100. To Balcarres, June 25, 1798.
56. Ibid., July 27, 1798.
57. Ibid., July 31, 1798.
58. *Fortescue, op. cit.*, pages 562–563 and 566.

It could not be expected that white planters in the West Indies would see as far ahead as the British Government or its representative on the spot. They saw in Maitland's Convention only a recognition by Britain of rebellious slaves which was bound to have a very bad effect on the Negroes of all the islands. Had not Governor Orde admitted years back that "our power over those people in such an island as this hangs in the thread of opinion—touch it too often, it certainly will break?"[59] Balcarres, who had at first advocated the entire abandonment of St. Domingo and had been prepared to pronounce "*EVACUATE*,"[60] only voiced colonial sentiment when he hysterically denounced Maitland's right to make a convention for Jamaica. "It would be thought somewhat odd if the City of London should send over an immense quantity of provisions and clothing for the use of the *sans culotte* army assembled for the purpose of invading England!"[61] The Duke of Portland, Home Secretary, in a secret and confidential letter, tried to quiet Balcarres's fears. The Convention would secure the tranquillity and safety of Jamaica. Balcarres was urged to give the leading Jamaicans "a right impression of the measure in question" and point out to them the securities attached to the convention by making Toussaint entirely dependent on Britain and America for the means of subsistence; and, finally, Portland admitted that the Government had "no alternative but must adopt and maintain the convention to the best of our power."[62] If the British could not themselves retain St. Domingo, they could see to it that the French would bleed to death in the island.

Thus ended the British attempt to conquer St. Domingo. "The secret of England's impotence," wrote Fortescue, "for the first six years of the war may be said to lie in the two fatal words St. Domingo."[63] It was British greed for sugar that saved the French Revolution in Europe. "After long and careful thought and study," Fortescue summarises, "I have come to the conclusion that the West Indian campaigns, both to Windward and Leeward, which were the essence of Pitt's military policy, cost England in army and navy little fewer than 100,000 men, about one-half of them dead, the remainder permanently unfit for service." In return, Britain could show only the British islands of Grenada and St. Vincent in ruins, the acquisition from the French of insignificant Tobago, Martinique, badly damaged and with difficulty held, and St. Lucia, so wasted as to be no more than a naval station. "For this

---

59. C.O. 71/20. June 3, 1791.
60. C.O. 137/100. To Maitland, July 4, 1798.
61. Ibid. To Portland, Sept. 16, 1798.
62. C.O. 137/101. Jan. 6, 1799.
63. *Fortescue, op. cit.*, page 325.

England's soldiers had been sacrificed, her treasure squandered, her influence in Europe weakened, her arm for six fateful years fettered, numbed and paralysed."[64]

Fortescue was concerned only with the military side of the expedition. To him Pitt was fighting a new dynamic force with antiquated weapons. He therefore failed to grasp Britain's greatest, if negative, gain. French colonial superiority was smashed, even though Britain had not succeeded in the attempt to acquire that colonial monopoly which the war had seemed to promise—*a colonial monopoly which must logically have postponed the abolition of the slave trade for decades.*

---

64. Ibid., page 565.

CHAPTER SIX

The Significance of the West Indian Expeditions

It is impossible to understand the great efforts made by Britain to acquire St. Domingo, the lives and money lost, unless one has grasped the essential point of the superiority of the French sugar islands. In the words of Professor Holland Rose, "when five or six valuable islands were to be had, to all appearance with little risk except from the slaves, ministers would have been craven in the extreme not to push on an enterprise which promised to benefit British commerce and cripple that of France."[1] Would later historians, one wonders, have condemned the expeditions had they been successful?

The vast expense entailed by St. Domingo showed that the British Cabinet meant business. St. Domingo was important not merely for its intrinsic worth; it could also be used as a pawn, a valuable concession in the diplomatic bargaining. It was not merely St. Domingo, or even all the French colonies in the West Indies, at which Britain aimed, but all the foreign West Indian possessions. It is perhaps quite understandable that an "Army" historian should fail signally to realise the economic significance of the Dutch colonies, and should condemn Dundas for "truckling to a parcel of greedy merchants,"[2] and the expedition to Demerara as "undertaken, almost avowedly, not for the furtherance of any object in the war, but to secure the profits of a clique of merchants who had ventured their capital, from motives the reverse of patriotic, in the Dutch colonies."[3] But even in 1799, despite

---

1. J. H. Rose: William Pitt and the Great War (London, 1911), pages 222–223.
2. Fortescue, op. cit., page 442.
3. Ibid., page 432.

repeated failures, Dundas was of opinion that the acquisition of Surinam was highly desirable, if it could be secured without a great expenditure of men and money.[4] Grenville wished at the end of the war, if the internal situation of France and Holland were agreed on to Britain's satisfaction, to restore all the French and Dutch colonies except the Cape of Good Hope and Ceylon. Dundas opposed this. If they were restored, the colonies that would remain with Britain would not be worth keeping.[5]

The very structure of St. Domingo imperatively demanded the continuance of the slave trade. By 1789 St. Domingo needed 40,000 slaves a year. No offer of St. Domingo would have been made to Britain by French colonial planters, infuriated by the mere fear that the National Assembly would interfere with the basic structure of the colonial system, unless those planters were convinced that Britain would not herself do the same and would not abolish the slave trade. When Article 5 of the Capitulations, signed in 1793, was agreed to, guaranteeing the internal structure of St. Domingo, it meant, logically, that the slave trade could not be abolished. Without the 40,000 slaves a year the great colony would have been useless to its owners.

The British did not only agree on paper but stuck so rigidly to the conditions that they actually imperilled, if they did not destroy, the success of the expedition. By the Capitulations the privileges of the Mulattoes in St. Domingo were to be those enjoyed by the Mulattoes in the British colonies. The St. Domingo planters demanded this; the British Cabinet assented, even though Dundas realised the fanatical lengths to which the French planters carried their racial dissensions. Williamson repeatedly pointed out how much easier the British conquest would be were the Mulattoes in St. Domingo conciliated. "If I had it in my power," he wrote to Dundas in one letter, "to grant the people of colour a ratification of the Decree of Louis Quatorze in 1685, which gave them full and equal privileges with the whites, I make no doubt but we should at this moment be in quiet possession of the whole of the Western and Southern provinces."[6] The British Cabinet never agreed to this. "Great care should be taken," Dundas warned Williamson, "to excite the jealousy of the whites as little as possible, in taking advantage of the service of the mulattoes."[7] If Britain gave way to the French planters on this point, British sovereignty would not have been accepted if the still more fundamental point of the slave trade was at all in doubt.

4. *Dropmore Papers*, Vol. IV, page 513. March 31, 1799.
5. Ibid., Vol. VI, pages 37–38. Nov. 24, 1799.
6. C.O. 137/92. Jan. 17, 1794.
7. C.O. 137/93. July 5, 1794.

Further, Fortescue blames the British Government for not saving the lives of the British soldiers by raising black troops to do fatigue work and act as labour corps. As early as 1790 Grenville had written to Effingham strongly urging the utility of such black troops.[8] Effingham promptly pointed out the various difficulties.[9] Williamson, on his arrival, at once saw the impossibility of persuading the planters of its advantages, and recommended that the Government should purchase slaves from the different plantations,[10] who could, after service, be resold at the same price.[11] But the planters, French as well as British, were opposed to any such measure, and permission to raise black troops came from home only in 1795 when it was too late.[12] Even then British commanders were forbidden in the most positive terms to promise emancipation after five years' service to Negro recruits.[13] Whatever British ministers individually wished for, they were obviously determined not to quarrel with the St. Domingo planters. If emancipation was not to be granted to those of the blacks who might be persuaded to leave their fellows and join the British, the acceptance of St. Domingo, with its numbers of slaves in revolt, meant of necessity the continuation of the slave trade for years.

It was this very necessity to continue slavery and with it the slave trade—for St. Domingo could not exist without it—which was the decisive political factor in the conflict. We have seen that the declaration abolishing slavery by the revolutionary commissioners in St. Domingo was a bid for black support against the aristocratic white planters supported by Britain. A year later the difficulties of defence drove the French Convention to the ratification of this measure, not only for St. Domingo but for all the French colonies. We would as little deny the idealism of the French Convention as we would that of the British humanitarians. But the spontaneous abolition of slavery had the soundest political motives. "Citoyens," cried Danton, "c'est aujourd'hui que l'anglais est mort! Pitt et ces complots sont déjoués."[14] Professor Holland Rose laments the lapse of the question of abolition in the years 1795 and 1796 as "a public misfortune; for the slaves, despairing of justice from England, turned to France. . . . Here was our chief difficulty in the West Indies owing to the refusal of Parliament to limit the supply of slaves or to alleviate their condition, we had to deal with myriads of blacks, exasperated by their former hardships, hoping everything from France, and able to support climatic changes which

8. C.O. 137/88. Oct. 6, 1790.
9. Ibid. Sept. 12, 1790.
10. C.O. 137/89. To Grenville, Dec. 19, 1790.
11. Ibid. To Grenville, March 20, 1791.
12. *Fortescue, op. cit.*, page 452.
13. Ibid., page 469.
14. *Cochin, op. cit.*, Vol. I, page 15. Feb. 4, 1794.

dealt havoc with the raw English levies. In truth, the success of the West Indian expeditions depended on other factors besides military and medical skill. It turned on political and humanitarian motives that were scouted at Westminster. The French Jacobins stole many a march on the English governing classes; and in declaring the negro to be the equal of the white man they nearly wrecked Britain's possessions in the West Indies."[15]

It is perhaps by tracing Pitt's activities in regard to abolition that we can best follow the course of the abolition movement in the minds of the most powerful governing section of the day.

Pitt had manifested his great interest in the question of abolition in many ways. It was he who had introduced the timid Rev. Newton to the Privy Council;[16] it was by his "particular direction" that several extra clerks had been engaged by the Privy Council to hasten their investigation;[17] and Pitt wrote to the French Ambassador in London asking for the most exact information procured by the French Government on the population, annual importation, births and deaths of the slaves in the French colonies.[18] Yet it was about this very time that Clarkson, in the spring of 1788, had an interview with Pitt, in which Pitt pretended total ignorance of the question of the slave trade,[19] the effect, no doubt, commented Wilberforce's biographers, of constitutional reserve.[20]

The explanation is quite inadequate. Pitt was at this time negotiating with France for abolition. What is far more likely is that he did not yet wish to come out into the open. For, despite his pledge to Wilberforce that the latter's illness would not be allowed to injure the cause,[21] and his repetition of this pledge to Granville Sharp,[22] Pitt was very careful not to expose his hand.

---

15. *Rose, op. cit.*, pages 238–239.
16. *Wilberforce, Correspondence*, Vol. I, page 114.
17. B.T. 3/20. Nov. 15, 1788.
18. *Chatham Papers*, G.D. 8/333. France: Diplomatic Papers and Despatches. April 15 and April 23, 1788.
19. *Clarkson: History*, page 274. "I had removed doubts and given birth to an interest in favour of our cause." See also *Prince Hoare: Memoirs of Granville Sharp* (London, 1820), page 421 (footnote).
20. *Life of Wilberforce*, Vol. I, page 163.
21. Ibid., Vol. I, page 170. Wilberforce to Wyvill, April 5, 1788. "To *you* in *strict confidence* I will intrust, that Pitt, with a warmth of principle and friendship that have made me love him better than I ever did before, has taken on himself the management of the business, and promises to do all for me if I desire it. . . . This is all I can say now; I might add more were we side by side on my sofa."
22. Granville Sharp's Report to the Abolition Committee, April 21, 1788—"He had a full opportunity of explaining that the desire of the Committee went to the entire abolition of the slave trade; Mr. Pitt assured him that his heart was with us, and that he considered himself pledged to Mr. Wilberforce, that the cause should not suffer any injury from his indisposition, but at the same time, that the subject was of great political importance, and it was requisite to proceed in the business with temper and prudence." *Abolition Committee's Proceedings*, Add. Mss. 21255, folio 14.

The notice he gave respecting the slave trade in May 1788 was marked by such careful reticence, so deliberate an avoidance of his personal opinion on the general question, that Fox declared that Pitt had left them completely in the dark.[23] By the time Dolben's bill to provide temporary regulations for the transport of slaves was being debated, however, Pitt was prepared to discuss the general question and to vote for "the utter abolition of a trade which was shocking to humanity, contrary to every humane, every Christian principle, and to every sentiment that ought to inspire the breast of man."[24] The bill met with some opposition in the House of Lords, though Pitt expressed his surprise how any human being could resist it.[25] So strongly did he feel on the matter that he was determined that, if it failed, he and his opponents could not remain in the same cabinet,[26] and he forced the King to keep Parliament in session until the bill became law.[27]

The opposition of the Jacobins to send relief to the white planters in St. Domingo drew from Pitt the bitter gibe that the French preferred their coffee "au caramel,"[28] and in 1792 Wilberforce's diary struck the first ominous note: "Pitt threw out against slave motion on St. Domingo account."[29] From London to Inverness Pitt's sincerity was questioned.[30] In the debate in 1795 on the question of abolition in 1796, Pitt, while still proclaiming his adherence to immediate abolition, thought it dangerous at a time when the state of the colonies was particularly tender and vulnerable.[31] Wilberforce's measure was defeated by 78 to 61, a vote in his opinion so "infamous" that he found in it an argument for parliamentary reform.[32] By 1796 Dundas could with justice taunt Wilberforce that he was further from attaining his end than he had been four years ago.[33] In that year Pitt expressed his opinion that if Wilberforce's motion for abolition was not likely to succeed, he would have

---

23. *Parl. Hist.*, Vol. XXVII, pages 498–499. May 9, 1788.

24. Ibid., page 598. June 17, 1788.

25. *Wilberforce, Private Papers*, page 20. Pitt to Wilberforce, June 28, 1788. But even this mild measure was strongly opposed by the Liverpool merchants as involving "the total ruin of the bulk of the African commerce." In a letter to Lord Hawkesbury, in which he confined himself to Dolben's bill "without touching upon the merits of the assumed or pretended general question of humanity," John Tarleton expressed the hope that Pitt would obviate the mischief "by quashing the bill at once." The Liverpool merchants, he declared, deprecated hasty and violent measures at the end of the session, but were "not averse to any regulations wisely conceived and maturely digested." *Liverpool Papers*, Add. Mss. 38416, folio 9. May 25, 1788.

26. *Dropmore Papers*, Vol. I, page 342. Pitt to Grenville, June 29, 1788.

27. *Klingberg, op. cit.*, page 106.

28. *Stoddard, op. cit.*, page 169.

29. *Life of Wilberforce*, Vol. I, page 341.

30. Ibid., Vol. I, page 344. Dr. Dickson to Wilberforce.

31. *Parl. Hist.*, Vol. XXXI, page 1342. Feb. 26, 1795.

32. *Life of Wilberforce*, Vol. II, page 84, to Wyvill, Feb. 28, 1795.

33. *Parl. Hist.*, Vol. XXXII, page 751. Feb. 18, 1796.

preferred it to remain in temporary oblivion until it might be brought for-ward with more safety and unanimity.[34] The motion was defeated by 74 to 70—"10 or 12 of those who had supported me," is Wilberforce's bitter entry in his diary, "absent in the country or on pleasure. Enough at the opera to have carried it;"[35] and he confessed later, when his Slave-carrying Bill was counted out, "with Pitt by the West Indians," that he had occasionally felt a sinful anger about the slave-carrying Bill and the scandalous neglect of his friends.[36] In 1797 Pitt had changed to such an extent that he tried to per-suade Wilberforce to accept the compromise of a West Indian planter, Ellis, that the duty of passing ameliorating measures for the Negroes should be left to the colonial legislatures.[37] Wilberforce refused, whereupon Pitt, in Wilber-force's phrase, "stood stiffly" by him, and in the ensuing debate expressed his decided objection to the very suggestion he had made as "only a substitute for that abolition which the honour of the country and the safety of the islands so loudly called for."[38]

The full extent of Pitt's defection from the cause can be seen from the discussions on the prohibition of the slave trade to the conquered French and Dutch colonies. Lecky condemns Pitt strongly for this. "It was in the power of Pitt," he writes, "by an Order of Council to prevent it, but he refused to take this course. It was a political and commercial object to strengthen these new acquisitions, and as they had so long been prevented from supplying themselves with negroes they were ready to take more than usual. The result was that, in consequence of the British conquests, and under the shelter of the British flag, the slave trade became more active than ever. . . . It was computed that under his administration the English slave trade more than doubled, and that the number of negroes imported annually in English ships rose from 25,000 to 57,000."[39]

With the conquest of Trinidad in 1797, and the opening thereby of ex-tensive virgin soil to British enterprise and British capital, Pitt was induced to favour a compromise by which the slave trade, on the insistence of aboli-tionists as well as West Indian planters of the older islands, was to be stopped to the acquired possessions, but these new lands were to be developed by

34. Ibid., page 895. March 15, 1796.
35. *Life of Wilberforce*, Vol. II, pages 141–142. March 15,1796.
36. Ibid. Vol. II, page 147. May 15, 1796. This was not the first time—or even the last—that the cause of abolition suffered from such neglect; there were no signs of such neglect before the war. The motion of 1793 was lost, as the Abolition Committee confessed, "in a great measure by the absence of some of our ablest friends; a circumstance which the advocates of the trade did not fail to improve to their advantage." *Abolition Committee's Proceedings*, Add. Mss. 21256, folio 85(v). Aug. 20, 1793.
37. Just what this meant we shall have ample occasion to see later.
38. *Parl. Hist.*, Vol. XXXIII, page 289. Apl. 6, 1797.
39. Cit. *Kingberg*, page 116.

labourers transferred from the older islands. Pitt had evidently forgotten his arguments in earlier years about the dreadful mortality attending the opening of new lands. "Lloyd's Coffee House is in a roar of merriment," Stephen reported to Wilberforce, "at the dexterous compromise Mr. Pitt has made between his religious friends and his and Dundas's West Indian supporters. Well may the slave merchants laugh at this wise plan of giving them a new market in the old islands, where payment is more secure, for the sake of not opening to them an equal one in a new settlement, with such unsafe paymasters as new settlers generally are." Stephen was quick to see the danger to the abolitionist cause from the foundation, "on abolition principles," of a colony which was certain to prove incapable of keeping up its numbers or existing without supplies from Africa. "Really," he wrote in criticism of Pitt, "my charity does not go so far as to believe it possible he can be innocent of indirect and selfish views on this occasion."[40]

Stephen spoke not for himself alone when he wrote bitterly to Wilberforce that "Mr. Pitt, unhappily for himself, his country and mankind, is not zealous enough in the cause of the negroes, to contend for them as decisively as he ought, in the cabinet any more than in parliament."[41] With the remarkable increase in the British slave trade as a result of the destruction of rival mercantile marines during the war and the great need of slaves in the foreign colonies now in British possession, the slave trade agitation was at a low ebb. Between 1797 and 1804 the Abolition Committee held no meetings; Wilberforce's "delenda est Carthago" was soon heard no more in the House; and Stephen lugubriously prophesied that it was the slave trade which would bring the scourge of heaven on England and lead to her ruin. "Dundas will go on to waste our last energies between the tropics, Pitt will support him, and you and your friends will support Pitt, till Africa has no longer a foe to fear in Great Britain. It is for this that Pitt was made eloquent, and great, and if you will, virtuous."[42]

Was Stephen wrong, or even ungenerous? Wilberforce's secret reflections for June 27, 1797, speak of the great provocation he received when Pitt put off his Slave-carrying Bill; "I was near resenting it on the spot."[43] In 1799 we find the once rising hope of the stern unbending abolitionists writing to Lord Hawkesbury that he had summoned a Cabinet meeting to deal with the slave trade: "what I wish to propose rests almost wholly on political grounds, and

40. *Life of Wilberforce*. Vol. II, pages 259–263. The letter is dated 1798.
41. Ibid., Vol. II, page 225. The date is 1797.
42. Ibid., Vol. II, page 256. To Wilberforce, Sept. 20, 1797.
43. Ibid., Vol. II, page 286.

has in view the future security of our West India possessions."[44] A few days later the Duke of Portland explained to Lord Hawkesbury that at the meeting Pitt admitted that his communication was merely what he "thought himself called upon to do in consequence of the notice he had given in the House of Commons."[45] An unusually sure instinct convinced Wilberforce in 1802 that the grief he felt on reflecting that he had not talked to Pitt on abolition was useless: "I deliberately think it would have done no good."[46] And a month later Pitt excused himself, on the ground of a rest which had been recommended, from attending Wilberforce's motion; most certainly and eagerly would he have supported it, had he been able to attend, even though he saw no chance of its being carried.[47]

The question of the Guiana Order—the desire of the abolitionists to prohibit the slave trade to the conquered Dutch colonies, likely to be returned at the peace, stopped by an Order in Council—confirms, if confirmation is still needed, the unpopularity of the Abolition cause, and shows the extent of Wilberforce's pleading and the strength of Pitt's hold upon him. Wilberforce was very explicit in his reasons for desiring this Order. What he was considering was "the effects on our old West India islands of the immense region of Dutch Guiana being cultivated to its full extent." The superior fertility of the soil and lower costs of production would drive the older British Islands out of all foreign markets, and consequently, he emphasized, the British West Indian planters, that is, of the older islands, strongly advocated the prohibition of the slave trade to Dutch Guiana and its restoration at the end of the war, provided the Dutch did not then continue the slave trade and produce the ruinous competition they dreaded.[48] It was to prevent this latter possibility that Brougham was at that time in Holland urging the Dutch to abolish the slave trade, and the abolitionists in Britain were pressing for the Guiana Order, because of the good effect it would have on the Dutch and the possibility that it might induce them on their part to abolish the trade.[49]

Wilberforce begged Pitt in September 1804 to issue the proclamation. It would take only half an hour, the forms were ready in the Council Office, and he himself was personally interested, as he would have to face attacks on him by a certain section of his party.[50] But delay followed delay, whilst the slave trade went on increasing. Wilberforce accused Pitt of procrastination, the delay

44. *Liverpool Papers*, Add. Mss. 38192, folio 101. July 9, 1799.
45. Ibid., Add. Mss. 38191, folio 245. July 12, 1799.
46. *Life of Wilberforce*, Vol. III, page 96. April 27, 1802.
47. *Wilberforce, Private Papers*, page 31. May 31, 1802.
48. *Wilberforce, Correspondence*, Vol. 1, pages 328–331. To Lord Harrowby, Sept. 29, 1804.
49. Ibid., Vol. I, page 331. Wilberforce to Stephen, Oct.2, 1804.
50. Ibid., Vol. I, page 312. Sept. 14, 1804.

tried his patience and temper "more almost than in any other part of the long course of abominations," and made him "sick of this bad world."[51] When the Order was sent to him it was so unsatisfactory that he begged Pitt to withhold its publication and considered the advisability of having recourse to parliament, a course which the abolitionists had rejected in favour of "the spontaneous determination of government."[52] The Order as then framed was worse than none, and though he longed to enjoy a charming spring day,[53] he was forced to town to see Pitt. He could do nothing but "write and call, again and again"[54]—all to no effect. "Procrastination in one whom you used to call the General," he moaned to Muncaster, "has increased to such a degree as to have become absolutely predominant."[55] Wilberforce himself relates how others considered him the dupe of Pitt, and how his supporters did not share his optimism. "I saw certain significant winks and shrugs, as if I was taken in by Pitt, and was too credulous and soft etc; but I of course saw them as if I had seen them not." Yet this was a question involving 12,000, or 15,000 human beings annually, and a vast investment of capital, amounting to 18 millions in the last war, in a foreign settlement which might be relinquished at the end of the war.[56]

In 1805 Pitt tried to persuade Wilberforce, out of tenderness for the susceptibilities of his political friends, to postpone his notion, but Wilberforce refused to "make that holy cause subservient to the interest of a party."[57] When the motion was brought forward, the Irish members, consistently favourable to abolition, were, strangely enough, hostile, and all Wilberforce's usual supporters, Fox alone excepted, silent, Pitt for the first time saying nothing in support of abolition.[58] How many men must have concurred with

51. Ibid., Vol. II, pages 33–34. To Stephen, 1805.

52. Ibid., Vol. II, page 15. Wilberforce to Pitt, March 30, 1805.

53. *Life of Wilberforce*, Vol. III, page 231.

54. Ibid., Vol. III, page 232. June 4, 1805.

55. Ibid., Vol. III, pages 232–233.

56. Ibid., Vol. III, pages 233–234. It should be mentioned that the Order in Council which Pitt would not issue was issued in 1805 by Castlereagh, an inveterate opponent of abolition. The Government's object was candidly stated. It was to prevent as much as possible the employment of British capital in the cultivation and improvement of the conquered colonies until their future fate was decided. Many complicated regulations were drawn up, upon the principle of permitting imports of slaves only to replace losses in the existing stock and of prohibiting such imports under any pretence whatever for new cultivation. "By this limited but liberal supply," it was emphasized, "you will find the old planters disposed, from motives of self-interest, not only to watch the new cultivators but to check each other." C.O. 324/103. Circulars to Governors, 1794–1815, folios 78–96. Aug. 21, 1805. Castlereagh endeavoured, in his own words, "to steer a middle course, applying strict regulations in the first instance, and leaving their relaxation, in cases of evident hardship, to the discretion of the Governors abroad." *Correspondence, Despatches and other Papers of Viscount Castlereagh* (London, 1848–1853), Vol. III, page 5. (Referred to hereafter as *Castlereagh, Correspondence*.) Castlereagh to the Lord Chancellor, July 21, 1805.

57. *Life of Wilberforce*, Vol. III, page 211.

58. Ibid., page 212. Diary, Feb. 28, 1805.

Somers Cocks, a consistent abolitionist, in his violent attack on Pitt: "it had frequently occurred to him that if the Rt. Hon. gent, had employed the fair honourable influence of office, the great object which he professed to have had so cordially in view would, long ere this, have been obtained."[59] In 1807 Hibbert taunted the House that abolition, though, according to the abolitionists, indisputably enjoined by every principle of justice and humanity, and demanded for twenty years by the voice of the public and the union of the greatest talents within the House, had not succeeded until it received the protecting hand of His Majesty's Minister in either House. "There must be some mistake in the application of these great principles to the measure."[60]

It perhaps might not be out of place to attempt some explanation of the confusing part played by the great British minister. Men do not act absolutely in accord with economic tendencies which, a hundred years later, when they have run their full course, we can distinguish with a clarity impossible at the time. If that were so the writing of history would be a matter of geometrical deduction and extremely simple. We may take it that at the beginning Pitt did feel very strongly about abolition, and or seeing that the slave trade was not nearly as valuable as people conceived it to be, and was in some respects positively harmful, threw himself into the cause. Wilberforce and the abolitionists, however, ignorant of or blind to the responsibilities of the British Government to the French planters, continued with their agitation for abolition during the war. They did not see that not only would the question of the French colonies, even if temporarily, affect the position of the British Prime Minister, at least for the duration of the war, but that the whole question of the French Revolution had radically altered the possibilities of reform in Britain. Pitt affords the best example of the effect of the Revolution on a statesman who was concerned with the fortunes of the empire as a whole, and not with the particular grievances of any small and politically uninfluential section of it, the slaves.

The outbreak of war produced a great change in popular sentiment in Britain. All measures of reform were postponed on the ground that they smacked of Jacobinism, to which the indiscretions of men like Clarkson in associating with political thinkers and radicals lent some colour.[61] The rising tide of liber-

---

59. *Parl. Deb.*, Vol. II, page 654. June 13, 1804.
60. Ibid., Vol. VIII, page 980. Feb. 23, 1807.
61. *Life of Wilberforce*, Vol. I, page 343. "What business had your friend Clarkson to attend the Crown and Anchor last Thursday? He could not have done a more mischievous thing to the cause you have taken in hand." Dundas to Wilberforce, July 18, 1791. "You will see Clarkson, caution him against talking of the French Revolution; it will be ruin to our cause." Wilberforce to Muncaster, Oct. 1792.

alism in Great Britain was checked by the French Revolution.[62] Pitt's natural genius was for reform and improvement, not for war and reaction.[63] The reasons given by Klingberg for Pitt's vacillation in issuing the Guiana Order really explain Pitt's altered attitude to the abolition in general; the opposition of some West Indian planters, his slender majority in Parliament, the condition of Europe, and Klingberg conceived that the best evidence of Pitt's sincerity was the fact that neither Wilberforce nor Clarkson ever lost faith in him.[64] It is reasonable, too, to suppose that Pitt considered that his first and main task was to save Britain and Europe from the French Revolution, and he was at the mercy of those reactionary commercial forces, incarnated in Hawkesbury. These forces, powerful enough before the war, for instance, to strip his Irish commercial treaty of its more liberal provisions, were immensely strengthened by the war. Pitt's backsliding over the question of abolition was paralleled by his backsliding over the question of parliamentary reform.

In the country the cause of abolition seemed lost. Since 1792 the trade had been carried on to a greater extent than at any former period;[65] it was one-fourth more, at least, than what Parliament had determined it ought to be,[66] while in Britain they were "trifling and trimming between our consciences and our purses."[67] Between 1792 and 1804, according to Wilberforce, 300,000 additional Negroes had been imported into the West Indies, and 140,000 into Jamaica alone.[68]

Eden wrote complacently in 1801 that "the slave trade (I speak of it only in a commercial view) promises to open new sources of mercantile profit. The demand for negroes must, for some years to come, be very great; St. Lucia, Martinico, and Trinidad may still be supplied, although the 'not happier island in the stormy waste,' St. Domingo, should continue to be deemed too pure a soil for slaves to dwell in."[69] This extension of the slave trade would, he anticipated, create at the peace a greater demand for British manufactures in Africa than usual. His figures of the tonnage of British vessels which cleared outwards for Africa tell their own tale.[70]

---

62. *Ragatz, op. cit.*, page 253.
63. C. M. MacInnes: *England and Slavery* (Bristol, 1934), page 149.
64. *Klingberg, op. cit.*, pages 115 and 125 (footnote). But we have already had reason to think Clarkson's testimony worthless, and we have seen how Wilberforce was considered by some the dupe of Pitt.
65. *Parl. Hist.*, Vol. XXXII, page 746. Feb. 18, 1796.
66. Ibid., page 897. March 15, 1796.
67. *Life of Wilberforce*, Vol. III, page 446. Wilberforce to Muncaster, April 14, 1802.
68. *Parl. Deb.*, Vol. II, page 454. May 30, 1804.
69. *Sir F. M. Eden: Eight Letters on the Peace; and on the Commerce and Manufactures of Great Britain* (London, 1802), page 70.
70. Ibid., pages 95–96.

Table 6.1.

Year	Tons	Year	Tons
1789	19,493	1795	18,234
1790	26,921	1796	23,251
1791	32,590	1797	23,477
1792	40,479	1798	39,310
1793	16,484	1799	41,778
1794	29,034	1800	38,966

It seemed that the economic interests defending the slave trade, however powerful they had been before the war, had now become much more powerful. British naval supremacy and the occupation of the French, Dutch and Spanish colonies meant not merely that Britain became the sole slave carrier, but that as a result there was a tremendous increase in the British slave trade.

It is against this background that we must consider the attempt of the bill of 1799 to prohibit the trading for slaves on the coast of Africa within certain limits. In the very early days of the abolition movement, the abolitionists had contemplated, as a corollary of the abolition, the beginning of an honourable and natural commerce with Africa, not for slaves, but for those natural productions in which Clarkson was so interested, and which, in his interview with Pitt, caused such sublime thoughts to rush in upon the minister, "some of which he expressed with observations becoming a great and dignified mind."[71] Thus the Sierra Leone Company came into being. With the aid of about seven hundred Negroes, men, women and children, who had run away to Nova Scotia,[72] over four hundred blacks who swarmed the streets of London in a distressed condition, and together with sixty whites, chiefly women of the lowest sort, in ill-health and of bad character,[73] all sent out at the expense of Government to Sierra Leone, the undertaking was begun. Wilberforce expatiated on the benefit which would accrue to British manufactures when once Africa had acquired a taste for them and reached such a state of civilization as to make returns,[74] among which the abolitionists placed in the forefront sugar and cotton. Some West Indians thought the undertaking big enough, if only in conception, to excite alarm, and feared that the precedent set to foreign nations with African possessions might prove detrimental to

---

71. *Clarkson: History*, page 273.
72. *Life of Wilberforce*, Vol. I, page 322.
73. *Substance or the Report of the Court of Directors of the Sierra Leone Company to the General Court*, Oct. 19, 1791, page 3.
74. *Auckland Papers*, Add. Mss. 34427, folio 123(v). To Eden, Nov. 23, 1787.

those countries which already possessed West Indian colonies.[75] But the fear was unfounded; as far as sugar was concerned the African output could not have equalled the growth of the smallest West Indian island.[76]

The bill, introduced by Henry Thornton in 1799, prohibited the trade, as Grenville was careful to emphasize, on merely about one-fourth of the whole of the coast on which the slave trade was carried on.[77] Nevertheless, the answer of Parliament, in this period when the slave trade was at its height, when in the next year Dolben's annual Regulating Bill was not passed because the House was counted out, was a decided negative. No measure attacking the slave trade in any way, however small, could be tolerated. "This celebrated Sierra Leone Company, these *Amis des Noirs*, these dealers in ivory and benevolence, at the expense of the blood and treasure of other men,"[78] met with a sharp rebuff. The Duke of Clarence saw in the bill an attempt to "disfranchise the West India merchants and planters, to depopulate Liverpool, and deprive some thousands of industrious and respectable men of their birthright as British subjects."[79] In the House of Commons Wilberforce was no more successful. He was, he confessed, "shocked to see P. and all the rest opposing bill for limiting from part of African coast, like entire abolition, alas!"[80] but he was able to conquer, in a Christian way, his indignation at the coolness with which Pitt put off the debate when he had manifested an intention to answer Pitt's speech, and so left misrepresentations unrefuted. Pitt was not interested in the Sierra Leone Company, despite all his eloquence about the civilization of Africa and his interest in African productions. "To the cause of abolition," writes his most famous biographer, referring to the Sierra Leone Company, "he gave the support of his eloquence and his influence in parliament; but he gave no decided lead in these and cognate efforts, a fact which somewhat detracts from his greatness as a statesman in this formative period."[81]

What a shock it must have been for Wilberforce, who had worked "like a negro"[82] in the cause, even to the extent, to his great grief, of breaking the Sabbath,[83] who, one of his opponents said, never could hear the slave trade mentioned without starting as if he saw a ghost and exclaiming abolition!

---

75. *Chatham Papers*, G.D. 8/352. West India Planters and Merchants, Resolutions. May 19, 1791.
76. *Strictures and Occasional Observations upon the System of British Commerce with the East Indies*, page 40.
77. *Parl. Hist.*, Vol. XXXIV, page 1106. July 5, 1799.
78. Ibid., page 1110. Earl of Westmorland.
79. Ibid., page 1099.
80. *Life of Wilberforce*, Vol. II, page 331.
81. J. H. Rose: *William Pitt and National Revival* (London, 1911), page 473.
82. *Life of Wilberforce*, Vol. I, page 281. To Mr. Hey, Nov. 3, 1790.
83. Ibid., Vol. I, page 290.

abolition![84] Once it had been his proud boast that his interest in abolition enlivened his waking and soothed his evening hours, that he carried the topic with him to his repose, and often had the bliss of remembering that he had demanded justice for millions, who could not ask it for themselves.[85] Little hope in the dark days of the end of the century of justice to Africa! Her sufferings had been, and were still to be, the theme that had arrested and engaged his heart.[86]

There was to be yet another shock for him. The Sierra Leone blacks proved little amenable to the beneficent influences of civilization. "They have made the worst of all possible subjects," he complained sorrowfully to Dundas, begging him for a military force to take the colony under protection and quell all tendency to insurrection, "as thorough Jacobins as if they had been trained and educated in Paris."[87] At the end of our period the grandiose schemes once entertained had faded. "I presume," wrote Auckland privately to Grenville, "that the parties, finding themselves involved in an expensive and embarrassing project, would be glad to transfer that concern to the broader shoulders of the public."[88]

---

84. *Parl. Deb.*, Vol. VII, page 586. Gen. Tarleton, June 10, 1806.
85. *Parl. Hist.*,Vol. XXIX, page 1073. April 2, 1792.
86. Ibid., page 1065.
87. *Melville Papers*, Add. Mss. 41085, folios 33–35. Aug. 1, 1800.
88. *Dropmore Papers*, Vol. VIII, page 266. Aug. 10, 1806. See too *Castlereagh, Correspondence*, Vol. VIII, page 4: "The circumstances of the colony of Sierra Leone, the state also of our funds, and above all the sentiments recently expressed by our Directors, place, in my mind, out of all question, the necessity of surrendering up the settlement at a very early period. . . . A regard for the colonists, whom the Government unquestionably, as I conceive, will feel it to be their duty to protect, makes me desirous of suggesting to Your Lordship the necessity of taking early measures for that purpose." Henry Thornton to Castlereagh, Jan. 1, 1805.

CHAPTER SEVEN

The Abolition of the Slave Trade

At the end of the eighteenth century the natives of Africa supp'd full with horrors. By 1807 the whole situation had undergone such a transformation that now it was not only the leaders, but even the dwarfs and pigmies, who favoured abolition.[1] What influence did economic factors exert in this transformation?

We have already referred, in our discussion of the Guiana Order, to the breach in the ranks of the anti-abolitionists which resulted from the rivalry between the older British islands and the conquered ones. As early as 1794 this self-interest had induced planters like Vaughan and Barham to support Wilberforce's bill for the abolition of the foreign slave trade. By 1804 the fear of the growing cultivation of the conquered Dutch settlements had neutralised many of the West Indian body,[2] and some of them began to talk of abolition and offered a three years' suspension.[3] It was one such planter who wrote to Wilberforce: "I am a West Indian and have some little property there, and I am far from thinking that the abolition of the slave trade will be the ruin of the West Indies."[4] The West Indians eventually decided against the suspension, but the breach widened, the abolitionists helping to widen it. One wonders, however, with what feelings the West Indians listened to Pitt's appeal to them in 1804, when he asked whether, by the importation of slaves

---

1. *Parl. Hist.*, Vol. XXIX, page 358. Mr. Drake, April. 19, 1791, declared that whilst the leaders were in favour of abolition, the dwarfs and pigmies were against it.
2. *Life of Wilberforce*, Vol. III, page 180. To Grenville, June 27, 1804.
3. Ibid., Vol. III, page 165. Diary, Dec. 16, 1803.
4. Ibid., Vol. III, page 182. Dr. Coulthurst, Oct. 20, 1804.

since 1792, the original property embarked in the trade had been improved. The whole of that importation had been directed to the cultivation of new land, which competed with the older property, new colonies had arisen to rival the old ones, and the sudden and great increase of the black population was a danger, especially at a time when "the planters have been, year after year, applying, as they are doing now, for the interference of government on their behalf, on account of having produced more sugar than they can find purchasers for all over the world."[5]

The West Indian planters needed little encouragement. The slave trade, in Ellis's opinion, ought to be restricted to the old colonies and prohibited to Trinidad, because in the former case the property had been acquired before any idea of abolition was entertained.[6] In 1806 a Government measure to abolish the foreign slave trade and make permanent and universal the temporary Order in Council passed for Guiana was introduced. It was attacked by inveterate opponents as General Tarleton of Liverpool as an attempt to "come by a side wind on the planters."[7] Gascoyne, also of Liverpool, thought the bill a violation of faith, if any hope had been held out to the conquered colonies that they would be treated in the same manner as the British;[8] while to Lord Sheffield the measure seemed "a curious mixture of the sentimental in respect to the trade in slaves, and of a job in favour of our old West Indian settlements, for the ruin of our new acquisitions in those parts."[9] They were right. The slave trade could hardly have been immoral when it concerned the new colonies and moral when it concerned the older ones. And, moreover, if the trade was to be abolished and the conquered islands could not be cultivated for want of Negroes, there was neither policy nor expediency in wasting the troops and resources of the country in reconquering islands, the possession of which must be altogether nugatory.[10]

Further, with Britain squeezed more and more by Napoleon's blockade, it seemed to some, as for example Sir C. Price, speaking at the instance of several very respectable merchants of the City of London, that the measure would be injurious to the country in general and to London in particular. "This was not a time to shut a door by which we were enabled to export manufactures to the amount of £2,800,000."[11] Lord Sheffield objected to

---

5. *Parl. Deb.*, Vol. II, page 551. June 7, 1804. It is difficult to realise that Pitt is here condemning the results of his own military policy.
6. Ibid., page 652. June 30, 1804.
7. Ibid., Vol. IV, page 918. April 25, 1806.
8. Ibid., page 919.
9. Ibid., Vol. VII, page 235. May 16, 1806.
10. Ibid., Vol. II, page 657. Mr. Dent, June 13, 1804.
11. Ibid., Vol. VI, page 1023. May 1, 1806.

Britain's relinquishing a trade which held out the best prospects to her, at a time when the only direct carrying trade left was to Africa and the East and West Indies, when Americans and neutrals participated so very largely in the East and West Indian trade, and when Britain was shut out from so large a proportion of the world.[12]

In defence of the bill it was urged that slaves were to be considered as raw material, and it had always been an axiom that it was highly impolitic to export to foreign states any raw material which was afterwards to be worked up into manufactured articles.[13]

It was economic argument against economic argument, and the Government's case was unanswerable. Even in time of war, declared the Attorney-General who sponsored the motion, it was British subjects and British capital which supplied Negroes to their rivals in Cuba, St. Domingo, Martinique, Guadeloupe and many parts of the South American continent, mainly from the Danish islands, St. Croix and St. Thomas. As the colonies were not only the sources of the prosperity but the foundation of the maritime strength of the European countries, it was contrary to sound policy that Britain should afford them the means of rivalling her own colonies, and of attaining a high degree of commercial prosperity.[14]

These words might well have been spoken by an abolitionist before 1792, before the war gave Britain an opportunity of securing the coveted and valuable possessions of her rivals. Plus ça change, plus ç'est la même chose. A die-hard West Indian opponent like Sir William Young approved the principle of the bill, which he considered as a boon to the West Indian merchants;[15] the Bishop of London rejoiced that political consideration no less than the dictates of morality were in favour of it;[16] and the Earl of Buckinghamshire, once a believer in regulation rather than abolition of the trade,[17] was now convinced that the interest of the West Indian colonies would be considerably advanced by the measure.[18] Not all the arguments of Sheffield could shake Prime Minister Grenville's conviction that it was a measure which was called for by every dictate of sound policy.[19]

---

12. Ibid., Vol. VII, pages 235–236. May 16, 1806.
13. Ibid., page 34. Earl of Moira, May 7, 1806.
14. Ibid., Vol. VI, pages 597–598. March 31, 1806.
15. Ibid., pages 805–806. April 21, 1806.
16. Ibid., Vol. VII, page 229. May 16, 1806.
17. *Dropmore Papers*, Vol. I, page 308. To Granville, March 2, 1788.
18. *Parl. Deb.*, Vol. VII, page 235. May 16, 1806.
19. Ibid., page 32. May 7, 1806.

The foreign slave trade abolished, it was next the turn of the slave trade in general.

The abolitionists took no chances. Grenville reminded his hearers of Pitt's population statistics in 1791, bringing them up to date by showing that the average excess of deaths over births in Jamaica in the three years ending in 1798 or 1800 was only 1/24th per cent.[20] According to Lord Howick, who, too, in the House of Commons, referred to Pitt's statistics, the excess of deaths over births in eight parishes of Jamaica was in 1804–1805 only 258.[21] Hibbert gave away what little case the West Indians had by admitting that the old colonies required annually only 7,000 imported slaves,[22] and Whitbread declared, in support of abolition, that it had been proved by Pitt, "from the most undeniable calculations, that the islands and the empire at large would gain in revenue, in seamen, in commerce, in strength, and in profit, by the abolition."[23]

By 1807 the only town still really interested in the slave trade was Liverpool; London carried it on only to a very small extent, while in Bristol four ships in five did not deal in slaves.[24] But the war had made Liverpool less and less dependent upon the slave trade. Whereas in 1792 the vessels engaged in it were about one-twelfth of the total tonnage of the port, in 1807 they were only one-twenty fourth.[25] It was absurd, with the great increase in industry and trade, to speak of abolition as likely to prove ruinous to the country or any one port. Anti-abolitionists feared it would cause the loss of the whole of Liverpool's revenue from dock duties, which revenue was estimated, however, at only £5,000 annually. This fear had no foundation in fact. In 1772, when there were 175 ships engaged in the African trade, 100 of which belonged to Liverpool, the dock duties were £4,552; in 1779, as a result of the American War, when only 28 ships sailed to Africa, 11 of these from Liverpool, the dock duties were £4,957.[26]

The tonnage engaged in the trade to Africa, according to Lord Howick, was in 1805 not quite 1/52nd part of the whole export tonnage, excluding Ireland and the coastal trade. The seamen employed in the African trade were not quite 1/23rd part of those engaged in general trade. The gaps, therefore, which would be occasioned by abolition, could easily be filled up.

---

20. Ibid., Vol. VIII, page 658. Feb. 5, 1807.
21. Ibid., page 949. Feb. 23, 1807.
22. Ibid., page 985.
23. Ibid., page 1052. Feb. 27, 1807.
24. Ibid., Vol. VII, pages 1022–1023, May 1, 1806.
25. Ibid., Vol. VII, page 612. June 10, 1806.
26. Ibid., Vol. VIII, page 948. Lord Howick, Feb. 23, 1807. These figures were quoted from Clarkson: Impolicy, page 132.

The proportion of capital, moreover, embarked in the African trade, on the average of ten years preceding 1800, was 1/24th part of the whole capital of the export trade, but as a result of the Slave-carrying Bill and the bill to prohibit the importation of slaves into the conquered colonies, this capital had been further reduced by four-sevenths, so that in 1807 the proportion was estimated at not more perhaps than 1/80th of the capital in the whole export trade.[27] Neither Liverpool nor any other port could therefore be ruined by the abolition of what was merely a remnant of a once flourishing trade. And the Liverpool representative was at hand to affirm emphatically that, whatever might have been supposed, the inhabitants of the town of Liverpool were by no means unanimous in resisting the abolition of the slave trade, and could, significantly, look to the East, as Liverpool had been looking since 1792,[28] and plead for the abrogation of the East India Company monopoly as compensation for any loss which the slave trade might occasion to British merchants.[29]

The abolition legislation was enacted at a black and critical period in West Indian history. The idea that the slave trade was abolished despite the fact that it was profitable is a legend which would have surprised no one so much as the men who were chiefly responsible for the measure.

It might be thought that with the new century the British West Indies would have regained their pre-eminent position. East Indian competition had failed. St. Domingo was ruined, its whole exportable produce in 1801 was not one-third of what it had been in 1789.[30] So many slaves had died during the course of the rebellion and the war against Bonaparte that even Toussaint's enlightened constitution of 1801 recognised the necessity of the slave trade, and Pitt admitted later that a treaty signed with Toussaint had allowed the latter to import slaves.[31] The decrees of consuls, black or white, could not fill up the gaps in the population of St. Domingo.[32]

The St. Domingo Negro insurrection had at the outset given a great fillip to the distressed areas in the British West Indies. Immense orders for British sugar came from Hamburg, Riga, and in general from all Europe, at prices so enormous as to encourage a large export,[33] and to raise the spirits of the

---

27. Ibid., pages 947–948.
28. *Liverpool Papers*, Add. Mss. 38228, folios 153–154. Public Meeting of Liverpool Merchants held "for a participation of the trade to the East Indies," Nov. 23, 1792.
29. *Parl. Deb.*, Vol. VIII, pages 961–962. Mr. Roscoe, Feb. 23, 1807.
30. *Eden, op. cit.*, page 19.
31. *Parl. Deb.* Vol. II, page 562. June 8, 1804.
32. *Eden, op. cit.*, page 18.
33. *Dropmore Papers*, Vol. II, page 29. Buckingham to Grenville, Feb. 6, 1791.

Dominica planters.[34] Numbers of St. Domingo planters emigrated to Jamaica, where they turned their attention to the growth of coffee.[35] But even this temporary advantage could not reconcile Jamaica to the example afforded to their slaves of "such a precedence of the triumph of anarchy over all order and government."[36]

The occupation of the French colonies was very advantageous to Great Britain,[37] but for the British West Indies it was disastrous. The produce of the conquered colonies was admitted on an equal footing with that of the British colonies, to glut and depress the home market. No wonder the most ardent supporters of the Peace of Amiens were the West Indian planters.[38]

With the renewal of war the difficulties of the British colonies increased. The continental blockade and the American neutral trade shook the edifice of the British colonial system to its very foundations. It seemed that, whatever the state of the world, these wretched colonies were doomed.

Even in 1799 the West Indian merchants had submitted to Pitt conclusive evidence that Great Britain did not command the colonial trade or the supply of Europe with colonial produce. Between March 8 and September 10, 1799, 146 American ships had entered Hamburg laden chiefly with sugar and coffee; the total from places other than Britain was 230; while the British ships, most of them small, numbered only 211, and did not carry colonial produce only.[39] It was in this very year 1799 that speculations, as a result of British prosperity which flowed from the destruction of French colonial trade, reached such a height that the inevitable financial panic ensued. Eighty-two firms, most of them connected with leading West Indian houses,

---

34. C.O. 71/20. Gov. Orde, April 2, 1791.

35. C.O. 137/91. Dec. 3, 1792: *Chatham Papers*. G.D. 8/349. Aug. 15, 1796.

36. C.O. 137/90. Petition of House of Assembly, Nov. 4, 1791. Dundas in reply emphasized the advantages, but lamented that they had not been obtained without exposing Jamaica to danger. Jan. 7, 1792. See also *Liverpool Papers*, Add. Mss. 38231, folios 62–63, where Baron de Montboisier, writing to Hawkesbury, July 12, 1796, hoped that an enlightened minister would not be influenced by Jamaica's narrow and selfish calculations.

37. The duties collected in St. Domingo from Sept. 20, the beginning of the British occupation, to Nov. 9, 1793, were £58,889.4.6d. (C.O. 137/92. Nov. 8, 1793). Williamson trusted that the exports from St. Domingo to Jamaica would, when sent to Britain, add considerably to the revenue (Ibid. To Dundas, Feb. 9, 1794), and flattered himself that the expenses attending the operations in St. Domingo would in comparison appear small (C.O. 137/93. To Dundas, April 28, 1794). For the quarter ending Dec. 31, 1793 St. Domingo sent the following quantities to British ports: coffee, 644,751 lbs; sugar, 91,593 lbs; cotton, 56,339 lbs; cocoa, 66,944 lbs (J. H. *Rose: William Pitt and the Great War*, page 223.)

38. Britain's trade with the conquered islands amounted, 1796–1800, to one-third of the trade with the British islands, as far as tonnage was concerned, and to somewhat above one-third, reckoning in imports from the conquered islands, and not quite one-third, in exports to them (*Eden, op. cit.*, pages 66–68).

39. *Parl. Deb.* Vol. IX, page 96. Mr. Hibbert, March 12, 1807.

with engagements amounting to some £2,500,000, failed. British sugar exports to the continent immediately declined by 60 per cent.[40]

The continental blockade aggravated the situation. The Committee set up in 1807 to investigate the commercial state of the West Indian colonies discovered that the main evil, to which all others could ultimately be referred, was the very unfavourable state of the foreign market, in which formerly the British merchant enjoyed nearly a monopoly, but where he could not then enter into competition with the planters, not only of the neutral, but of the hostile colonies. We seem to be again in the pre-war period, 1807 was 1789 writ large. The one devil of the British West Indies, exorcised by the war, had been replaced by seven, and the last state of the islands was worse than the first.

While the hostile colonies enjoyed a facility of intercourse with Europe, under the American neutral flag, by means of which a market was found for their produce, at charges little exceeding those of peacetime, the British planters were burdened with all the inconvenience, risk and expense arising from a state of war.[41] The costs of American freight and insurance were so much lower than the British that the continental buyer paid 8/11d less for sugar valued at 40/- per cwt., and the Mediterranean purchaser 12/6d less. The position was so serious that it appeared to the Committee of 1807 "a matter of evident and imperious necessity to resort to such a system, as by impeding and restricting, and as far as possible preventing the export of the produce of the enemy's colonies from the places of its growth, shall compel the continent to have recourse to the only source of supply, which, in that event, would be open to it."[42]

Pitkin's statistics for the increase of American neutral trade occasioned by the European wars[43] show the full extent of British West Indian distress.

---

40. *Ragatz, op. cit.*, page 286.
41. *Report, 1807*, page 5.
42. Ibid., pages 5–6.
43. T. Pitkin: *A Statistical View of the Commerce of the United States* (Hartford, 1816), page 137. Note the decrease, 18 months after the Peace of Amiens.

Table 7.1.

Year	Coffee (lbs.)	Sugar (lbs.)
1791	962,977	74,504
1792	2,134,742	1,176,156
1793	17,580,049	4,539,809
1794	33,720,983	20,721,761
1795	47,443,179	21,377,747
1796	62,385,117	34,848,644
1797	44,521,887	38,366,262
1798	49,580,927	51,703,963
1799	31,987,088	78,821,751
1800	38,597,479	56,432,516
1801	45,106,494	97,565,732
1802	36,501,998	61,061,820
1803	10,294,693	23,223,849
1804	48,312,713	74,964,366
1805	46,760,204	123,031,272
1806	47,001,662	145,839,320
1807	42,122,573	143,136,905

This was the net result of the enforcement of the Navigation Laws in the British islands. The Americans turned to the foreign ones, and with the destruction of rival mercantile marines America became the sole carrier of foreign colonial goods. But even that was not all. The grandiose schemes of a self-supporting empire which the Privy Council for Trade had entertained in 1783, the attempt to keep the Americans out of the British colonies, broke down. All the witnesses examined in 1807 spoke of the necessity of the American trade, and the Committee agreed that the West Indian–American trade was very convenient and advantageous to the colonies, which they could not relinquish, without detriment, unless they were compensated in other ways. They were writing after the event; the year 1806 marked the breakdown of the Navigation Laws in the West Indies, and the abolition bill followed hard upon the heels of the American Intercourse Bill of 1806.

The outlook for the West Indies was black indeed. Since 1799, the Committee reported, there had taken place a progressive deterioration in the situation of the planters, as the result of a progressive diminution in the price of sugar, while the duty[44] and the expenses attendant on cultivation had increased, so that by 1806 the price could not pay for the cost of production. The West Indians considered ten per cent a fair profit on their capital; from 1800 it had gradually diminished to 2½ and 1½ per cent, until, in 1807, there

---

44. As a result of the need of increasing the national revenue to continue the war.

was no profit at all.[45] Hibbert reminded the House of a Report of the Sugar Distillery Committee, to the effect that when the consumer of sugar paid 63/- per cwt., not one shilling went into the pockets of the grower. In 1787 the planter got about 19/6 per cwt. profit, in 1799, 10/9d, in 1803, 18/6d, in 1805, 12/-, in 1806, nothing.[46] The West Indians were "at last reduced to the hard necessity of continuing their estates at a very heavy loss, as they cannot be rendered productive in other culture."[47] A West Indian merchant, Thomas Hugham, warned the Committee of 1807 that the pressure on the planters was "fast approaching to that crisis, that nothing but inevitable ruin can be the consequence, unless some alteration in the circumstances takes place."[48] The distress, in the despairing words of Mr. Bosanquet, was universally so great that it would not be materially increased by the total annihilation of the properties. Bosanquet himself, agent to the planters in the sale of their produce, was not, we may be sure, the only one who would not exchange an estate in Britain producing four per cent for one in the West Indies supposed to produce ten.[49]

In Jamaica the distress was so acute that the Assembly declared that "a faithful detail would have the appearance of a frightful caricature."[50] There were only three topics of conversation, debt, disease and death. Between 1799 and 1807, 65 plantations were abandoned, 32 were sold under decrees of the Court of Chancery to meet claims against them, and in 1807 suits were pending against 115 others.[51] The profit on capital invested in the West Indies was, according to Wilberforce, quite inconsiderable, being a mere four per cent in Jamaica and not exceeding five or six in the other islands. The number of executions on property was truly alarming, mounting in twenty years to no less than thirty millions in the currency of the islands.[52] Barham, a West Indian planter, withdrew his former opposition to abolition, which had been based on the argument that it would lead to an extensive contraband trade. The colonists were at that time little disposed to enter on such a trade, their profits were not one-third of what they used to be, and, as a consequence, the temptations to speculation were curtailed.[53]

---

45. Report, 1807, page 4.
46. Parl. Deb., Vol. IX, page 98, March 12, 1807.
47. Ibid., page 88, West Indian Petition to Parliament, Feb. 27, 1807.
48. Report, 1807, page 35.
49. Ibid., pages 38–39.
50. Feb. 25, 1805.
51. Ragatz, op. cit., page 308.
52. Parl. Deb., Vol. II, page 452. May 30, 1804.
53. Ibid., page 463. Similarly Sir William Young, another West Indian, May 1, 1806. Ibid., Vol. VI, pages 1022–1023.

The West Indians petitioned Parliament for relief in February 1807. Wilberforce was happy that the question was raised before the abolition bill was passed, because the distress complained of in the petition could not be imputed to abolition.[54] He realised only part of the truth, and that the less important part. Abolition was the direct result of that distress.

This was the situation in 1806, when Pitt had disappeared from the scene, and Fox and Grenville came in determined upon abolition.[55] It was no five days' fit of philanthropy that inspired them. Grenville warned the House of Lords that to encourage the continuance of the slave trade, for the purpose of cultivating new lands, would be to ruin the planters. "Are they not now distressed by the accumulation of produce on their hands, for which they cannot find a market; and will it not therefore be adding to their distress, and leading the planters on to their ruin, if you suffer the continuation of fresh importations?"[56] Abolition provided the only remedy for the acute distress of the islands. In 1806, so great was the glut of West Indian produce, as a result of the continental blockade, some 80,000 or 90,000 hogsheads in London, and about 150,000 or 160,000 in the whole of Britain, that Lord Temple, following a precedent set in 1800 when Great Britain was suffering from a serious grain shortage, submitted a proposition for the use of sugar and molasses, together with grain, in the breweries and distilleries.[57] The great stock of sugar on hand, in the opinion of Lord Henry Petty, himself an eager abolitionist, called loudly for legislative interference, and he introduced measures to encourage the exportation of sugar and the consumption of rum.[58]

Opponents, like all opponents, simply could not, or would not, understand the position. "We might as well say," declared veteran Stephen Puller, "oh, we will not have our chimney swept, because it is a little troublesome to the boy, as that we should give up the benefit of the West Indies on account of

---

54. Ibid., Vol. IX, page 101. March 12, 1807.

55. Wilberforce surrendered the leadership in the hope that their patronage of the measure would "have great weight in neutralizing some who might otherwise be active enemies; and in converting into decided friends some who might otherwise be neutral." *Dropmore Papers*, Vol. X, page 464. To Grenville, May 20, 1806.

56. *Parl. Deb.*, Vol. VIII, pages 658–659. Feb. 5, 1807. See too speech of Mr. Jacob, Feb. 27, 1807. Ibid., page 1050. Abolition, he argued, would furnish ample compensation to the planters, as it would tend to enhance the value of their existing Negroes and plantations, while a continuation of the traffic would, "by operating to increase the means of cultivation, serve to extend the produce which was already superabundant, and thus lead to the ruin of the planters, more immediately and effectively." Compare also Castlereagh to Manchester: "At a time like the present, when it is found that by the too great increase of colonial produce, the markets of the world are over-stocked, and the price proportionally reduced . . . it becomes the interest of the West Indian planter to prevent the increase of cultivation and the breaking up of new lands." C.O.137/121. Jan. 19, 1808.

57. *Parl. Deb.*, Vol. VIII, pages 238–239. Dec. 30, 1806.

58. Ibid., pages 840–841, Feb. 17, 1807.

the supposed hardships of the negro."[59] At a time of war, when empires were tumbling like nine pins around them, was not strict economy imperative? asked Machiavellian Windham; "were they not called to attend to candle ends and cheese-parings?"[60] Hibbert resorted to threats, pathetic threats. Had the long intercourse between mother country and colonies grown insipid by its harmony, did they need, as in the case of married couples who lived too much together, something like the *amantium irae* to stimulate regard, and rekindle mutual affection? If so, if they were only making a moral or philosophical experiment upon the passions of the colonists, it would be well to be careful not "to tickle them into a frenzy, or, what perhaps was more to be apprehended, pinch them to death."[61] Almost on the eve of abolition the agent for Jamaica, Edmund Lyon, was repeating all the exploded arguments that the West Indies were the most valuable appendages of the empire, that by abolition the islands would lose the benefits of the planters' services in the various capacities of jurors, magistrates and militia men, and that abolition would occasion diminished commerce, diminished revenue, and diminished navigation, and in the end remove the great cornerstone of British prosperity.[62] When a system is doomed, the last, perhaps the only, resource of its defenders is to live in the past. To the end some of the West Indians never realised that the Industrial Revolution had transformed and was still transforming Britain, that under the new conditions "the exportation of a piece of British broadcloth is more beneficial to us than the re-exportation of a quantity of Bengal muslin or of West India Coffee of equal value."[63]

In Parliament there was surprising unanimity in the determination to wash out "the foul stain from the pure ermine of the national character."[64] Mr. Lushington refused to "balance imports and exports against justice and humanity."[65] The time had arrived when the arm of the slave dealer must be arrested, and when men who were anxious to grow rich must first learn to be humane.[66] Young noblemen argued that nothing was really politic or expedient that was not conformable to the principles of humanity and justice.[67]

---

59. Ibid., Vol. IX, page 60. March 6, 1807.
60. Ibid., page 136. March 16, 1807.
61. Ibid., page 93. March 12, 1807.
62. *Dropmore Papers*, Vol. IX, pages 14–19. To Grenville, Jan. 16, 1807. Compare, however, that anonymous planter who wrote to Grenville, Jan. 1807, cordially wishing the measure success. "I give it as my decided opinion that both interest and humanity combine in putting an effective stop to the further importation of slaves." Ibid., pages 27–29.
63. *Eden, op. cit.*, page 129.
64. *Parl. Deb.*, Vol. VIII, page 977. Sir John Doyle, Feb. 23, 1807.
65. Ibid., page 963.
66. Ibid., page 965. Mr. Fawkes.
67. Ibid., page 969. Lord Mahon.

The real object of the trade, it was said, was "to enable the slave merchants of Liverpool and other places to gormandize more turtle, to swallow more venison, and to drink more claret."[68] Some "obiman" seemed to have cast his spell not only upon Grenville,[69] as Earl St. Vincent suggested, but upon the majority of members.

The abolition bill passed the Commons by a huge majority, 283 to 16.[70] To Wilberforce the charge which had come over the House seemed nothing short of marvelous. "How wonderful are the ways of providence!" he had recorded in his diary with reference to the Foreign Slave Trade bill of 1806, "how God can turn the hearts of men!"[71] During the debates on the abolition bill, he marvelled at the "astonishing eagerness of House; six or eight starting up to speak at once, young noblemen, etc., and asserting high principles of rectitude."[72] "How astonishing," he wrote later, "is our success, and the eagerness and zeal of the House now, when the members have been so fastidious as scarce to hear a speech about it! Six or eight getting up at once, and the young noblemen especially . . . everybody taking me by the hand; and several voting with us for the first time."[73] That Pitt and Fox should both have died before abolition was carried, and that now Grenville, "without any particular deference from court," should carry it triumphantly, amazed Wilberforce. "How popular abolition is, just now. God can turn the hearts of men."[74] Wilberforce's outlook was intensely religious, but Parliament was converted not by the truths of religion and the principles of humanity but by economics.

The bill was passed, but the parliamentarians sought to present it to the world in the best possible light. Lord Hawkesbury objected to the declaration that the slave trade was "contrary to the principles of justice, humanity

---

68. Ibid., Vol. II, page 927. Earl Stanhope, July 3, 1804.

69. Ibid., Vol. VIII, page 669. Feb. 5, 1807. Presumably a reference to the famous character of those and our times, the West Indian "obeah man"

70. By a strange irony which he no doubt failed to appreciate, it fell to Windham, who had changed from an eager supporter of abolition (*Clarkson: History*, page 161: "Rather let Liverpool and the islands be swallowed up in the sea than this monstrous system of iniquity be carried on"—Windham at the second meeting of the "influential men"), into one of those who favoured the compromise of colonial self-determination (H. of C., April 3, 1798 and March 1, 1799), to circularise the colonial governors on the eve of abolition. Windham advised them to assure the planters that Parliament had never lost sight of their interests, and impressed on them the necessity of urging this point and any other which might remove impressions unfavourable to the measure and of endeavouring "by every means to render the decision of Parliament upon this great question as satisfactory to the colonies as it is hoped it will prove conducive to their final advantage and to the general benefit of mankind." (C.O. 324/103. Circulars to Governors, 1794–1815. March 7, 1807). "Domine non sum dignus" must surely have been Windham's comment.

71. *Life of Wilberforce*, Vol. III, page 260. April 5, 1806.

72. Ibid., Vol. III, page 296. Feb. 23, 1807.

73. Ibid., Vol. III, page 299. Feb. 25, 1807.

74. Ibid., Vol. III, page 295. Feb. 11, 1807.

and sound policy." In his opinion the words "justice and humanity" reflected on the African trader, and he therefore moved an amendment excluding those words, and confining the necessity of abolition solely to the inexpediency of continuing the slave trade.[75] Lord Chancellor Erskine opposed the amendment, which would take away the only ground on which other powers could be asked to co-operate in the abolition of the trade.[76] The amendment, declared the Earl of Lauderdale, would omit the most essential words in the bill. He warned the House that it would lend colour to the suspicion in France voiced to him by one of the French ministers whilst he was in Paris, that Britain was abolishing the trade merely because, with her colonies well-stocked with Negroes, she could afford to do so, whilst France, with colonies ill-stocked and deficient in produce, could not abolish it without conceding to Britain the greatest advantages and sustaining a proportionate loss. "How," asked Lauderdale, "in thus being supposed to make no sacrifice ourselves, could we call with any effect upon foreign powers to co-operate in the abolition?"[77] The House on the division voted for the original version.

By thus giving all the credit to humanity and none to sound policy a distorted view was presented which it is the purpose of this thesis to correct.

---

75. *Parl Deb.*, Vol. VIII, page 679. Feb. 6, 1807.

76. Ibid., pages 680–681.

77. Ibid., page 681–682. See also Grenville's letter to Lauderdale, when the latter was in Paris. "If discussions should proceed, pray do not overlook the slave trade. I think it appears clearly that Bonaparte is not much influenced by the motives of justice or humanity on which we act, and indeed how could he? But I really think we might shame him by an official note so as to make it very difficult for him to refuse his concurrence, supposing other things adjusted." *Dropmore Papers*, Vol. VIII, page 262. Aug. 8, 1806. In an article—not ratified—of the 1806 treaty with America, Britain, while proposing abolition, made no reference to the "sound policy" which had figured so largely in the debates; and in the treaty of 1814 between Britain and Spain, the King of Spain expressed his fullest concurrence with the sentiments of His Britannic Majesty "with respect to the injustice and inhumanity of the traffic of slaves," and resolved to "co-operate in the cause of humanity." F.O. 94/294.

PART II

THE ABOLITION OF SLAVERY

Relief from this monopoly would be cheaply purchased by granting the West India proprietors the full amount of the compensation proposed.

—William Clay, June 11, 1833.

CHAPTER EIGHT

The Abolitionists and Emancipation

This thesis concentrates on the economic aspect of abolition and emancipation. It would, however, be a mistake to underestimate the humanitarian forces. The Government was subjected to the pressure of strong economic interests tending towards emancipation, but it would give a distorted view not to realise the powerful part played by the humanitarians, which in this particular question assumed the proportions of a nation-wide crusade.

(a) The Abolitionist Programme up to 1807

It is frequently said that the abolitionists had never concealed their intention of working for complete emancipation,[1] that they had not forgotten slavery, and that they decided to attack the slave trade first, not merely because it was the easier to destroy, but because they believed that its destruction would certainly and quickly bring to an end the whole slave system.[2] We know to-day that emancipation ultimately followed abolition. But 1807 and 1833 are clearly distinct dates, and the abolitionists, as an organised body, not only eschewed and disowned, for some time, any idea of emancipation, but did not, until very late, envisage the abolition of slavery by an act of Parliament. They believed abolition would come inevitably, but not by legislative action. Pitt, Wilberforce, Adam Smith had emphasized the superiority of free labour.

---

1. *MacInnes, op. cit.,* page 156.
2. *R. Coupland: The British Anti-slavery Movement,* page 87.

But emancipation as the actual destruction of private property was not for a long time visualized.

The alarmed West Indians naturally distorted the aims of the abolitionists and accused them of desiring emancipation. The abolitionists were frequently forced to rebut these accusations. In 1788 the Abolition Committee stated explicitly that however acceptable a temperate and gradual abolition of slavery might be to the wishes of individuals, it never formed any part of their plan.[3] In 1792, and again in 1797, in the face of persistent misrepresentations, the Committee felt it incumbent upon them again publicly to declare their uniform adherence to the original purpose of the institution of the society, the abolition of the slave trade.[4]

In Parliament, too, the abolitionists took pains to disclaim the intentions foisted upon them. They proceeded, declared the Bishop of Rochester, upon no visionary notions of equality and imprescriptible rights of men; they strenuously upheld the gradations of civil society.[5] In other words, attacks on the slave trade were not to be construed as attacks on slavery. William Smith spoke of the silly confusion of abolition and emancipation.[6] The Bishop of St. Asaph looked to abolition to produce all the amelioration in the condition of the slaves that was practicable or desirable, and visualized no further consequences whatever.[7]

Such freedom for the slaves as the abolitionists had in mind was nothing revolutionary. Planters, they knew, might be induced to consent to the abolition of the slave trade, but would be certain to oppose by every means in their power the emancipation of the slaves. All that the abolitionists aimed at doing by Parliamentary legislation was to abolish the slave trade.[8] Abolition, they hoped, would lead to amelioration of the condition of the slaves and that, in turn, in the nature of things, to ultimate emancipation. It was pretty generally and rather industriously rumoured that it was the design of the abolitionists to propose, in addition to abolition, the immediate emancipation of the Negroes. That intention, declared Wilberforce, he could never have entertained for a moment.[9] Emancipation, said Pitt, was a delicate point. The Africans were not yet ready for such a boon; and until they had been "relieved from everything harsh and severe, raised from their present degradation, and put under the powerful protection of the law," to talk of

3. *Abolition Committee's Proceedings.* Add. Mss. 21255, folio 50(v.) Aug. 12, 1788.
4. Ibid., Add. Mss. 21256, folios 40(v) and 96(v). Jan. 31, 1792, and March 29, 1797.
5. *Parl. Hist.*, Vol. XXXIII, page 1119. July 5, 1799.
6. *Parl. Deb.*, Vol. VII, page 601. June 10, 1806.
7. Ibid., Vol. II, page 931. July 3, 1804.
8. What a French writer calls "cette solution bâtarde." *Gaston-Martin, op. cit.*, page 41.
9. *Parl. Hist.*, Vol. XXIX, page 1057. April 2, 1792.

emancipation was insanity.[10] It was a fundamental error in the opponents of abolition to think either that emancipation would be the immediate effect of abolition, or that abolition would not be accomplished at all, with safety, until the Negroes were fit for emancipation.[11]

In all this there was no suggestion of reforming colonial society by legislation. Emancipation by legislative measures did not, before 1807, form any part of the programme of the abolitionists, and indeed they were prepared to oppose it when proposed by others. The day after the overwhelming success of the bill abolishing the slave trade, Earl Percy introduced a bill for the gradual abolition of slavery. Anti-abolitionists rejoiced; "it showed the cloven hoof which had been attempted to be concealed."[12] Wilberforce was glad that the notion had been made, as it gave him an opportunity to show the distinction made by his party between abolition and emancipation. The sole point they had in view was the abolition of the slave trade; anti-abolitionists had always confused the two objects, abolitionists had distinguished them.[13]

(b) The Slave Trade Felony Bill and the Registry Act

The Slave Trade once abolished, the abolitionists directed their attention not to emancipation, but to those supplementary measures, with which they had feared to burden the abolition, and which aimed at closing all the loopholes to evasion left by the abolition act. The abolitionists had anticipated the difficulties of completely extirpating the traffic, but they had underrated the wickedness of the slave trader and the infatuation of the planter. The trade was still carried on, under the more innocent denominations of wood and ivory. Lurking in some dark corner was almost always to be found a hoary slave trader, who accompanied the vessel as a kind of supercargo and whose experience enabled it to escape detection. The profits were enormous, one successful adventure was sufficient to cover three or four failures, while the pecuniary penalties were a woefully inadequate deterrent. "While you levied your pence, the wholesale dealers in blood and torture pocketed their pounds, and laughed at your two-penny penalty." Therefore Brougham, in 1811, introduced a bill making the slave trade felony, to punish such an

---

10. Ibid., page 340. April 19, 1791.
11. *Parl. Deb.*, Vol. II, page 550. Pitt, June 7. 1804.
12. Ibid., Vol. IX, page 143. Sir C. Pole, March 17, 1807.
13. Ibid., pages 143–144. See *Life of Wilberforce*, Vol. III, page 70, for Wilberforce's idea that Napoleon probably knew nothing of abolition and confounded it with emancipation. In 1814, too, when France was being urged to abolish the slave trade, Macaulay reported that Malouet confused abolition and emancipation. "I set him right in this particular and said that we confined our views entirely to the former." Ibid., Vol. IV, page 186. Macaulay to Wilberforce, June 1, 1814.

offence with something at least equal to the punishment imposed for stealing an oyster. He warned the slave trader that if this were found insufficient, the punishment would be made capital,[14] and the bill, despite Canning's plea for caution and the apathy of the House, became law.[15]

The slave trade might be abolished and made felonious, but the situation of the West Indian Islands and the prevalence of smuggling still made possible infractions of the law, a possibility which would be increased on the termination of the war. Stephen, for instance, deprecated the retention of Dutch Guiana as likely, among other reasons, to lead to a contraband introduction of slaves to a fearful extent from Dutch Surinam, and their exportation from Demerara, to the older West Indian Islands.[16] The solution for this was the registry of all the slaves in the British colonies, to which the abolitionists now directed all their energies.

The registration of the slaves contained an imputation that the abolition act had been violated. Those who had before asserted that abolition would be useless because of the facilities for smuggling, were now quick to resent the implication that their law-abidingness could not be trusted. In Barbados no such violation had taken place; even before abolition, with its superabundant slave population, it had retained few imported Negroes.[17] From Demerara the Governor reported that no importation had taken place contrary to the Abolition Act.[18] The Governor of Jamaica repudiated the idea,[19] which the West Indian merchants and planters of Glasgow condemned as an assumption, founded on injurious suspicions, "which at once proceeds to apply a violent remedy for the cure of an imaginary disease."[20] Wilberforce alleged that there had been a considerable illicit importation into Jamaica between 1808 and 1812, mainly from Cuba and the Spanish Main, and, in the absence of positive proof which could not possibly be obtained, gave as his reason the significant increase in the Tax Roll Returns of 1811.[21] The planters argued

---

14. As was eventually done in 1824.

15. *Parl. Deb.*, Vol. XVII, pages 659–673; Vol. XIX, pages 234–238. Brougham's Speeches, June 15, 1810 and March 5, 1811.

16. *Report on the Mss. of Karl Bathurst* (Historical Manuscripts Commission, London, 1923), page 351 (Referred to hereafter as *Bathurst Mss.*), Stephen to Bathurst, June 12, 1815.

17. Ibid., page 431. Wilberforce to Bathurst, private, Jan. 1, 1817.

18. C.O. 111/22. May 29, 1816. Governor Murray added that from the character of the inhabitants and the difficulties attending the deed, he was well assured that there was not the slightest foundation for apprehending any violation of the law in the future.

19. C.O. 137/142. August 17, 1816. The Duke of Manchester, too, declared his confident opinion and belief that there was no desire on the part of the planters to increase the number of their slaves by such means. While this may well have been true of Jamaica and the other over-stocked islands, it could not have applied to Demerara and Trinidad.

20. C.O. 137/143. March 5, 1816.

21. *Bathurst Mss*, pages 414–415, 416–419, 428–432. Private letters of Wilberforce to Bathurst, June 29 and July 4, 1816, and Jan. 1, 1817.

that this difference arose only from the superior accuracy of the enumeration in 1811,[22] and Bathurst, the Colonial Secretary, explicitly exonerated them of any infraction of the law, and recommended the Registry Act as one not to correct an existing evil, but to prevent the occurrences of an evil which, without some such regulation, would probably arise.[23]

The registry was first decreed for the crown colony of Trinidad in 1812, as an experiment. It proved very unpopular. The planters claimed that it turned the minds of the slaves to general emancipation by imposing emancipation as a penalty on the proprietors in particular cases![24] The post of Registrar was a sinecure, which permitted its holder to rival the Governor in luxury at the expense of the inhabitants.[25] Governor Woodford made the danger-ous admission that the planters were accustomed to obey only such orders of Government as suited their personal convenience. The Order in Council was too methodical, too precise, it would "confound persons of *ordinary abili-ties*," the Governor himself could not manage to make one of the returns, far less the ignorant French, Spanish and coloured slave owners; it aimed at too much, and with the frequent returns and the duplicate registry to be sent to Britain,[26] it was a severe hardship on the island.[27] Considerable simplification was necessary.[28] When such language came from the Governor, it is not sur-prising that so many departures were made from the original scheme, so many concessions granted as to the time of registering slaves and making returns, that no effectual step was taken to execute the Order until eleven months after its arrival in Trinidad. After the time decreed for the registration of slaves, no fewer than 4,000 returns had been made, and the total number of slaves was 5,000, or twenty-five per cent, more than was expected. These, Stephen emphasized in a very able memorandum, could only have been in-troduced into the island subsequent to the promulgation of the Order. The higher price of slaves in Trinidad and its more fertile soil, compared with the sterility and redundant slave population of the older islands, encouraged this importation. The returns included an unusually high proportion of personal to plantation slaves, which could only be explained by the assumption that considerable numbers had been imported by merchants as personal slaves, to

22. *Parl. Deb.*, Vol. XL, page 977. Mr. Henry Goulburn, June 8, 1819.
23. Ibid., Vol. XXXIV, page 910. May 30, 1816.
24. C.O. 295/31. Petition of the Proprietors to Gov. Monro.
25. Ibid., April 23, 1813.
26. See *Bathurst Mss.*, page 352. Stephen to Bathurst, June 12, 1815: "Without a duplicate registry *here*, I would not give a farthing for the plan."
27. C.O. 295/37. Woodford to Goulburn, October 15, 1815. Woodford thus described his letter: "It is not as methodical as the order in council, but I hope it is a little more intelligible."
28. C.O. 295/38. Registrar to Woodford, Feb. 1, 1815.

be kept until such time as the planters, always distressed and short of cash, were able to purchase them.[29]

It has been necessary to deal in such detail with the Trinidad Registry to show what difficulties Parliament would encounter in the colonies which had local legislatures. What chance was there of securing that co-operation from the legislative colonies which the Government and West Indian champions in Parliament considered desirable? If only one-fourth of a measure could be obtained in the colonies, said Lord Holland, himself a West Indian proprietor, that proportion was better than the whole measure passed by the Imperial Parliament, which would only be imperfectly executed in the colonies.[30] The Registry gave the planters an important advantage, in a perfectly valid title to their slaves, of which they were not slow to avail themselves when the abolitionists began to demand emancipation.[31] But they were not content with this. They claimed that the Negroes interpreted the bill as conceding emancipation which was opposed by their masters.[32] Their friends in Britain were not idle. "Great diligence is used in cultivating a support for us in parliament, and I am glad to say we make a progress,"[33] the Jamaica agent wrote in March 1816, and Wilberforce was compelled to admit that "the stream runs most strongly against us."[34]

The Barbados insurrection of 1816 played right into the hands of the planters. It was admitted on all sides that the Negroes had entertained incorrect notions of what was intended. Inevitably an attempt was made to throw the blame on the abolitionists. Wilberforce again denied the accusation that they were aiming at emancipation: "it might be supposed that our opponents would have abandoned this position after we had gone on for twenty-seven years constantly refuting it. But no, they still persevere." As he put it, "the artillery they had loaded so high against us bursts among themselves, and they impute to us the loading and pointing of it."[35] The tactics were only too obvious. The colonists objected to discussions in Parliament but spoke their mind freely in the presence of their slaves. The slaves were treated as quadrupeds, devoid of intelligence or reason, and the planters objected when they merely behaved like men. When the colonists themselves, by their constitutional claims, showed the slaves that there was dissension in the camp

---

29. C.O. 295/34. This memorandum, an excellent instance of Stephen's watching brief on behalf of the Negroes, entitles him to be regarded as the ablest of the abolitionists.
30. *Parl. Deb.*, Vol. XXXIX, page 851. March 4, 1819.
31. C.O. 137/161. Committee of Correspondence to agent Hibbert. Dec. 15, 1824.
32. C.O. 137/142. Manchester to Bathurst, Jan. 26, 1816; April 23, 1816; Sept. 6, 1816.
33. Quoted in *R. L.Schuyler: Parliament and the British Empire* (New York, 1929), page 129.
34. *Life of Wilberforce*, Vol. IV, page 282. Feb. 24, 1816.
35. Ibid., Vol. IV, pages 287–288.

of their rulers, what less could be expected from the slaves? Jamaica objected to Parliamentary legislation "upon a subject of mere municipal regulation and internal police."[36] Barbados denied that the best understandings and the purest motives were an adequate substitute for the want of local knowledge essential to the work of legislation.[37] The abolitionists retorted that no law could be expected from the colonies; Wilberforce warned Bathurst against a law which might conform to Parliament's wishes in words but not in substance;[38] and the abolitionists asserted the right of Parliament to pass such a law in opposition to "the monstrous pretensions of those petty assemblies."[39]

These disputes alone would have encouraged the slaves to cut the Gordian Knot. But, further, the insurrection was directly instigated by some ill-disposed people, probably "poor whites," to discredit the home Government.[40] At any rate it had that effect. Wilberforce was urged to withdraw his measure, to which he agreed, in order to turn his attention to the foreign slave trade and discontent at home. The Registry Act was left to the colonial assemblies, and it has been well said that its withdrawal was a greater victory for the West Indies than the repeal of the Stamp Act had been for the continental colonies.[41]

(c) The Abolitionists up to 1823

In all this there was nothing whatever said of, or to suggest, emancipation. The word occurs in 1818, when Castlereagh cautioned Wilberforce against "pressing for too entire a change, in short for slaves' emancipation," until abolition had been decreed by the other powers.[42] At a council of the abolitionist leaders it was decided not to work for emancipation at that time.

The abolitionists did not make emancipation their programme until 1823. Until then they repeatedly affirmed that they looked to the abolition of the slave trade to produce, out of self-interest on the planters' part, all the ame-

---

36. C.O. 137/143. House of Assembly, Oct. 31, 1815.
37. C.O. 28/85. Petition of Assembly and Council, Jan. 17, 1816.
38. *Life of Wilberforce*, Vol. IV, page 292. May 17, 1816.
39. *Bathurst Mss.*, page 353. Stephen to Bathurst, June 12, 1815.
40. C.O. 28/85. Gov. Leith to Bathurst, April 30, 1816: "The mischievous delusion of those who have availed themselves of every circumstance to inflame the minds of the slaves." Col. Codd to Leith, April 25, 1816: "This idea (emancipation) seems to have been conveyed by mischievous persons and the indiscreet conversation of individuals on the measure." Rear Admiral Harvey, April 30, 1816: "an idea which had been industriously propagated amongst the negroes by ill-disposed persons."
41. *Schuyler, op. cit.*, page 149.
42. *Life of Wilberforce*, Vol. IV, page 368.

lioration in the state of the Negroes that they desired. In a memorandum on "subjects for action and deliberation for abolitionists" in 1810, Wilberforce, for example, made no reference whatever to emancipation. His primary concern was to render the abolition act more effective and to secure the general abolition of the slave trade.[43] He hoped to encourage improvements in the West Indies by circulating books on the management of the Negroes, and thought of "firing a pamphlet" at the planters, "to awake them and alarm them."[44] In the debate on the Registry Bill, he again denied the charge that they had changed ground, and were now aiming at emancipation. Their main object was the abolition of the slave trade which, they hoped, would, by degrees, produce a natural transition from slave labor to free.[45] This transition would "most safely be produced by gradual manumission, by education, by improving the situation of the slaves, and encouraging marriages among them."[46] The abolitionists were so explicit in the distinction they drew between amelioration and emancipation that it is surprising that they should have been misinterpreted, then or now. In 1814 a suggestion was made to Wilberforce that all Negroes illicitly imported into any part of the British dominions should immediately be declared free. Wilberforce turned it down.[47] What his aim was he stated clearly: "our object and our universal language was and is, to produce by abolition a disposition to breed instead of buying. This is the great vital principle which would work in every direction, and produce reform everywhere."[48] Nothing could be clearer or more authoritative than the doctrine of the African Institution. They looked to "an emancipation of which not the slaves but the masters should be the willing instruments or authors."[49]

(d) Gradual Emancipation

There are three reasons which accounted for the revolutionary departure of the abolitionists in 1823 from their former object. The institution of colo-

---

43. Ibid., Vol. III, page 483.

44. Ibid., Vol. III, pages 481–482. Letters to Manning and Macaulay, Oct. 1809.

45. *Parl. Deb.*, Vol. XXXIV, pages 1157–1158. June 19, 1816.

46. Ibid., Vol. XXXVIII, page 304. Sir Samuel Romilly. April 22, 1818.

47. Ibid., Vol. XXVIII, page 803. July 20, 1814.

48. *Life of Wilberforce*, Vol. IV, pages 365–366.

49. *Parl. Deb.*, NS, Vol. XIX, page 1469. Report of the institution in 1815, quoted by Lord Seaford, June 23, 1828. See also Ibid., NS, Vol. X, pages 1094–1095, where Canning. March 16, 1824, emphasized that the abolitionists had always disclaimed emancipation; and C.O. 137/161, where the Jamaica Assembly, Dec. 15, 1824, demanded the repeal of the Registry Act on the ground that, when it was passed, a pledge had been given that emancipation was not contemplated. Sir George Stephen expressed later his firm belief that the most sanguine abolitionist never contemplated actual emancipation in 1813. *Sir George Stephen: Anti-Slavery Recollections* (London, 1854), page 21.

nial registers revealed a diminishing population[50] quite at variance with the policy of amelioration. Public opinion in Britain was shocked by the flagrant cases of cruelty on the part of the slave owners and the immoral perversion of justice in the slave colonies, and a Hodge, a Rawlins and a Huggins were taken as typical of the generality of West Indian planters. But the fact which more than any other turned the religious section of Britain against the planters was the persecution of the missionaries.

The Methodists were greatly disliked in the colonies. The planters claimed that they instilled dangerous notions into the heads of the slaves, which were subversive of discipline on the plantations and of the general state of slavery. From the intimacies, wrote Woodford from Trinidad, which they contracted with the Negroes, their presence was always a source of uneasiness.[51] In his opinion they were not persons of responsibility, they should be forbidden to administer the sacraments, and it was only the protection afforded them by the British Government which restrained him from expelling them.[52] In Demerara they were looked on with jealousy and mistrust by the majority of the planters, and deemed "hot headed fanatics anxious to convert everything into persecution, and to set up a claim of merit upon it, haranguing their ignorant hearers on the abstruser mysteries of our religion ill fitted to the scale of their understandings, instead of instructing them in the plainer precepts of the Gospel and of enforcing those moral duties that are of so much consequence to the class of which their hearers are composed."[53] In Jamaica the missionaries had to face the same opposition,[54] while the Governor of Barbados, in accordance with the traditional attitude since the seventeenth cen-

---

50. It might seem strange that the population should have diminished when the birth and death rates were, it will be remembered, approximately level in 1788. But abolition must have meant a certain dislocation in an economy which was based on the receiving of a certain number of new recruits. Moreover, there was the same personnel in the directing staff, the same methods of feeding, etc. It might well have taken some time for the planters to realise where their real interest lay. Further, the intercolonial slave trade was responsible for the transfer of numbers of slaves from the older islands to the more fertile, new colonies, and we have already seen what Stephen and the abolitionists thought of this arrangement. Finally, the history of the sugar colonies everywhere shows a tendency for the slave population to decrease in direct proportion to the increased output of sugar.

51. C.O. 295/39. To Bathurst, Feb. 8, 1816.

52. C.O. 295/48. To Bathurst, Jan. 26, 1819; C.O. 295/46. June 24, 1818; C.O. 295/39. Feb. 8, 1816. See also C.O. 295/48. Woodford to Goulburn, Jan. 27, 1819: "As I have heard and seen nothing of the *Methodizzes* since the last took himself off, I hope I am quit of them, but let me entreat of you to do what you can abt a Bishop for us."

53. C.O. 111/12. Bentinck to Liverpool, Jan. 6, 1812.

54. See C.O. 137/183. Nov. 12, 1832; C.O. 137/188. Jan. 20, 1833. Mulgrave to Goderich, where the Governor declared it would be useless to institute legal proceedings against those who had taken part in the demolition of Methodist Chapels, and impossible to reprimand or dismiss so many magistrates, "sustained as I fear these gentlemen would be by the applause and encouragement of no inconsiderable part of the community." The Attorney General was unable to obtain affidavits against the offenders, and there was no hope of securing a conviction by any jury in Jamaica.

tury, opposed the building of churches on the ground that permission to the Negroes thus to assemble would turn their minds to plots and insurrections.[55]

The colonists always asked for clergymen of the Established Church to replace the missionaries and, in their defence, it was urged that even in Britain there were laws against irregular preaching. "If teachers," asked Barham, "will mix poison in the cup of salvation, can those be blamed who will not suffer it to be handed round?" It was unfair that when a system, which was just and proper in Britain, was introduced into the West Indies, "you have the whole army of Saints besieging His Majesty's council to get the law rejected."[56] But the home Government refused to permit any violation of the law of toleration in the colonies.[57] The climax came with the destruction of the Methodist chapel in Barbados in October 1823. Printed copies of a handbill were circulated in Barbados apprizing the inhabitants of the "great and signal triumph over Methodism" and of the flight of the "agents to the villainous African Society," and calling upon the other colonies to follow the laudable example of the Barbadians, and put an end to Methodism and its chapels all over the West Indies.[58] This was going too far. The trial for conspiracy and subsequent death of the missionary Smith in Demerara added fuel to the flames of indignation in Britain, and Smith and Shrewsbury became the rallying cries of the future.

Thus it was that the abolitionists found themselves in 1823 almost forced by colonial recalcitrance and colonial misconduct to advocate emancipation. Emancipation, however, was to be gradual. Slavery was to wither away. In the words of Buxton, on whom the leadership of the cause had devolved, there was to be "nothing rash, nothing rapid, nothing abrupt, nothing bearing any feature of violence." The precise date of the abolition of slavery he would not give. In fact it would never be abolished. "It will subside; it will decline; it will expire; it will, as it were, burn itself down into its socket and go out. . . . We shall leave it gently to decay—slowly, silently, almost imperceptibly, to die away and to be forgotten."[59] Canning, the apostle of gradual-

---

55. C.O. 28/92. Nov. 4, 1823.

56. *Parl. Deb.*, Vol. XXXIV, pages 1203–1204. June 19, 1816.

57. See C.O. 137/165, for the disallowance of the Jamaica Slave Act of 1827. "It is the settled purpose of His Majesty's Government to sanction no colonial law which needlessly infringes on the religious liberty of any class of His Majesty's subjects," Huskisson to Keane, Sept. 22, 1827. The Jamaica Assembly declared that the disallowance of the Act "must shake the confidence of the island in their (His Majesty's Ministers) wisdom and justice." Ibid., Dec. 14, 1827.

58. C.O. 28/94. The island agent, in a letter to Bathurst, excused the act as "committed under peculiar circumstances of aggravated feelings, directed against an influence which was considered as highly prejudicial and dangerous to the interests of the island." Ibid., May 3, 1824.

59. *Parl. Deb.*, NS, Vol. IX, pages 265–266. May 15, 1823. According to Sir George Stephen, the first hint of the possibility of ultimate emancipation was given in a report of the African Institution in 1822, but it was "only casually alluded to, and in so quiet a manner that it seems rather to have

ness, was there to urge still greater caution and prudence. "There are knots which cannot be suddenly disentangled, and must not be cut." What was morally true must not be confounded with what was historically false, and they must not legislate as if it was for a new world, "the surface of which was totally clear from the obstruction of antecedent claims and obligations."[60] They were faced with "conflicting prejudices and opposite extravagancies of principle," and it was not, nor could it be made, a question merely of right, of humanity, or of morality.[61]

The policy agreed upon was that the Government should prepare various reforms designed to ameliorate the condition of the slaves and prepare them for an indefinite day when they would be fit to be made freemen.[62] These reforms Government would enforce in the crown colonies and submit to the independent legislatures for that "full and fair co-operation" which Britain had a right to expect. In case of resistance, a resistance not of reason but of contumacy, Canning pledged himself to take the necessary steps, but he had secured his aim. The question was left in the hands of the executive.

The abolitionists were as desirous as anyone else that these reforms should be undertaken by the colonists themselves, because of the good effect it would have on the minds of the slaves. But past experience made them sceptical, and their fears were to be amply justified. The colonists were the authors of the evils complained of, and how could it be expected that they would legislate against themselves? "To leave the slaves in *their* hands, what is it less than to recommend the lamb to the protection of the wolf?"[63]

In the crown colony of Trinidad, where it was hoped the influence of Government would secure the acceptance of the measure, the opposition was determined and prolonged. One of the members of the council asserted that as much had been done by the planters to improve the condition of their slaves as could have been done by any gentlemen of Britain under similar circumstances: "unless they divested themselves altogether of their worldly concerns and assumed the office of apostles and missionaries they could

---

escaped from the writer's pen unconsciously, than to have formed the object of any scheme in actual contemplation. I have reason to believe that it did not, and that had the question been directly put, the design of emancipation would have been disavowed." *Stephen, op. cit.*, page 59.

60. Ibid., pages 278 and 282. See Ibid., NS, Vol. XIV, page 1156, where the Lord Chancellor hesitated to say that slavery was contrary to the genius of the British Constitution. March 7, 1826.

61. Ibid., NS, Vol. X, pages 1093 and 1198, March 16, 1824.

62. By omitting to state this time Canning had, in the opinion of Sir F. Blake, acted like a person who had built a very fine house only to discover later that a material part of it was wanting—the staircase. *Parl. Deb.*, NS, Vol. XI, pages 1425–1426. June 15, 1824.

63. *An Address to the Public on the State of Slavery in the West India Islands.* From the Committee of the Leicester Auxiliary Anti-Slavery Society (London, 1824), page 10.

do no more."[64] The Order in Council had produced not amelioration but deterioration, which would continue.[65] The planters replied to the Government's suggestions with rudeness[66] and sarcasm,[67] the Protector and Assistant Protector of Slaves were described as salaried informers,[68] and the Order in Council of November 1831, enforcing a reduction of the working hours of the slaves, as villainous.[69] Multifarious and disreputable obstacles were thrown in the way to impede and discredit the measures of Government,[70] and one of the assessors refused to try cases arising out of the Order in Council and walked out of court.[71]

If this was the fate of "the slow and silent course of temperate but authoritative admonition" in Trinidad, what was to be anticipated from the independent colonies? The Order in Council was sent to the latter in the form of heads of bills, which the Governor was to submit to the legislature. In Barbados there was no one in whom the Governor could confide without

---

64. C.O. 295/65. Mr. Burnley, October 7, 1824. Mr. Barham taunted the African Institution that even they, if they changed places with the planters, would be unable to do more: "as to the pseudo philanthropists and trading philanthropists, I believe they would do much less." *Parl. Deb.*, Vol. XXXIV, page 1199. June 19, 1816.

65. C.O. 295/71. Woodford to Horton, May 3, 1826, quoting Mr. Burnley.

66. C.O. 295/67. One Fitzgerald, manager of a plantation, wrote in the returns decreed of the nature and particulars of slave offences, that the plantation had become "of mere nominal value since the promulgation of the silly Orders in Council of the 24th June 1824, which have almost paralyzed and rendered useless the best efforts of the poor manager." Big wigs and evil advisers had destroyed the former good feeling between master and slaves, only "to put £3000 cy in the pocket of a craving lawyer—as much as would support six modest managers like myself." He hoped the salary of the worthy slave protector would be increased, "whose disinterest [sic] endeavours to prevent black carcases from being roughly handled are so deserving of applause." In describing the punishment he wrote—"23 stripes on that part which my Lord Chesterfield strongly recommends to be the last to enter and the first to retire on all presentations at levies and to name which in the presence of ladies is considered a great breach in the laws of politeness," and much more in the same vein. The Governor was forced to restrain these improper expressions by a proclamation of Jan. 30, 1826. C.O. 295/70.

67. C.O. 295/92. Mr. Jackson, at a public meeting, Jan. 14, 1832: "Because we are not idle, do not read the new novels till sometime after they are published . . . because we do not go to Newmarket . . . because we have private concerts instead of operas, and amateur concerts instead of the pantomimes of Drury Lane and the melodramas of Covent Garden—for these most excellent and unanswerable reasons His Lordship contends that we are incapable of understanding our own affairs, or taking care of our own interests, far less of embracing those comprehensive and enlightened views of general policy and justice by which it is tacitly understood the measures of government are so notably distinguished. Local knowledge and practical experience are held to be impediments to a wise system of legislature."

68. Ibid. Board of Cabildo to Gov. Grant, Jan. 4, 1832.

69. Ibid. Article in the Gazette Extraordinary, Mar. 25, 1832. The Order was called "that 121-pronged scourge invented by the 'saints' of Downing Street to goad to madness the oppressed, insulted and bitterly persecuted West Indian planters."

70. Ibid. Grant to Goderich, confidential, June 10, 1832.

71. Ibid. Grant to Howick, April 30, 1832. See C.O. 295/93, for the remarks of Taylor (Aug. 23) and Stephen (Aug. 25) on the contumacy displayed in all the crown colonies. Stephen suggested that assessors should henceforth be drawn from the whole body of society, which would serve to introduce the free people of colour.

giving away the fact that these heads of bills were recommendations from the home Government,[72] and when, out of duty, he wrote to the most likely member of the council, he received no reply.[73] With the Demerara insurrection before them, the Barbados Assembly refused to pass a slave code which was to be "a mere catalogue of indulgencies to the blacks." They would not co-operate. "If it is determined that we shall be the victims of fanaticism, prejudice and injustice, we must submit, but neither threats nor persuasion will ever induce us to put the finishing hand to our own political, perhaps natural existence."[74] "The axe was uplifted, ready to strike at the root of the most venerable and sacred institutions,"[75] but theirs was not the hand that would wield it.

Everything depended on Jamaica, whose position as the largest colony made it certain that its decision would have great weight either way. But the Jamaica Assembly was even more extreme. A bill was passed unanimously to repeal the Registry Act,[76] and so strong was public feeling that the Governor dared not put the home Government's proposals to the Assembly in the form his instructions ordered.[77] The Governor thought the reluctance to part with power over the slaves strange in such an age,[78] and he too could find no one to whom he could entrust the bills.[79] The Assembly declared its determination to embrace every favourable opportunity for making such enactments as might be deemed prudent and advisable,[80] but by 1831 they were still impressed with the necessity of proceeding "deliberately, gradually, and even almost imperceptibly."[81] The opposition in the colony was unanimous, it was no temporary ebullition of a small discontented party, but the feeling of every person of property.[82] Jamaica's answer to the Government, like that of Trinidad and Barbados, was an emphatic No.

The colonists thought it unfair that whilst they were stigmatized as devils, the perfection of angels was expected of them.[83] There was much truth in

---

72. C.O. 28/92. Warde to Bathurst, most confidential, and private and confidential, July 2 and Aug. 23, 1823.
73. Ibid. Warde to Bathurst, private and confidential, Sept. 10, 1823.
74. C.O. 28/95. Nov. 15, 1825.
75. C.O. 28/107. Council to Gov. Lyon, in Lyon's of March 11, 1831.
76. C.O. 137/154. Manchester to Bathurst, Dec. 23, 1823.
77. Ibid., Manchester to Bathurst. Oct. 13 and Nov. 10, 1823.
78. Ibid., Manchester to Bathurst, Dec. 24, 1823.
79. C.O. 137/163. Manchester to Bathurst, private, May 6, 1826.
80. C.O. 137/161. Assembly to Manchester, Nov. 26, 1824.
81. C.O. 137/179. Numerous and respectable meeting of the Freeholders of the parish of Portland, Aug. 15, 1831.
82. C.O. 137/180. Agent Burge to Goderich, Sept. 5, 1831.
83. C.O. 28/92. Report of a Debate in Council on a Despatch from Lord Bathurst to Sir Henry Warde, printed, Sept. 3, 1823. Speech of Mr. Hamden, page 25.

this, but that was no reason why they should promptly proceed to behave like devils. The home government's recommendations that the whip should be abolished in the fields did not allow for the colonists' "abstract admiration" of what seemed to them a necessary instrument of correction. "Once establish this rule and then adieu to all peace and comfort on plantations."[84] The postponement of punishments until the day after the offence had been committed proceeded, in the opinion of a local meeting in Trinidad, on the groundless assumption that punishments were inflicted under the impulse of ungovernable passion.[85] As regards the abolition of female punishments, the planters claimed that it was found necessary to punish women even in civilized societies,[86] that flogging was "the most humane, prompt and efficacious mode to crush disorderly behaviour,"[87] and that the alternative, confinement in the stocks, was uneconomical.[88] Flogging was the only way in which the insolent tongues of the women could be restrained,[89] and its abolition would be an injustice to the male slaves.[90] Colonial sentiment on the subject can be summed up in the words of Mr. Burnley of Trinidad: "the idea appears to me so monstrous and extraordinary that I hardly know how to approach the subject."[91] It was indeed impossible to retain slavery and abolish coercion.

The "compulsory manumission" suggestion met the same fate. The Jamaica agent thought it full of danger to every interest in the colonies, as, in its best consequences, it would tend to emancipate the most valuable of the slaves.[92] So hostile was opinion in Jamaica to every suggestion emanating from home that the Governor dared not recommend, as he had been ordered to do, the emancipation of female children under certain conditions, but proposed waiting until "the dread of innovation which now pervades the whole

---

84. Ibid., page 24.

85. C.O. 295/60. Resolutions of Arima General Meeting, Sept. 29, 1825. See also *Parl. Deb.*, Vol. XXXVIII, page 310. Mr. A. Grant, April 22, 1818: "Why use the odious and invidious term of a cartwhip, implying a brutal infliction of severity. Instead of a necessary correction?"

86. C.O. 28/92. Sept. 3, 1823. Speech of Mr. Hamden: "I doubt whether a milder discipline would be necessary for the *poissardes* of Paris, or the furies of Billingsgate, than for their hardy spouses. Are not women flogged in houses of correction in England?" Page 21.

87. C.O. 295/60. Resolutions of the Quarter of Point-a-Pierre, Oct. 20, 1823. Compare Mr. Hamden, *op. cit.*: confinement was "a mode of punishment for women not without serious objections on the score of humanity."

88. C.O. 295/65. Woodford to Bathurst, Feb. 10, 1825.

89. C.O. 295/59. Woodford to Bathurst, Aug. 26, 1823; C.O. 295/60. Commt at Chaguanas to Woodford, Aug. 20, 1823; C.O. 295/71. Woodford to Horton, confidential, July 3, 1826. Also C.O. 111/56. Protector of Slaves half yearly report, Nov. 1826.

90. C.O. 295/59. Woodford to Bathurst, Aug. 6, 1823. Burnley spoke of the "attempt to arrest an immutable law of nature by a British Order in Council"—it would give a superiority to the women. C.O. 295/60. Hamden thought that the men would be sorry to see the women who had "a tendency to the Amazonian cast of character," placed beyond the reach of chastisement. C.O. 28/92.

91. C.O. 295/60.

92. C.O. 137/166. To Horton, April 2, 1827.

community here shall have passed away."[93] In Demerara the Court of Policy refused to adopt the principle of manumission *invite domino*: "it is more for their consistency and for the interests of their constituents that it should be done *for* them than *by* them."[94] Trinidad went even further. The price paid for manumissions went up enormously, while the number of manumissions declined. The possibility of sworn appraisers pronouncing an unjust decision had not been contemplated or provided for.[95]

The policy of gradual emancipation adopted in Britain had as its foundation the religious and moral improvement of the Negroes. One of the first steps in this direction was the abolition of the Negro Sunday market,[96] as compensation for which the home Government recommended another day in the week for the slaves. Barbados alleged the depression as the justification of her refusal to surrender one-sixth of an already attenuated income.[97] (If this reform, or any others, had to wait for West Indian prosperity, the slaves might as well have waited for the Greek Kalends.) Jamaica refused, and the Governor feared that it must be left to "the operation of time and the change of circumstances and opinions which is slowly but surely leading to the improvement of the habits and manners of the slaves."[98] In other words, if and when Sunday trading was abolished, the Negroes would not get another day in the week.

By 1830, therefore, the net result of the Government's policy of admonition and recommendation was nothing. The Whigs replaced the Tories and a new policy of fiscal bribery was attempted. Stephen had once made

93. C.O. 137/154. Manchester to Bathurst, Oct. 13, 1823.
94. C.O. 111/55. D'Urban to Bathurst, private, July 4, 1826.
95. C.O. 295/72, Woodford to Bathurst, Aug. 8, 1826; Woodford to Bathurst, private and confidential, Dec. 19, 1826; C.O. 295/73. Stephen to Horton, Oct. 5, 1826. C.O. 295/85—List of Manumissions in Trinidad.

Table 8.1.

Year	Personal Slaves	Plantation Slaves
1825	124	38
1826	121	46
1827	118	49
1828	95	33
1829	72	15
1830 (To Oct. 29)	26	6

96. See an interesting letter in C.O. 137/152. A Jamaica Proprietor to Bathurst, Edinburgh, Feb. 18, 1821, urging abolition of Sunday Markets: "If the Whigs claim the credit of abolishing the slave trade, let the Tories have their actions registered in heaven in a way they may not be ashamed of."
97. C.O. 28/92. Mr. Hamden, Sept. 3, 1823.
98. C.O. 137/148. Manchester to Bathurst, confidential; July 10, 1819.

an interesting suggestion that the continuation of West Indian preference over East India sugar should be used as a bargain for amelioration.
"Let us have reform of oppression and deliverance from national guilt, in
exchange for our Indian trade and our money." He recommended that
the scale of import duties on colonial produce might be made inversely
proportionate to the advances made by the colonial legislatures in the
mitigation of slavery.[99] Barham pointed out the pernicious error of supposing that general emancipation could arrive by multiplying individual
emancipations, and recommended that the nation should buy all West Indian property in order to conduct its experiments.[100] Wilberforce wanted a
national fund for buying amelioration from the planters. Canning turned
down his scheme. "If a shop for such payments is once opened, there will
be no want of customers; for what West Indian now would not part with
his estate at half or one-fourth its value?"[101] But by 1831 something had to
be done. The Whig Government held out the hope of fiscal concessions
to those colonies which adopted Government's recommendations; the
hot-tempered parent, having failed to persuade the children to obey her
commands, now held out a sugar plum as the bribe of obedience.[102] Not a
single legislature accepted the offer on the terms stipulated, which Jamaica
described as "fiscal oppression . . . a most tyrannical threat, subversive
of the sacredness of property, (which) could only have emanated from a
revolutionary government."[103]

All this was undisguised contumacy; and yet the Government at home did
nothing. The mother country suffered her voice "to roll across the Atlantic
in empty warnings and fruitless orders."[104] For this there were four reasons.
In the first place, the difficult question of constitutional right was raised;
secondly, the West Indians had powerful friends in the Cabinet and Parliament; thirdly, there was the general fear of a Negro revolution; and in the
fourth place, the abolitionists were guilty of serious mistakes. These reasons
call for closer examination.

---

99. E. J. Stapleton (ed.) Some Official Correspondence of George Canning (London, 1877), Vol. 1,
page 115. Stephen to Canning, March 16, 1823. (Referred to hereafter as Canning, Correspondence).
100. Barham, op. cit. pages 6 and 35.
101. Wilberforce, Correspondence, Vol. II, page 477. Canning to Wilberforce. Jan. 4, 1824.
102. Parl. Deb., Third Series, Vol. XIV, page 1107. Sir Adolphus Dalrymple, Aug. 3, 1832. Gov.
Woodford had suggested such a concession, by reduction of duties, on two occasions. C.O. 295/59.
July 13, 1823; C.O. 295/62. May 7, 1824.
103. C.O. 137/179. Numerous and respectable meeting of the Freeholders of the parish of Portland, Aug. 15, 1831.
104. Parl. Deb., NS, Vol. XXV, pages 1190–1191. Brougham, July 13. 1830.

(e) Constitutional Claims

It was only to be expected that the colonial victory over the Registry Bill would lead in the future to a reiteration, even an exaggeration, of the claims of the colonies to govern or misgovern themselves and their slave population, without interference from the Imperial Parliament. Canning practically gave the colonies a blank cheque in this respect: "no feeling of wounded pride, no motive of questionable expediency, nothing short of real and demonstrable necessity, shall induce me to moot the awful question of the transcendental power of Parliament over every dependency of the British Crown."[105] But Canning was only one of a number of the Cabinet who wished the question to be shelved, under the guise of executive freedom of action. Sir George Murray was willing to make recommendations and to impress upon the West Indian body the necessity of doing something, but the measures to be adopted should not be prescribed positively and dogmatically. The almost necessary result of dictating to an assembly over which they had no direct influence was to produce resistance; and although means might be found of overcoming that resistance by force, it was much better to avoid producing it if possible.[106] Wellington agreed with Murray, they had no right to give orders to the colonial assemblies.[107]

The home Government was undoubtedly influenced by the memory of the North American colonies. They had already been warned by one of the West Indians; "by persisting in the question of right we lost America . . . we might perhaps light up a flame between the mother country and the colonies which would one day be deeply deplored."[108]

The West Indians quoted the Declaratory Act, and Liverpool at least was impressed with the gravity of the situation. In the crown colonies, where Britain's rights were unquestioned and unquestionable, they could proceed experimentally. But what of the colonies with independent legislatures? "I can quite understand," he wrote to Canning, "the right of the mother country to legislate externally for all her dominions and even to enforce such external legislation by internal regulations if necessary; but it always appeared to me that between the questions of taxation and internal legislation (purely as such) there were many much stronger arguments in support of the right of

---

105. Ibid., NS, Vol. X, pages 1105–1106. March 16, 1824.

106. *Despatches, Correspondence and Memoranda of Field Marshal Arthur, Duke of Wellington* (London. 1867–1880), Vol. IV, page 658. Murray to Wellington, Aug. 19, 1828. (Referred to hereafter as *Wellington, Despatches.*)

107. Ibid., Vol. IV, page 642. Wellington to Murray, Aug. 20, 1828; page 556. Wellington to Stephen, July 25, 1828.

108. *Parl. Deb.*, Vol. XXXI, pages 781–2. Mr. Marryat, June 13, 1815.

taxation than in that of internal legislation."[109] The West Indians in Parliament did not question the right of the mother country to legislate—even if it was "polemical legislation"[110]—for the colonies.[111] All they said was that it was not expedient; not so the West Indian colonists. The Barbados Assembly was quick to resent anything savouring of dictation,[112] while the Trinidad Council considered its business "to represent and defend interests, not to register edicts."[113] It was in Jamaica, inevitably, that the colonial claims were most loudly proclaimed. The Assembly spoke in terms of independence,[114] they refused to acknowledge any more allegiance to Great Britain than to Canada, or to be cited to the bar of British opinion to defend their laws and customs.[115] "As for the king of England," asked Mr. Beaumont, "what right I should be glad to know has he to Jamaica except that he stole it from Spain?"[116] The Governor reported that, "the undoubted rights of the British Parliament have been wantonly and repeatedly denied, (and) unless the arrogance of such pretensions is effectually curbed, His Majesty's authority in this colony will exist but in name."[117]

The abolitionists, with that growing tradition which emphasized that protection of natives could not be expected from the men on the spot, argued, with justice, that it was useless to expect reforms from the colonists and that the Imperial Parliament had an undoubted right to interfere to enforce those reforms. The argument that the colonies were a part of the Empire but that the Imperial Parliament could not interfere in their internal affairs appeared to Stephen "a solecism in policy," which put Jamaica on the same footing as Hanover.[118] Wilberforce was prepared to concede that the size of Jamaica made its pretensions plausible,[119] but Stephen condemned the Government's policy as "a hopeless and most culpable devolution of the duties of the mother country."[120] The abolitionists realised as well as anyone else the danger of legislating at home in the teeth of hostile local opinion, they understood the danger of that power of inertness which the colonists might

109. *Bathurst Mss.*, page 560. Jan. 9, 1824, private and confidential.
110. *Parl. Deb.*, Vol. XXXIII, page 329. Lord Holland, March 22, 1816.
111. See Ibid., NS, Vol. XV, page 1341, where Ellis, a West Indian, did not support the colonial legislatures and regretted their refusal to co-operate. May 19, 1826.
112. C.O. 28/93. Warde to Bathurst, confidential, Oct. 21, 1824.
113. C.O. 295/60. Mr. Burnley.
114. C.O. 137/183. Manchester to Goderich, Nov. 13, 1832.
115. C.O. 137/186. Memorial of the Jamaica deputies to Britain, Nov. 29, 1832.
116. C.O. 137/183. Manchester to Goderich, secret and confidential, Dec. 16, 1832.
117. Ibid., Manchester to Goderich, Dec. 16, 1832.
118. *Wellington, Despatches*, Vol. IV, page 555. Stephen to Wellington, July 24, 1828.
119. *Bathurst Mss.*, page 416. Wilberforce to Bathurst, private, July 4, 1816.
120. *Canning, Correspondence*. Vol. I, page 114. Stephen to Canning, March 16, 1823.

exercise sullenly,[121] and knew that no imperial enactments would be of any force without a reform of the administrative and judicial department in the colonies. Of what use, Stephen had asked, would be a Registry Act without a judge to enforce it?[122] Colonial officials were forbidden to own slaves or to manage estates, and the Governor of Barbados had to ask for independent judges, independent magistrates and independent law officers to enforce the Abolition Act.[123]

(f) West Indian Defenders in Britain

The West Indians had powerful friends in Britain, who, like Canning, saw in their conduct "much to blame, indeed—much to excuse—something to pity, but nothing to punish."[124] One of Canning's best friends was a West Indian,[125] and one of his most important constituents was one of the richest planters in Demerara.[126] No wonder he constantly harped on the fearfulness and delicacy and "most awful importance" of the West Indian question.[127] So powerful was the opposition that they had to face that the abolitionists, if they wished for an interview with ministers, dared not give too long notice, because that would afford the latter an opportunity of conferring with their West Indian friends.[128] Unhappily, wrote Wilberforce to his son about Canning's pledge in 1823, "government is under the influence, from personal friendship, of some great West Indian proprietors, and therefore I fear they will not follow up their own resolutions."[129] Splendid dinners, with costly viands and soothing speeches, did the rest.[130] Wellington refused to "plunder the proprietors in the West Indies in order to acquire for themselves a little popularity in England."[131] Wilmot Horton was the persistent

---

121. *Parl. Deb.*, NS, Vol. XV, page 1351. Ellis, May 19, 1826.
122. *Life of Wilberforce*. Vol. IV, page 240. Stephen to Wilberforce.
123. C.O. 28/111. Smith to Stanley, June 1, 1833. See C.O. 295/72 for Return of Public functionaries in Trinidad owning or interested in slaves, Oct. 3, 1826.
124. *Parl. Deb.*, US, Vol. X, page 1205, March 16, 1824.
125. *Life of Wilberforce*, Vol. V. page 129. Wilberforce to his son. May 17, 1823. The friend referred to was Ellis.
126. C.O. 111/24. Canning to Bathurst. Sept. 12, 1817.
127. *Canning, Correspondence.* Vol. I, page 134. To Liverpool, Jan. 9. 1824.
128. *Life of Wilberforce*, Vol. V, page 124. Wilberforce to Macaulay. April 8, 1822. See also *Bathurst Mss.*, page 579, where Canning, April 9, 1825, informed Bathurst of a request of "the Saints, under the title of the Anti-Slavery Society," for an interview to discuss the refractoriness of Jamaica, and suggested that he could "jog them on to the next week" if he could not see Bathurst before that.
129. *Life of Wilberforce*, Vol. V. page 265. Feb. 6, 1826.
130. H. Richard: *Memoirs of Joseph Sturge* (London. 1864), page 90. Sturge's address at the Friends' Yearly Meeting, 1830.
131. *Wellington, Despatches*, Vol. V, page 603. Memorandum for Sir George Murray respecting the Order in Council for Demerara, May 16, 1829.

advocate of just and equitable compensation to the planters.[132] Wilberforce implored Bathurst to be fair to the abolitionists.[133] Huskisson opposed their tactics,[134] he soon followed Canning's example in resigning his post as one of the Governors of the African Institution after Buxton's resolutions of May 1823,[135] and feared the consequences of an impatient interference to effect in a few years by legislative interposition what in his view was not attainable by statutory enactments.[136]

As a result the West Indians were given more than enough rope, with which they immediately proceeded to hang themselves. Their spokesmen in Parliament pleaded for time. "This country ought not to complain, or to think thirty years too long for a moral position to find its way across the Atlantic." So deep-rooted and inveterate an evil as slavery could not be removed by a single act of legislative benevolence; there was no such magic in legislation, the omnipotence of Parliament could work no such miracles.[137] Roman Catholic emancipation in Britain had not been won in a day.[138] Palmerston advised the colonists to take advantage of the strong feeling to deal tenderly with their interests.[139] While Wellington hoped the Jamaica Assembly would be persuaded to omit the clause referring to the missionaries from the otherwise good slave law of 1827.[140] But while their friends pleaded, colonial recalcitrance increased. The leaders in the colonies seemed to Huskisson insane. "They seem bent upon raising a cry against themselves, and as the weakest they must go to the wall, if they force on a contest of

132. R. W. Horton: *First and Second Letters to the Freeholders of the County of York on Negro Slavery* (London, 1830). The agent for Jamaica thanked him for his "many instances of candour and fair dealing upon our colonial concerns" (C.O. 137/166. April 2, 1827). The agent for Demerara sent McDonnell's work on "Considerations on Negro Slavery" to him as "a sincere and able friend to the West Indies" (C.O. 111/47. Nov. 16, 1824). Gov. Woodford hoped he would not remain anonymous as an author of a pamphlet, that "the colonists may know what an able advocate they possess in you" (C.O. 295/74). Feb. 27, 1827).

133. *Bathurst Mss.*, page 428. Jan. 1, 1817. See also page 565. Canning to Bathurst, March 21, 1824: "You will be happy to hear that you are restored to favour with the West Indians. As to the Saints I cannot say."

134. *Corry, op. cit.*, Vol. II, pages 699–701. Huskisson to Gladstone, Nov. 2, 1823.

135. *Huskisson Papers*, Add. Mss. 38745, folio 81. "It appears to me not immaterial that the President of the Board of Trade and member for Liverpool should get out as soon as he can." Huskisson to Canning, Nov. 2, 1823. Canning's resignation is in *Canning, Correspondence*, Vol. I, pages 124–125. Canning to Macaulay, Oct. 26, 1823. See also *Life of Wilberforce*, Vol. V, page 127, where Wilberforce wrote to Macaulay, May 10, 1822, informing him of the refusal, in very civil letters, of Canning, Lord Harrowby and Wellington to attend a meeting of the African Institution.

136. *Huskisson Papers*, Add. Mss. 38745, folios 182–183. To Joseph Sandars, Jan. 22, 1824, agreeing with his withdrawal from the Liverpool Anti-Slavery Society.

137. *Parl. Deb.*, NS, Vol. XIV, pages 1164–1165. Lord Dudley and Ward, H. of L, March 7, 1826.

138. Ibid., Third Series, Vol. XII, page 613. Lord Seaford (formerly Charles Ellis), April 17, 1832.

139. Ibid., NS, Vol. XIV, page 919. Feb. 28, 1826.

140. *Wellington, Despatches* Vol. IV, page 642. Wellington to Murray, Aug. 20, 1828.

authority with this country."[141] That was exactly what happened to the colonies, they paid the price of their intransigence. No wonder Brougham could thank them for their contumacy.[142] Was it that they clung to the last hope of intimidating the politicians at home? Possibly. At any rate they alienated public opinion in Britain. Their "cuckoo song" of ruin and cries for assistance ill accorded with their contumacy, and even a friendly-disposed man like Wellington got tired of them and treated a deputation of the West Indian body in London very roughly.[143]

(g) Fears of a Negro Revolution

There was one very strong reason why the British Government was most reluctant to intervene to enforce its recommendations on the contumacious assemblies. They knew, and the West Indians saw to it that they should not forget, that if the authority of the local legislators was overridden by the Imperial Parliament, the slaves might rise in a body and make the British colonies a number of St. Domingos. In the West Indian colonies the public mind was ever tremblingly alive to the dangers of insurrection.[144] The West Indians therefore deprecated even discussions on the state of slavery. So influential a person as the Duke of York wrote that the unfortunate countenance given by the Parliament to Buxton's propositions of 1823 had raised a flame in the colonies which could never be quenched.[145] Slavery was the sore part of the West Indian system. "The frequent handling of it served to irritate but not to cure it; the fretful inter-meddlings with it by persons in this country only served to make it worse."[146] To bring forward the subject of the abolition of slavery in Parliament was to shed blood and provoke rebellions in the West Indies.[147] But unfortunately it was an age in which the risk of discussion could not be avoided.[148]

Ministers were fully alive to the danger of public discussions respecting the state of slavery in the West Indies. But they had no more power sum-

---

141. *Huskisson Papers*, Add. Mss. 38752, folios 26–27. Huskisson to Horton, Nov. 7, 1827.

142. "I feel deeply impressed with gratitude to the West India planters, God knows, more than I expected to feel, for their advancement of the cause by fulfilling all I have ever ventured to predict of them; but I never expected to live to feel such weight of obligation to the whole West India legislature, towards whom I now beg leave to express my most unbounded gratitude." Speech at the second general meeting of the Anti-Slavery Society, April 30, 1825. Quoted in *The Quarterly Review*, Vol. XXXII, 1825, page 514.

143. W. Smart: *Economic Annals of the 19th Century* (London, 1910–1917), Vol. II, page 545.

144. C.O. 28/88. Combermere to Bathurst, Jan. 5, 1819.

145. *Bathurst Mss.*, page 547. To Bathurst, Oct. 15, 1823.

146. *Parl. Deb.* Vol. XXXIV, page 1185. Mr. Pallmer, June 19, 1816.

147. Ibid., NS, Vol. IX, page 256. Mr. Baring, May 15, 1823.

148. Ibid., Vol. XXXIV, page 1211. Lord Castlereagh, June 19, 1816.

marily to stop parliamentary discussions on this subject than upon any other popular question.[149]

The West Indians said that these frequent discussions unsettled the minds of Negroes. They would never admit that the Negroes were men, with feelings, desires and aspirations of men. The planters might think the state of slavery eternal, ordained by God, but why should the slaves think the same? They were not all stupid and docile, they had a peculiar facility for acquiring information about anything concerning their degraded state,[150] and thought that every ameliorating measure, every parliamentary discussion granted them emancipation. Thus they confounded the abolition of the slave trade with the abolition of slavery.[151] Every new Governor, they imagined, brought out emancipation in his pocket;[152] and the serious Demerara insurrection in 1823 was attributed by the Governor to the Negroes' misconception of the discussions that had recently taken place.[153]

The abolitionists were blamed for these discussions and the ferment in the Negro mind. Canning held them responsible for the Demerara insurrection,[154] but he would have blamed everyone and everything which brought into the limelight a subject which had no attractions for him.[155] What was there in the policy of amelioration which would provoke insurrection?[156] De Tocqueville tells us that revolutions occur when circumstances begin to improve, but the Negroes knew their masters too well to doubt that the masters would not willingly agree to improvements in their condition. And if the masters

149. *Huskisson Papers*, Add. Mss. 38745, folios 58–59. To J. Bolton, Oct. 19, 1823. Huskisson added an important statement which the planters would have done well to digest. "The West Indians, I fear, will greatly deceive themselves if they infer from what has now happened at Demerara, that it will damp the intemperate zeal which brought forward the question last year; and that it will not be renewed again, and every year, with increasing effect and acrimony of debate; unless the Government shall be able to show by the proceedings in the West Indies a cordial spirit of co-operation on the part of those colonies in those measures of melioration to which the Government itself stands pledged."
150. C.O. 295/87. Gov. Smith to Goderich, July 13, 1831: "The slaves have an unaccountable facility in obtaining partial and generally distorted information whenever a public document is about to be received which can in any way affect their condition or station."
151. C.O. 137/119. Gov. Coote to Castlereagh, June 27, 1807; C.O. 137/120. Gov. Coote to Castlereagh, Dec. 4, 1807 and Simon Taylor to Thomas Hugham, Jan. 7, 1807.
152. C.O. 111/44. D'Urban to Bathurst, May 5, 1824; C.O. 137/183. Mulgrave to Howick, private, Aug. 6, 1832; C.O. 28/111. Smith to Stanley, May 23, 1833.
153. C.O. 111/39. Murray to Bathurst, Aug. 24, 1823.
154. *Life of Wilberforce*, Vol. V, page 201. Macaulay to Wilberforce, Nov. 11, 1823.
155. *Huskisson Papers*, Add. Mss. 38752, folio 26. Huskisson to Horton, Nov. 7, 1827: "it was a subject upon which he (Canning) did not willingly converse, and it had no attractions for me to induce my talking to him upon it."
156. *Report of the Committee of the Society for the Mitigation and Gradual Abolition of Slavery throughout the British Dominions* (London, 1824), page 6: "Was there anything in the gift of Sunday as a day of rest; or in the mitigation of corporal punishment; or in the removal of restraints on manumission which would have a tendency to promote discontent and insurrection among the slaves?."

deprecated discussions four thousand miles away, what was to be said of their own stupid and intemperate behaviour in publicly discussing the question of slavery, and in giving vent to their feelings of rage and indignation in the presence of intelligent domestic slaves?[157]

In short, it was the owners themselves who were responsible for the agitated minds of the slaves, though it would have been too fearful a risk to provoke and incite the slaves to revolt in order to justify their own arguments for non-intervention by the home Government.[158] In one instance, however, the Negro insurgents in Demerara were actually armed and led by a white man, and another circulated a story upon different plantations that the Prince Regent had declared freedom for the slaves and ordered them to arm their defence.[159] Governor Warde from Barbados ascribed the false reports of a speedy emancipation of the slaves to the continual discussions of the whites and the evil designs of a few planters.[160] In Trinidad the Governor considered public discussions unwise,[161] but the planters printed surreptitiously and circulated some ill-advised resolutions which he had deemed it expedient not to publish in the Island Gazette, owing to the disturbed minds of the slaves.[162] Governor Grant earnestly recommended the planters not to give way to angry feelings or to discuss the subject of slavery on occasions obviously objectionable,[163] but the planters showed no restraint. The slaves could easily have been kept quiet if such was the desire of those who should have guided their endeavours; "it would almost appear to be the actuating motives of some leading people here to drive the government to abandon its principles, even at the risk and by the means of exciting the slaves to insurrection."[164] From Jamaica came the same news; the slaves were collectively well-disposed, and the planters' meetings and resolutions were more calculated to disturb them than any casual report that some benefit was intended for them by the home Government which their masters wished to withhold.[165]

157. See *Bathurst Mss.*, page 415. Wilberforce to Bathurst, private, June 29, 1816: "Never did we use any such language, especially where the slaves could hear of it."

158. See *Report of the Committee of the Society for the Mitigation and Gradual Abolition of Slavery*, page 13. If so many plots had been discovered in order to oppose the abolition of the slave trade, it would have been strange if there had been a dearth of them "at a time when such claims were likely to be regarded as the best expedient to avert the deprecated reformation of a system in which almost all the colonists supposed their interests as well as their character to be more or less involved."

159. C.O. 111/20. Acting Gov. Carmichael to Bathurst, July 31, 1812.

160. C.O. 28/92. Warde to Bathurst, June 14, 1823.

161. C.O. 295/59. Woodford to Bathurst, Aug. 6, 1823.

162. Ibid., Woodford to Bathurst, Dec. 5, 1823.

163. C.O. 295/92. Grant to Planters' deputation, Jan. 1832.

164. Ibid., Grant to Howick, April 30, 1832.

165. C.O. 137/172. Belmore to Goderich, July 20, 1831.

By 1832 the situation in the colonies had become serious. The Demerara insurrection had been put down by force, but the spirit of discontent remained alive, and the Negroes, outwardly impassive, were agitated, jealous and suspicious.[166] A revolt broke out among the slaves in Jamaica in 1832; the leaders were slaves employed in situations of the greatest confidence, who were consequently exempted from all hard labour.[167] Delay was dangerous, not only for the sake of the intrinsic humanity and policy of emancipation, but in order that expectation and conjecture should cease.[168] Nothing was so dangerous as the undefined and vague expectations of the Negro mind.[169] Suspense paralyzed the planters' efforts and drove the slaves to sullen despair.[170] The Demerara rebellion had set the ball rolling, nobody could say where it would stop.[171] By 1832 it was not a question of Negro rebellions if but Negro rebellions unless emancipation.[172] In Britain, St. Domingo was on everyone's lips and in everyone's mind; emancipation was the only way in which the catastrophe of a servile and racial war could be averted. As the Tsar of Russia was to realise thirty years later, it was better to begin the abolition of slavery from above than to wait until it began to abolish itself from below.

(h) Abolitionist Propaganda

In 1823 the West Indians had been urged to set their house in order. Ten years later they had done practically nothing to comply with the wishes of the Government and people of Britain. Why was contumacy thus allowed to continue unrestrained for so long, when it must have early been evident that the colonists were neither to be cajoled nor intimidated? For this long respite the colonists could thank not their pretensions to independence, nor the fear of the slaves, nor the strength of the West Indian interest, nor their powerful friends, so much as the policy and shortcomings of the abolitionists themselves.

The opprobrium which the West Indians heaped on the abolitionists testifies indeed to the effectiveness of abolitionist propaganda. The abolition-

---

166. C.O. 111/44. D'Urban to Bathurst, May 5, 1824.
167. C.O. 137/182. Belmore to Goderich, May 2, 1832.
168. C.O. 111/44. D'Urban to Bathurst, May 5, 1824.
169. Ibid., D'Urban to Bathurst, May 15, 1824.
170. C.O. 28/111. Smith to Goderich, May 7, 1833.
171. C.O. 28/92. Warde to Bathurst, confidential, Aug. 27, 1823.
172. Daniel O'Connell: "The planter was sitting, dirty and begrimed, over a powder magazine, from which he would not go away, and he was hourly afraid that the slave would apply a torch to it." (*Parl. Deb.*, Third Series, Vol. XIII, page 77, May 24, 1832). Buxton: "He was convinced that it was absolutely indispensable that this question should be settled, and further, that if it was not settled in that House, it would be settled elsewhere, in another and more disastrous manner." (Ibid., Third Series, Vol. XVI, page 827. March 19, 1833). Stanley: "They were compelled to act; for they felt that take what course they might, it could not be attended with greater evil than any attempt to uphold the existing estate of things." (Ibid., Third Series, Vol. XVIII, page 538, June 10, 1833).

ists were accused of hawking for subscriptions in all directions,[173] of sending their emissaries to disturb every market town in the Kingdom,[174] and their itinerant adventurers everywhere with petitions ready prepared,[175] which they took cut and dried from their pockets.[176] The bona fides of their leaders was questioned, their agitation was attributed to interested motives,[177] they were accused of false humanity[178] and the misdirection of their benevolent activities,[179] of ignorance of the British colonies,[180] and in general of unfairness to the colonists.[181] The colonists attacked them violently. The two Houses of Assembly of St. Vincent called them innovators, visionaries,

---

173. *Parl. Deb.*, NS, Vol. XXI, page 1697. Mr. Hudson Gurney, June 3, 1829.

174. Ibid., NS, Vol. X, page 1159. Mr. Baring, March 16, 1824.

175. Ibid., page 1012, Mr. Watson Taylor, March 15, 1824.

176. *Correspondence between John Gladstone, M.P. and James Cropper on the present state of slavery in the British West Indies and in the United States of America, and on the importation of sugar from the British settlements in India* (Liverpool, 1824), page 25. Gladstone's letter, Dec. 15, 1823 (Referred to hereafter as *Gladstone-Cropper, Correspondence*).

177. Wilberforce was accused of having inherited a West Indian estate which he sold preparatory to his abolition labours (*Life of Wilberforce*, Vol. V, page 352, foot-note). Stephen, according to John Bull, had done the same, and Buxton was forced to deny that he had ever owned a hogshead of sugar or an acre of land in the West Indies (Cit. *Klingberg*, pages 186 and 189, footnotes).

178. C.O. 137/172. "An Enemy to Cant and Humbug" wrote to the freeholders of Jamaica, in the *Jamaica Courant and Public Advertiser*, Sept. 15, 1832: "One noble personage, Lord Grosvenor, knows no law which authorizes slavery, and *wonders* that our slaves are not emancipated! . . . His hundred thousands would make thousands comfortable. His starving countrymen may think of this, and he would fain blind their eyes with his humanity and slave-emancipating mania!" Mr. Bernal, of Rochester, accused the abolitionists of having called "affected religion and bastard morality" to their aid (*Parl. Deb.*, Third Series, Vol. I, page 651. Nov. 23, 1830).

179. See *Parl. Deb.*, NS, Vol. XVIII, page 1047. March 6, 1828. James Wilson told "his compassionate brethren over the way, who were for galloping away thousands of miles from their own country and seeking to bestow their benevolence everywhere but in those places where it was most wanted, 'look at home, go to Ireland and Scotland.'" Tory philanthropy in Michael Sadler joined hands with Cobbett and Attwood to draw attention to the white, the infant slaves at home, who labored fifteen hours a day. (Ibid., Third Series, Vol. XIV, page 1256. Aug. 8, 1832).

180. *Quarterly Review*, Vol. XXIX, 1823, page 495. Wilberforce and Buxton had never seen the West Indies; Macaulay and Stephen had left years before. See too C.O. 28/92, Mr. Hamden in a debate in the council, Sept. 3, 1823: "An honest assembly forming their judgments on the representations of West Indian society, given by Messrs. Wilberforce, Macaulay, Stephen and Buxton, could not do less than bind us in chains of iron."

181. C.O. 137/172. "An Enemy to Cant and Humbug"—"we take them to be ignorant, conceited, interested intermeddlers in our business. They are all this, and mischievous to boot. They seek our ruin . . . one from interest—a second from the vanity of having and using influence—a third from a fanatic feeling—a fourth because he is mad and must do mischief—a fifth from spite." Also, C.O. 137/186, Memorial of the Jamaica deputies, Nov. 29, 1832—"We are represented as the outcasts of civilization—as the oppressors and persecutors of the miserable African, and where we had a right to look for sympathy and succour we have had the mortification to find our misfortunes met by a portion of our fellow subjects with the triumph and ridicule of declared enemies." Lord Dudley and Ward thought misrepresentations natural "in this struggle for the prize of vituperative eloquence, to be awarded by pious men and sympathizing ladies." (*Parl. Deb.*, NS, Vol. XIV, page 1161.—March 7, 1826.) Baring condemned the "kind of quackery abroad," which excited a feeling as if the slaves were in a most miserable and abominable condition" (Ibid., NS, Vol. XVIII, page 1035, March 6, 1828), and thought it "a little hard, because parliament and the people find their moral sense improved, to throw the whole connexion of their sins upon the colonies." (Ibid., NS, Vol. XV, page 221. April 14, 1826.)

counterfeit philanthropists and fanatics, and likened them to tigers and hy-
enas.[182] Colonial Governors commented caustically on the garbled versions,
the wrong impressions and falsifications of colonial events and occurrences
in the abolitionist press.[183] The abolitionists became so unpopular that they
dared not let it be known that suggestions emanated from them,[184] and Wilberforce had cause to be grateful that he lived in a country in which the law
afforded protection from personal injury.[185]

The abolitionists, their opponents complained, directed their arguments
more to the sympathy than to the conviction of their audiences.[186] The
question of slavery was considered one of conscience rather than of judgment, and persons quieted their consciences for the year by subscribing to a
missionary society or signing a petition against Negro slavery.[187] But it was in
this appeal to the sentiments and religion of the people that the strength of
the abolitionists lay, for only the people of Great Britain could abolish slavery. Why then was this appeal to the religion and morality and justice of the
people of Britain, on which Wilberforce boasted that he relied,[188] not made
before 1833? In the first place Wilberforce was quite unfit to be the leader
of this revolutionary crusade—for emancipation was a revolutionary change.
Wilberforce's conservative outlook was an asset when, as before 1823, the
contest was fought out mainly in Parliament. But even then he was thought
too moderate by many,[189] and the man who had sat on the secret committee to investigate and repress popular discontent in 1817,[190] whose house
the masses nearly attacked, for his support of the Corn Law of 1815,[191] who
thought Russell's first Reform Bill too radical,[192] was hardly the person to give
the lead when the centre of gravity was shifting from Parliament to the con-

---

182. *Parl. Deb.*, NS, Vol. XI, page 1413. Wilberforce. June 15, 1824.

183. C.O. 137/160. Manchester to Horton, private, Dec. 19, 1825; C.O. 137/165. Manchester to Horton, private, Dec. 7, 1827; C.O. 111/49. D'Urban to Horton, Dec 27, 1825.

184. See for instance *Liverpool Papers*. Add. Mss. 38578, folio 11, Stephen's appeal to Peel, Aug. 8, 1811, on behalf of a Negro, John Wise. Stephen admitted that if there was a chance of obtaining justice, the knowledge that the Negro had the patronage of the African Institution would preclude it. See too *Canning, Correspondence*, Vol. I, page 228, where Macaulay begged Canning, Oct. 8, 1824, not to divulge that a suggestion about female slaves had come from him, as that would render it much more obnoxious to the West Indians.

185. *Wilberforce, Private Papers*, page 180. Wilberforce to his son Samuel, April 25, 1818. See too Wilberforce's diary, April 22, 1818, "I used to fear I was too popular." (*Life of Wilberforce*, Vol. IV, page 378.)

186. *Quarterly Review*, Vol. XXIX, 1823, page 488.

187. *Parl. Deb.*, NS, Vol. IX, page 348, Mr. Baring, May 15, 1823.

188. *Life of Wilberforce*, Vol. IV, page 291.

189. *Parl. Deb.*, Vol. XXXVIII, page 298, Wilberforce, April 22, 1818.

190. B. Coupland: *Wilberforce*, pages 411–417.

191. Ibid., pages 406–408.

192. *Wilberforce, Private Papers*, page 265. Wilberforce to his son Samuel, March 4, 1831.

stituencies. He realised, of course, the need of this signal,[193] but it was impossible for him to give it. Wilberforce lacked the single-mindedness of purpose which is so essential in leaders of great causes, and Stephen urged him in vain to devote himself entirely to the Negroes.[194] Wilberforce remained Wilberforce[195] and the cause of emancipation suffered. Stephen, more restless than his leader, was restrained. He grew quite sick of the West Indies, and lost all patience with a policy the aim of which was merely "to load the shelves of a minister with laboured memorials, to haunt him with conferences for years, and at last to be turned round by the whisper that a governor stands well with great men, and must not have his toes trod upon."[196]

The second reason for postponing the general appeal to the feelings of the public was that the abolitionists feared that they would be joined by men of ulterior motives. "How," Stephen asked Wilberforce, "is a cry to be raised without the help of the disaffected, or of men who will take widely different ground from what you or I could decorously or even conscientiously defend?"[197] But by 1828, when the interested men had joined the ranks, uninvited, Stephen was convinced that the only remedy for the "very unfortunate sedative" of leaving the issue in the hands of Government was an appeal to the people at large.[198] Of this the Government was mortally afraid. Castlereagh had already objected to the way in which the abolition-

---

193. *Bathurst* Mss., pages 414 and 418. Wilberforce to Bathurst, private, June 29 and July 4, 1816. Wilberforce opposed the female anti-slavery associations (*Life of Wilberforce*, Vol. V, page 264. To Babington, Jan. 31, 1826.)

194. *Life of Wilberforce*, Vol. III, pages 486–487. Stephen to Wilberforce, 1810—"If you, who *must* be the public leader, are to be only a battering-ram to be pushed forward, instead of a forehorse in the team to pull as well as guide the rest, the cause is lost, the abolition is undone. It will sink under the weight of your daily epistles; your post privilege will be the bondage of Africa, and your covers the funeral pyre of her newborn hopes. Millions will sigh in hopeless wretchedness, that Wilberforce's correspondents may not think him uncivil or unkind, and that no anonymous or unknown supplicant may have his individual tale, whether true or false, neglected." Compare Stephen to his wife: "I have been all day at work for the negroes, and I hope to be so tomorrow and Thursday. Hitherto I have not much misspent this year 1816." C. E. Stephen: *The Right Honourable Sir James Stephen. Letters with Biographical notes* (printed for private circulation only, 1906), page 4, Jan. 2, 1816. Stephen once put off an appointment to go to Harrow with his wife: "My time is quite consumed with these African matters, and I feel that it would be very unjustified if I indulged myself at the expense of sacrificing the opportunities of contributing my pittance of aid towards these great interests." (Ibid., page 5, Jan. 5, 1816.) "The last ten years of my life," wrote Stephen in 1829, "have been very busy ones, devoted not exclusively but mainly to promoting, as far as was compatible with the duties of my office, the extinction of slavery." (Ibid., page 16. To Alfred Stephen.)

195. "It was a common saying of him (Wilberforce) . . . that you might safely predicate his vote, for it was certain to be opposed to his speech." *Stephen, op. cit.*, page 79.

196. Ibid., Vol. IV, pages 240–241. Stephen added: "I really think that we shall do nothing effectual to check colonial crimes till we blazen them to the English public, and arm ourselves with popular indignation."

197. Ibid., Vol. III, page 550.

198. *Wellington, Despatches*, Vol. IV, page 554. Stephen to Wellington, July 24, 1828.

ists boasted of numerous petitions,[199] and Wellington begged Stephen to remember St. Domingo.[200]

"Colonial abuses, colonial obduracy, colonial hypocrisy, were the only topics for agitation, but colonial castigation and colonial emancipation were tabooed."[201] The abolitionists continued to rely for success upon aristocratic patronage, parliamentary diplomacy and private influence with men in office. The African Institution, which had not condescended to look below the station of Member of Parliament for aid, died of its own dignity in 1827, and was replaced by the Anti-Slavery Society, equally addicted to moderation, compromise and delay.[202] It deprecated extreme measures and feared popular agitation. "It was therefore necessary that another order of men, of bolder and more robust, if somewhat less refined, natures should now appear to take the work in hand, not so much to supersede as to supplement the exertions of their more wary and hesitating colleagues."[203]

By 1830 these new men appeared on the scene. Sturge set himself to evoke that moral insurrection among the people which was necessary to abolish slavery root and branch. George Stephen bettered the instruction of his opponents and placarded the walls of London. The Agency Committee was set up,[204] agents were sent everywhere, and the divergence over the question of compensation nearly split the party. Otway Cave refused to allow the wishes or convenience of individuals, however eminent or meritorious, to weigh again the lives and liberties of millions, and introduced resolutions which might be called a declaration of the Rights of the Negro.[205] Slavery was bound to fall, as soon as the abolitionists desisted from their petty war of outposts.[206] The famous Pownwall amendment at the great meeting of the Anti-Slavery Society in May 1830 showed the state of public feeling. Buxton had proposed the usual resolutions, "admirably worded; admirably indignant, but—admirably prudent." Then Pownwall rose to put his amendment and

---

199. *Wilberforce, Correspondence*, Vol. II, page 501. Wilberforce to Macaulay.

200. *Wellington, Despatches*, Vol. IV, pages 556–557, July 25, 1828.

201. *Stephen, op. cit.*, page 98.

202. Ibid., page 77. "Like its predecessor, the African Institution, the Anti-Slavery Association drooped under an accumulation of political bias and aristocratic ascendancy, and worse than either, of tame monotony."

203. *Richard, op. cit.*, page 79.

204. *Stephen, op. cit.*, page 168. While the "Anti-Slavery Reporter" still confined itself to the antiquated duty of dissecting and criticising the slave codes of the colonies, the Agency Committee was a hundred miles ahead and accelerated the accomplishment of the work by at least one generation.

205. *Parl. Deb.*, NS, Vol. XXI, pages 1744–1746, June 4, 1829. Cave was the only teller for the ayes, and was opposed among others by William Smith.

206. Ibid., NS, Vol. XXV, pages 1228–1229. Otway Cave, July 16, 1830. Cave thought the slaves entitled to take by force, if Government refused to intervene, what force and not right had dispossessed them of.

make history. It was a spark to the mine. Buxton deprecated, Brougham interposed, Wilberforce waved his hand for silence, but eventually Wilberforce was compelled to put the amendment, "which was carried with a burst of exulting triumph that would have made the Falls of Niagara inaudible at equal distance."[207] The policy of the new men was admirably stated by one of Sturge's friends: "Sin will lie at our door if we do not agitate, agitate, agitate. We must all become Radicals and Unionists, for if we sit down quietly with our hands before us government will laugh at us. The people must emancipate the slaves, for the government never will."[208]

(i) The Emancipation Movement after 1830

In the midst of the humanitarian ardour in Britain came the successful French Revolution of 1830 to increase the pressure of the reform movement in Britain. The agitation for emancipation was postponed until the Reform Bill was passed. Not only did the Reform Bill, by abolishing the rotten boroughs, diminish the strength of the West Indian interest in Parliament, but in the same way as the revolutionary wave in France had given rise to the Friends of the Blacks, so the powerful reform movement in Britain gave great impulse to that demand for the reform of all abuses, of which slavery was the greatest and most obvious.

In the humanitarian and religious excitement there was nothing in any way savouring of economic considerations. The people were spontaneously moved by the conviction that slavery was a disgusting and immoral system, and therefore it had to go.

The colonial system was a system which killed the labourers in thousands, at a rate at which, Buxton calculated, the earth would have been depopulated in fifty years.[209] In Britain the mortality in the coal mines was equally excessive; but the inference was not that sugar must be cultivated and coal produced.[210] The reform of the system of sugar production was the first step on the road to reform of inhuman conditions in general. Whilst the convicts and prostitutes of New South Wales were reproducing, whilst America teemed with life, the West Indies remained desolate. What the Spaniards had done on the continent for gold, the British were doing in the islands for sugar.[211] This alarming mortality was accompanied by an appalling inflic-

207. *Stephen, op. cit.*, pages 120–122.
208. *Richard, op. cit.*, pages 101–102. Letter to Sturge from a friend in London, March 28, 1833.
209. *Parl. Deb.*, NS, Vol. XVIII, page 1042. March 6, 1828. The slave population had decreased by 52,000 in 11 years preceding 1832. (Ibid., Third Series, Vol. XIII, page 45. May 24, 1832.)
210. As Wilmot Horton inferred. Ibid., NS, Vol. XV, page 514. April 20, 1826.
211. Ibid., Third Series, Vol. XIII, page 54. T. B. Macaulay, May 24, 1832.

tion of punishments which, in Demerara, one of the crown colonies, in the *improved* state of society in 1829, amounted to over 20,000 per year, or one punishment a year for every third slave. If the laboring classes in Britain had been punished in the same proportion, between six and seven million punishments would have been inflicted.[212] These punishments in Demerara meant upwards of two million lashes annually.[213] If this was Demerara, what must have been the condition of the slaves in the legislative colonies?

Furthermore, in 1833, whilst some of the white colonists were talking and plotting treason, the free people of colour, a numerous class, were steadfastly loyal. They were men of property,[214] and compared favourably with the impecunious whites.[215] In refinement, morals, education and energy they were superior to the whites, who had nothing but old rights and prejudices to maintain their illiberal position.[216] Emancipation would deprive the whites of their traditional position, which had imbued them with a love not only of the labour of their slaves but of power over them,[217] but on the free people of colour depended the preservation of the colonies.[218] Whatever was valuable in human society was manifestly at stake in the colonies. "The ultimate end of human society—the security of life, property and reputation—must be preferred to its subordinate ends—the enjoyment of particular franchises."[219]

Whilst in Parliament the Government was bartering for colonial cooperation and gilding the bitter pill by their gift of twenty millions,[220] outside Parliament the opposition to slavery had become a settled religious feeling. The apostles might have recognized slavery, but the people were better Christians than the apostles.[221] Petitions to Parliament were measured by

---

212. C.O. 111/68. Stephen to Hay, Feb. 18, 1829.

213. *Parl. Deb.*, Third Series, Vol. XIII, page 45. Buxton, May 24, 1832.

214. Ibid., NS, Vol. XVII, pages 1424–1426. Petition of Free People of Colour of Jamaica, presented by the Earl of Harrowby, June 29, 1827. In Trinidad, in 1821, £756.14s. was given in poor relief to whites, only £70.13s. to free coloured people; in 1822 the figures were £1030.9.6d and £216.13s. (C.O. 295/62).

215. It was said that out of 45 members of the Jamaica Legislature not ten of them had any landed property, many were not solvent but were bankrupt attorneys and slave managers. Not one of them could, after paying his debts, raise half-a-crown in the pound. Admiral Fleming, *Parl. Deb.*, Third Series, Vol. XVIII, pages 467 and 472, June 7, 1833.

216. C.O. 28/111. Smith to Stanley, May 23, 1833.

217. Ibid. Smith to Stanley, July 13, 1833.

218. Ibid. Smith to Stanley, May 23, 1833: "You will see a large policy in present circumstances in bringing these castes forward. They are a sober, active, energetic and loyal race; and I could equally depend on them if need came, against either slaves or white militia."

219. C.O. 295/93. Stephen to Howick, Aug. 25, 1832.

220. See C.O. 137/88. Mulgrave to Stanley, Aug. 5, 1833; and C.O. 28/111. Smith to Stanley, July 13 and July 19, 1833, for the effects of the increased compensation on the colonial planters.

221. This was a question asked by Lord Wynford. *Parl. Deb.*, Third Series, Vol. XVII, page 1341. May 17, 1833.

the yard,[222] gradual emancipation was denounced as perpetual slavery,[223] and London was treated to the spectacle of black-coated delegates from all over the country walking down the Strand to memorialize the Government. The treatment of the West Indian Negroes was a stain upon a Christian age and upon a country professing itself Christian.[224] The reformation of the system had been blinked and delayed until the agitation acquired a force and momentum which made further trifling impossible. The slave owners might have vested rights, but the slaves had vested wrongs.[225] Even Cobbett abandoned his bitter attacks on the abolitionists. Whilst still stressing the conditions of the factory workers at home, he refused to be a party to any scheme which would take an additional farthing from the pocket of the people of Great Britain in order to make compensation to the planters.[226]

As with the Reform Bill, so with the Emancipation Act, the people of Great Britain did not get all they had worked for. The planters, on the other hand, got perhaps more than they deserved. Emancipation was gradual after all, the apprenticeship system left the slaves half bond and half free,[227] and led to many difficulties in the future. The great change was still to be consummated. But a new life had begun for the blacks.

---

222. Ibid., Third Series, Vol. XIII, page 1180. Lord Suffield, July 2, 1832, presented a petition signed by 146,000 persons, 76 yards long.

223. Ibid., Third Series, Vol. XVII, page 839. Lord Suffield, May 2, 1833.

224. Ibid., page 1217. Stanley, May 14, 1833.

225. Ibid., Third Series, Vol. XIX, page 1069. Andrew Johnston, July 22, 1833.

226. Ibid., Third Series, Vol. XV, page 1179. Feb. 27, 1833. Cobbett had in the past frequently pilloried Wilberforce and, on his flight to America after the suspension of Habeas Corpus in 1818, had exulted that in America there were no Wilberforces. Cobbett wrote of missionary Smith: "There is more outcry about the death (a natural one) of this mischievous canter than there was about all the cuttings and killings of 1817 and 1819. This fellow was laboring to plunge a whole colony into bloodshed. He was tried and condemned, and then he was *pardoned*. He has since *died*. What, was the fellow to be immortal?" Cit. *Smart*, Vol. II, page 179 (footnote).

227. *Parl. Deb.*, Third Series, Vol. XVII, page 1248. Viscount Howick, May 14, 1833. O'Connell, an ardent advocate of emancipation, lashed the ministerial plan with his sarcasm: "There had been nations of hunters, and of shopkeepers, and of agriculturists, and of masters and slaves; but never before had they heard of a nation of masters and apprentices. An old woman of eighty was to become an apprentice, and she was to be told that, if she lived till ninety-two, she would be out of her time, and might commence a life of gaiety and jollity on her own account. They were to send out stipendiary magistrates to compel the negroes to work—it would be more wise to call in the police to scold and punish the servants in every house in London." (Ibid., Third Series, Vol. XVIII, page 313, June 3, 1833.)

CHAPTER NINE

The Foreign Slave Trade

The abolitionists had not confined their anathemas and humanitarianism to the British slave trade. After 1807 they turned their attention to the twin problems of improving the condition of the Negroes and of abolishing the slave trade in general. The deity of the African Institution was not, as some feared, asleep in 1815, he was only journeying.[1] The era of a general peace in Europe seemed a providential opportunity for securing the repose of Africa.

The power first approached was France. With her mercantile marine destroyed, St. Domingo under a black Emperor, and almost all her colonies and African settlements in British hands, the task might have seemed easy. But the intensive preparations made on the morrow of the peace to renew the slave trade augured ill for the success of the abolition cause. The Amis des Noirs were in bad odour, and to Wilberforce's suggestion that the pro-pagandist committee of literary men be set up, Humboldt replied: "toute le monde se gendarmera contre cette sociéte." Public opinion was more con-cerned with the taxes on drink than with Africa,[2] and it was impossible to get articles on abolition inserted in the press.[3]

The abolitionists and the government turned therefore to flattery and persuasion. Wilberforce hoped for much from the virtues, humanity and religious feelings of Louis XVIII;[4] while Grenville felt sure that his long resi-

---

1. *Parl. Deb.*, Vol. XXXI, page 1128. Mr. Barham, July 5, 1815.
2. *Life of Wilberforce*, Vol. IV, pages 182 and 213–214. May 15, 1814 and Sept. 16, 1815.
3. Ibid., Vol. IV, page 212. Gen. Macaulay to Wilberforce, Oct. 8, 1815.
4. *Parl. Deb*, Vol. XXVII, page 639. May 2, 1814.

dence in England had implanted in his breast an indignant abhorrence of the slave trade.[5] Shall it be said, Stephen wrote eloquently to Louis XVIII, that France by her sordid example stood between the repentance of Europe and the deliverance of Africa?[6]

Not content with flattery the abolitionists would even have gone the length of coercion. They demanded that none of the French colonies should be restored except in return for an explicit promise that no slaves would be imported into them.[7] When at Vienna Britain had to be content with a French abolition in five years, the abolitionists were bitterly disappointed. Consequently they began to importune the Cabinet to grant a colony to France as compensation for immediate abolition, an idea which Clarkson had picked up in Paris.[8] They evidently thought that abolitions was worth not only one island but anything and everything.[9] Liverpool preferred a grant of money to the cession of a colony, and authorised Wellington to offer two millions and even three.[10] But he was prepared to surrender a colony in return for immediate abolition, and in order to dissuade the French from attempting the reconquest of St. Domingo. It must, however, be a West Indian colony, and he chose Trinidad in preference to Guiana, which could provide cotton for British manufactures.[11] The French in their turn suggested Mauritius.[12] But Britain was not to be so easily duped. Canning realised the extent of the importations into the French island of Bourbon, off the east coast of Africa. If France were given Mauritius as well, there would be no limit to their importations, and from

---

5. Ibid., Vol. XXVIII, page 305. June 27, 1814.

6. *Life of Wilberforce*, Vol. IV, page 174.

7. Ibid., Vol. IV, page 172. Wilberforce to Liverpool; Ibid., Vol. IV, page 182. Wilberforce to Macaulay, May 21, 1814, telling him to remind Castlereagh; *Castlereagh, Correspondence*, Vol. IX, page 401. Wilberforce to Castlereagh, March 28, 1814; Ibid., Vol. X, page 47 and 49. Macaulay to Castlereagh, May 29 and May 30, 1814.

8. *Castlereagh, Correspondence*, Vol. X, page 103. Wellington to Castlereagh, Sept. 2, 1814; Vol. X, page 117. Clarkson to Castlereagh, Sept. 10, 1814. See also Vol. X, page 110, Castlereagh to Wellington, Sept. 9, 1814. "I suspect the notion is picked up in some of those conversations which he provokes with the Philanthropists at Paris, and is thrown out, if not *insidiously*, to force us into some offer of this description in the vain hope of its being accepted. Mr. C. is not, as I believe, partial to the Government, and extremely likely to impute to them the having fallen short in their exertions upon this point."

9. *Liverpool Papers*, Add. Mss. 38416, folios 334–334(v). Liverpool to Wellington, private, Sept. 7, 1814. See too Add. Mss. 38566, folios 184–185. Wilberforce to Liverpool, Aug. 31, 1814, private.

10. Ibid., Add. Mss. 38416, folios 336–337. Liverpool to Wellington, private, Sept. 7, 1814.

11. *Castlereagh, Correspondence*, Vol. X, page 132. Liverpool to Wellington, Sept. 23, 1814. See too Ibid., Vol. XII, page 35, where Stephen, in 1818, suggested that Britain had more than one colony "which it would be real policy and advantage to transfer to her without a consideration, much more for such a benefit as even the temporary trade of Hayti."

12. *Wellington, Despatches*, Vol. I, page 296. Wellington to Canning, Sept. 21, 1822.

the two islands they could easily supply their West Indian colonies by a legitimate intercolonial trade.[13]

As regards Spain, Britain's assistance in the struggle with Napoleon seemed to hold out reasonable hope of success. But Spain after 1814 began to talk of abolition in eight years, and, with what seemed to Liverpool "sheer perverseness," insisted on continuing the slave trade north of the Equator,[14] while still desiring a continuation of the British subsidy. Britain could not afford to become purchasers on such extravagant terms of indulgences for Africa.[15] Eventually in 1818 a treaty was signed by which Spain, in return for £400,000, agreed to abolish the slave trade. The treaty was opposed in Parliament. Britain could not continue to be the general paymaster of Europe.[16] Sir Oswald Mosley denied that it was for Britain to teach Spain humanity and feared that the redemption of each African slave would mean slavery for thousands in the Spanish colonies in South America struggling to throw off the mother country's yoke;[17] while Lord Althorp thought the treaty was inspired by an ambition to be distinguished as the most charitable of all nations.[18]

Canning had argued in 1810 that the removal of the Portuguese Court to Brazil, the very home of slavery, and not any want of zeal or humanity, was responsible for Portugal's failure to adhere to the commercial treaty of 1808.[19] But in 1815 Portugal, too, though not a single step had been taken towards gradual abolition, demanded an extension of the limit to eight years, a demand which Liverpool thought inconceivable and unreasonable.[20] Spain and Portugal could not be allowed to continue the slave trade for eight years when France had consented to five.[21] Everything centred around Brazil, after her successful struggle for independence. By a treaty signed in 1810 Portugal had agreed expressly to abolish the slave trade, with such exceptions as were

---

13. Ibid., Vol. I, page 327. Canning to Wellington, Sept. 30, 1822. This is quite at variance with Canning's assurance to Wilberforce, Oct. 31, 1822, that "I have no objection at all to reconsider the question of the Mauritius. Indeed, I was personally and still am rather inclined to it." Ibid., Vol. I, page 474.

14. *Castlereagh, Correspondence*, Vol. XI, page 41. Liverpool to Castlereagh, Oct. 2, 1815. See too *Liverpool Papers*, Add. Mss. 38578, folio 28, where Liverpool wrote privately to Castlereagh, Nov. 20, 1818: "It can only be from ignorance and perverseness that the Spanish Government continue the trade north of the Line."

15. Ibid., Vol. X, page 112. Castlereagh to Liverpool, Sept. 9, 1814.

16. *Parl. Deb.*, Vol. XXXVII, page 244. Sir Gilbert Heathcote, Feb. 9, 1818.

17. Ibid., page 250.

18. Ibid., page 336. Feb. 11, 1818. The treaty was eventually approved by the Commons by a surprisingly small vote, 56 to 4.

19. Ibid., Vol. XVI, page 13. ****** March 12, 1810.

20. *Liverpool Papers*, Add. Mss. 38578, folios 21–21(v). Liverpool to Castlereagh, secret and confidential, Jan. 8, 1815.

21. Ibid., folios 16–17. Liverpool to Castlereagh. Dec. 9, 1814.

deemed necessary to supply the deficiency of population in Brazil. In 1822, therefore, Canning could justly describe it as monstrous to suppose that a provision made for the purpose of protecting the interests of Portugal in her colonial possessions could continue in force when Brazil had ceased to be a colony.[22] Further, Brazil was looking to the European powers for recognition. Such recognition could only be purchased by a frank surrender of the slave trade.[23] The one great question which hung about Britain's neck was the slave trade, and the one great mart of legal slave trade was Brazil. This legal slave trade was the pretext for all the slave trading carried on illegally, in violation of treaty as well as of law. There was the danger that France would recognise Brazilian independence, with the continuance of the slave trade. "We may come too late with our offer contingent upon its discontinuance, and we shall have missed, and missed irrecoverably, an opportunity of effecting the greatest moral good of which human society is now susceptible, (and) of getting rid of the most perplexing discussions with which the counsels of this country are embarrassed."[24]

If this did not succeed, there were still two courses which might be pursued with success. The first was that the colonial produce of countries which had not legally and effectually abolished the slave trade should be boycotted. This early attempt at sanctions was, in Canning's opinion, a regulation wholly within the power of every independent government.[25] The second course was that the Pope's co-operation should be sought with the Roman Catholic powers.

This desire to secure the abolition of the slave trade by all the European powers was dictated by two motives, the first humanitarian, the second economic.

Nothing in all these negotiations is so astonishing as the popular pressure exerted on the British Government. The foreign slave trade aroused in Britain a spontaneous warmth of feeling which was to be equaled only in the days preceding emancipation. In thirty four days from June 27, 1814, no fewer than 772 petitions, bearing nearly a million signatures, were presented to the House of Commons.[26] Wellington wrote that the people were ready to go to

---

22. *Wellington, Despatches*, Vol. I, page 381. Canning to E. M. Ward, Oct. 18, 1822.

23. Ibid., Vol. I, page 329. Canning to Wellington, Sept. 30, 1822.

24. *Canning, Correspondence*, Vol. I, pages 61–63. Memorandum of Canning for the Cabinet, circulated about Nov. 15, 1822.

25. *Wellington, Despatches*, Vol. I, pages 326 and 329. Canning to Wellington, Sept. 30, 1822. Liverpool had suggested this to Castlereagh as far back as Dec. 9, 1814. See *Liverpool Papers*, Add. Mss. 38578, folio 18.

26. *Klingberg, op. cit.*, page 146.

war for abolition,[27] and the Government was warned that at the Congress of Vienna the British plenipotentiary must speak for Africa.[28] Liverpool wrote to Wilberforce: "If I were not anxious for the abolition of the slave trade on principle, I must be aware of the embarrassment to which any government must be exposed from the present state of that question in this country."[29]

The sons of Wilberforce speak of the "friendly violence" the abolitionists exercised on the Government.[30] The phrase is as correct as it is picturesque. Wilberforce's policy was to apply to ministers in particular instances to show them that "our attention is wakefully directed to the subject, and that they also must be awake."[31]

Between this humanitarian pressure and the pressure of the industrial bourgeoisie striving for the removal of monopolies, the Government were in serious difficulties. No wonder slave questions nearly drove Huskisson mad.[32] This is not to say that the humanitarian agitation accomplished nothing. "Without the unceasing efforts of Wilberforce and his friends, Castlereagh and his government would have accomplished but little. . . . Without the sustained and eager insistence of an organised public opinion in this country, the responsible statesmen would have allowed the iniquitous traffic to continue under the pretext that it was impossible to do otherwise."[33] Liverpool confessed this candidly. "The question of the abolition of the slave trade," he wrote privately to Wellington, "is become so embarrassing that it would be expedient to purchase it by some sacrifice though it should be refused."[34] It was this popular feeling which explains why the negotiations for abolition were continued long after it was obvious that they were futile. "Whole loads of humbug" were brought every year upon the table of the House of Commons merely to gratify the feelings of the country.[35] "We shall never succeed," Wellington admitted to the Earl of Aberdeen, "in abolishing the foreign slave trade. But we must take care to avoid to take any steps which may induce the people of England that we do not do everything in our power to discourage and put it down as soon as possible."[36]

On the whole ministers were convinced that the abolitionist agitation did more harm than good. Wellington wished the question to be kept out

27. Ibid., pages 147–148.
28. *Life of Wilberforce*, Vol. IV, page 197.
29. Ibid., Vol. IV, page 209. Sept. 7, 1814.
30. Ibid., Vol. IV, page 133.
31. Ibid., Vol. IV, page 79. Wilberforce to Macaulay, Nov. 4, 1812.
32. *Huskisson Papers*, Add. Mss. 38752, folio 26. Huskisson to Horton, Nov. 7, 1827.
33. *The Cambridge History of British Foreign Policy* (Cambridge, 1922), Vol. I, page 499.
34. *Liverpool Papers*, Add. Mss. 38416, folios 334(v)–335. Sept. 7, 1814.
35. *Parl. Deb.*, NS, Vol. IX, page 349. Mr. Baring, May 15, 1823.
36. *Wellington, Despatches*, Vol. V, page 15. Sept. 4, 1828.

of discussion by public bodies and by the press.[37] Castlereagh was strongly impressed with "the sense of prejudice that results, not only to the interests of the question itself, but of our foreign relations generally, from the display of popular impatience which has been excited and is kept up in England on this subject." Foreign nations could not be persuaded that this sentiment was unmixed with views of colonial policy, and they saw in this very impatience of the nation "a powerful instrument through which they expect to force at a convenient moment the British government up on some favourite object of policy."[38] The executive should be left to pursue negotiations with its ordinary means of influence and persuasion, instead of being expected to purchase concessions on this point almost at any sacrifice.[39]

The zeal of ministers was often, and perhaps unfairly, questioned. It was only on the subject of the slave trade, said Brougham, that Government said they could do nothing.[40] Mr. Phillips expressed his doubts whether a declared and active opponent of the abolition of the British slave trade, down to the very period of its enactment, could be an adequate representative of the deep interest felt by Parliament and the country on that great question.[41] He compared the French promise to abolish in five years to the gamester's resolve to stop gambling after one last throw, or the highwayman's determination to abstain from acts of violence after one last winter.[42] "We cannot barter away the rights of others," said Grenville; "the lives and liberties of the nations of Africa have not been placed by our Creator at the disposal of France and England."[43]

But what could the Government do? Ministers pleaded and remonstrated. Abolition was unpopular in France, no law would pass the chambers, juries would not convict.[44] It had taken twenty years for abolition to become law in

37. *Wilberforce, Private Papers*, pages 145–146. Wellington to Wilberforce.

38. Compare Lord Clancarty to Castlereagh, from Brussels, Jan. 5, 1821, referring to the Dutch minister and the slave trade—"If this business, in which he knows we are much interested, should be again thrown open, it would give an advantage to him in another, on which this government is extremely anxious, viz. the settlement by convention of the rights of trade and establishment, particularly in the Indian Archipelago, and generally in the seas eastward of the Cape." (*Castlereagh, Correspondence*, Vol. XII, page 342.)

39. Quoted in *The Cambridge History of British Foreign Policy*, Vol. I, page 496. Castlereagh to Liverpool, Oct. 25, 1814. For Wellington's view see *Wellington, Despatches*, Vol. I, page 270. Wellington to the Rt. Hon. J.C. Villiers, Sept. 3, 1822.

40. *Parl. Deb.*, Vol. XVII, page 663, June 15, 1810.

41. Ibid., Vol. XXVIII, page 292. June 27, 1814.

42. Ibid., page 293.

43. Ibid., pages 322 and 331. June 27, 1814.

44. *Wilberforce, Correspondence*, Vol. II, page 292. Canning to Wilberforce, Oct. 25, 1814; *Bathurst Mss.*, page 496. Sir Charles Stuart to Londonderry, April 16, 1821; *Wellington, Despatches*, Vol. I, pages 295–296. Wellington to Canning, Sept. 21, 1822; Ibid., Vol. I, page 325. Canning to Wellington, Sept. 30, 1822.

Britain. It was not consistent with the progress of the human mind to adopt valuable truths at once.[45] They could not dictate to France. Did the British wish to bind all the world? Malouet had asked Macaulay.[46] It was not to be expected, Castlereagh urged, that France should be taught morality at the point of bayonet. "Morals were never well taught by the sword; their dissemination might sometimes be made a pretext for ambition, but the real object could not be long concealed; and it was to the light of experience, to the promulgation of wisdom and not to the exercise of violence, or the influence of war, and they could look with any prospect of success for the abolition of the slave trade."[47] Castlereagh recognised the difficulties of the situation. "My feeling is," he wrote to Liverpool, "that on grounds of general policy we ought not to attempt to tie France too tight on this question."[48] In framing a stipulation for an unwilling government, what guarantee would they have for its observance? So he begged the House to "moderate their virtuous feelings, and put their solicitude for Africa under the dominion of reason."[49] Much had been gained and Parliament ought to be satisfied.[50]

The government had indeed done its best. "The very principles," Liverpool repeatedly urged, "upon which some of them had opposed the abolition led them, when the traffic was by law abolished, to carry the law, if possible, into complete execution."[51] If humanitarian considerations were not sufficient to encourage ministers, they could always be influenced by economics. As Wilberforce wrote to Stephen about Castlereagh: "you have hit on the bait for him, if he be to be caught at all, by the exhibition of political consideration affecting our own interests, rather than any prospects of general philanthropy—not that he would not recognise these."[52]

With the foreign slave trade humanity and economics went hand in hand. The West Indian planters, who had persistently opposed the abolition of the British slave trade, were now the loudest advocates of the cause of humanity. The French said that Britain's pleas of having abolished the slave trade on the grounds of religion, justice and humanity were "all moonshine, mere hypocrisy,"[53] and thought that Britain merely sought to inflict upon the

---

45. *Parl. Deb.*, Vol. XXVIII, page 280. Castlereagh, June 27, 1814.
46. *Life of Wilberforce*, Vol. IV, page 186. Diary, June 4, 1814.
47. *Parl. Deb.*, Vol. XXVIII, pages 279 and 284. June 27, 1814.
48. Quoted in *The Cambridge History of British Foreign Policy*, Vol. I, page 451. May 19, 1814.
49. *Parl. Deb.*, Vol. XXVIII, pages 391 and 393. June 28, 1814.
50. Quoted in *The Cambridge History of British Foreign Policy*, Vol. I, page 499. Castlereagh to Liverpool, Jan. 26, 1815.
51. *Parl. Deb.*, Vol. XXIII, page 1189. July 23, 1812.
52. *Life of Wilberforce*, Vol. V, page 3 Aug. 19, 1818.
53. Ibid., Vol. IV, page 189. Diary, June 13, 1814, recording an interview with Liverpool.

French colonial possessions a portion of the evils which the partial abolition had brought upon her own.[54] They were wrong. Abolition had not been detrimental to the British West Indies. What was detrimental was the continuation of the slave trade to countries where the soil was vastly more fertile than in the old exhausted British islands. Brazil, Cuba, and other places were, in fact, in the position the British colonies had enjoyed in 1750. The West Indies, deprived of further importations, could not possibly hope to compete with those more fertile colonies unless the latter found themselves, by abolition, with a deficiency of labourers.

Hibbert and Jamaica had looked forward with dread to the end of the war, when France would be again in possession of extensive colonies in the West Indies.[55] Marryat thought that, in assisting Spain in her contest with Napoleon, they were fighting for liberty with one hand and slavery with the other.[56] Lord Holland, a West Indian proprietor, kept the slave trade before the House of Lords as persistently as Wilberforce kept it before the House of Commons. Britain seemed, in his opinion, to forget that she had ever entered into the merits of the question or adopted such grave resolutions.[57] With his new-born humanity, he denounced the slave trade as "a system of man-stealing against a poor and inoffensive people,"[58] and thought that "at Paris, at Madrid, and at Rio de Janeiro the cause has been very coldly, or at least very inefficiently, supported, if it has not actually been betrayed."[59] William Smith pointed to the strange fact that Wilberforce's address to the Prince Regent in 1814, concerning the total annihilation of the slave trade, had been supported and eulogized by the member for Liverpool, the member for Bristol, and a West Indian proprietor who might almost be considered the official agent for the colonial interest.[60] It was Barham, another West Indian, who introduced a bill to make penal the employment of British capital in the foreign slave trade, and even to make the insurance of ships in a slave trade voyage criminal. He wished to prevent British subjects from lending money on the security of property belonging to countries in which the slave trade had not been abolished. The temptation to lend money on these terms was

---

54. *Wellington, Despatches*, Vol. I, page 170. Wellington to Macaulay, May 8, 1821; Ibid., Vol. I, page 323. Canning to Wellington, Sept. 30, 1822.
55. *Parl. Deb.*, Vol. XVII, page 687. June 15, 1810.
56. Ibid., page 676.
57. Ibid., Vol. XVI, page 11****. March 12, 1810.
58. Ibid., Vol. XXVIII, page 349. June 27, 1814.
59. *Wilberforce, Private Papers*, pages 152–154. Lord Holland to Wilberforce, Nov. 13, 1815.
60. *Parl Deb.*, Vol. XXVII, page 647. May 2, 1814.

great. The price of slaves in the British Colonies was four times as high as the price in Cuba, and the profits were therefore proportionately great.[61]

The West Indian colonists always harped on the ruinous effects of the continuance of the slave trade. So long as it was permitted to continue, nothing which ministers might do on their behalf would be of any avail.[62] In 1830 the West Indian body in London suggested five remedies to meet the increasing distress of the colonies. The fifth read: "to adopt more decisive measures than any that have hitherto been employed to stop the foreign slave trade; on the effectual suppression of which the prosperity of the British West India Colonies, and the consequent success of the measures of amelioration now in progress in them, ultimately depend."[63] Their great adversary, stated the Jamaica envoys to Britain, was the prodigious increase of the slave trade. "The colonies were easily reconciled to the abolition of a barbarous commerce, which the advanced civilization of the age no longer permitted to exist; but they have thought, and apparently with reason, that the philanthropists should not have been satisfied with the extinction of the British trade."[64]

It was not the West Indian planters alone who recognised the economic advantages of the general suppression of the slave trade. Canning knew that this was the only thing which could save them from utter ruin,[65] and the abolitionists saw it as clearly as Canning. It is a mistake to think or assume that economic considerations found no place in abolitionist propaganda.

---

61. Ibid., Vol. XXX, pages 657–658. April 14, 1815; and Vol. XXXI, page 172. May 5, 1815. Marryat objected to the bill as tending to interdict all British trade with Brazil, Caracas and Buenos Ayres, which amounted to ten millions annually (Ibid., page 173). Mr. Baring said that every commercial body in Britain would petition against it (Ibid., page 174). After various amendments, the bill passed the House of Commons. In the House of Lords the second reading was moved by the Marquis of Landsdowne (Ibid., page 557. June 1, 1818). Greenville supported it, and Liverpool recommended it as the act of a West Indian proprietor, who "could not be supposed to be actuated by any of the wild ideas which were entertained by some men on the subject" (Ibid., page 851. June 16, 1815). Lord Ellenborough thought it loosely described, a crude act of legislation, "much more defective in mercy and in sense than any bill which he had ever known. . . . Because he might wish to protect the black man, he would not therefore subject the white man to definite prosecution and punishment" (Ibid., page 850). He remarked on the "savage character" of the bill, thought it "an emanation of that fanatical irregularity of mind, which would render that excellent measure the abolition of the slave trade odious in the West India islands" (Ibid., page 1064. June 30, 1815), and feared that the slave trade could never be put down so long as slavery was allowed to exist (Ibid., page 851). The Earl of Westmorland objected to the risk to which the innocent were exposed by the provisions of the bill (Ibid., page 606), and the bill was defeated.

62. C.O. 137/153. Committee of Correspondence of the Jamaica Assembly to agent Hibbert, Feb. 7, 1822.

63. H. of C. Sess. Papers, Accounts and Papers, 1830–1831. Vol. IX, No. 120. Statements, Calculations and Explanations submitted to the Board of Trade relative to the Commercial, Financial and Political state of the British West India Colonies since the 19th of May, 1830. Letter from Keith Douglas, Oct. 30, 1830, page 84. (Referred to hereafter as Statements to the Board of Trade).

64. C.O. 137/186. Memorial of Jamaica deputies, Nov. 29, 1832.

65. Canning, Correspondence, Vol. I, page 63. Memorandum for the Cabinet, Nov. 15, 1822.

Brougham knew as well as Wilberforce that if the slave trade was continued to Brazil and Cuba, the British planters would be undersold in every market.[66] The sanguine and general wish, and even expectation, which prevailed in Britain, that an explicit renunciation of the slave trade would be secured from France, was not confined to those who on general grounds were opposed to the slave trade. It extended to almost every individual connected with the colonies, who anticipated from the revival of the French slave trade the eventual ruin of the British West Indies.[67] Lord Grenville, in condemning the Government's policy of giving France five years of grace, refused to deal with the inexpediency of such a policy. It had not the weight of a feather in the balance when compared with the moral argument. But he admitted that it was unnecessary to urge economic considerations which were obvious to all. "You are well apprized what ruinous speculations this revival of the slave trade will infallibly produce in the French islands; you know by what inevitable consequence these must expose your own planters to an unequal and uncommercial competition."[68]

The French slave trade, which everyone dreaded so much, meant St. Domingo. Wilberforce declared that it "would in itself be an immense vortex of human calamity," and that its cultivation, in the five years allotted to France, would mean a sacrifice of 500,000 lives. "As a matter of policy some individuals, connected with the West India trade, might think that they should be seriously injured by the monopoly that France would acquire."[69] It was to prevent this that Liverpool had been prepared to offer France a colony or a grant of money. He was sure that France would only lose character and credit by an attempt to reconquer St. Domingo, which would certainly prove abortive. "I do not believe that the parties in the island will come even to any compromise with the French government which is not founded upon the independence of the colony and its right to trade with other countries as well as with France."[70]

For not only would the French reconquest of St. Domingo—or Hayti, to give it its new name—prove as ruinous to the British colonies as its competition had been in pre-war days, but Britain would lose by it a substantial trade, which Stephen computed at a more than £700,000 per annum. The exports from Hayti exceeded those from any British colony with the exception of Jamaica. Stephen sent a memorandum to Lord Castlereagh in preparation for

66. *Parl. Deb.*, Vol. XVII, page 665. Brougham, June 15, 1810; Ibid., Vol. XXXVI, page 1325. Wilberforce, July 9, 1817.
67. *Castlereagh Correspondence*, Vol. X, page 48. Macauley to Castlereagh, May 29, 1814.
68. *Parl. Deb.*, Vol. XXVIII, page 332. June 27, 1814.
69. Ibid., pages 272 and 274. June 27, 1814.
70. *Castlereagh, Correspondence*, Vol. X, pages 133–134. Liverpool to Wellington, Sept. 23, 1814.

the Congress at Aix-la-Chapelle.[71] Its main theme was that "it would be of unspeakable importance to Great Britain if means could be found to induce France to release her claim of sovereignty in Hayti, or, if this cannot be accomplished, at least to prevent her from asserting that claim by war." If the independence of Hayti was maintained, Britain "might . . . perhaps have, at no far distant period, a West Indian island worth more to our manufacturers than all our sugar colonies collectively, and without any drawback for the expenses of its government and its protection in time of war." Britain, he suggested, was to offer mediation between the Haytian chiefs and the French Government, on the basis of the independence of Hayti. By this she "might easily secure this commerce to herself, with all the advantages herein before pointed out, and even obtain perhaps a conventional monopoly of it, if this were an object we could inoffensively and decorously pursue. Of course, any appearance of a self-interested purpose would spoil all."

It was against this background that Stephen dealt directly with the slave trade. The possession of Hayti would hold out a dangerous temptation in time of war to the British colonists. The distress which undoubtedly existed in every island in which the Abolition Act was effectively enforced would encourage them to resort to the French flag for slaves; whereas the French had in the past obtained their slaves from British traders, the British colonists would in the future patronise the French. These arguments, Stephen admitted, impeached the policy of Britain's Abolition Act, and show what a serious view he took of the situation. In all this there was nothing whatsoever of humanitarianism or religion, and yet Stephen visualized a war for abolition. "It is politic to consider if the people of England are thus to lose their commerce, their money, and their benevolent hopes, by the moral apostacy of France, and her breach of solemn engagements, they may not add to it the loss of their temper; and whether, at some not far distant crisis, the peace of Europe may not be broken on the slave coast."

It will be useful now to consider why all these arguments, economic and otherwise, failed, and why France, Spain, Portugal and Brazil continued a traffic so utterly at variance with all the established religion and elementary justice. We have seen how the abolitionists blamed their own Government. On other occasions they found a scapegoat in the humanitarian Tsar. Brougham very early voiced the dissatisfaction the abolitionists felt at the Tsar's lukewarmness. "As for Alexander and the allies, they may cheaply enough be abolitionists, having not one Negro—as I doubt not the Bourbons

---

71. Ibid., Vol. XII, pages 4–35. Sept. 8, 1818.

are all for abolishing villenage. This liberality at other people's expence is, I believe, the whole amount of the magnanimity we hear so much of."[72] It should have been obvious that the Tsar had enough slaves in his own dominions on whom he could practise emancipation.[73] Clarkson's mission to Aix-la-Chapelle was a conspicuous failure; all that he obtained was an interview lasting an hour and a half, and an assurance from the Tsar that he entirely entered into their views.[74] The Tsar had agreed at Vienna to boycott the produce of slave-trading countries, but a decided preference was given to Brazilian produce. Wilberforce, in anger, thought that it was "a breach of faith of which any private man who should be guilty would forfeit for ever the character of a man of honor."[75] On behalf of his party, he wrote a strong letter to the Tsar expressing their disappointment, and plainly intimating that they would have an unfavourable opinion of his religious or moral character if he did not honestly exert his influence on their behalf at Verona.[76] The Tsar, however, did nothing, and Wellington, when the Congress was over, had to give him a piece of his mind.[77]

But the Tsar's tergiversation is an inadequate explanation of the failure to suppress the slave trade. It grieved Wilberforce that a great and high-minded people, a nation of cavaliers like the French, should continue the slave trade, while Britain, who had been called a shop-keeping nation, had given it up.[78] Canning wrote that the moral feeling was wanting as much in the French people as in the Government.[79] In Brougham's opinion so cold-blooded and base a prosecution of the slave trade could only have been perpetrated by French politicians of the worst school,[80] while Grenville wrote to Wilberforce that the French people were utterly and almost universally incapable of being moved by any moral considerations.[81]

All these appeals to nobility of character and chivalry, to virtuous feelings and high principles were nonsense. The British ministers knew that it was not national prejudices or national ignorance they were warring against,

---

72. *Wilberforce, Correspondence*, Vol. II, page 287. Brougham to Wilberforce. The date is probably 1814.

73. *Parl. Deb.*, NS, Vol. IX, page 349. Mr. Baring, May 15, 1823.

74. *Life of Wilberforce*, Vol. V, page 4. Clarkson to Wilberforce, Oct. 11, 1818. Clarkson was sent as the "nemo" who should apply his lever to Alexander. It was safer for him to go than Wilberforce or Macaulay. "He would be regarded as half Quaker, and may do eccentric things with less offence than you or I could." Ibid., Vol. V, page 3. Wilberforce to Stephen, Aug. 19, 1818.

75. *Liverpool Papers*, Add. Mss. 38578, folios 31–32. Wilberforce to Liverpool, Sept. 4, 1822.

76. *Life of Wilberforce*, Vol. V, pages 136–137. Wilberforce to Macaulay, Nov. 20, 1822.

77. *Wellington, Despatches*, Vol. I, page 618. Wellington to Canning, Nov. 29, 1822.

78. *Parl. Deb.*, Vol. XL, page 1543. July 7, 1819.

79. *Wellington, Despatches*, Vol. I, page 474. Canning to Wilberforce, Oct. 31, 1822.

80. *Wilberforce Correspondence*, Vol. II, page 287. Brougham to Wilberforce, 1814.

81. Ibid., Vol. II, page 300. Dec. 23, 1814.

but economic interest and the desire for commercial gain. Wellington wrote to Liverpool: "I did not tell Mr. Clarkson that it was a question of national vanity. It is one of profit; and those interested in carrying on the trade, who are the only persons who have any information on the subject, with very few exceptions, operate upon the national vanity by representing the question not only as one purely English, but as one of English profit and monopoly."[82] It may be presumed that those British forces which, as we shall see, were anxious to abolish the monopoly, would at least not view with any lack of interest the strong humanitarian appeal which aimed at achieving what they themselves were anxious to achieve.

In short the slave trade continued because it was profitable. It seemed to Canning as if those who continued the abominable traffic had a malicious pleasure in defeating the calculations of benevolence.[83] But Wellington gives us the real reason. The profits of a single voyage—and each ship could make two or three voyages a year—amounted to 300 per cent. On the other hand, the deterrent risks were negligible, the chances of punishment slight, and the punishment itself, when inflicted, ridiculously small in comparison with the crime, in which the rate of insurance for each trip did not exceed fifteen per cent.[84] The slave traders resorted to all kinds of ingenious and disreputable tricks in order to evade the law. On the papers of the vessel the tonnage was over-estimated, to enable it to carry a larger number of slaves.[85] False papers were used to convey the impression of laudable and honest commerce.[86] The slaves were left on shore until the time of embarkation, and until any watchful cruiser had been decoyed away. Frequently the flags of states which had not abolished the slave trade were used by subjects of states which had agreed to abolition as the cover for their own slave trade, and in at least

---

82. *Castlereagh, Correspondence*, Vol. X, pages 119–120. Wellington to Liverpool, Sept. 12, 1814.

83. *Wellington, Despatches*, Vol. I, pages 323–324. Canning to Wellington, Sept. 30, 1822.

84. Ibid., Vol. I, page 551. Minute of Wellington upon the slave trade, read at the Congress of Verona on Nov. 24, 1822.

85. *H. of C. Sess. Papers, Accounts and Papers*, 1824, Vol. XXIV. Class B, Correspondence with British Commissioners relative to the Slave Trade, pages 13–14. Gregory and Fitzgerald to Canning, April 29, 1823; Ibid., page 166. Gregory to Canning, June 1823; Ibid., Class A, Correspondence with Foreign Powers relative to the Slave Trade, page 22. Canning to Consul-General Chamberlain, Oct. 25, 1823. See also Ibid., *Accounts and Papers*, 1825, Vol. XXVII. Class B, Correspondence with Foreign Powers relative to the Slave Trade, pages 64–65. Chamberlain to Canning, Sept. 18, 1824. By this false estimate, it was legal to ship at the rate of four slaves for each real *bona fide* ton, instead of five slaves to every two tons.

86. Ibid., *Accounts and Papers*, 1823, Vol. XIX. Class B, Correspondence with Foreign Powers, page 9. Gregory and Fitzgerald to Londonderry, Sept. 20, 1822; "In the case of the Dos de Fevreiro, these documents were coupled with private letters of the same tenor, so numerous, so uniform, and so strong, that nothing short of the positive proofs found, of her being actually engaged in obtaining a cargo of slaves, could efface the impression of innocent and laudable commerce, made by the contents of these papers. . . . Papers of that description are used as a common means of deception."

one instance the slave traders did not hesitate to resort to violence to resist capture.[87]

These slave traders, however, could not have succeeded to the extent to which they did but for Government connivance and encouragement in France, Spain, Brazil and Cuba. The treaties signed at various times agreeing to abolition were mere scraps of paper. Colonial opinion in the French, Portuguese and Spanish colonies was unanimously in favour of the prosecution of a trade which was vital to their development.

In France the Government openly encouraged the trade. Slaves were landed in large numbers in the colonies, while men of war were in the harbours doing nothing.[88] When complaints were lodged with France consuls abroad, they pleaded that they had received no instructions.[89] In such conditions, what would be the use of a registry bill, on the lines of the law in force in the British colonies, with provisions for a reciprocal residence of agents to inspect the registers in each respective colony? Were not slave ships publicly fitted out at Havre and Bordeaux? Were not shares in the ventures of those ships openly on sale in all the seaports? Or would the fact, so well ascertained, that the French vessels filled with Negroes sailed from the coast of Africa, have been at all strengthened by the evidence that their cargoes were landed at Martinique in the face of a British supervisor?[90]

The same remissness was displayed by the Brazilian authorities. Violators of the abolition laws remained at large, confident that the penalty of the law would not be visited on them in the event of a second capture.[91] "These governments and the officers employed under them, consisting of individuals of the place, personally interested or immediately connected with those who are, easily dispense themselves from the rigorous enforcement of the

---

87. Ibid., page 28. Gregory and Fitzgerald to Londonderry, July 24, 1822. "These Spanish vessels were of large size, formidably manned and armed; purposely fitted out in order to carry into effect a determination of illegal slave trade by force of arms." Two British seamen were killed and five wounded.

88. C.O. 295/79. Letter of W. Neilson from Martinique, Oct. 20, 1827.

89. *H. of C. Sess. Papers, Accounts and Papers*, 1824, Vol. XXIV. Class A, Correspondence with Foreign Powers, page 60. Consul Parkinson to Canning from Pernambuco, March 21, 1823. A French ship had arrived from Martinique with one hundred and odd "passengers": "The circumstance of a French Vice Consul, and a Commander of a French Man of War, voluminously instructed as they are known to be on most points, being left without directions how to act against a daring violator of the laws of France excites remark *even here*."

90. *Wellington Despatches*, Vol. I, page 328. Canning to Wellington, Sept. 30, 1822. Wellington realized that even an effective register "would affect not a tenth of the existing evil, and (would) impose a hardship upon our own colonies which is neither required nor deserved." But he thought that its establishment would show governors, colonists and the public that the king was in earnest. (Ibid., pages 452–453. To Canning, Oct. 28, 1822.)

91. *H. of C. Sess. Papers, Accounts and Papers*, 1823, Vol. XIX. Class B, Correspondence with British Commissioners, page 110. Hayne to Londonderry, Feb. 16, 1822.

laws."[92] A British merchant, who had resided many years in Brazil, assured Wellington that it was useless to listen to the professions and promises of the Brazilian Government. The agriculture of the country was carried on exclusively by slaves from the districts prohibited by treaty. Vast fortunes had been made by the leading houses, but the trade was universal. "The government *may prohibit* their importations at the *principal* ports . . . but I am certain it will *leave it to be understood* at the time that *liberty will be given to land them on any contiguous part of the coast*, because the nation to a man, I am persuaded, will acquiesce in nothing short of this. It were as reasonable to make a treaty with their Government to give up the country altogether. It is by this alone that they subsist, and they are not a race of people to abandon their property to the *caprice of their rulers*."[93]

Cuba reinforced the moral of the story. The Spanish laws were defective, loosely and vaguely worded. Their execution was not committed to any particular department, and they were therefore neglected by all.[94] The British Commissioners could do nothing but protest and remonstrate; their protests were treated as waste paper, their remonstrances mingled with the air. They were always well received by the island authorities and promised redress, as far as it was possible, but the illicit slave trade increased and was daily carried on more systematically.[95] Vessels landed their cargoes on the coast, some even at the mouth of the harbor, and then came in in ballast professedly from the Danish island of St. Thomas.[96] The Governor was placed in a very delicate situation. However much he may have wished to execute the laws, he was surrounded by people who represented to him that the prosperity of the island depended upon the continuance of the traffic, that efforts to suppress it would probably be unsuccessful, and would bring upon him general unpopularity and odium.[97] The capital employed in the trade was in 1823 upwards of two and a half million dollars. By the subdivision of the shares, a large section of the population was directly concerned in the traffic.[98] The vessels fitted out were sometimes so large that they could not possibly have been the venture of a single individual. The ostensible proprietor was only

92. Ibid., 1824, Vol. XXIV. Class B, Correspondence with British Commissioners, page 14. Gregory and Fitzgerald to Canning, Sierra Leone, April 29, 1823.

93. *Wellington, Despatches*, Vol. IV, pages 370–371. W. A. Kentish to Wellington, April 13, 1828.

94. *H. of C. Sess. Papers, Accounts and Papers*, 1823, Vol. XIX, Class B, Correspondence with British Commissioners, page 99. Kilbee and Jameson to Londonderry, July 22, 1822.

95. Ibid., page 101. Aug. 2, 1822.

96. Ibid., 1824, Vol. XXIV. Class B. Correspondence with British Commissioners, page 174. Kilbee and Jameson to Canning, April 16, 1823.

97. Ibid., 1825, Vol. XXVIII. Class A, Correspondence with British Commissioners, page 67. Kilbee to Canning, June 14, 1824.

98. Ibid., page 142, Kilbee to Canning, Jan. 1, 1825.

"screening more cautious participators, who would be let into their respective shares of the advantages in the event of the success."[99] It was difficult for the British Commissioners to secure information where so many were directly implicated, where slave evidence was not accepted, and where no reward was offered to informers.[100] What a paradise Cuba was for the slave trader we can see from a letter of some French merchants in St. Jago de Cuba: "We consider there is no longer any risk upon our coast. . . . The sales meet with no opposition, and are carried on in some measure publicly."[101]

In this battle between morality and economies, the dice were heavily loaded against morality. British ministers realized that only self-interest would induce the French, Brazilian and Spanish Governments to consent to abolition. Canning confessed frankly to Wilberforce that he looked "for some sense of interest (if it can be created) rather than for any compunctious sentiment for the conversion of the mob as well as ministry."[102] Castlereagh was not satisfied with putting Clarkson's precis of the "Impolicy" before the Allied ministers. He added the proofs in the later chapters, that abolition was not ruinous, "a conclusion," he wrote to Wilberforce, "which many will listen to, who might be deaf to a moral appeal."[103] He stated this even more clearly in a letter to Clarkson himself: "I should have been most entirely satisfied to rest our case upon your short analysis, had I been arguing only with persons influenced by humane and moral considerations; but, as ministers are often hard-hearted persons when they consider themselves the guardians of public interests, I was very desirous of bringing before them the latter chapters of the same work, which go to prove, I think unanswerably,

---

99. Ibid., 1823, Vol. XIX. Class B, Correspondence with British Commissioners, page 29. Gregory and Fitzgerald to Londonderry, Sierra Leone, July 24, 1822.

100. Ibid., pages 95 and 99. Kilbee and Jameson to Londonderry, March 3, 1822, and July 22, 1822.

101. Ibid., 1825, Vol. XXVII. Class B, Correspondence with Foreign Powers, page 21. L. Dutocq and Co. to G. Segand and Son, Dec. 29, 1824. The British Commissioners had to face the same difficulties in Surinam. See Ibid., 1823, Vol. XIX. Class B. Correspondence with British Commissioners, page 136. Lefroy to Londonderry, Sept. 20, 1822: "So far from cordially co-operating with me, if any good has been effected since I have been here, it has been effected only by the most irksome and continuous extra judicial importunity on my part, which ought not to have been necessary, and at the utmost expense possible of trouble and expostulation to your Lordship and His Majesty's Ambassador in Holland." Lefroy suggested a Registry Act, which might in some degree be crippled, but could not be entirely defeated. In a letter to Joseph Planta, Oct. 24, 1822, page 140, he said that the Dutch men of war stationed there might as well have been away as far as the suppression of the slave trade was concerned. On Dec. 23, 1822, page 147, he repeated to Canning: "It is painful to me to be obliged to impugn the authorities here, at a period so long since the execution of the treaty, but I should be trifling with you and His Majesty's government, if I did not repeat my conviction that without much more energetic conduct on the part of those authorities, the slave trade in this colony will never be overcome."

102. *Wellington, Despatches*, Vol. I, page 474. Canning to Wilberforce, Oct. 31, 1822.

103. *Castlereagh, Correspondence*, Vol. X, page 199. Nov. 11, 1814.

that abolition is not incompatible with the prosperity of colonies and with the interest of the planters."[104]

Castlereagh was right. The British Commissioners in Havannah knew that the suppression of the trade would be produced not by moral but by economic forces.[105]

In view of the necessity of the slave trade to such countries as Brazil and Cuba, it was natural that Britain's efforts to persuade them to abolish the trade were attributed to selfish economic motives. In Cuba it was universally believed that abolition was a measure which Britain, under the cloak of philanthropy, but really influenced by jealousy of the island's prosperity, had forced upon Spain, and the illicit traders considered that they were thwarting the selfish views of Great Britain.[106]

This belief did no justice to the humanitarian aspect of the question which was so strong in Britain. But we can adduce one more instance to show the important part played by the economic aspect in the general abolition of the slave trade.

We have referred elsewhere to the suggestion that the produce of slave trading countries should be boycotted. This suggestion met with the cordial approval of the West Indian philanthropists. Marryat thought that the slave trade was being assisted by the fact that Britain conveyed the produce of Brazil to Europe. "We had in the beginning abolished it on the grounds of justice and humanity; but we had afterwards admitted policy into the calculation, and it was much to be feared our policy made us swerve from our purer

104. Ibid., Vol. X, page 201. Nov. 11, 1814.

105. *H. of C. Sess. Papers, Accounts and Papers*, 1823, Vol. XIX. Class B, Correspondence with British Commissioners, page 95. Kilbee and Jameson to Londonderry, March 3, 1822: "The low prices of colonial produce, which diminish the demand for negroes and the ability to pay for them, will be the best check to this illicit traffic." Page 101, Aug. 2, 1822: "We have no hesitation in giving it as our opinion that, but for the large stock of negroes imported during the three years previous to the abolition, and the present very low price of sugar, the slave trade would, at this moment be as brisk and extensive as during any period whatever." Page 105, to Canning, Jan. 23, 1823: "We have no hesitation in giving it as our opinion that this diminution is to be attributed solely to the general distress, as well agricultural as commercial, which has existed here for some time, and by no means to any increased exertions on the part of the authorities for the suppression of the traffic." Ibid., 1824, Vol. XXIV. Class B, Correspondence with British Commissioners, page 174, they repeated: "Latterly indeed, the traffic has not been so brisk, but this is principally to be attributed to the present depressed state of commerce and agriculture" (April 16, 1823). In Sierra Leone, however, the Commissioners thought that the trade would only be suppressed when a moral feeling had arisen among the Portuguese people; at that time no such feeling seemed to exist. Ibid., 1825, Vol. XXVII. Class A, Correspondence with British Commissioners, page 3. To Canning, May 15, 1824.

106. Ibid., 1825, Vol. XXVII. Class A, Correspondence with British Commissioners, page 143. Kilbee to Canning, Jan. 1, 1825.

motives."[107] In 1814 Lord Holland definitely recommended such a boycott by the great powers of the North and of Germany.[108]

Only the British West Indies would gain by the boycott. Were the boycott made general, Britain would be the greatest loser, for Britain monopolized the Brazilian carrying-trade. Hence Britain attempted to persuade the Continental Powers to adopt the boycott. Wellington was to propose it at Verona. If his proposal were met with the enquiry, whether Britain was also prepared to exclude the produce of slave-trading countries which came not for consumption but for transit, he was to express his readiness to refer that proposition for immediate consideration to his Government.[109] No answer was made to Wellington's proposal, though he observed "those symptoms of disapprobation and dissent which convince me not only that it will not be adopted, but that the suggestion of it is attributed to interested motives not connected with the humane desire of abolishing the slave trade!"[110] What was worse, Wellington later reported that he had reason to believe that the suggestion would be made, but by Russia, and would be intended as a blow to Britain.[111] Canning summed up the whole question for the Cabinet: "the proposed refusal to admit Brazilian sugar into the dominions of the Emperors and the King of Prussia was met (as might be expected) with a smile; which indicated on the part of the continental statesmen a suspicion that there might be something of self-interest in our suggestion for excluding the produce of rival colonies from competition with our own, and their surprise that we should consent to be the carriers of the produce which we would fain dissuade them from consuming."[112]

The boycott failed because the Brazilian carrying trade was too important, economically, to Britain to be sacrificed on the altar of humanity. Certainly the British statesmen wished the slave trade, on ethical grounds, to be abolished, but they had to choose between the conflicting forces of humanity and economic interest, and it was these contradictory forces which produced all the vacillation and uncertainty of these years. Canning, for instance, thought that abolition of the slave trade by Brazil could justifiably be made a *sine qua non* of recognition. "But there are immense British interests engaged in the trade with Brazil, and we must proceed with caution and good heed; and take the commercial as well as moral feelings of the country with us."[113]

107. *Parl. Deb.*, Vol. XVII, page 676. June 15, 1810.
108. Ibid., Vol. XXVIII, page 656. July 11, 1814.
109. *Wellington, Despatches*, Vol. I, page 329. Canning to Wellington, Sept. 30, 1822.
110. Ibid., Vol. I, page 453. Wellington to Canning, Oct. 28, 1822.
111. Ibid., Vol. I, page 585. Wellington to Canning, Nov. 26, 1822.
112. *Canning, Correspondence*, Vol. I, page 62. Memorandum for the Cabinet, Nov. 15, 1822.
113. *Wilberforce, Correspondence*, Vol. II, page 466. Canning to Wilberforce, Oct. 24, 1822.

If morality and economics were not at variance with each other, all would be well. If they proved to be incompatible, one or the other would have to go. From 1820 onwards, right up to 1863, we get a conflict between the social and economic conscience in the British Empire, between the humanitarian movement for the abolition of slavery and the slave trade and the economic drive towards the abolition of monopolies and laissez-faire. Canning made those two divergent and irreconcilable forces quite clear in a letter to Wilberforce: "you argue against the acknowledgment of Brazil unpurged of Slave Trade . . . you are surprised that the Duke of Wellington has not been instructed to say that we will give up the trade with Brazil, (for that is, I am afraid, the amount of giving up the import and re-export of her sugar and cotton), if Austria, Russia and Prussia will prohibit her produce. In fair reasoning, you have a right to be surprised, for we ought to be ready to make sacrifices when we ask them, and I am for making them; but who would dare to promise such a one as this without a full knowledge of the opinions of the commercial part of the nation?"[114]

The merchants soon voiced their opinion. Wilberforce had, significantly, defended the Spanish treaty of 1818 on the ground that the grant to Spain would be more than repaid to Britain in commercial advantages by the opening up of a great continent to British industry. "If, indeed, we only considered it upon the most simple commercial footing, as a common mercantile regulation, we should find it abundantly recompensed by the result."[115] In 1824 Sir James Mackintosh presented a petition from one hundred and seventeen merchants of London for the recognition of the independence of South America. The petitioners were, in a word, the city of London.[116] Not only London, but Liverpool and Manchester came out in favour of South American Independence. The President, Vice-President and members of the Chamber of Commerce of Manchester declared, in a petition to the House of Commons, that the opening of the South American market to British industry would be an event which must produce the most beneficial results to British commerce.[117]

The full importance of Brazil will be seen in a later chapter. For the present it is sufficient to notice that the British merchants thought the trade

114. *Wellington, Despatches*, Vol. I, pages 474–475. Oct. 31, 1822. An extract from the letter can be found in *Life of Wilberforce*, Vol. V, page 138.

115. *Parl. Deb.*, Vol. XXXVII, page 248. Feb. 9, 1818.

116. Ibid., NS, Vol. XI, page 1345. June 15, 1824. David Ricardo was among the signatories. Hume, in supporting Mackintosh, urged Wilberforce to devote his attention to the independence of St. Domingo, and wondered that he had not thought of it before, in his zeal for the welfare of the Negroes (Ibid., page 1406).

117. Ibid., pages 1475–1477. Presented by Sir J. Mackintosh, June 23, 1884.

valuable, superior to all other considerations. They were logically bound to oppose anything which might upset that trade. The Brazil trade depended in the last resort on the slave trade. Hence by 1833 we find a decided revulsion of feeling against that humanitarian policy which had stationed cruisers on the African coast and established forts and garrisons in unhealthy spots in Africa, in an attempt to extirpate the slave trade at its source. This opposition to humanitarianism assumed the guise of economy, humanitarianism or defeatism.

Notwithstanding all Britain's efforts and sacrifices, Wellington argued not less than 80,000 slaves had been exported annually from Africa between 1800 and 1822, this number being double the annual export in any year preceding 1800.[118] Britain had not been able to effect much, and this very lack of success was used as an argument to justify the cessation of all efforts in the future. The British Commissioner at Surinam had once warned his Government that "the slave trade is not a practice to be overcome by gentle admonitions or merely negative prohibitions, or anything short of the energetic measures pursued by the British Government."[119] Yet the British cruisers were now to be withdrawn, and the British establishments in Africa abandoned.

As early as 1824 Wilberforce had condemned the Government's African expenditure as too economical.[120] Goderich computed it in 1827 at not less than half a million a year.[121] The expense exceeded the value of all the trade, import and export, in every year.[122] Hume put the exports from the coast at never more than £150,000 in any year from 1787 to 1823; in 1824 they were only £154,000. The imports amounted to £118,000 in British goods and £119,000 in foreign. This was the great extent of commerce for which the country was to make such a vast sacrifice of human life.[123] The African establishments were expensive appendages which, at their best, were of little

---

118. *Wellington, Despatches*, Vol. III, page 345. Wellington to Bathurst, July 4, 1826.

119. *H. of C. Sess. Papers, Accounts and Papers*, 1823, Vol. XIX. Class B, Correspondence with British Commissioners, page 128. Lefroy to Londonderry, May 1, 1822.

120. *Life of Wilberforce*, Vol. V, page 225. Wilberforce to Macaulay.

121. *Wellington, Despatches*, Vol. IV, page 131. Goderich to Wellington, Oct. 1, 1827.

122. Ibid., Vol. IV, page 667. Wellington to William Allen, Aug. 26, 1828. Allen had written, Aug. 23, suggesting means of reducing the expense by £30,000 a year. His proposals included a civil instead of a military governor; proper attention to the cultivation of the soil, particularly cotton, to render Britain independent of America; and measures on the most liberal scale with regard to education for the people of colour, to promote morals and religion. (Ibid., pages 658–659.) Wellington replied that the expense could not be reduced by diminishing the staff, that the governor's salary would be inadequate without his perquisites as a military officer, and that the only means of economising was by withdrawing the European troops. (Ibid., pages 667–668.)

123. *Parl. Deb.*, NS, Vol. XXV, page 398. June 15, 1830. Buxton reminded Hume that the imports of all the West Indian islands were only £864,000, and that therefore the proportion of Sierra Leone was infinitely greater. (Ibid., page 400.)

avail in achieving the aim for which they had been intended, and, at their worst, tended only to disturb a valuable trade with Brazil.

Huskisson's earliest biographer claimed it as a credit to him that he took the first step towards the accomplishment of an object which, in common with every friend of humanity, he had earnestly at heart, the gradual reduction of the establishments on the slave coast of Africa.[124] Gen. Gascoyne of Liverpool regretted that Sierra Leone was abandoned on the ground of economy and not on that of humanity.[125] It was humanity against humanity; humanity had dictated the establishment of Sierra Leone, humanity now demanded its abandonment.[126] "There were some persons in this country under a humane delusion; but why were they to delude the whole Parliament of England?"[127]

By 1833, therefore, the slave trade was allowed to take its course, undisturbed and unmolested. Strong economic interests supported the abolitionist crusade for emancipation in the British colonies. These same interests opposed any tampering with the foreign slave trade, on which their profitable commerce with Brazil depended. So vast was the slave trade which was still carried on that the Act of 1833 was only a very small part of a triumph which was not to be consummated until long after.

The "lamentable and disgraceful change"[128] which came over Britain after 1833 can only be explained by the importance of the Brazil trade. By 1838, according to Buxton, 150,000 Negroes were annually imported into Brazil and Cuba alone.[129] In 1839 Buxton attacked the cruiser system as useless. Sturge re-established the Anti-Slavery Society on a purely pacific basis. Carlyle questioned the morality of a policy which could put the whole world in a turmoil. Gladstone opposed any interference with the trade; "it was not an ordinance of Providence that the Government of one nation shall correct the morals of another." Cobden and "The Times" joined hands. Bright, the representative of Manchester, was, says Mathieson, obviously quite alive to the fact that Lancashire supplied most of the goods that were used in the barter of slaves.[130] Leave the slave trade alone, it was said, it will commit suicide. Britain could no more afford to alienate Brazil in 1840 than she

124. *The Speeches of the Right Honourable William Huskisson with a Biographical Memoir*, Anonymous (London, 1831), Vol. I, page 163. (Referred to hereafter as *Huskisson, Speeches*.)
125. *Parl. Deb.*, NS, Vol. XX, page 495. Feb. 23, 1829.
126. Ibid., page 496.
127. Ibid., NS, Vol. XXV, page 405. Gen. Gascoyne, June 15, 1830.
128. The phrase is Lord Denman's.
129. C. Buxton (ed.): *Memoirs of Sir Thomas Fowell Buxton* (London, 1848), page 436.
130. For all this see W. L. Mathieson: *British Slave Emancipation 1838–1849* (London, 1932), pages 33–34; and Sir George MacMunn: *Slavery through the Ages* (London, 1938), page 133.

could alienate the Southern States in 1860. Powerful interests were exasperated by the policy of humanitarianism which one critic thus described: "The utmost latitude, one might almost say licentiousness, of means—public money to any extent—naval armaments watching every shore and every sea where a slave-ship could be seen or suspected—courts of special judicature in half of the inter-tropical regions of the globe—diplomatic influence and agency such perhaps as this country never before concentrated on any public object."[131]

The eventual suppression of the slave trade was due to two causes. The first was the cessation of the demand by the victory of the North in the American Civil War, followed twenty years later by the abolition of slavery in Brazil and Cuba. The second was the advent of the steam cruiser. The fast slave clipper could not out-distance the cruiser as it had out-distanced the sailing frigate; and the slave trader's need of secrecy militated against his adoption of the new device, for steamers meant coaling stations.[132]

---

131. *Parl. Deb.*, Vol. LXXXI, pages 1158–1159. Mr. William Hutt, June 24, 1845.
132. For this see J. H. Rose: *Man and the Sea* (Cambridge, 1935), chap. XII.

CHAPTER TEN

East India Sugar

We have dealt with the humanitarian forces which were clamouring for emancipation, without which no account of the emancipation movement would be adequate or comprehensible. We have now to investigate the nature of those economic interests which gave it such momentum. The controversy over the East India sugar duties reveals the interested men and their ulterior motives which sullied the cause of humanitarianism and religion.

With the failure of the earlier campaign to secure the introduction of sugar from the East Indies on a footing of equality with sugar from the West, King Cotton threatened to oust King Sugar. The attention of Manchester merchants, and consequently of the East India Company, was directed not merely to ensuring the Indian market for Lancashire manufactured goods but to providing returns by India in the form of raw cotton. The American War of 1812 had shown the danger of dependence on foreign supplies and turned Lancashire's eyes to the Levant and the East Indies. John Gladstone was the first private trader to venture into the new field. When his ship, the "Kingsmill," returned in September 1815 laden with the raw cotton purchased with its outward cargo of British manufactures, the effect was electric. Private traders swarmed into the East India trade and reduced the American prices.[1] Indian cotton exports increased

---

1. *T. P. Martin: Some International Aspects of the Anti-Slavery Movement, 1818–1823.* Journal of Economic and Business History, Vol. I, No. 1, Nov. 1928 (Cambridge, U.S.A.), page 141.

from 6,972,790 lbs in 1816 to 31,007,570 lbs in 1817, and more than doubled again in 1818, actually in the latter year exceeding the American supply. By 1820 they had dropped to 23,125,825 lbs, while in 1822 they formed only four per cent of the export from the United States.[2] Post-war stagnation and the inherent superiority of the American cotton, together with the rise of Brazil as a supplier of the raw material, made it impossible for the free labour of the east to compete with the slave labour of America.[3] Indian raw cotton had to be content with its monopoly at Canton, the Liverpool of the East, where it sold for well over a million sterling every year, and where, with British woolens, Cornwall tin and Bengal opium, it was exchanged for China tea.[4]

The failure of the cotton experiment meant that some other export crop had to be found to solve the problem which dated back to 1770, the equation of India's balance of payments. The East India Company turned therefore to sugar. The use of sugar, as a dead weight to ships returning from India, became essential to the existence of the trade with that country.[5] Hence the

2. See *Customs* 5/5–11. From these we get the following table:

Table 10.1.

Year	E.I. Exports	U.S. Exports
1816	6,972,790	50,329,520
1817	31,007,570	59,358,525
1818	67,456,411	66,398,245
1819	58,856,261	60,762,080
1820	23,125,825	87,030,229
1821	8,831,706	91,355,222
1822	4,554,225	100,018,143

(I have not been able to find these figures in the Returns of the Inspector-General, H. of C. Sess. Pap., A and P.)

3. For this see A. *Redford (ed.): Manchester Merchants and Foreign Trade, 1794–1858* (Manchester, 1934), pages 144 and 217–220. Indian cotton was suitable only for the manufacture of coarse cloths; owing to bad preparation for the market, it was extremely dirty. See E. *Baines: History of the Cotton Manufacture in Great Britain* (London, 1835), page 308: "It is the worst in the English market; owing to the negligent cultivation and packing." In 1831 the East India Company declared: "This most valuable and important article has been, for a series of years past, declining in the scale of our external trade." H. *of C. Sess. Papers, Accounts and Papers*, 1831, Vol. VI, No. 320 (c), page 30. The cotton imports from Brazil for the years 1816–1822 were: 1816—20,052,230 lbs; 1817—16,338,861; 1818—24,987,979; 1819—20,860,865; 1820—29,198,155; 1821—19,535,786; 1822—24,705,206. (*Customs* 5/5–11.)

4. C. N. Parkinson: *Trade in the Eastern Seas, 1793–1813* (Cambridge, 1937), pages 88–89.

5. Petition from the Merchants, Shipowners, and others, concerned in the trade to the East Indies, presented to the House of Commons by W. W. Whitmore, March 3, 1823. *Parl. Deb.*, NS, Vol. VIII, pages 337–338.

campaign was begun for the equalization of the duties and the abolition of the preference in favour of West Indian sugar.

The West Indians naturally opposed this "unheard of injustice."[6] India, they argued, was an independent empire, not a colony subject to the restrictions of the colonial system. Britain's tenure was insecure, India's separation was not far distant. Why should the West Indian planter, for such a speculation, be reduced to a mere nonentity?[7] The importation of sugar in large quantities from the East would injure Britain's maritime strength, as the ships in the Indian trade were navigated by Lascars.[8] East India sugar was not, as its advocates asserted, free grown. Slavery existed in India. "The substance is not altered by the name, and whether a man is called a ryot or a slave is a matter of entire indifference."[9] The sugar from the East was not entirely the produce of British India. Large quantities came from Java, Singapore and the Philippines, for which British cotton goods were given

---

6. *T. Fletcher: Letters in vindication of the rights of the British West India Colonies* (Liverpool, 1822), page 16. These letters were an answer to letters written by James Cropper to Wilberforce.

7. *Parl. Deb.*, NS, Vol. VII, page 679. Mr. Barham, May 17, 1822. See too speech of Charles Ellis, page 677; and *Quarterly Review*, Vol. XXXII, 1825, page 519.

8. *Parl. Deb.*, Vol. XXVII, page 202. Alderman Atkins, Nov. 26, 1813. See too *Memorandum on the Relative Importance of the West and East Indies to Great Britain* (London, 1823), page 32.

9. *Quarterly Review*, Vol. XXXII, 1825, page 519; *Fletcher, op. cit.*, page 33; "Men are not bought and sold, but they are subject to a slavery of another and peculiar kind—that singular division of society into castes. . . . There is perhaps not a more depressed or abject race of men in the world than the lower ranks of the Hindoo:" and page 36: "However then the question may be debated on political and commercial grounds, let us hear no more of the superior *humanity* of employing labourers at 3d. per day in the East, rather than slaves in the West;" G. *Saintsbury: East India Slavery* (London, 1829), page 32: "India is a slave territory, as Jamaica is a slave colony." The East Indians made excuses—e.g., Cropper: "To so small an extent and of such a nature is slavery in Bengal that many who have resided years in that country are not aware of its existence." *Letters to William Wilberforce, M.P., recommending the encouragement of the cultivation of sugar in our dominions in the East Indies as the natural and certain means of effecting the total and general abolition of Slave Trade* (Liverpool, 1822), page IV (Referred to hereafter as *Letters to Wilberforce*); Z. Macaulay: "It must be recollected, as a justification of the Company, that they had obtained dominion over countries which had been previously under the Hindoo and Mogul Government. They therefore could not be blamed if, when they came into possession of those countries, they found principles acted upon with which, however adverse to their feelings, it would be unsafe to interfere, without due caution." *Debates at the General Court of Proprietors of East India Stock on the 19th and 21st March 1823 on the East India Sugar Trade,* page 35. (Referred to hereafter as *East India Sugar Debate, 1823.*) It is difficult to recognize here the moving spirit of the abolitionist party.

in exchange.[10] In addition to all this, East India sugar was vastly inferior to that from the West.[11]

The West Indian planters claimed that their Eastern rivals enjoyed advantages which made competition impossible. The cheapness of labour, the abundance of food and unlimited extent of the richest soil, capable of irrigation and intersected with navigable rivers—all these advantages gave the Bengal farmer a pre-eminence over the cultivators in the old British colonies.[12] India had other articles which she could cultivate for export and was not dependent on sugar.[13] The home market was glutted,[14] the British West Indies were not adequate for the supply of Great Britain and even had a surplus for export, and consequently the introduction of East Indian sugar,

10. *Fletcher, op. cit.*, page 27; *Memorandum on the relative importance of the West and East Indies to Great Britain*, page 31; *To the Consumers of Sugar* (n.d.), page 2. A Select Committee on the affairs of the East India Company was told in 1831 that the Chinese were more skilled in the manufacture of sugar than the Bengalese (Mr. Gisborne, page 58), and that sugar was on the increase in Java, and needed only a foreign demand (Mr. Maclaine, page 83)—*H. of C. Sess. Papers, Accounts and Papers*, 1831, Vol. VI, No. 320 (c). Huskisson said that Bengal imported more sugar from China and Java than she sent to Europe (*Huskisson, Speeches*), Vol. II, page 200. May 22, 1823). During the years 1827–1833 the following quantities of sugar, given in round numbers in cwt., were imported from countries in the East. (*Customs* 5/16–22.)

Table 10.2.

Year	Singapore	Philippines	Java
1827	5,500	8,749	952
1828	22,628	912	
1829	14,689	17,325	
1830	38,535	33,780	5,950
1831	23,794	39,348	4,773
1832	43,415	28,924	14,653
1833	33,369	32,531	21,774

11. *Saintsbury, op. cit.*, page 5; *Memorandum on the relative importance of the West and East Indies to Great Britain*, page 31.

12. C.O. 137/140. Report from a Committee of the House of Assembly, 1813. Marryat claimed that the free Hindoo labourer cost about six shillings a month, the West Indian slave almost as much a day (*Parl. Deb.*, Vo. XXVII, page 203. Nov. 26, 1813). The West Indians were so impressed with the cheapness of East India labour that Governor Woodford from Trinidad advocated the introduction of East Indian immigrants as likely to prove or disprove the argument that free labour was cheaper than slave (C.O. 295/33. Woodford to Bathurst, Oct. 3, 1814).

13. *Gladstone-Cropper, Correspondence*, page 21. Gladstone, Nov. 5, 1823; *Addresses and Memorials to His Majesty from the House of Assembly at Jamaica, voted in the years 1821 to 1826* (London, 1828), page 10: 1821; *Statements to the Board of Trade*, page 89, Meeting of Standing Committee of West Indian Planters and Merchants, Dec. 29, 1830.

14. *Parl. Deb.*, NS, Vol. VII, page 680. Mr. Barham, May 17, 1822. "They were about to admit the produce of the East Indies into a market which was already glutted. If this system were persisted in, they might as well give up their West Indian colonies."

on the large scale which would follow equalization of the duties, would spell ruin for the West.[15]

Before 1820 this assertion would have been absurd. The high freight rates normally prevented Indian cotton or Indian sugar from competing effectively with the products of the West. Bombay was farther from Liverpool than Demerara or the United States. Indian cotton, before the vast increase after 1815, sold in Britain only when Arkwright's machinery had outrun all other supplies. In 1814, when a 10/- preference had been fixed in favour of West Indian sugar, the East Indian freight rates were 17/- to 18/- per cwt. With the failure of the cotton venture the freight rates dropped. They became, in Gladstone's phrase, unnaturally low,[16] and East India sugar was brought sometimes for as little as 6/- per cwt. The East Indian traders, as M'Queen expressed it, were reduced to choosing for ballast between the sand of the Ganges and raw sugar. The West Indian planters therefore appealed to Government for increases in the sugar duties commensurate with the decline in the freight rates from India.[17]

The West Indians did not base their case on sympathy or charity alone. The monopoly was theirs, not of grace but of right. The colonies had chartered rights, and they claimed the continuation of these rights on the grounds of principle and policy. Their exclusive possession of the home market was their just reward for the restrictions imposed on them by the colonial system.[18]

While the West Indians demanded monopoly, the East Indians asked (at least so they said) only for fair treatment. "Your petitioners ask for no exclusive favour, preference or protection to themselves; all that they require is to be placed upon an equal footing with the West Indians both in the amount

---

15. *Fletcher, op. cit.,* page 29; C.O. 28/81. Petition of Committee of Merchants and Planters to Governor Beckwith, Oct. 2, 1812. Marryat emphasized that the East had ruined the West wherever the two had competed, e.g., indigo and cotton. *Parl. Deb.,* Vol. XXVII, page 203. Nov. 26, 1813.

16. *Huskisson Papers,* Add. Mss. 38744, folio 153. Charles Ellis to Huskisson, March 29, 1821. Gladstone had by this time quitted the East Indian Trade.

17. For all this see *Parkinson, op. cit.,* page 88; *Martin, op. cit.,* pages 143–144. Fletcher, in 1822, insisted that the 10/- preferential duty should be increased, *op. cit.,* page 16. As long ago as 1813 Jamaica had raised the cry for such an increase as would exclude all hopes of bringing East India sugar to the home market. According to a report of a Committee of the Assembly a ten per cent preference was a cruel mockery, and a fifty per cent duty was necessary in order to enable them to compete with the East. C.O. 137/140.

18. *Fletcher, op. cit.,* page 27; *Memorandum on the relative importance of the West and East Indies to Great Britain,* page 30. In view of the colonial system Jamaica claimed their monopoly "not as a boon, but as a right for which a valuable consideration is given by the monopoly of their market for every article of her (Britain's) growth or manufacture" (C.O. 137/140. Report from Committee of House of Assembly, 1813). Did the colonists mean, as William Smith, the abolitionist, asked, that British manufactures were dearer than others, and that it was only the monopoly which restrained them from resorting to other markets? (*Parl. Deb.,* Vol. XXVII, page 205. Nov. 26, 1813)

of duties and in the classification of qualities."[19] While the duties on East Indian products were grievous in themselves, in comparison with the duties on those from the West Indies they were prohibitory, and Whitmore, in a moment of wrath, warned the House to remember North America.[20]

Anyone listening to the West Indians would have imagined that they were demanding a prescriptive right, as old as the colonies themselves. But the right dated back only to 1814. And as the East Indians pertinently pointed out, such a claim could only be preferred by the old colonies. In the same year that the unfavourable duty was imposed on sugar from the East, the sugar from the conquered West Indian colonies was admitted on an equal footing with that from the older islands. The Government seemed to be "not entirely exempt from a certain sympathy with the growers of sugar by slave labour, and a corresponding dread of the competition of sugar the produce of free labour." Was the West Indian claim based on length of possession? If so Bengal had been British longer than half of the West Indian colonies. Did it rest on the fact that slavery was so desirable an institution in itself that, wherever it existed, it was entitled to peculiar favour and protection? Then this was "a partiality of the most monstrous and unjustifiable description."[21] Furthermore, what would have become of the older British colonies had the rich St. Domingo plum fallen into Britain's lap? Wilberforce, in the debate on equalization of the duties in 1823, asked the West Indians what had become of the supposed pledges given to them when the conquered colonies were allowed to compete with them in the home market.[22] And in any case why should the West Indians assert their claims to a preferential duty in the article of sugar only? Why was it not extended to cotton and indigo?[23]

The East Indians had two strings to their bow, the one humanitarian, the other economic. They claimed that their sugar offered "a better and cheaper, as well as a humane guiltless compensation for any possible injury the West Indies may sustain from the removal of the protecting duty."[24] Conscious that its quality, strength and price could not enable it to compete advantageously with the sugar from the West Indies, they were anxious, their opponents

---

19. *Parl. Deb.*, NS, Vol. VIII, page 338. Petition of Merchants, Shipowners etc., concerned in the trade to the East Indies, March 3, 1823.

20. Ibid., NS, Vol. XVII, pages 815–817. May 15, 1827. The duty on East Indian coffee was 84 per cent, on West Indian 56; on East Indian rum 20 s. on West Indian 8/6d; on East Indian cotton 5 per cent, on West Indian nothing.

21. For all this see *East and West India Sugar; or a refutation of the claims of the West Indian colonists to a protecting duty on East India sugar* (London, 1823), page 14–15, 20, 23, 25, 40. The author was Zachary Macaulay.

22. *Parl. Deb.*, NS, Vol. IX, page 462. May 22, 1823.

23. Macaulay, *op. cit.*, pages 22 and 24.

24. Ibid., page 71.

derided, "to help it off by an appeal to moral feeling."[25] The unrestricted importation of East India sugar, Seely asserted, possessed the power of abolishing the slave trade everywhere.[26] The West Indians seemed strangely perverse and selfish. They could not compete with Brazil and Cuba, and yet they sought, with what Hume called a dog-in-the-manger attitude, to restrain those who alone could.[27]

If the sugar from the East could really drive out the Brazilian and Cuban product from the European market, that was, for the West Indian planters, a consummation devoutly to be wished.[28] But the East Indians went further. It would tend to improve the economy of the British islands, by forcing the planter to withdraw his poor soil from cultivation and retain only land of superior fertility.[29] It would do more. The great grievance of the West Indian planters, the root cause of their distress, was the slave system. East India sugar would abolish West Indian slavery. By substituting East for West Indian sugar, the Peckham Ladies' African Anti-Slavery Association were informed, they were undermining the system of slavery in the safest, easiest and most effective manner.[30] Liberty and property were the foundation of good agriculture, without them it could not flourish.[31] Macaulay was convinced that the existence of West Indian slavery depended upon the continuance of the protecting duty.[32] Remove the duty and slavery would fall immediately. The planter would learn that "the cautious economy of the freeman consumes less than the heedless profusion of the slave."[33] Indeed, the introduction of East India sugar would abolish slavery in Brazil and Cuba.[34]

The East Indians did not confine their appeals to the friends of humanity. Their attack had a sharper economic point. The West Indians had based their legal right to the monopoly of the home market on the ground

---

25. *To the Consumers of Sugar*, pages 7–8.

26. J. B. Seely: *A few hints to the West Indians on their present claims to exclusive favour and protection at the expense of the East India interests* (London, 1823), pages 38, 48, and 94. Seely thought that this glorious opportunity of stopping the importation and the use of slaves deserved the serious attention of "the excellent Mr. Wilberforce." Compare Cropper: "The most certain means to destroy the foreign slave trade will be found to be the encouragement of the cheaper productions of free labour in our own dominions." (*Letters to Wilberforce*, page VI.)

27. *Parl. Deb.*, NS, Vol. XXV, page 835. June 30, 1830. Hume was himself an East Indian proprietor.

28. *Fletcher, op. cit.*, pages 12 and 44–45.

29. *East India Sugar, or an Inquiry respecting the means of improving the quality and reducing the cost of sugar raised by free labour in the East Indies* (London, 1824), page 17.

30. W. Naish: *Reasons for using East India Sugar* (London, 1828), page 3.

31. *Ibid.*, page 6.

32. *East India Sugar Debate, 1823*, page 34.

33. *Manifesto against African Slavery, issued by the Liverpool Anti-Slavery Society* (1830?), page 13. The author was William Roscoe. (Referred to hereafter as *Manifesto against African Slavery*).

34. *Seely, op. cit.*, page 38.

that they were subject to the restrictions of the colonial system. With the concession in 1825 of free trade to all parts of the world, subject only to the conditions of the Navigation laws, their right to the monopoly disappeared.

The East Indian attack was concentrated on the monopoly. Would no half measures, no compromise, nothing but unqualified monopoly, satisfy the West Indians?[35] Were the West Indians entitled to the enjoyment of the monopoly merely because they had enjoyed it for a length of time? "It would be to contend, that because a great many people who used to be employed in the manufacture of cotton, or other articles, by hand, are thrown out of employ by the invention of machinery, a tax upon machinery should therefore be levied. . . . It would be to say that because the conveyance by canal has been found much more cheap and convenient than the old mode of conveyance by waggon, a tax should therefore be laid upon canal conveyance."[36] The West Indians pleaded that they had invested their capital in the cultivation of sugar and were therefore entitled to a continuance of the protecting duty, "a claim which might be urged with equal force in the case of *every* improvident speculation."[37] If for this they were entitled to protection, as well might any other clans of men seek protection from the Legislature. The manufacturer who had invested capital in the rude and badly constructed machinery formerly used in the cotton manufacture might seek protection against the superior machinery of an Arkwright, or the man who had invested capital in poor and unproductive land claim protection by a tax upon the more productive land of his neighbours. "If such an absurdity as this be suffered to exist, we may next look for a proposal to supersede the introduction of foreign wines by raising grapes in hothouses; and such a tax upon all improvements, as will drive the country back from civilization to barbarism."[38] They were called upon to depart from the ordinary principles of commerce, in order to benefit the West Indians.[39] Hume trusted that the good sense, the honest feeling and the patriotic spirit of the people of Britain would never allow the continuance of such a monopoly, for all restraints and monopolies were bad.[40]

The East Indians, so quick to demand the abolition of the West Indian monopoly which was contrary to their interests, were themselves among

---

35. Ibid., pages 81–82.
36. *Report of a Committee of the Liverpool East India Association, appointed to take into consideration the restrictions of the East India Trade* (Liverpool, 1822), pages 21–22. (Referred to hereafter as *Report of a Committee of the Liverpool East India Association.*)
37. *Macaulay, op. cit.,* page 37.
38. *Report of a Committee of the Liverpool East India Association,* pages 22–23.
39. *East India Sugar Debate, 1823,* page 12. Mr. Tucker, who seconded the motion for equalization of the duties.
40. Ibid., pages 40–41.

the great monopolists of the day. How could the monopolists of the China trade well declaim against monopolies in general? In the great East India sugar debate in 1823, Mr. Tucker, while denying the West Indian claims to a prescriptive monopoly, stated clearly that he was not one of those sweeping theorists who opposed all restrictions whatever, and defended the China trade monopoly and the monopoly of salt.[41] Some proprietors realized how the Company was laying itself open to attack. "That part of the community who are not connected with India, and above all that part who are deeply interested in the West India Colonies, will (not) give credit to this Court for the same disinterested feelings. . . . They will ask whence this new light and enlarged views of unrestricted commerce which now influence the Court of East India stock proprietors, who, from the days of Elizabeth to the year 1814, were entire possessors of the trade of India."[42] Barham was astonished at the quarter whence this cry of a free trade proceeded.[43] Marryat thought it extremely amusing to hear those interested in one of the most outrageous monopolies that ever existed in any country in the world declaiming on the advantages of free trade.[44] What the East Indians wanted was not free trade, but equalization of the duties. When they got their share of the spoils in 1836, they became as ardent monopolists as their former rivals, firmly opposed to any extension of their original free trade principles by the equalization of the duties on foreign slave-grown sugar.

The East Indians were on safer ground when they argued not so much against the monopoly, but against a monopoly which was expensive. Macaulay reminded the West Indians that the monopoly had been given them expressly for the purpose of supplying Britain with sugar cheaper than she could obtain it elsewhere, and not in order that she should pay a higher price for it than her neighbours.[45] Ricardo drew a parallel between the sugar duties and the corn laws. The poor soil of the West Indies, like the poor soil of Britain, was to be protected from the competition of the richer soil of other countries. It would be cheaper to purchase sugar from the East Indies and pay a tax directly to the West Indies for doing so.[46] The West Indians may have invested a large capital in the sugar trade, but Britain was not therefore bound to take sugar from them at double the price which would be paid elsewhere.[47]

---

41. Ibid., page 9.
42. Ibid., page 25, Mr. Carruthers.
43. *Parl. Deb.*, NS, Vol. VII, page 680. May 17, 1822.
44. Ibid., NS, Vol. IX, page 459. May 22, 1823.
45. *Macaulay, op. cit.*, page 103.
46. *Parl. Deb.*, NS, Vol. VII, page 691. May 17, 1822.
47. Ibid., NS, Vol. IX, page 458. May 22, 1823.

It was indeed the people of Britain who suffered from the West Indian monopoly, which alone maintained the wretched system of colonial bondage.
According to Naish, the people of Britain paid to the colonists £1,700,000
annually in bounties.[48] Cropper put the figure at £1,200,000.[49] Whitmore
estimated that bounties and protecting duty cost the taxpayer two millions
sterling a year,[50] while the Brazilian Association of Liverpool reckoned that
the bounty amounted to eight shillings per hundredweight.[51] Buxton quoted
with approval "a very able pamphlet written lately by an intelligent merchant of Liverpool, a Mr. Cropper," to the effect that the tax to the West
Indians amounted to no less than one and a half millions annually, and from
his own estimate he assured the House that the consumer paid at least one
million a year extra in consequence of the West Indian monopoly, for the
sole benefit of the West Indian merchants.[52] The Liverpool Anti-Slavery
Society protested against the application of public money to the support of
a disgraceful, inefficient and sinking system,[53] while Cropper thought the
continuance of such a system of oppression, of wickedness, of impolicy and
of folly, which if left to itself would unquestionably fall by its own weight,
almost incredible in an enlightened age.[54]

The sugar duties, according to the propagandists of the East, was not a
petty question affecting only the trifling interests of shipowners and agents.
It was a great public question in which the millions of Britain and India were
concerned. The fertility of the soil alone would explain the lower costs of
production in India.[55] If a population of less than one million could produce
200,000 tons of sugar, what might not one hundred millions produce? The
East Indians could, according to this economic arithmetic, grow sugar sufficient for the consumption of the world.[56] The West Indians, declared Seely,
had in their eagerness for gain totally forgotten the third party concerned,
the consumer. Was it just to force the price of an article by restrictive du-

48. *Naish, op. cit.*, page 12.
49. *J. Cropper: Letters to Wilberforce*, page V.
50. *Parl. Deb.*, NS, Vol. IX, page 445. May 22, 1813. The West Indians replied that the protecting duty had conferred no benefit, and that the bounty amounted to £844,444. Cit. *Klingberg*, page
248, (footnote).
51. *J. Cropper: Another Bonus to the Planters: or the advantage shown of an equitable purchase of the
Monopoly and Bounty on West Indian Sugar* (London, 1833), page 6.
52. *Parl. Deb.*, NS, Vol. VII, pages 674–675. May 17, 1822.
53. *Manifesto against African Slavery*, page 11.
54. *Gladstone-Cropper, Correspondence*, page 7.
55. *Macaulay, op. cit*, pages 91–93. The length to which some of the East Indians carried their
propaganda can be seen from Naish's address to the Peckham Ladies' Anti-Slavery Association.
According to him, not only could the East Indians raise sugar at 14/- per cwt., which in the West
cost 19/6, but the fixed capital required to raise 250 tons of sugar was in the East £800, in the West
£45,000. (*Naish, op. cit.*, pages 5–6.)
56. *Report of a Committee of the Liverpool East India Association*, page 46.

ties above its value, for the gain of, comparatively speaking, a small body of men?[57] Macaulay was more outspoken. "They have no more right to claim the continuance of a protecting duty on sugar, to the manifest wrong of India and of Great Britain, than they had before a right to claim the continuance of the Slave Trade, to the manifest wrong of Africa."[58]

It was high time to revise this "beetle-eyed" policy towards India for the sake of "bolstering up the rotten cause of the holder of slaves in the West Indies."[59] The admission of East India sugar would be of enormous importance to British industry and commerce.

British industrialists realized this, and in this conflict between East and West the Lancashire merchants were active on the East Indian side. On May 4, 1821, the Manchester Chamber of Commerce presented a petition to the House of Commons deprecating a preference to one colony over another, and particularly a preference to a settlement of slaves over a nation of free men. Whereas in the former it was only the wants and desires of the few proprietors which caused a demand for foreign productions, a trade with a people possessing civil privileges had no assignable limit.[60] The Napoleonic wars had seen the end of the former competition between Indian textile exports and the Lancashire cotton industry, and the Manchester merchants hoped to develop a large market in India for Lancashire goods. To attain this, India must develop large-scale production for export, in order to pay for the manufactured goods in raw material. Among these export crops prominence was given to cotton and sugar.[61] The failure of the cotton experiment made the equalization of the sugar duties imperative. In Macaulay's words, the only limit to the growing demand of India for British manufacturers was the power of obtaining adequate returns.[62] The removal of the protecting duty would increase the manufacture of cloth in Britain and the cultivation of sugar in India.[63]

Equalization of the duties would not, so the East Indians argued, be detrimental to British shipping; in fact it would add forty per cent to its employment.[64] It was alleged that if the West Indian trade decreased—as it would if the duties were equalized—there would be a proportionate decrease in British agricultural exports to the West Indies. Macaulay, from a parliamentary

57. Seely, op. cit., page 9.
58. Macaulay, op. cit., page 29.
59. Seely, op. cit., page 89.
60. Martin, op. cit., page 146.
61. Redford, op. cit., pages 144 and 219.
62. Macaulay, op. cit., page 99.
63. Report of a Committee of the Liverpool East India Association, page 51.
64. Ibid., page 56.

document, replied that taking together grain, provisions, fish and all kinds of exports of that description, from Britain to the West Indies, from January 1822 to January 1823, the whole amount was only £266,000, including even the bottled ale and porter which were to be consumed by the Creoles. "Why this was not so much as several of their brewhouses in London consumed in grain alone in the course of a year. . . . Any town in England with 15,000 inhabitants consumed more agricultural produce in the course of a year than the whole population of the West Indian islands."[65] The West Indies were claiming a seventeenth century position in a nineteenth century Empire.

India, with a population of one hundred and twenty millions, could not be sacrificed to the interest of the West Indies with their population of less than one million,[66] and it seemed to the East Indian philanthropists an act of pure justice that India should be recompensed in some way for the destruction of her native cotton manufactures.[67] In 1829 Huskisson, in presenting a petition from Liverpool against the East India Company's charter, emphasized approvingly that British exports to the East, which, in 1813, had amounted to less than £1,600,000, were in 1828, £5,800,000, or one-eighth of the total exports of the country. In 1812 there were 28,000 tons of British shipping employed in the trade with India. In 1828 the figure was no less than 109,000 tons, and Huskisson admitted that the difficulty then was to find returns from India to Europe.[68]

---

65. *East India Sugar Debate, 1823*, page 32.
66. *Report of a Committee of the Liverpool East India Association*, page 19.
67. Smart, *op. cit.*, Vol. II, page 161.
68. *Huskisson, Speeches*, Vol. III, page 442. May 12, 1829. The following table, prepared from *Customs 8*, shows the growth of Britain's trade to the East Indies and China. For convenience's sake I have used round numbers only. The volume in each case is put in brackets after the particular year.

Table 10.3.

Year	Exports to E.I. and China (official value)	Total Exports (official value)
1814 (2)	£1,471,720	£31,224,723
1815 (3)	1,789,020	68,087,379
1817 (6)	2,462,947	44,570,653
1819 (10)	1,990,718	35,657,029
1820 (12)	2,978,451	40,242,773
1821 (14)	3,639,746	43,113,655
1824 (20)	3,684,224	51,713,203
1826 (24)	4,240,424	40,332,854
1827 (26)	5,627,296	51,279,101
1828 (28)	5,827,924	52,019,728
1830 (30)	6,522,642	61,152,353
1832 (35)	6,377,507	65,025,278

After 1817, the E.I. figures include the exports to Mauritius, but these were never very high. In 1828, they were only £217,753; in 1829, £255,522; in 1832, £271,416.

What was the relation between the East Indians and the abolitionists? Klingberg confines it to co-operation[69] and blandly says that this movement, like many other humanitarian movements, enlisted the support of all kinds of people.[70] Burn is of the opinion that the importance of the controversy regarding the preferential duties in connection with the question of slavery can easily be exaggerated,[71] though he acknowledges that the support which the emancipation movement secured from a number of wealthy and fairly influential men was obtained at considerable costs, and cast doubts on the bona fides of the whole emancipation group.[72]

Let us consider more closely the connection between the economists and the humanitarians. Huskisson refused the East Indian demand in 1823 for a Select Committee of Inquiry on the ground that discussion would not be confined to the mere commercial question, but would be conducted principally with reference to "the fearful and delicate subject of the state of slavery."[73] The East India sugar debate in 1823 was like any other debate on slavery. A West Indian proprietor, Plummer, assured the proprietors that the slaves were happy and that the cheerful sound of the song was far more prevalent in the hours of labour than the cries of punishment.[74] Macaulay replied with such a diatribe against slavery that Hume, who followed him, deprecated the discussion: "If the slave trade were ten times worse than it had been stated to be, they were not met to consider that question."[75]

The East Indians were strong advocates of emancipation,[76] and "brought a new support to the humanitarian and religious sentiment which had animated the anti-slavery movement."[77] To Ricardo, slavery was the infamous system, the shocking system, on which no one could for a moment reflect without shuddering. Wilberforce was a most benevolent individual.[78] Cropper, in his numerous publications, never missed an opportunity of attacking the system of slavery, on economic and humanitarian grounds. Thomas Whitmore, one of the leaders of the East Indians in Parliament, was vice-

69. *Klingberg, op. cit.*, page 203.
70. Ibid., page 192.
71. W. L. Burn: *Emancipation and Apprenticeship in the British West Indies* (London, 1937), page 85.
72. Ibid., pages 87–88.
73. *Huskisson, Speeches*, Vol. II, page 197. May 22, 1823.
74. *East India Sugar Debate, 1823*, page 22.
75. Ibid., page 36.
76. See *Castlereagh, Correspondence*, Vol. VIII, page 94, for an interesting letter from Castlereagh to Robert Dundas, Dec. 13, 1807. The East India Company had suggested that they should take over the Portuguese settlements in East Africa. Castlereagh pointed out that the annual exports to India did not exceed £30,000 to £40,000 and added: "I cannot but think it is brought forward on the grounds of anti-Slave Trade and not commercial policy."
77. *Martin, op. cit.*, page 144.
78. *East India Sugar Debate, 1823*, page 20.

president of the Anti-Slavery Society,[79] and it appears that Wilberforce had once hesitated between Whitmore and Buxton in the selection of his successor.[80] The abolitionists gave the East Indians a quid pro quo by supporting the demand for equalization of the sugar duties.

The entry in Wilberforce's diary for May 22, 1823, the date of Whitmore's motion about the sugar duties, is: "None interested for the question but the East Indians and a few of us anti-Slavers, and the West Indians and government against us."[81] In fact, the two tellers for the East Indian side were Whitmore and Buxton.[82] The latter expatiated on the great importance of the East Indies. The value of the trade had increased in a most extraordinary degree, there seemed to be no saying to what extent it might increase, no return was so valuable as sugar.[83] When it was proposed to relieve the West Indies of some of the restrictions on their trade and permit them to export to foreign countries, Buxton expressed the hope that, in return for this concession, the restriction upon the importation of East India sugar would be removed.[84] Wilberforce, in the debate in 1823, repeated an assertion he had formerly made, "that if the whole system of the West Indies were inquired into, it would be found that the most unprofitable, to be maintained with the greatest expenditure of men and money, and after all, to be the most insecure, of any of the possessions of the Crown."[85] Bennet was disinclined to give preference to any class of men, least of all to those "who had vested their capital in dealing in human flesh."[86] William Smith, one of the abolitionist veterans, urged that the people of Britain should, by reduction of the duties on East India sugar, have the satisfaction which they craved by five hundred petitions.[87] In fact, of all the abolitionists, only one, Brougham, pleaded for caution; equalization of the duties would very speedily lay waste the whole of the West Indian archipelago.[88]

Zachary Macaulay was not merely a proprietor of the East India Company; he was also one of the nine signatories who demanded in 1823 a meeting of the General Court to discuss the sugar question.[89] From Macaulay's argu-

79. R. Coupland: The British Anti-Slavery Movement, page 124.
80. W. L. Mathieson: British Slavery and its Abolition, 1823–1838 (London, 1926), page 125.
81. Life of Wilberforce, Vol. V, page 180.
82. Parl. Deb., NS, Vol. IX, page 467.
83. Ibid., NS, Vol. VII, page 675. May 17, 1822.
84. Huskisson, Speeches, Vol. II, page 110. April 1, 1822.
85. Parl. Deb., NS, Vol. IX, page 462. May 22, 1823.
86. Ibid., NS, Vol. V, page 508. May 4, 1821.
87. Ibid., NS, Vol. XVII, page 836. May 15, 1827.
88. Ibid., NS, Vol. VII, page 698. May 17, 1822.
89. East India Sugar Debate, page 5. This important fact is mentioned, so far as I am aware, only by Ragatz, op. cit., page 363.

ments we are led to wonder whether the humanitarian had not given way to the economist. Nothing more damaging to the cause of humanitarianism could be imagined, unless it was the support of James Cropper. According to Burn the attacks on Cropper's disinterestedness were unfounded,[90] while in the opinion of Ragatz "his was one of those occasional cases in which conduct is not primarily influenced by self-interest though they may accidentally coincide."[91] But it was well known that Cropper was the greatest importer of East India sugar into Liverpool.[92] He was the founder and head of the independent East India house, Cropper, Benson and Company of Liverpool.[93] Gladstone, in the celebrated correspondence between the two men, poured withering scorn on the humanitarian whose cotton came from slave labour in the United States.[94] Cropper replied that the connection had ceased, to which Gladstone retorted with telling effect; "it would be rather a curious coincidence were we to find that this cessation was coeval with his becoming a public writer against slavery: and in that case is it not rather remarkable that he should not have been induced to turn author until his slave cotton agency had ceased?"[95]

Cropper was fully aware that his own private interests rendered his motives liable to suspicion.[96] Yet George Stephen welcomed him as an acquisition, his pen being as fluent as his purse.[97] According to Cropper's own explanation, it was the result of the successful East Indian competition with the West Indies in the article of indigo which had encouraged him to enter, without hesitation, extensively into the East Indian trade.[98] "I saw that hideous monster, slavery, gasping, as it were, in the agonies of death, seeking for support which could alone continue its existence. . . . I could not suffer the fear of reproaches, on account of being interested, to get the better of paramount feelings of humanity and duty. I durst not encounter the reproaches of my own conscience."[99]

Cropper knew the strong desire felt by many warm friends to the cause that they should keep perfectly clear of all commercial considerations. He discussed the abolition of slavery in Europe, in the Northern States of the Union and in certain parts of South America. "Were we to consider all these

90. *Burn, op. cit.*, page 88.
91. *Ragatz, op. cit.*, page 436.
92. *Gladstone—Cropper, Correspondence*, page 15, Gladstone's letter, Nov. 5, 1823.
93. *Ragatz, op. cit.*, page 364.
94. *Gladstone—Cropper, Correspondence*, page 16, Gladstone's letter, Nov. 5, 1823.
95. Ibid., page 37. Nov. 22, 1823.
96. *J. Cropper: Letters to Wilberforce*, page VII.
97. *Stephen, op. cit.*, page 84.
98. *J. Cropper: Letters to Wilberforce*, page 2, May 3, 1821.
99. *Gladstone—Cropper, Correspondence*, page 55. Nov. 27, 1823.

meliorating changes as the effects of benevolent feeling and Christian principle, we should find many things irreconcilable with those views; whilst, if we admit the powerful co-operation of another principle, these difficulties will be removed. There can be no doubt that a reduction in the price of labour, probably (as in many places at present) to the lowest scale of subsistence, rendered slave labour unprofitable, and produced its abolition in many parts of Europe. . . . (That) emancipation has not been extensive where slave labour is profitable, shows that the efforts of benevolent men have been most successful when co-operating with natural causes."[100]

The abolitionists themselves did not steer clear of these commercial considerations. The Agency Committee instructed its agents not to place too much reliance on cases of colonial cruelty. Colonial statistics were far more useful, while "the general principles of religious duty and commercial policy give a more solid foundation for appeals to the public judgment."[101]

Macaulay and Cropper were only two of a number of people who stood to gain by emancipation. What motive was uppermost in their mind is unimportant. The economic factor was there.[102] The abolitionists needed all the support they could get, from any quarter whatever. But the whole significance of the East India sugar question is missed by considering it in the abstract. It was part of a general movement of the mercantile community against, firstly, the West Indian monopoly, because it was unprofitable, and secondly, all monopolies in general. The campaign to reduce the East India sugar duties failed for the simple reason that it merged into the broader question of free trade. The conflict had begun between two inconsistent forces, the social conscience making for emancipation, and the economic conscience striving towards free trade. By 1826 the attention of the mercantile community was directed towards Brazil as well as India, and we shall see in the later chapter how some of the protagonists of East India sugar moved logically forward towards the abolition of all monopolies and the removal of all discriminating duties. As the prelude to this later movement the East India sugar controversy is of paramount importance. For our immediate purpose, what it is essential to grasp is that the demand for equalization was an economic attack by the mercantile interest on the West Indian monopoly.

100. J. Cropper: *A Letter addressed to the Liverpool Society for promoting the Abolition of Slavery, on the injurious effects of high prices of produce, and the beneficial effects of low prices, on the condition of slaves* (Liverpool, 1823), pages 8–9 and 23. We seem almost to be listening to the economist Merivale.

101. *Stephen, op. cit.*, page 140.

102. Martin emphasizes the economic considerations which, from the very beginning of the African Institution, were linked with strong philanthropic motives. Giving a list of the Vice-Presidents and Directors, he adds that it is hardly necessary to comment on their business connections. *Op. cit.*, pages 137–138.

The campaign failed. The industrialists wanted cheap sugar, not East India sugar; free trade, not an East Indian instead of a West Indian monopoly, and the Brazilian trade was of vast importance. Brazil was to India in 1830 what St. Domingo had been in 1793.

It now remains for us to see what was the attitude of the Government in the controversy. The West Indian system, in Macaulay's words, stood "marked with the strongest features of impolicy and injustice."[103] Yet the duties were not equalized before 1836. Until the West Indian problem had been solved the Government considered it exceedingly improper to reduce the East India sugar duties.[104] Faced on the one hand with the strong West Indian interest and on the other with the pressure of the powerful commercial and industrial forces, each vociferously urging its rights, the Government were between the upper and nether millstones. As with the agitation for emancipation and with the question of Brazil, they compromised.

How was it, asked Huskisson, that this alleged cheap sugar from the East had not been brought to Europe by those countries which had no West Indian colonies, but which, prior to the French Revolution, had possessed factories in India?[105] How was it that the dearer West Indian sugar could find a sale abroad?[106] How was it that the cheap East India sugar did not drive out its rivals?[107] These arguments, not all fair or clear, showed the difficulties of the Government's position. The question, said Huskisson, could not be considered in the abstract. "Far was he from agreeing that the House might press hard upon a West Indian, because the West Indian happened to be an owner of slaves. That the West Indian was an owner of slaves was not his fault but his misfortune; and if it was true that the production of slavery was more costly than that of free labour, that would be an additional reason for not depriving him of the advantage of his protecting duty."[108] Free trade was a very sound principle, but all extensions of it were attended with great difficulty, and should be proceeded in with circumspection and with due

---

103. Macaulay, *op. cit.*, page 99.

104. *Parl. Deb.*, Third Series, Vol. XVI, page 326. Lord Althorp, March 6, 1833.

105. *Huskisson, Speeches*, Vol. II, page 197. May 22, 1823.

106. Ibid., Vol. III, page 141. May 15, 1827. Why should Huskisson have overlooked the bounty paid to the planter on export? This bounty alone enabled him to compete with his Brazilian and Cuban rivals.

107. Ibid., Vol. III, page 141. Huskisson also argued that those employed in manufacturing muslins would not turn to the cultivation of sugar (Vol. II, page 199). Why not? Had not sugar displaced cotton in the West? He reminded the East Indians that, as far as cotton was concerned, which they hoped to introduce on a large scale, every ounce was produced by the slave labour of Brazil and U.S.A. (Vol. II, pages 199–200).

108. Ibid., Vol. II, page 198. May 22, 1823.

regard to other general interests already widely established.[109] They ought to be cautious how they dealt with the vested interests of the West Indian capitalists.[110] The sting of Huskisson's compromise was in the tail. "The time must come, and could not be far distant, when the subject would be ripe for consideration, and when it would be imperative duty of Parliament to enter into a full investigation of all the circumstances connected with it."[111]

When that time came the issue had changed. It was no longer East India versus slave-grown sugar, or even free-grown versus slave-grown sugar. Morality and economics were opposed to each other, and the East Indians were put to the test of showing whether, as they had argued, their own sugar, freed from adverse duties, was capable of holding its own with the slave product of Brazil and Cuba.

---

109. Ibid., Vol. III, pages 138–139. May 15, 1827.

110. *Parl. Deb.*, NS, Vol. XIX, page 1213. June 9, 1828.

111. *Huskisson, Speeches*, Vol. III, page 146. May 15, 1827. Huskisson had an awkward time. In June 1828, he presented a petition from the merchants of Calcutta respecting the trade with India. The petitioners complained of the inconvenience felt and injury sustained by the unequal duty, and were indignant that their articles should be treated as if they were not the produce of a British possession. Huskisson added: "Looking to the trade with the Indian Archipelago—looking to the various new sources of trade and commerce which were springing up—but more particularly looking to the probable intercourse between India and the liberated states of South America, he was perfectly satisfied that a field would be opened for the employment of British capital, much more extensive than was imagined by those who had not narrowly considered the subject" (Ibid., Vol. III, page 356. June 16, 1828). And in 1829, on Grant's motion for the reduction of the sugar duties, Huskisson argued that the West Indian interest need not fear any injurious rivalry from the East! All Europe and America were free to trade in East India sugar, yet they took very little of that article; thus proving how groundless were the apprehensions of the West Indian merchants that the admission of East India sugar into the British market, on something like equal terms with their own, would be injurious to them (Ibid., Vol. III, page 456. May 25, 1829).

CHAPTER ELEVEN

The Distressed Areas

By the beginning of the nineteenth century the British West Indies were making neither men nor fortunes.[1] A change of system was inevitable: "if it were not very vicious in many respects it is becoming so unprofitable when compared with the expence that for this reason only it must at no distant time be nearly abandoned."[2]

The East Indian was not the sole competition within the Empire which the West Indian planters had to face. A more dangerous rival was Mauritius. Mauritius had been retained at the peace settlement in 1815 and immediately began to petition for a reduction of the heavy duties with which, as an eastern colony, its produce was burdened. Its very existence as a colony, it was said, was at stake. The extent of its productions was so circumscribed that if they were all thrown into the London market, they would probably produce no sensible effect upon the price of the article, and would affect neither the revenue nor the private interests of their brethren of the western colonies. Its slave population distinguished Mauritius from the other colonies

---

1. *Burn, op. cit.*, page 32.
2. *Liverpool Papers*, Add. Mss. 38295, folio 102. An anonymous correspondent to Lord Bexley, July 1823. Compare Lord Suffield's view of slavery: "In the first place he considered it to be most impolitic, because it was unproductive to those engaged in it. If it did produce profit he should say that it was unjustifiable, insomuch as that profit would be derived from a moral wrong." *Parl. Deb.*, Third Series, Vol. XIII, pages 6–7. May 24, 1832.

in the east, and therefore the planters begged that it should be put on the same footing as the slave colonies of the west.[3]

The Mauritius petitions were not granted until 1825. In the meantime the slave trade was carried on in all its horrors. Canning had opposed the cession of Mauritius to France because its proximity to the very fountain of slaves would have been a great temptation to carry on the slave trade to an enormous extent. The Mauritius planters did not hesitate to take advantage of their favourable geographical position. The slave trade was carried on, in Buxton's words, as notorious as the sun at noon-day.[4] It was not a question of desperate adventurers, but a regular, systematic and unceasing importation, to such an extent, and in a manner so open, as to reflect, in the strongest manner, on the highest authorities in the island.[5] Consequently he demanded an official inquiry, warning Parliament that, if they refused to act, "there is an end of our abolition labours. No more high-sounding treaties with the Imaun of Muscal, or the king of Madagascar—no more exultations at our righteousness, no more remonstrances against the hollowness of France! England will stand as the worst of slave traders, and the chief of convicted hypocrites."[6]

The Government denied the allegations of the abolitionists. In Horton's opinion an inquiry would have been a waste of time.[7] He thought that the humanitarians' case was weak, and that much of their future power and popularity depended on the issue.[8] To Bathurst's mind the humanitarian agitation had degenerated into "a controversy in which the cause of humanity has by the heat of a long-continued contest soured . . . into malignity."[9] Horton acquitted the Governor of all knowledge or participation, but the "easiness" of his character made him fear that it was possible that he had been systematically juggled and deceived. The question was not a farce; at least, if it were, it was the most serious in which Buxton had ever performed.[10]

The Mauritius planters had not continued the slave trade out of viciousness or perverseness. What the slave trade meant to them can be seen from

3. *H. of C. Sess. Papers, Accounts and Papers*, 1825, Vol. XIX, No. 236, pages 11, 15, 17 and 23. Petitions of Oct. 23, 1816; May 5, 1821; May 25, 1824.
4. *Parl. Deb.*, NS, Vol. XVI, page 606. Feb. 21, 1827.
5. Ibid., Vol. XV, pages 1014–1015. May 9, 1826.
6. Ibid., page 1037.
7. Ibid., page 1049.
8. *Bathurst Mss.*, page 611. Horton to Bathurst, Aug. 16, 1826.
9. Ibid., page 608. Bathurst to Horton, Aug. 3, 1826.
10. Ibid., page 611. Horton to Bathurst, Aug. 16, 1826.

the terrific increase in the growth of sugar. The output increased sixtyfold between 1810 and 1822. In the four years 1819–1822, while the price of sugar had been reduced nearly one-half, the production had quadrupled.[11]

Huskisson, however, in his masterly exposition of the colonial policy of the country, contended in favour of equalization of the duties that no serious prejudice could result to the West Indian planter as the quantity of sugar grown in Mauritius was not considerable.[12] Some 10,000 or 12,000 hogsheads might find their way into the British market, which, without equalization, would be sent to Europe and thus determine the price in the general market.[13] Huskisson could no more have meant this than the Government have meant their denials of the patent fact that Mauritius had for years violated the abolition laws.[14] The Mauritius exports to Britain alone nearly

11. *Parl. Deb.*, NS, Vol. XV, pages 1025–1026. Buxton, May 9, 1826. The following table shows the increase of the Mauritius output as compared with the East Indian exports. The Mauritius figures are the total export, the East India to the United Kingdom only. The former are taken from *L. J. Ragatz: Statistics for the Study of British Caribbean Economic History, 1763–1833* (London, 1927), page 20, Table XX; the latter from *Customs* 5/4–14.

Table 11.1.

Year	Mauritius	East India (direct and indirect)
1815	20,049 cwt.	124,319 cwt.
1816	82,963	127,163
1817	65,834	125,893
1818	79,083	162,395
1819	56,788	205,527
1820	155,247	277,228
1821	204,100	269,158
1822	234,036	226,371
1823	274,008	219,580
1824	243,345	271,848

The East India figures, which are given to the nearest cwt., are substantially the same as those in *Ragatz: Statistics*, page 21, Table XXII.

12. *Huskisson, Speeches*, Vol. II, page 325. March 21, 1825.

13. Ibid., Vol. II, page 424. June 3, 1825.

14. The Government subsequently admitted that the laws had been violated.

quadrupled in the years 1825 to 1828, and in 1831 exceeded half a million hundredweight or more than one-third of the export from Jamaica.[15]

The increased production was due to two causes: the slave trade, which had stocked the island with slaves, and the substitution of sugar for coffee. In opposing the equalization of the duties, abolitionists and West Indians joined hands. Brougham could not explain it except by assuming that the policy had been to give bounty and protection to the masters of slaves and to withhold it from the masters of freemen.[16] We must not, like Brougham, blind ourselves to the fact that British policy was, as we shall see, based on making Britain the emporium of sugar and the supplier of the world. The introduction of Mauritius sugar proved disastrous to the West Indies by increasing the surplus in a market already overstocked, but it did not, as East India sugar would have done, raise the vexed question of the relative merits of free grown and slave grown sugar. Mauritius taught the lesson which Brazil and Cuba were to improve upon, that slavery, in given conditions, with an unexhausted and fertile soil and paucity of labour, was economically a profitable method of production. The West Indies could not compete with the slave labour of East, nor could they with the slave labour of Mauritius or the slave labour of Brazil and Cuba. They could hold their own only against rocks as sterile as themselves.

It was not merely that the West Indian snails could not hope to keep pace with the tortoises elsewhere, but even among the snails themselves there were great inequalities. Mauritius was not the only sugar island which had been retained in 1815. Trinidad and Demerara had also been acquired, and the Committee set up in 1831 to investigate the commercial state of the West Indies admitted that this extension of the sugar colonies was one of the

---

15. The following statistics, compiled from *Customs* 5/16–22, show the rate of increase. (The export for 1825 to Britain was 93,723 cwt. *Ragatz: Statistics*, page 20, Table XX.)

Table 11.2.

Year	British Imports (to nearest cwt.)
1826	186,782
1827	204,344
1828	361,325
1829	291,567
1830	485,710
1831	517,552
1832	541,768
1833	529,352

16. *Parl. Deb.*, NS, Vol. XVII, page 843. May 15, 1827.

most operative causes of existing distress. They made it clear, however, that the acquisition of more fertile, and therefore valuable, possessions could not be admitted as giving to any part of the more ancient Empire a right to be compensated for the depreciation of its produce. "It would be as reasonable for an English landholder to complain of the effect of the corn and cattle of Ireland, admitted on the principle of the Union, as for a planter in Jamaica to urge that his produce is become cheaper since Demerara has been added to the British Dominions."[17]

The fertility of these new colonies was a striking contrast to the exhausted soil of the old colonies. Cropper constantly emphasized that the West Indian colonies, with the tendency of soil to deteriorate under slave cultivation, could no longer maintain a profitable slave economy able to compete with the vast territory of the United States—or for that matter of Brazil—which permitted the planter to abandon the soil as soon as it was exhausted.[18] In Trinidad and Demerara it was not so much the extent of territory as their natural fertility which rendered them superior to the older islands. In fact the Jamaica and Barbados of 1820 had to compete with Jamaica and Barbados of 1750. Governors expatiated on the fertility of Trinidad, where the labour on coffee and cocoa estates was comparatively an amusement,[19] and where the returns from a sugar estate were beyond the conception of any person not well-informed on the subject.[20] In the older islands, whilst the exhaustion of the soil required the laborious operations of digging and manuring, the slave produced only one hogshead of sugar on an average; in Trinidad, the soil being very rich, no manure was needed, and the average output was not less than three hogsheads per slave.[21] The land in Trinidad, moreover, required replanting only once in ten years, whereas in the older colonies the land had to be replanted every second year.[22] The canes in Trinidad produced saccharine matter in proportion of 2.5 to 1 compared with the older islands.[23]

The same thing was true of Demerara. In 1800 a resident in the colony extolled its importance, prophesied that its cultivation would be doubled in the course of twenty or thirty years, and argued against its restoration to

17. H. of C. Sess. Pap, Reports Committees, 1831–1832, Vol. XX, No. 381. Select Committee appointed to inquire into the Commercial state of the West India Colonies, page 15. (Referred to hereafter as Select Committee, 1831–1832.)
18. J. Cropper: The support of Slavery Investigated (Liverpool, 1824), page. 9.
19. C.O. 295/78. Farquharson to Murray, Oct. 12, 1828.
20. C.O. 295/80. Grant to Murray, Oct. 12, 1828.
21. C.O. 295/78. Farquharson to Murray, Oct. 12, 1828.
22. Ibid., Marryat claimed that the land in the old islands needed replanting every three years, in Trinidad once in every twenty or more. C.O. 295/79. Marryat to Murray, Aug. 19, 1828.
23. C.O. 295/79. Marryat to Murray, Aug. 19, 1828.

its former indolent possessors.[24] It was estimated that the relative fertility of Demerara and Barbados, as judged by exports, was in the proportion of four to one.[25] In Demerara it took 200 days' labour to produce 5,000 lbs of sugar, in Barbados 400. In the former sugar was produced without any outlay of capital for manure, in the latter it required twenty-five per cent of the labour of the plantation.[26] Huskisson, in opposing the Chancellor of the Exchequer's reduction of the sugar duties in 1830, emphasized that the distress in the older islands was much greater than that in Demerara and Trinidad, and that two of the most fertile of the older colonies, Barbados and Antigua, did not produce more than one-third of the sugar from Demerara.[27] The Select Committee of 1831 recommended that the loans which the Government intended to make to the colonies should be confined to the older islands, as if extended to the more recently acquired colonies they might serve as a stimulus to increase production.[28] The West Indian planters had asked for an increased bounty on export, which the Committee dared not recommend: "a bounty given in common to Dominica and to Demerara may have the effect of bringing to market from the new acquisition an augmented quantity of sugar, to compete with more limited produce of the old possession."[29]

24. *Windham Papers*, Add. Mss. 37879, folio 116. Samuel Sanbach to his uncle, April 13, 1800.
25. C.O. 111/16. Codd to Bathurst, Nov. 18, 1813.
26. *Select Committee, 1831–1832*. Page 180. Evidence of John P. Mayers, agent for Barbados.
27. *Huskisson, Speeches*, Vol. III, pages 596–597. June 21, 1830. Huskisson probably meant the two islands separately. From the following table, taken from *Ragatz: Statistics*, page 20, Table XVII, we can see the competition from Trinidad and Demerara.

Table 11.3.

Year	Antigua cwt	Barbados cwt	Jamaica cwt	Trinidad cwt	Demerara & Berbice cwt
1812	187,822	156,196	1,455,954	118,407	236,899
1822	102,934	156,662	1,413,675	178,989	586,305
1823	135,466	314,538	1,417,725	186,981	663,857
1824	222,200	245,802	1,451,325	180,093	680,598
1828	176,966	338,855	1,463,974	265,703	802,319
1829	156,657	270,860	1,386,392	292,833	865,616
1830	138,431	295,793	1,352,356	156,427	828,132
1831	169,031	322,777	1,395,892	240,764	900,890
1832	133,472	244,024	1,416,186	233,200	815,398
1833	115,932	350,462	1,238,574	206,680	830,015

Comparing the years 1812 and 1833, the Antigua output had diminished by nearly one-half, and the Barbados figure had more than doubled. Trinidad exports were nearly 50 per cent higher, while Demerara and Berbice had multiplied three and a half times. Jamaica remained practically stationary until 1832, but in the next year there was a decline of more than 10 per cent. (For the years 1825–1827 there are no details, island by island.)
28. *Select Committee, 1831–1832*, page. 20.
29. Ibid., page 18.

There was only one thing that restrained the full development of these two colonies, their limited slave population. To remedy this they strained the letter of the law to the utmost. The cost of a slave in Barbados or Antigua was only £35 or £40, in Demerara and Trinidad it was from £80 to £90.[30] Slaves were needed, if the cultivation was to be extended, and this was the background to the intercolonial slave trade of the twenties which reached enormous proportions. Specious arguments were adduced to justify this slave trade, for it was nothing less. The toil of the slaves was lighter in a fertile soil, their provision grounds were more fruitful (removing the danger of famine) and were worked with less labour, the humane regulations enforced by Orders in Council in the crown colonies were highly advantageous to the slaves and it was easier for them to purchase their freedom. If the Order in Council could not go to the slaves, the slaves should be encouraged to go to the Order in Council, and so great was the need of labourers that the planters of Trinidad and Demerara expressed their willingness to accede to any conditions laid down by the Government. Applications for the removal of slaves in large batches inundated the Governors and Colonial Office, and bankrupt planters of the older islands saw in this removal a means of getting rid of their superabundant slave population. Between 1808 and 1821, 7,775 slaves were imported into Demerara, and a further 1,750 were introduced by the end of 1825.[31] In the nine years ending in 1821 the Trinidad slave population was augmented by 3,815 recruits from the older colonies.[32] This slave trade was carried on under the innocent guise of domestics attendant on the persons of their owners and it was not until 1825, when it had become notorious, that the Consolidated Slave Act laid down stringent regulations designed to mitigate the horrors and diminish the extent of an evil totally at variance with Britain's contemporary efforts to induce perverse and immoral foreign nations to suppress the traffic.[33]

As a result of the vast extension of sugar cultivation in the colonies acquired in 1815 the British market was overstocked. This excessive production was not a temporary but an increasing evil,[34] and the Committee of 1831 asserted that this overproduction was the original cause of West Indian

---

30. *Huskisson, Speeches*, Vol. III, page 610. June 21, 1830.
31. C.O. 111/37 and C.O. 111/54.
32. C.O. 295/55.
33. See Appendix Three for "Pièces Justificatives" on the Intercolonial Slave Trade.
34. *Statements to the Board of Trade*, page 9. Statement extracted from various communications received from the House of Assembly of Jamaica.

depression, the difference between the war period and 1831 being only in the circumstances of aggravation.[35]

To imagine that this question of overproduction is an exaggeration is to commit a grave error. Poulett Thomson, Vice-President of the Board of Trade, estimated that the West Indies sent to Britain twenty-five per cent more sugar than was wanted in the country.[36] Stanley put the surplus at one million hundred weight in 1833;[37] John Wood, the member for Preston, reduced it to one-eighth,[38] while the West Indian planters declared that it would require the extinction of one-fourth of the cultivation to bring the prices up to the required point.[39] So long as there was this surplus, the West Indian monopoly was a nominal and not a real one, and we shall see presently exactly what this surplus implied.

To remedy this deep-rooted evil the West Indians asked for palliatives, and would have resorted to the old expedient of using sugar in the distilleries. So long as the war continued, the war-time depression remained, and it could be argued that distillation from sugar was justified. But Lord Auckland pointed out that this expedient would only remove some twelve of the 70,000 hogsheads which were lying unsold in 1808,[40] and the barley counties raised a great howl against this invasion of their rights. They should not depart, one member said, from "the fundamental principles of public economy, so decidedly laid down by Hume, Stuart and Smith in this country, and by Turgot and Condorcet in France. The uncertain wealth of speculation should not be supported by the sacrifice of the certain benefits of agriculture."[41] Everyone admitted the justice of the West Indian case, everyone spoke to them words of commiseration, but everyone sent them to the next door.[42] A few dissentient peers strongly reprobated a policy which sanctioned the temporary relief of those who had embarked their capital in one branch of industry by imposing hardships on those whose capital was engaged in promoting national prosperity through the means of another branch of industry.[43] If the West Indians were granted relief, as well might Parliament make good the losses of those merchants and manufacturers who had hazarded their property in Buenos Ayres, while it had been in British hands. If they were successful, there would be no end to their applications

35. *Select Committee, 1831–1832*, page 21.
36. *Parl. Deb.*, Third Series, Vol. II, page 790. Feb. 21, 1831.
37. Ibid., Third Series, Vol. XVII, page 1209. May 14, 1833.
38. Ibid., NS, Vol. XXV, page 322. June 14, 1830.
39. *Statements to the Board of Trade*, page 90. Jan. 19, 1831.
40. *Parl. Deb.*, Vol. X, page 733, Feb. 25, 1808.
41. Ibid., Vol. XI, page 58. Mr. Brand, April 13, 1808.
42. Ibid., page 518, Mr. Barham, May 23, 1808.
43. Ibid., page 1115. June 30, 1808.

in the future. The planters pleaded that Britain as a result of the war was on the verge of famine. But the idea of famine never would have entered their heads if there had not been a vast surplus of sugar for which no market could be found. "Sweet gentlemen! They have sought a very far fetched argument in support of their saccharine cause!"[44]

The use of sugar in the distilleries in 1830 would have been a pill to cure an earthquake.[45] The planters argued that it was difficult to act in concert or combination to reduce production.[46] Overproduction was therefore inevitable in West Indian economy.[47] The West Indians could not work out their own salvation, they must therefore be forced to be free. Time was when the sick man of the British Empire might have been supported though not permanently restored by cordials.[48] The time for cordials was over. A major operation was necessary.

The West Indians had long been urged to overthrow the despotism of King Sugar. The American War of 1812 gave a temporary stimulus to the cultivation of cotton. Stephen, the abolitionist, and Marryat, the West Indian, recommended it on the ground that the lighter labour involved would tend to ameliorate the condition of the slaves.[49] Governor Woodford of Trinidad was instructed to encourage the cultivation of provisions,[50] and Macaulay advised the West Indians in their own interest to cultivate their own corn and rear their own cattle instead of raising so unprofitable an article as sugar.[51] But here the vicious system which prevailed in the West Indies intervened. Corn and rice, the Governor of Demerara asserted, could be raised in any quantity and cattle reared sufficient to supply all the islands and render them independent of the United States. But unfortunately these humble paths to certain profit were

---

44. *Windham Papers*, Add. Mss. 37886, folios 125–128. "Observations on the proposal of the West India Merchants to substitute sugar in the distilleries instead of barley" (anonymous). The date is probably 1807.

45. Althorp refused the demand in 1831. The revenue from malt would that year show an increase of £800,000, which he would not be justified in hazarding. *Parl. Deb.*, Third Series Vol. III, page 375. March 11, 1831. The West Indians then asked that molasses should be allowed in the distilleries. The proposition was opposed, among others, by Michael Sadler, who championed the interests of the community. "A wholesome beverage might be made from that article, but the people of England did not like it." Ibid., Third Series, Vol. V, page 82. July 20, 1831.

46. Ibid., Vol. XI, page 507. Mr. Barham, May 23, 1808.

47. *Statements to the Board of Trade*, page 12. Statement of Mr. J. R. Smith: "It is one of the peculiar features of production in the West India Colonies, that it is not practically reducible to such a moderate extent as would bring it within the demand for the consumption of Great Britain."

48. *Parl. Deb.*, Vol. XI, page 526. Mr. Hibbert, May 23, 1808.

49. Ibid., Vol. XXVI, pages 967 and 973. June 29, 1813.

50. C.O. 295/30. Woodford to Bathurst, Aug. 3, 1813.

51. *East India Sugar Debate, 1823*, page 32.

overlooked by people whose whole attention was absorbed in the expectation of obtaining rapid fortunes by the growth of sugar, coffee or cotton;[52] and the mercantile creditor, who stipulated that the produce should be remitted to him for the sale, on which he gained a commission in addition to his interest, found the sale of corn and rice in a nearby market of no advantage to him.[53]

When the Governor of Trinidad could write that whereas twenty-five pounds of beef cost on the neighbouring continent eighteen pence, the price in Trinidad was as high as two shillings per pound,[54] the position was serious. The grant of Crown lands was therefore made on the condition that sugar should not be cultivated. A proposal from a Mr. James Hamilton to set up establishments for breeding cattle, horses and mules on a large scale was welcomed by Huskisson as tending to a beneficial employment of the land.[55] Both Twiss and Taylor of the Colonial Office resisted any petition for permission to grow sugar on new lands. Taylor said that sugar cultivation had evil effects on the slaves.[56] This was undoubtedly true, but equally true was it that the object was to prevent the extension of sugar cultivation. In fact it is even possible that the policy was to make things as difficult as possible for the planters. In 1832 some members of the Trinidad Council petitioned for the abolition of the slave tax of one pound currency per head. The comment of the Colonial Office is illuminating. It was "of very great importance that this tax should be continued; instead of rendering slave labour cheaper it is desirable to render it dearer."[57] The various Orders in Council sent out by the home Government would, in the long run, have diminished production by reducing the hours of labour. In 1824 the Government determined "to maintain entire and unbroken the maxim that the owner of the slave has no title to his labour, except during six days of the week."[58] The Order of November 1831 reduced the working day of the slave to nine hours, which the Trinidad

---

52. C.O. 111/16. Murray to Bathurst, June 22, 1813.
53. Ibid. Codd to Bathurst, Sept. 6, 1813. "The consignees of West India property resided in London, Liverpool and Glasgow. Bristol too was a favoured spot; and the slaves were scarcely more the property of the planters than the planters themselves were the property of their consignees and creditors on this side of the Atlantic." *Stephen, op. cit.*, page 113.
54. C.O. 295/33. Woodford to Bathurst, Oct. 3, 1814.
55. C.O. 295/75. The date of Hamilton's letter was July 14, 1827.
56. C.O. 111/68. No date, but probably 1829.
57. C.O. 295/93. The Council's petition was enclosed in Governor Grant's despatch of August 29, 1832.
58. C.O. 111/49. Bathurst to D'Urban, July 9, 1825.

proprietors considered "a sentence of confiscation of the property of all the sugar planters in the island."[59]

All these palliatives had little effect. The West Indians were no nearer the possession of a real monopoly of the home market. By 1833 indigo had long disappeared in face of the competition from the East, and tobacco had gone. Trinidad cocoa succumbed under the competition of the Brazilian product,[60] and the cotton of Demerara and Berbice, once a substantial amount, was

---

59. C.O. 295/92. Edward Jackson to Gov. Grant. Dec. 31, 1831: "Upon what principle," Jackson asked, "save that of a most unjust and oppressive invasion of property, can it be reconciled that the master in England may by law exact twelve hours labour from children in the heated and sickly atmosphere of a cotton-manufactory, and the West India proprietor is prohibited from employing the full grown workman under the cool and airy shade of the mill or boiling house in a much lighter work for more than nine hours."

60. Trinidad Governors always urged the pleasant nature and light labour of cocoa cultivation. In Jan. 1819 the cocoa planters asked for a reduction of the duty (C.O. 295/49) and Gov. Woodford recommended a preference for Trinidad cocoa in purchases under the Treasury's authority (C.O. 295/53. Dec. 1, 1821). But even the reduction of the duty did not make the use of cocoa general (C.O. 295/55. Woodford to Bathurst, April 2, 1822). Trinidad, one planter urged, should be made a cocoa island, and the Negroes employed in distilling poisonous rum and growing bad sugar should be made to plant cocoa (C.O. 295/63. Henry Graham to Woodford, n.d.). Woodford assured Horton that the encouragement of cocoa would be the greatest boon to the slave population, and enclosed a letter from London in which it was stated that a Government contract for 80 tons of cocoa had been confined to Brazil cocoa, when there were in the docks enough British plantation cocoa to supply three such contracts (Ibid., Dec. 7, 1824). Governor Grant submitted that it was "good policy to take for consumption a staple article of our own colonies, when furnished at the lowest remunerating price, and forming employment and the means of subsistence to the bulk of the population through the medium, in a great degree, of free labour, in preference to getting it from a foreign country even at a lower price" (C.O. 295/89. Grant to Goderich, Jan. 4, 1831). This was hardly an argument to appeal to a country which was soon to demand cheap food, and to emphasise the cost rather than the nature of the production. The following figures, taken from *Ragatz: Statistics*, page 14, Table II and *Customs* 5/17–22, show the competition of Brazil with the West Indian product.

Table 11.4.

Year	Trinidad lbs.	Total B.W.I. lbs.	Brazil lbs.
1828	104,047	449,598	1,174,1686
1829	300,873	678,850	2,442,456
1830	411,989	711,867	1,308,694
1831	1,017,835	1,451,792	1,711,614
1832	387,225	590,276	2,198,709
1833	1,755,144	2,120,527	2,502,803

It should be noted that the Trinidad product in 1814 was 1,576,400 lbs.

by 1833 a mere drop in the ocean of the American and Brazilian product.[61] With the growing popularity of coffee and the increase in the number of coffee houses in London the West Indies had to face the competition of the East Indies, Brazil, Ceylon and Singapore.[62] King Sugar remained in all his unprofitable isolation, with no rival to threaten his supremacy, and no more profitable article likely to outbid him for the allegiance of his bankrupt subjects.

Such a situation called for drastic measures. The distress of the colonists, said Stanley in 1833, could be traced to one plain and undeniable cause— they had overstocked the market. The owners of property in the West Indies, he affirmed, proceeded with enterprises not warranted by the circumstances

---

61. The following table shows the gradual abandonment of cotton in the West Indies (*Ragatz: Statistics*, page 16, Tables VII and VIII).

Table 11.5.

Year	Demerara and Berbice lbs	Total B.W.I. lbs
1818	8,457,345	10,446,885
1820	5,074,853	6,472,454
1822	6,526,318	8,556,668
1824	3,733,970	5,718,102
1829	3,108,679	4,424,683
1830	1,785,227	3,161,132
1831	1,433,894	1,994,785
1832	1,267,606	1,640,649
1833	1,109,889	1,539,984

In 1812 the figures were: B.W.I., 13,265,289; Demerara and Berbice 9,437,473 lbs.

62. *Ragatz: Statistics*, page 15, Table IV, and *Customs* 5/14–22. The figures are in pounds avoirdupois.

Table 11.6.

Year	B.W.I.	E.I. & Ceylon	Brazil	Singapore, Java, Philippines etc.
1825	24,940,989	4,513,290	6,132,371	....
1826	24,700,504	5,520,354	3,854,752	....
1827	29,011,812	1,392,099	6,002,680	4,479,719
1828	29,451,872	2,767,313	3,013,816	4,596,293
1829	26,582,613	1,739,057	3,393,928	4,551,267
1830	27,043,261	3,202,207	3,242,513	3,833,283
1831	19,687,107	4,337,016	9,151,771	3,168,332
1832	24,465,433	5,605,666	6,661,151	4,775,268
1833	28,517,813	3,910,114	3,341,733	2,313,061

It is clear that the E.I. figures for 1825 and 1826 include Singapore etc. In addition, Cuba, Hayti and various parts of South America were sending large quantities to Britain. Hayti sent over four million lbs. in 1831 and Cuba nearly five million in 1832.

of the colonies or the demand for sugar in the European markets.[63] This was positive madness. Only one thing could save the West Indians, a reduction of the quantity of sugar brought to market.[64] The trouble with these colonies was that the sugar which they produced was not only expensive but that it was greater than the demand of the mother country while at the same time inadequate to allow Britain to command the export trade. In other words what was wanted was that the West Indians should have a real monopoly of the home market, with no surplus for export, while the British sugar refining industry would capture the entire European market by making Britain the emporium of all the sugar of the world. Stanley's assertion was not so much incorrect as dishonest. But what did that matter? Any stick was good enough to beat the West Indians with—St. Domingo, East Indies or Brazil. What mattered was that the West Indians had to be beaten.

Whatever the shortcomings of Stanley's argument, his object was clear. Baring had previously objected that emancipation would mean that the black freeman would cease to cultivate sugar,[65] and would "pass his hours basking in the scorching sunshine of a luxurious but languid climate." Emancipation would treble the price of sugar. Was the country prepared to pay some six millions annually "for the pleasure of performing costly experiments in humanity"?[66] Stanley replied that "as far as the amount of the production of sugar is concerned, I am not quite certain that to some extent a diminution of that production would be matter of regret—I am not quite certain that it might not be for the benefit of the planters and of the colonies themselves, in the end, if that production were to be diminished."[67]

We have now to consider this question of overproduction in relation to the foreign market. The twenty-five per cent surplus which could not be sold at home came into competition in the European markets with the Brazilian and Cuban product. While Britain in the main monopolized the Brazilian carrying-trade, America monopolized the Cuban, but the sugar of both places was taken in large quantities to Britain, some in foreign ships, for subsequent

63. *Parl. Deb.*, Third Series, Vol. XVII, page 1209. May 14, 1833.
64. Ibid., Third Series, Vol. VI, page 1330. Althorp, Sept. 12, 1831. Althorp therefore refused to reduce the high war-time duties on sugar, remembering Huskisson's warning that every shilling off the sugar duties would mean a loss of £150,000 annually to the revenue (*Huskisson Speeches*, Vol. II, page 235. March 8, 1824). Althorp preferred to reduce the duties on sea-borne coals and candles, after which the suggestion that the sugar duties should be reduced seemed to him unreasonable (*Parl. Deb.*, Third Series, Vol. II, page 795. Feb. 21, 1831). The parlous state of the West Indies afforded the best prospect of obtaining those reforms demanded alike on humanitarian and economic grounds.
65. *Parl. Deb.*, Third Series, Vol. III, page 1463. April 15, 1831.
66. Ibid., Third Series, Vol. XVIII, pages 492–493. June 7, 1833.
67. Ibid., Third Series, Vol. XVII, pages 1209 and 1211–1212. May 14, 1833.

re-exportation.[68] The Brazilian and Cuban sugar dominated the European market in much the same way as the sugar of St. Domingo had done in pre-war days.[69] The West Indians laid the blame for everything at the door of the slave trade. According to their own estimate their cost of production had been increased by 15/10d per cwt. by the abolition of the slave trade, but it

68. *Customs* 5/6–22. The figures are to the nearest cwt.

Table 11.7.

Year	Brazil		Cuba	
	Br. Ships	For. Ships	Br. Ships	For. Ships
1817	50,822	....	35,594	....
1818	46,466	....	77,022	....
1819	59,373	....	19,700	....
1820	80,446	....	62,634	....
1821	105,410	....	74,844	....
1822	28,469	....	71,128	3,728
1823	70,719	719	122,048	....
1824	87,693	....	98,809	15,970
1825	67,491	5,220	69,684	16,796
1826	12,241	....	34,404	12,550
1827	77,202	....	64,939	21,049
1828	97,393	....	20,780	10,783
1829	55,203	....	64,346	35,670
1830	85,749	8,801	57,900	60,438
1831	359,975	2,647	75,611	36,531
1832	144,022	3,293	145,927	64,917
1833	197,983	215	89,495	49,609

The great increase in 1831 was due to a temporary act admitting foreign sugar for refining purposes.
69. *Statements to the Board of Trade*, page 58. The following figures show the importation of Cuban and Brazilian sugar, jointly, into Hamburg and Prussia, and separately into Russia.

Table 11.8.

Year	Hamburg	Prussia	Russia	
			Cuba	Brazil
1822	63,886	120,502		
1823	84,378	188,823		
1824	68,798	207,801	616,542	331,584
1825	66,817	265,035	729,156	217,039
1826	51,210	302,359	539,782	131,790
1827	81,402	413,216	553,297	208,450
1828	93,682	404,203	823,242	204,704
1829	75,441	415,134	935,395	415,287

The Hamburg figures are in boxes and chests, the Prussian in cwt., and the Russian in poods, one pood being equivalent to 36 lbs.

is significant that the Committee of 1831 refused to accept this figure and suggested that the difference in price was to be found in natural causes, that is, the superior fertility of the soil in Brazil and Cuba.[70]

Under these circumstances the West Indians found artificial support imperative in order to enable their surplus to compete with their rivals. The bounty on refined sugar exported and the drawback on raw sugar exported both went to the planter, and were an encouragement to him to produce. Consequently, the price in the home market was determined by the price obtained abroad, and the West Indian monopoly ceased to be a monopoly in all but name. By 1833, Britain was not merely paying a high price for sugar at home, as a result of the quantity taken out of the home market by the premium on export, but this bounty was being paid in order to enable the West Indians to upset the Continental market and compete with Britain's best customer. It was necessary therefore to diminish West Indian production at all costs.

The planters were mere nominal owners, but the merchants, the real owners, were unwilling to advance any more money in an unprofitable undertaking. In St. Christopher only three of the hereditary proprietors remained in the island,[71] scarcely an ancient name existed in possession of its patrimony, and those who had been driven to the possession of it found it an encumbrance instead of an advantage. The struggle of the West Indian planters was not for a restoration of their former prosperity, but for bread, not for the acquisition of power, but to avert the knife from their throats.[72] In Jamaica seventeen estates in the parish of Hanover had not paid, in November 1831, the taxes due in August, and very few had settled the contingent accounts.[73] The distress was equally felt in the newer islands. It was so extreme that Marryat declared the situation of the West Indians to be one of annihilation rather than distress,[74] and Whitmore assured the House that even in the Lapland prosperity was the rule, while in the West Indies distress was the rule and prosperity the exception.[75] Their rum could not be sold in the United States and it was better to throw it into the sea than to carry it to Britain.[76] No person, said Lord Redesdale, would advance a shilling on West

---

70. *Select Committee, 1831–1832*, pages 16–17.

71. Ibid., page 126. Evidence of James Colquhoun, agent for the Leeward Islands.

72. Ibid., page 120. Petition of Council and Assembly of St. Christopher, 1825, presented by Anthony Brown, agent for the Antigua and Montserrat.

73. Ibid., page 24. Evidence of Alexander Macdonnell, Secretary to the Committee of West Indian Merchants, quoting a letter from Mr. Robert Hibbert of Jamaica, Nov. 8, 1831.

74. *Parl. Deb.*, NS, Vol. XXV, page 308. June 14, 1830.

75. Ibid., NS, Vol. XI, page 732. May 13, 1824.

76. *Select Committee, 1831–1832*, page 112. Evidence of James M'Queen, West Indian Merchant in Glasgow.

Indian property.[77] To quote the words of a modern writer, "by 1833 the West Indies were not an inferno, but they were (what is often less easy to defend) an anachronism."[78] These were the colonies that found themselves in opposition to the most powerful interest in Britain, the industrial bourgeoisie.

77. *Parl. Deb.*, NS, Vol. XV, page 385. April 19, 1826.
78. Burn, *op. cit.*, page 73.

CHAPTER TWELVE

The Industrialists and Emancipation

The part played by the industrial and commercial forces has never been given its proper place in the history of the emancipation movement. The abolitionists could not prevent these interested men with their ulterior motives from enlisting on their side in their moral crusade. The Emancipation act was a triumph—even though an incomplete one—for the industrialists, as it was a triumph—also incomplete—for the humanitarians, and we shall see what catastrophic effects were to ensue to humanity from the divergent views of industrialists and humanitarians.

Before 1825 the British West Indies had been of considerable value as entrepôts for the export trade to the rising states of South America. During the Napoleonic wars, with Britain driven in a corner by the Continental Blockade, the West Indian islands furnished the means of extending the sale of British manufactures.[1] In Trinidad it was urged that while abolition had ruined agricultural prospects, the colony would hold for ages as a commercial depôt, and if its gates were thrown open to all vessels and all commodities from all parts, the result would astonish the heads that devised and promoted the scheme.[2] Stephen estimated that probably two-thirds of the British

---

1. *Windham Papers*, Add. Mss. 37883, folio 209. A. Cochran Johnstone; "Hints for Mr. Windham's information relative to the West Indies," April 12, 1806. "Let all the ports of our West India Colonies be opened, without any invidious preference or distinction, and the result will be that Great Britain will find a new market for her manufacturers, extend her carrying trade, and hereafter derive greater advantages from the French colonies than even the power to which they belong."
2. C.O. 295/25. Attorney General to Governor Hislop, 1810.

exports to Jamaica, the greatest entrepôt of the indirect trade with South America, were re-exported to the Spanish and other foreign colonies, and he assured Lord Castlereagh that it would be a very large estimate to suppose that the British sugar colonies consumed in British manufactures and commodities more than one-tenth part of their value of their imports.[3]

The prosperity which accrued to the islands from this trade was altogether destroyed by the recognition of the independence of the South America States. There was no longer any need of an indirect trade. Huskisson in 1825 proposed to extend to certain West Indian ports the benefits and regulations of the warehousing system. This in his opinion would be attended with extraordinary advantages, for the wants of these new states, suffering from a lack of capital, were "best supplied as it were, in retail, and by small deliveries frequently renewed"; a large cargo was not easily disposed of and glutted the market.[4] But Huskisson was flogging a dead horse. The raison d'être of the entrepôts had disappeared, and this combined with the distress in the islands, which meant a reduction of the planters' purchasing power, produced a great decline in British exports to the Islands. The tremendous expansion of British industry and commerce was accompanied by the declining importance of the colonies which had once been the gems of the Empire. The West Indians were shrinking as markets. "Judged by the standards of economic imperialism, the British West India Colonies, a considerable success about 1750, had become a failure eighty years later."[5] The grapes the industrialists wanted could be gathered not from the West Indian thistles, but from the Brazilian, Cuban and Eastern vineyards.

The British industrialists constantly stressed the fact that the exports of British manufactures to Brazil, Cuba, St. Domingo, India and Batavia exceeded by fivefold those to the West Indies and offered a field for unlimited

---

3. *Castlereagh Correspondence* Vol. XII, page 13. Stephen's "Suggestions relative to Africa and colonial discussions that may have place in the Congress at Aix-la-Chapelle," 1818.
4. *Huskisson, Speeches*, Vol. II. Page 318. March 21, 1825.
5. *Burn, op. cit.*, page 52.

extension.[6] Pride of place went to Brazil, and in Liverpool there was a powerful Brazilian Association loudly proclaiming the importance of the Brazil trade.[7] We can understand now why Canning had taken a firm line in the question of its recognition, had threatened to resign over it, and when he had won his point wrote exultantly: "The nail is driven. . . . Spanish America is free, and if we do not mismanage our affairs sadly she is English. The Yankees will shout in triumph, but it is they who lose most by our decision."[8]

It is with this background in mind that we must consider the rising tide of denunciation against the colonies and the colonial system. Adam Smith had long before raised his powerful voice against the folly and injustice which had first directed the project of establishing the colonies.[9] Arthur Young too had written with asperity against all species of distant dominion and had called the colonies nuisances.[10] "That great lesson of modern politicks," he wrote, "the independency of North America ought to enlarge the horizon of our commercial policy," but the same exploded arguments and the same fallacies which had been used with reference to the tobacco colonies were repeated with reference to the sugar colonies. "This reasoning is not brought

---

6. *Parl. Deb.*, Third Series, Vol. XVIII, page 910. Petition from merchants and shipowners of Liverpool praying for the removal of all restrictions upon the importation of sugar for the purpose of refining, June 17, 1833. The importance of Brazil and the insignificance of the West Indies can be seen from the following table, compiled from *Customs 8*. (The relevant volume is given in each case in brackets after each year.)

Table 12.1.

Year	Brazil	B.W.I.
1821 (14)	£2,114,329	£4,704,610
1822 (16)	1,919,496	3,906,723
1823 (18)	3,357,173	4,360,624
1824 (20)	3,656,319	4,549,789
1825 (22)	4,116,130	4,433,630
1826 (24)	2,556,140	3,538,651
1827 (26)	3,757,014	4,241,672
1828 (28)	6,055,902	3,726,643
1829 (30)	4,566,010	4,739,048
1830 (32)	4,270,749	3,749,799
1831 (34)	2,392,662	3,729,522
1832 (35)	5,298,596	3,813,821
1833 (38)	5,982,821	4,401,991

7. See *Parl. Deb.*, Third Series, Vol. XVI, pages 284–287, for a petition, March 6, 1833, of the Association praying for a reduction of the excessive duties on Brazil sugar imported for refining.

8. Cit. *Cambridge History of British Foreign Policy*, Vol. II, page 74. Canning to Granville, Dec. 17, 1824.

9. *Smith, op. cit.*, Vol. II, page 397.

10. *Young, op. cit.*, Vol. IX, 1788, pages 95–96.

to show that the sugar islands are not of consequences; they have been mischievously made of great consequence: but they are not of the importance their advocates falsely contend for."[11]

With Young and Smith we see the beginning of a trend, which was to be accentuated later on. Young and Smith were the forerunners of Cobden and Bright. The movement gathered momentum after the Napoleonic wars and the development of free trade. The landed interest were quite ready to support their brethren in the colonies, but they drew a line, as in the question of the use of sugar in the distilleries, when the West Indians wished to encroach on their own monopoly, and were quite prepared to throw over some of the cargo of the sinking ship of Protection in order, if possible, to save the rest. Coke, a great landowner in Norfolk, compared the West Indies to ozier islands in the Thames.[12]

It seemed to the desperate planters as if a coalition had been formed for the destruction of the colonies.[13] America resisted, said Barham, and was lost. The West Indies could not resist but they might be ruined.[14] Nothing was true, he lamented, but what went to the West Indian condemnation, nothing was just but what went to West Indian ruin.[15] It was almost a hopeless case to stand up in the House of Commons and advocate the cause of the West Indies.[16] "The cause of the colonies altogether," wrote Hibbert, "but more especially that part of it which touches upon property in slaves is so unattractive to florid orators and so unpopular with the public, that we have and must have very little protection from Parliamentary speaking."[17] Monopoly was unpopular and slavery detestable, and the united odium of both was more than colonies could bear.[18] The colonies, said Hume, the leader in Parliament of that school which concentrated on the expensiveness of the colonial connection, were most expensive encumbrances, there was no end to the outlay required,[19] and he preached the reversal of the colonial system. Remove the iron chains which fettered the best exertions of the colonies,[20] let them manage their own affairs instead of being kept in leading strings

<hr/>

11. Ibid., Vol. X, 1788, pages 347–348. Ramsay, too, was so irritated by the way in which the public were "dinned with the sugar colonies as if they were some great national object" that he anticipated the little Englander of the middle of the nineteenth century. (MS. Vol., folio 64. "An address on the proposed bill for the Abolition of the Slave Trade.")
12. Parl. Deb., Vol. XI, page 817. Quoted by Marryat, June 3, 1808.
13. Addresses and Memorials to His Majesty from the House of Assembly at Jamaica, 1825, page 22.
14. Parl. Deb., Vol. XI, page 511, May 23, 1808.
15. Ibid., Vol. XXXIV, page 1192. Mr. Barham, June 19, 1816.
16. Ibid., Third Series, Vol. X, page 1238. Marquis of Chandos, March 7, 1832.
17. C.O. 137/166. Hibbert to Norton, April 2, 1827.
18. Parl. Deb., NS, Vol. XIV, page 1164. Lord Dudley and Ward, March 7, 1826.
19. Ibid., Third Series, Vol. I, page 472. Mr. Warburton, Nov. 12, 1830.
20. Ibid., NS, Vol. XXII, page 855. Feb. 23, 1830.

and subjected to the fluctuating management of Downing Street.[21] All this odium sprang from the desire of the industrialists to abolish an unprofitable monopoly. It was no theory of responsible government or dominion status which inspired them. Whether the Government was Tory or Whig there was no succour for the colonies but what God might vouchsafe.[22]

Indeed only God could help, for the West Indians had no case. Fitzgerald advocated the whole and entire protection which their interests had already received. He was prepared to defend the doctrine. "He would not be put down by sneers—he would treat them with contempt, as well as the coxcombry and conceit which prevailed in the measures he opposed."[23] Henry Goulburn presented a petition in 1833 from 1,800 persons of the highest respectability, at a meeting in London, against emancipation. He asked the House to mark the impulse given to trade and agriculture, and to look at the hamlets that had sprung into towns in consequence of the connection with the colonies. "Why did the right honourable gentlemen (Stanley) sneer at observations, the truth and justice of which were known to those who, from their connexion with trade, were interested in the prosperity of these places?"[24] The West Indians were in a desperate position and the only weapon they could find was defeatism. The colonies were a "damnosa hereditas," millstones round Britain's neck. If the colonial fruit showed no disposition, in accordance with the dictum of Turgot, to fall to the ground, it must be plucked from the tree.

This anti-colonial sentiment was part of the struggle waged by the industrialists against restrictions and monopolies in general. The anti-imperialist crusade which, with the exception of a few far-sighted idealists like Buller, Wakefield and Durham, was to be well-nigh universal in the forties, was part of the general movement towards a free trade, that movement against the landed class which began in France in 1789, triumphed in Britain in 1832 and 1846, and culminated in the American Civil War.

To date the beginning of the free trade movement from the agitation of Cobden and Bright is to commit a grave historical error. The Manchester School marked only the peak of a tendency which had its origins far back in the past, in the beginnings of the Industrial Revolution. Pitt was profoundly influenced by Adam Smith, and but for the intervention of the French Wars there is no saying how far he would have travelled on the road towards free trade. In 1815 a protest was entered in the Journals of the House of Lords

21. Ibid., Third Series, Vol. XI, page 834. March 23, 1832.
22. Ibid., Third Series, Vol. III, page 354. Mr. Robinson, March 11, 1831.
23. Ibid., page 537, March 18, 1831.
24. Ibid., Third Series, Vol. XVIII, page 111. May 30, 1833.

against the Corn Law of 1815, threatening the very keystone of the arch of Protection. In 1820 the Merchants of London presented a petition drawn up by Thomas Tooke, the author of the "History of Prices," in which it stated that "freedom from restraint is calculated to give the utmost extension to foreign trade and the best direction to the capital and industry of the country."[25] In the same year the Chamber of Commerce of Glasgow petitioned for the establishment of free trade and the removal of all restrictions upon commercial imports and exports. "If it should be found," said Mr. Finlay who presented the petition, "that the history of our commercial policy has been a tissue of mistakes and false notions, it surely was not too much to express a hope that that policy should be given up." Truly, as Finlay said, had Adam Smith been alive to hear his doctrines thus expounded, it would have afforded him inconceivable pleasure.[26]

Opposition to monopolies was indeed the order of the day. All monopolies, declared the merchants of Liverpool, which prohibited trade with any other country, and in particular the monopoly of the East India Company, were highly injurious to the general interests of the country.[27] The Company's Charter, however expedient or necessary when it was first granted, was in the altered state of the world in 1812 inconsistent with those principles which were universally admitted to be essential to the prosperity of commerce, and Liverpool's Corporation declared that British subjects possessed "an inherent right" to a free intercourse with any part of the world whatsoever.[28] By 1830 every merchant, every banker and every ship-owner in the town was opposed to the East India's Company's monopoly.[29]

We have already said that the majority of the East Indians, in the controversy over the sugar duties, desired not free trade but merely equalization, that is, a share in the West Indian monopoly. Some of the advocates of East India sugar, however, showed no desire to substitute King Stork for King Log. Cropper's arguments, the West Indian monopolists remonstrated, in their attempt to enlist all the vested interests on their side, proved that Brazilian and Cuban sugar should be admitted as well as East Indian, in fact that foreign corn, foreign cattle and foreign manufactures should be imported and the Navigation Laws repealed.[30] (The West Indians viewed the sugar duties in

---

25. Cit. *Cambridge Modern History* (Cambridge, 1934), Vol. X, pages 771–772.
26. *Parl. Deb.*, NS, Vol. I, pages 424–425 and 429. May 16, 1820.
27. Ibid., Vol. XXII, page 111. March 23, 1812.
28. Ibid., page 118.
29. Ibid., NS, Vol. XXIII, page 180. March 11, 1830. The petition was presented by Huskisson, the representative of Liverpool. Gascoyne, the other representative, presented another petition of the same sort and hoped that they would hear nothing of vested interests. "The interests of millions were not to be sacrificed for the sake of two or three thousand."
30. *Fletcher, op. cit.*, pages 27–28.

the abstract, and never related them to the general question of free trade.) Did Cropper mean, asked Gladstone, to advocate the introduction of Brazilian sugar?[31] What, asked Marryat, were the "other sugars," apart from East India, which the refiners begged for permission to refine?[32] How, taunted Ellis, could one reconcile the free trade doctrine of the advocates of East India sugar with the prohibitory duties which some of them wished to maintain on foreign sugar?[33] If, said Huskisson, in the days when the Government was trying to compromise between the two rivals, the importation of East India sugar were permitted, Britain might, upon the same principle, admit sugar from all the world.[34] It was this which was responsible for the failure of the East Indians to achieve their aim. One monopoly could not be abolished merely to substitute another, and the country was not ready for the sweeping change which was to be introduced in the later years. All the humanitarians would have been up in arms against the proposal to introduce slave-grown sugar into the home market.

Cropper had, for good or ill, definitely attached himself to the abolitionist group. His dual position of humanitarian and merchant intent on gain forced him, therefore, to compromise. Admit all sugars, he suggested, at a duty of thirty shillings per hundredweight, whether from India, the West Indies, China, Siam, Java, Cuba or Brazil, but attach to the two latter the condition of the abolition of the slave trade.[35] Had Cropper then forgotten his earlier arguments that in given conditions slavery was not only profitable but superior to free labour? Ricardo, an economist pure and simple, found himself in no such quandary. He would allow a competition not of East India sugar only, but of the sugar of South America, Cuba, Brazil and China.[36] "No exclusive protection should be granted to either the East or the West Indies, and we should be free to import our sugar from any quarter whatever. No possible injury could arise from this."[37]

In this delirium of free trade sentiments even the West Indies could not remain unmoved. Men's material interests produce inconsistencies and force them into incongruous attitudes which would excite surprise or ridicule were there not great issues at stake. In 1821 Marryat presented a petition from the merchants of London against the renewal of the charter of the West

---

31. *Gladstone-Cropper, Correspondence*, page 35. Nov. 22, 1823.
32. *Parl. Deb.*, NS, Vol. VII, page 695, May 17, 1822.
33. Ibid., NS, Vol. IX, page 451. May 22, 1823.
34. *Huskisson, Speeches*, Vol. II, page 200. May 22, 1823.
35. J. Cropper: *Relief for West Indian Distress, showing the inefficiency of protecting duties on East India sugar, and pointing out other modes of certain relief* (London, 1823), page 30. *Another Bonus to the planters*, page 10.
36. *Parl. Deb.*, NS, Vol. IX, page 459. May 22, 1823.
37. *East India Sugar debate, 1823*, page 19.

India Dock Company. He addressed the house upon "the impolicy as well as injustice of continuing, in an enlightened age like this, such monopolies, which were at once injurious to commerce and to the revenue of the country."[38] Such a theft of his opponents' clothes might well have excited derision, but the sledge-hammer of a Disraeli's sarcasm would not be used to crush insignificant wasps. There was not, Sir Isaac Coffin declared, much friendship in trade. "Each merchant sought his own interest, monopoly was the order of the day amongst them, and beggar my neighbour the object."[39] In 1830 Huskisson moved the equalization of the duty on rum imported into Scotland and Ireland with the duty on corn-made British spirits. The existing system, declared Bright, a West Indian, was a rigid monopoly, which ought to be immediately put an end to.[40] Some West Indians even went so far as to assert that Britain's monopoly of their market compelled them to buy their manufactured goods at a higher price than they would pay were free trade introduced.[41] The West Indians forgot that the whole world was equally compelled to consume British manufactures, because they were the cheapest and the best.[42] No wonder Whitmore vouched that the British industrialists would be prepared to give up their monopoly of the colonial market.

The brunt of this advance on the anti-monopolistic front had to be faced by the West Indians. In 1825 their legal claim to the monopoly of the British market was removed, when they were given permission to trade with every part of the world. Huskisson justified this innovation in British colonial policy on the ground that serious inroads had been made in the colonial system in general by the liberation of Brazil, St. Domingo and Cuba. A powerful argument was at hand in the separation of the North American colonies. "I would ask any man whether the disseverance of the United States from the British Empire, viewed as a mere question of commerce, has been an injury to this country? Whether their emancipation from the commercial thraldom of the colonial system has really been prejudicial to the trade and industry of Great Britain? . . . Is there no useful admonition to be derived from this example?" Modern commerce proved that whenever free scope was given to capital, to industry, to the stirring intelligence and active spirit of adventure, new roads would be opened to enterprise and new facilities afforded to the interchange of the productions of the different regions of the earth. Doubt-

---

38. *Parl. Deb.*, NS, Vol. IV, page 947. Feb. 28, 1821.
39. Ibid.
40. Ibid., NS, Vol. XXV, page 955. July 4, 1830. This naturally was not John Bright.
41. *Statements to the Board of Trade*, page 24. Statement of Mr. Woodburn, recently returned from Jamaica.
42. *Huskisson, Speeches*, Vol. III, pages 456–457. Huskisson, May 25, 1829.

less, Huskisson argued, the West Indies would underline the lessons taught by Ireland and the United States, that an open trade was infinitely more useful than any monopoly however exclusive.[43] Much of this was verbiage. Nothing could save the West Indies, but the act of 1825 showed in which direction the wind was blowing.

The West Indian monopoly presented a striking contrast to the towering eminence on which stood Britain's manufacturing skill and industry, "unshackled by bounties, unaided by useless monopolies, thriving with unrestrained freedom."[44] The strong drive against monopolies in general and the West Indian monopoly in particular as the embodiment of all that was restrictive and monopolistic came from the towns. Cropper was right when he wrote to Sturge that the important points on which to concentrate in the struggle for emancipation were the large towns.[45]

The attempt of the West Indians in 1824 to form a West Indian Company, with 40,000 shares at £100 each, was condemned as a plan for enlisting 40,000 persons on the side of the West Indian system and as tending to produce a considerable accession of power in a quarter already strong.[46] Whitmore, the leader of the East Indians in Parliament, strongly opposed the project on the ground that it would establish a baneful monopoly.[47] It was the West Indian monopoly which interested the industrialists, not the state of slavery in the colonies. Exclusive privileges, said Huskisson, member

---

43. *Huskisson, Speeches*, Vol. II, pages 306, 312, and 320–321. March 21, 1825. In July 1783 an Order in Council decreed free trade between Britain and the U.S.A. The results can be seen from the following table. T. Pitkin: *A Statistical View of the Commerce of the United States* (Hartford, 1816), pages 30 and 167–168.

Table 12.2.

Year	British Imports in £ sterling	Year	British Imports in dollars
1784	749,345	1792	15,285,428
1785	893,594	1795	23,313,121
1786	843,119	1796	31,928,685
1787	893,637	1797	27,303,067
1788	1,023,789	1798	17,330,770
1789	1,050,198	1799	29,133,219
1790	1,191,071	1800	32,877,059
		1801	39,519,218

44. J. Cropper: *A letter addressed to Liverpool Society for promoting the abolition of Slavery*, page 22.
45. *Richard, op. cit.*, page 84. Oct. 14, 1825.
46. *Parl. Deb.*, NS, Vol. XI, page 611. Mr. Sykes, May 10, 1824.
47. Ibid., page 612.

for Liverpool, were out of fashion.[48] The country was loaded with protecting duties on protecting duties, and monopolies on monopolies, and distressed by the millions of money taken out of the pockets of the people.[49] Every effort was made, on every possible occasion, whenever the West Indies were concerned, to prevent a reversion to "a system which science, and philosophy, and practical good sense had united to condemn and get rid of."[50] There was nothing, said Colonel Torrens, but a miserable system of restrictions and protections which were only obstructions.[51] Was the House, asked the member for Yorkshire, to take freedom of commerce and the extension of the employment of capital as the rule in legislating, or was it to increase monopolies by restrictions?[52] All monopolies ought, in his opinion, to be removed, as destructive to the progress of commerce.[53] They had too long truckled to the colonies. It was time that the present system should be abolished and a new one begun.[54] Any minister, said Ewart, the member for Liverpool, who should continue to impose fetters on British commerce would deserve impeachment.[55] This was strong language, but it showed the feelings of the industrialists.

The industrialists were not silent on the question of emancipation. Relief from the West Indian monopoly, declared Mr. Clay, would be cheaply purchased by granting the planters the full amount of the compensation

---

48. Ibid., NS, Vol. XXIII, page 180, March 11, 1830. Liverpool, which had rewarded Lord Hawkesbury with the freedom of the city for his exertions on behalf of the slave merchants, gave Huskisson in February 1826 a present of a service of plate, worthy of her greatness both in taste and magnificence, "as a testimony of (her) sense of the benefits derived to the nation at large from the enlightened system of commercial policy brought forward by him as President of the Board of Trade." (*Huskisson, Speeches*, Vol. I, page 115.)

49. *Parl. Deb.*, Third Series, Vol. I, page 475. Sir Henry Parnell (Queen's County), Nov. 12, 1830.

50. Ibid., page 476.

51. Ibid., Third Series, Vol. VI, page 1324. Sept. 12, 1831.

52. Ibid., Third Series, Vol. XVI, page 288. Mr. Strickland, March 6, 1833.

53. Ibid., Third Series, Vol. XVIII, page 911. June 17, 1833.

54. Ibid., Col. George Williams (Ashton).

55. Ibid., Third Series, Vol. XIX, page 793, July 17, 1833. The effect of the Reform Bill can be seen clearly in the change in Ewart's opinions. On Dec. 13, 1830 he advocated gradual emancipation, on behalf of the West Indian merchants and proprietors of Liverpool, as "alone consistent with sound policy and the principles of humanity" (Ibid., Third Series, Vol. I, page 1057). Two days later he presented a petition in favour of compensation for the planters and again emphasized that abolition must be gradual (Ibid., page 1183). On August 8, 1832, he supported most cordially the Orders in Council as "a progressive measure towards a general relief of the slave population of the West India Colonies" (Ibid., Third Series, Vol. XIV, page 1253). In 1833 however he expressed his regret that the Government experiments had not been such as to liberate so important a branch of the country's foreign trade as the trade with Brazil from the fetters that had hitherto bound it (Ibid., Third Series, Vol. XVI, page 287, March 6, 1833). A fortnight later he urged the necessity, in the interests of the people, of reducing not merely direct taxation but the indirect taxation arising from commercial restriction and monopoly, which pressed on the commercial relations of the country and impeded the comfort of all classes (Ibid., page 882, March 20, 1833).

proposed.[56] Ewart was willing to grant compensation to the planters on the specific condition that it should be accompanied by a stipulation for the unrestricted liberty of commerce.[57] Among those who voted for terminating the apprenticeship system at an earlier date than 1840, proposed in the ministerial plan, were representatives of Birmingham, Sheffield, Liverpool, Blackburn, Bradford, Durham, Hull, Wigan, Leicester, Cork, Dublin, and the Tower Hamlets, and the members for Yorkshire, Derbyshire and Northumberland.[58]

With the regard to the industrialists the Brazilian trade dominated the situation. What St Domingo would have effected in 1792 Brazil would effect in 1832. The West Indian monopoly meant not only that the planters had the monopoly of the home market but also that the refiners were confined to the use of British plantation sugar. In 1833, as in 1787, Britain wished to capture the European market.

The superiority of St. Domingo and Britain's opportunity of reversing in her favour an adverse balance in the Caribbean by its acquisition have already been described. We have seen too how the introduction of the sugar of the colonies conquered in the war was in the interest of the mother country but detrimental to the West Indies. This policy was continued for the duration of the war. The objection that instead of furnishing the enemy's colonies with a market for their produce they ought to be prevented from finding a market at all was, one writer urged, just in theory but impracticable. The writer argued at great length, in order to "combat a principle which seems to have taken hereditary root in the minds of the British planters, and had degenerated into a prejudice." No harm could be done to the West Indian planter, as if the amount sent to Britain increased, the amount sent to Europe decreased. In either case the competition was practically the same. The true security for the interest of the planters was that the duty paid on importation should be returned if the sugar was exported after being refined, and that no duty should be paid at all if the sugar was exported in a raw state.[59] In accordance with this principle sugar from Martinique was admitted in 1809, solely for the purpose, in the words of the Chancellor of the Exchequer, of expor-

56. Ibid., Third Series, Vol. XVIII, page 589. June 11, 1833. Clay was member for the Tower Hamlets.

57. Ibid., page 591.

58. Ibid., Third Series, Vol. XIX, page 1270. July 25, 1833.

59. *Windham Papers*, Add. Mss. 37883, folios 205–206. A. Cochran Johnstone: "Hints for Mr. Windham's information relative to the West Indies," April 12, 1806. The writer urged that Britain had enough sugar colonies, and suggested that Russia should be allowed to conquer Martinique and Guadeloupe, and the French driven totally out of the West Indies and never suffered to settle there again (folio 201).

tation.[60] Much more ominous for the future was the admission of Brazilian sugar in 1810. The West Indians, argued George Rose, himself a West Indian planter, would have no just cause of complaint unless their monopoly of the home market was encroached upon, though he admitted that by this measure a much larger quantity of produce would be sent to Europe.[61] Grenville opposed the measure. Every consideration of humanity, justice and policy required that the abolition of the slave trade should have been made a condition previous to entering into any commercial engagement with Portugal.[62]

With the growth of the free trade movement came an increased demand for the importation of foreign sugar for refining purposes. In 1828 Charles Grant emphasized that Cuba produced 90,000 tons and Brazil 60,000 tons of sugar annually, and that the carrying of the cargoes of such countries would confer a benefit on British shipping.[63] Admit all foreign sugars, said Hume; the price in Britain would depend on the price abroad.[64] Britain, said Huskisson, might be made the entrepôt of the sugar of the world, and might thereby give employment to her unemployed capital and operatives in refining that sugar for the markets of Europe. Indeed, he knew of no channel in which capital might be more beneficially expended than in refining sugar for the European markets, if the refining business was duly encouraged. Britain would become the sugar refiners of the world.[65] Why, asked Cropper, should Britain not supply the Continent with refined sugar as well as with manufactured cotton?[66]

Annual acts had been passed to permit the importation of foreign sugar until in 1831 the West Indians raised a sudden outcry against the practice. But, argued Poulett Thomson, it was a principle upon which they had always acted, and upon which they always must act, beneficially to Britain, the principle of making Britain the workshop of the world, by receiving the produce of foreign countries, and then employing their greater skill, their greater industry, their greater capital, their greater ingenuity, in working up that raw material and again selling it to different parts of the world. Not the slightest benefit would accrue to the foreign grower of sugar by its being refined in Britain, for otherwise it would only go to Hamburg or Amsterdam

---

60. *Parl. Deb.*, Vol. XIV, page 33. April 14, 1809. In 1813, owing to scarcity, Martinique sugar was admitted for home consumption as a temporary expedient. (Ibid., Vol. XXVI, page 107. May 13, 1813).

61. *Bathurst, Mss.* Page 145. Rose to Bathurst, Aug. 16, 1810.

62. *Parl. Deb.*, Vol. X, page 734. Feb. 25, 1808.

63. Ibid., NS, Vol. XIX, page 1208. June 9, 1828.

64. Ibid., page 1211.

65. *Huskisson, Speeches*, Vol. III, pages 454–455. May 25, 1829.

66. J. Cropper: *Relief for West Indian Distress*, page 9.

and the West Indians would have to face the same competition.[67] Did the foreign grower then, as Burge, the agent of Jamaica, asked, come to the British market for the mere purpose of amusement?[68] The principle, Poulett Thomson insisted, had been recognised by the legislature over and over again. It had been recognised in the articles of cotton, silk, and a variety of others.[69] Britain should, as much as possible, retain the business of refining for the whole world. She could do so either by giving a bounty on refining, which he thought inexpedient, or by admitting foreign sugar to be refined.[70]

If the Government needed any encouragement the industrialists were there to give it in person. The debates on the importation of foreign sugar went hand in hand with the debates on emancipation. The object, declared the member for Preston, ought to be to make Britain the depôt for all the sugar of the world, and "would the House, to gratify monopolists, consent to ruin our future resources?"[71] The subject, said George Wood, was one of great importance to the whole empire, but particularly so to the county of Lancaster.[72] The representative for Manchester spoke briefly but tersely on the vast importance of the subject to the great seat of the cotton manufactures which he represented.[73] James Oswald of Glasgow had been instructed to present a petition, bearing numerous respectable signatures, praying for a remittance of the excessive duties levied on Brazilian sugar imported for refining.[74] Ewart some time later presented a similar petition from the merchants and ship-owners of Liverpool, and requested that the exclusive colonial monopoly of the home market and the large bounty granted on re-exportation of colonial sugar might be particularly considered.[75] To Mr. William Clay, the existing restrictions on the importation of the raw material in the sugar industry were obviously so contrary to every sound principle of political science that it would be an unpardonable waste of the time of the House if he stopped to enforce an axiom in politics which no one disputed.[76]

The shipowners would have benefited as much as the industrialists from the admission of foreign sugar. British manufactures could be paid for only in Brazilian sugar and coffee, which would be carried in British ships were the admission of these articles permitted. Poulett Thomson emphasized that the

---

67. *Parl. Deb.*, Third Series, Vol. VI, pages 1343–1344. Sept. 12, 1831.
68. Ibid., Third Series, Vol. VII, page 732. Sept. 28, 1831.
69. Ibid., page 748.
70. Ibid., Third Series, Vol. XIX, page 1178. July 24, 1833.
71. Ibid., Third Series, Vol. VIII, page 362. John Wood, Oct. 7, 1831.
72. Ibid., Third Series, Vol. XVI, page 289. March 6, 1833.
73. Ibid., page 290. Mark Philips.
74. Ibid., page 291.
75. Ibid., Third Series, Vol. XVIII, pages 909–910. June 17, 1833.
76. Ibid., Third Series, Vol. XIX, page 1169. July 24, 1833.

importation of foreign sugar for refining was most beneficial to the interests of the British shipowners.[77] As a result of the prohibitory laws upwards of two millions of British capital, declared the Brazilian Association of Liverpool, were forced into other channels, giving employment to foreign shipping, and paying to foreign European States freights, commissions and charges, to the great loss of the British shipowners.[78] The introduction of foreign sugar, for use and consumption in Britain, it was said in the petition, would give employment to from 50,000 to 100,000 tons of British shipping.[79] Mark Philips of Manchester spoke of the extreme degree of hardship which arose from ships being deprived of return cargoes from Brazil, and told the House that in 1832 fifty-one vessels had sailed from Liverpool to Rio de Janeiro, not one of which could get a return cargo home.[80] The depressed state of the British shipping interest, according to a petition of shipowners in Liverpool presented by Ewart, was due mainly to the unjust and impolitic monopolies and restrictions, and they estimated that Brazil alone would furnish freightage for 120,000 tons of shipping annually, while St. Domingo, Cuba, Manilla and Singapore would provide cargoes for a further 200,000 tons.[81] Clay also championed the cause of the shipping interests, and stated that of four British vessels which had sailed monthly from Liverpool to Brazil in 1832, not one had returned with the produce with which their cargoes had been purchased.[82]

There was a third class which stood to benefit from the refining of foreign sugar, the sugar refiners. There was a large capital invested in the sugar refining trade, between three and four millions. Were the West Indian interests then, asked John Wood, alone to be regarded?[83] He trusted that they would not be protected at the expense of the sugar refiners.[84] The weight of London was thrown in the scale against the West Indians, Grote arguing that the refining of foreign sugar could not harm the West Indians.[85] In fact, argued John Wood casuistically, to prohibit the refining of Brazilian sugar would be to injure the West Indians, for it was well known that West Indian sugar would not refine unless mixed with Brazilian, when it refined extremely

77. Ibid., Third Series, Vol. VII, page 755. Sept. 28, 1831. John Wood agreed, Vol. VIII, page 362. Oct. 7, 1831.
78. Ibid., Third Series, Vol. XVI, page 285. March 6, 1833.
79. Ibid., page 285. It should be noted that the petitioners were asking for much more than the admission of foreign sugar for refining and subsequent exportation.
80. Ibid., page 290.
81. Ibid., pages 881–882. March 20, 1833.
82. Ibid., Third Series, Vol. XIX, page 1169. July 24, 1833.
83. Ibid., Third Series, Vol. VII, page 764. Sept. 28, 1831.
84. Ibid., NS, Vol. XXV, page 321. June 14, 1830.
85. Ibid., Third Series, Vol. XIX, page 793. July 17, 1833.

well.[86] In the words of Poulett Thomson, it was the bounden duty of the House, as it was its interest, to endeavour to assist the sugar refining industry, where such assistance could be afforded, as in this case, without injury to the rival interests of any other manufacturers.[87]

Indeed in 1831 the sugar refining industry was in desperate need of assistance. As a result of the prohibition of all sugar not the growth of the British plantations, the industry was on the verge of ruin. Where in 1814 there had been forty or fifty refiners in London, there was not one in 1831.[88] According to O'Connell there were no less than eleven sugar refineries in Dublin before the Union; in 1833 there were none.[89] The fact that the refiners were restricted to sugar from the British colonies, which was seven or nine shillings per hundredweight dearer than sugar sold on the Continent,[90] meant that the continental refiners were displacing the British in all European markets.[91] William Clay, the representative of one of the seats of the sugar refining industry, painted a black picture of a trade which, as he expressed it, was making a swift progress to absolute ruin.[92] Between 1818, when the exportation had been at its maximum, and 1826, the exports decreased by more than fifty per cent. The temporary acts of 1827, 1829 and 1830 produced a steady increase in consequence of the admission of foreign sugar. The act of 1830 expired in July 1831, and the export, which had been 150,000 cwt. in the first quarter of 1832 fell to 59,000 in the second quarter of 1833. In 1830 there had been 224 pans at work in the metropolis, in 1832, 183, in 1833, 70; a strong practical fact, in Clay's words, that spoke volumes. The depression was not confined to London. In Scotland all the pans had stopped working; in Liverpool two-thirds were out of employment; in Bristol not more than one-half were in use; in Hull two-thirds were idle. It might therefore be said that two-thirds of the sugar refining trade throughout the country was at a complete standstill. The distress was felt in trades indirectly connected with the refining industry. A builder, whose bill for work in the factories was £3,200 in 1830 and £3,300 in 1831, had, from 1832 until July 1833, earned only £3.7.6d. A carter connected with the factories had suffered losses amounting to fifteen pounds a day; a bricklayer who had formerly employed forty men a week now employed only two, and a cooper six instead of his

---

86. Ibid., Third Series, Vol. VIII, page 363. Oct. 7, 1831.
87. Ibid., Third Series, Vol. VI, page 1347. Sept. 12, 1831.
88. Ibid., Third Series, Vol. VII, page 765. Sept. 28, 1831.
89. Ibid., Third Series, Vol. XVII, page 75. April 13, 1833.
90. Ibid., Third Series, Vol. XIX, page 1168. Mr. Clay, July 24, 1833.
91. Ibid., Third Series, Vol. XVIII, pages 588–589. Mr. Clay, June 11, 1833.
92. Ibid., Third Series, Vol. XVII, page 74. April 3, 1833.

usual hundred.[93] It was not strange that Lord Althorp could speak not only of the depressed but of the oppressed state of the industry.[94]

The refining of foreign sugar, the industrialists also urged, would benefit the labouring population. At a time, said the Manchester representative, when the poor rates had increased in all but three counties in England it was the duty of the legislature to support every measure tending to increase the means of employment of the industrious labouring classes.[95] The merchants and shipowners of Liverpool expressed the hope that whilst the House was legislating for the benefit of the slaves in distant colonies, it would also consider the present condition and future welfare of the labouring population at home.[96] Moreover, urged the member for Preston with devastating logic, using an argument which was to enjoy great vogue in later years, why was the objection to foreign sugar not extended to cotton, indigo, dye-stuffs, and everything else that was the produce of Brazil? If such a proposition were acceded to, what would become of Britain's cotton manufacturers?[97] If, Ewart emphasized, the same restrictions had been applied to foreign cotton as then existed on foreign sugar, where would have been the power and consideration of Britain over the commerce of the world?[98]

The position of Cabinet Minister in those days must have been a thankless task. Between the conflicting and irreconcilable claims of planters and industrialists the Government were on the horns of a dilemma. But the time was passed when the West Indians could make an outcry against any measure which threatened their interests, and be listened to. The manufacturing, the mercantile and the shipping interests, even the rest of the colonies, could no longer be disregarded when the West Indies were in question.[99] Huskisson poured out the vials of his wrath on the Chancellor of the Exchequer's vacillating policy as ill becoming the finance minister of a great empire. Great interests were not thus to be trifled with. This kind of marching and countermarching was not a policy which should direct the commercial interests of a country like Britain. The Government could not "put forward laws as they would an advanced guard, with instructions to fall back, or to wheel to the right or to the left, as occasion might require."[100] Huskisson was voicing the

93. Ibid., Third Series, Vol. IX, pages 1165–1167. July 24, 1833.
94. Ibid., Third Series, Vol. XVIII, page 912. June 17, 1833.
95. Ibid., Third Series, Vol. XVI, page 290, Mark Philips, Mar. 6, 1833.
96. Ibid., Third Series, Vol. XVIII, page 910. June 17, 1833.
97. Ibid., Third Series, Vol. VIII, page 362. John Wood, Oct. 7, 1831.
98. Ibid., Third Series, Vol. XVII, page 75. April 3, 1833.
99. Ibid., Third Series, Vol. VIII, page 361. John Wood, Oct. 7, 1831.
100. *Huskisson Speeches*, Vol. III, pages 605 and 607. June 21, 1830.

feelings of the industrial section of the community, but he must have realised the difficulties of the Government's position.

It was not, as Poulett Thomson made clear, that the Government did not fully concur with the demands of the industrialist.[101] Why then had they not brought forward a measure to remove the impolitic restrictions on the refining of foreign sugar? The answer was that it was inexpedient, until the West Indian question was settled.[102] The Government were sensible of the disadvantages of delay, but so long as the question of emancipation was under discussion, it would not be desirable to open the matter.[103]

The Government was unwilling to make things more difficult than was necessary for the planters, and the refining of foreign sugar contained implications which made it necessary for the Government to proceed cautiously.

The result then was a compromise. Althorp had in 1831 distinctly admitted the right of the planters to the entire and complete monopoly of the home market.[104] Hume was prepared to accept the introduction of foreign sugar for refining on the distinct condition that every ounce of sugar refined should be exported and that the West Indian planters would have the entire supply of the home market.[105] Poulett Thomson agreed that, now that the system of Negro slavery was about to be abolished, the House should not depart from its principles of keeping, *so far as it was possible*, the monopoly of the home market for West Indian sugar.[106] Stanley made it clear that the apprenticeship system was intended to maintain the growth of sugar and perpetuate the system of slave labour.[107]

The plan, as eventually outlined by Althorp, embraced a distinct understanding that the produce of the West Indian colonies should have the power to exclude foreign sugar from the home market while the refining of foreign sugar would be permitted.[108] Compensation and Apprenticeship were not sufficient to buy the West Indians' consent to emancipation. The British West Indian monopoly was prolonged until 1852.

What were the implications of the campaign for the refining of foreign sugar? In the great debates on this question, which were in reality of much greater importance than the debates on emancipation, the great names we

101. *Parl. Deb.*, Third Series, Vol. XVI, page 288. March 6, 1853.
102. Ibid., Third Series, Vol. XVIII, page 593, Lord Althorp, June 11, 1833.
103. Ibid., page 912. Lord Althorp, June 17, 1833.
104. Ibid., Third Series, Vol. VI, page 1330. Sept. 12, 1831.
105. Ibid., Third Series, Vol. VII, page 766. Sept. 28, 1831.
106. Ibid., Third Series, Vol. XIX, page 1178. July 24, 1833.
107. Ibid., Third Series, Vol. XVIII, pages 504–505. June 7, 1833.
108. Ibid., Third Series. Vol. XIX, page 1174. July 24, 1833.

would expect are conspicuously absent. For foreign sugar meant slave-grown sugar, and could mean nothing else. Lord Sandon, a West Indian proprietor, expressed his regret that, whenever any arguments were adduced in the House for, or on behalf of, any suffering commercial interest in the West Indies, they were sure to be met, "by way of estoppel," by an allusion to the still stronger claims of suffering humanity.[109] But to imagine that the industrialists were thinking of the slave trade or slavery would be to labour under a delusion.

The admission of foreign sugar, though only for re-exportation, gave the Brazilian planters an opportunity to extend their production to meet the increased possibilities of trade with Britain. That could mean only slave-grown sugar. The slave trade would increase to an enormous amount, and in Brazil and Cuba there would be no power of enforcing those ameliorating measures on which the humanitarians had laid such store. It would be better, said Baring, to make the slave trade free, unless the ports of Africa could be hermetically sealed.[110] Any man, declared Hume, who agreed to the sugar refining bill agreed to promote the slave trade.[111] On what principle, asked Burge, could the refining of foreign sugar be justified consistently with the view the country had professed to take of the slave trade? Ought they, in spite of their own principles, to give support to the slave trade of other states? Ought they to encourage the slave trade because, if they did not, other states would?[112] The country said Godson, wished to be supplied with sugar the produce of free labour. That could be obtained neither from Brazil, nor from Cuba, nor from the French colonies.[113] It might be said, urged Peel, that they had nothing to do with the slaves of other states, and that their business was only to emancipate those in the British colonies. It might be so, legally speaking, but was there no moral responsibility?[114] The country, said Douglas, was hardly consistent in its wishes to abolish slavery in the colonies while it was anxious to benefit by the low price of slave-grown sugar.[115]

Who were all these men? Abolitionists? With the exception of Peel, they were all West Indian proprietors. Poulett Thomson therefore could casually dismiss their arguments as merely an adroit endeavour to excite in their

---

109. Ibid., Third Series, Vol. X, page 1250. March 7, 1832.
110. Ibid., Third Series, Vol. III, page 1463. April 15, 1831.
111. Ibid., Third Series, Vol. VI, page 1355. Sept. 12, 1831. Hume changed his views in a remarkable manner.
112. Ibid., Third Series, Vol. VII, pages 733–734. Sept. 28, 1831.
113. Ibid., Third Series, Vol. XVIII, page 221, May 31, 1833. Godson argued that it was only to the West Indies that they could look for the accomplishment of that great and desirable object, the production of sugar by free labour. He was interrupted by cries of Question! Question!
114. Ibid., page 356. June 3, 1833.
115. Ibid., Third Series, Vol. II, page 787. Feb 21, 1831.

favour the sympathy of those who generally took part against them.[116] The planters failed signally in this attempt. Buxton, with remarkable sophistry, argued that if it could be shown that the foreign sugar to be imported would be consumed at home, instead of being exported, he would vote against the bill. He had found that it required one-third more labour to refine sugar abroad and import it into Britain in a refined state instead of in a raw state. In permitting, therefore, foreign sugar to be refined in Britain they were substituting British machinery at home for slave labour abroad, and consequently to that extent diminishing slave labour and discouraging the slave trade.[117] Hume said that he had never heard anything more surprising than Buxton's declaration.[118] In 1833 the Brazilian Association of Liverpool petitioned for a remittance of the excessive duties on Brazilian sugar. Of the nine speakers only the last, Mr. Andrew Johnstone, referred to the question of slavery.[119] Dr. Lushington, one of the oldest of the abolitionists, was representative for the Tower Hamlets. His humanitarianism conflicted with his position as member for an important sugar refining district. In the great debate in July 1833 he emphasized the need of giving encouragement to manufactures, and urged the Government not to lose an hour in granting some relief to his constituents. Those whose interests he advocated asked for no bounty, no unfair advantage, no unjust monopoly.[120]

Keith Douglas, one of the ablest of the West Indians in Parliament, moved in 1832 for certain returns, the object of which was to show how the manufactures and commerce of Britain depended upon slave labour. The material for the whole cotton manufacture, of Manchester, Glasgow, and every little village, was supplied by compulsory slave labour. The proportion produced by free labour was less than one-fifteenth of the proportion produced by slaves. In the article of sugar, only one-twentieth of the total imports was free-grown; as regards coffee not above one-third of the quantity used in Britain was the produce of free labour. The raw material supplied by slave labour produced more than half of the country's manufactured exports.[121] Douglas thereby meant to insinuate that the West Indies were essential to Britain. But the West Indian interests had ceased to be the mighty interests he claimed them to be. The West Indians were thrown overboard, but slavery was not thereby abolished all over the world. In fact slavery and the slave trade increased and we give a false view of the emancipation movement if

---

116. Ibid., Third Series, Vol. VII, page 743. Sept. 28, 1831.
117. Ibid., Third Series, Vol. VI, page 1353. September 12, 1831.
118. Ibid., page 1355.
119. Ibid., Third Series, Vol. XVI, page 291. March 6, 1833.
120. Ibid., Third Series, Vol. XIX, page 117. July 24, 1833.
121. Ibid., Third Series, Vol. XIII, pages 1243–1246. July 2, 1832.

we do not present it in its proper context as part of the struggle of the industrial and commercial classes against monopolies. What gaps were left by the abolition of slavery in the West Indies would be filled up by the slave labourers of Brazil, Cuba, and the United States. Douglas's arguments prove conclusively that the reason why the West Indies fell was not because slavery existed but because slavery there was unprofitable. Had the West Indies been in the fortunate situation of America and Brazil, the humanitarians would not have found those powerful and dangerous allies who gave the struggle for emancipation its momentum. The industrialists shed crocodile tears over the few hundred thousand slaves in the British colonies. But emancipation in the West Indies meant the desolation of Africa on an unheard-of scale and all the rigours of slavery in Brazil and Cuba. The redemption of a few thousands meant the crucifixion of millions.

Epilogue

The Emancipation Act passed, public opinion underwent its lamentable and disgraceful change. Attention was distracted to the more pressing problems of internal politics, while the forces of free trade, organised in the Anti-Corn Law League, set themselves to extirpate monopolies root and branch and to put the finishing touches to the rough beginnings of 1833.

Industrialists and humanitarians had, for different reasons, worked to achieve the same aim. But whilst the humanitarians had proceeded on the principles that slavery was disgusting and that free labour was superior to slave, the industrialists wanted free trade and cheap food. In the nature of things the compromise of 1833 could not be of long duration.

It was in the midst of the industrial depression of 1839 that the cry was raised for the reduction of the duties on foreign sugar. The people of Britain, argued the industrialists, could not be excluded from the benevolent purposes of the abolitionists.[1] This new-born zeal on behalf of the poor might be sneered at as an attempt to sweeten the bitter draught of the New Poor Law with cheap sugar,[2] but in a country where the free trade movement was soon to reach its peak cheap food was a programme which had a powerful appeal.

The Government claimed that the people of Britain had done enough by emancipation to satisfy and quiet their consciences. Having granted the Negroes their freedom they were not justified in giving their attention exclusively to their interests and in endeavouring, by a mistaken pulley, to

---

1. *Parl. Deb.*, Third Series, Vol. LV, page 98. C. P. Villiers (Wolverhampton), June 25, 1840.
2. Ibid., Third Series, Vol. LVIII, page 355. Mr. Hamilton (Aylesbury), May 13, 1841.

force the cultivation of sugar in the West Indies. The unfortunate people of Bolton and Manchester would willingly change places with the people of Jamaica.[3] They had paid the money, said the Under Secretary of State for the Colonies, which they had advanced for a valuable purpose. The bargain was complete for which the payment had been made.[4] The Negroes were getting rich and would have nothing but quarto bibles with gilt edges in their chapels.[5] It was absurd to teach them to keep gigs and drink champagne by a tax levied upon the industrious classes at home.[6]

Moreover, there was no sense, said the industrialists, in rejecting slave-grown sugar merely because it was slave-grown. Where was the moral principle, asked T. B. Macaulay, the abolitionist, where was the great general law of humanity which permitted a man to wear slave-grown cotton, to smoke slave-grown tobacco, to enjoy a cup of slave-grown coffee, but forbade him to sweeten it with slave-grown sugar? To make this absurdity more complete, how could slave-grown sugar be imported into Newfoundland and Barbados and yet be forbidden in Yorkshire and Lancashire? The question must be looked at as one of expediency, unless it was desired to make Germany a Warwickshire and Leipzig another Manchester.[7] If the importation of slave-grown cotton were prohibited, a million and a half artisans would be thrown out of employment.[8] Such a boycott was a principle for individual agency, not a rule which could direct international commerce.[9] What right, asked Cobden, had a people who were the largest consumers and distributors of cotton goods to go to Brazil with their ships full of cotton, and then turn up the whites of their eyes, shed crocodile tears over the slaves and refuse to take slave-grown sugar in return?[10]

What dominated the situation was the importance of Brazil. The industrialists emphasized its gigantic resources, which might be developed to the great and lasting advantage of Britain.[11]

---

3. Ibid., pages 31–33. Lord John Russell, May 7, 1841.

4. Ibid., page 302. May 12, 1841.

5. Ibid., page 211. H. G. Ward (Sheffield), May 11, 1841.

6. Ibid., page 209.

7. Ibid., pages 190 and 193. Macaulay was Secretary at War. Howick too supported the Government.

8. Ibid., Third Series, Vol. LV, page 82. Mr. Ewart, June 25, 1840. Ewart was now member for Wigan.

9. Ibid., Third Series, Vol. LVIII, page 101. W. Ewart, May 10, 1841.

10. *J. Bright and J. T. Rogers (eds.); Speeches on Questions of public policy by Richard Cobden, M.P.* (London, 1878), pages 91–92. All slave-grown produce, said Grote, the member for London, must be prohibited if they wished to be consistent and to "take their stand upon the dignity of a moral and conscientious scruple." *Parl. Deb.*, Third Series, Vol. LVIII, page 114. May 10, 1841.

11. *Parl. Deb.*, Third Series, Vol. LVIII, page 100. Ewart argued that coffee was better than strong drink and that the reduction of the duties on coffee and sugar was a moral question of great importance.

Commerce was the great emancipator. It was not by gunboats on the West coast of Africa or by the warfare of duties that the iniquitous slave traffic on which Brazilian economy depended would be put down but by commerce and commercial intercourse.[12] Palmerston forgot his benevolent crotchet. They had given proof, he thought, of their zeal for the suppression of the slave trade, and if they forbade the importation of Brazilian sugar, Brazil would think that they did not really believe that free labour was cheaper than slave.[13] Look at the system of slavery more calmly, said Merivale; it would be found to be a great social evil indeed, but an evil differing in degree and quality, not in kind, from many other social evils which they were compelled to tolerate, such as the great inequality of fortunes, or pauperism, or the overworking of children.[14]

The West Indians were unable to compete with the cheap slave labour of Brazil without the monopoly and protecting duty. As compared with the years 1820–1830, the West Indian supply had decreased by 50,000 tons during the period 1830–1840.[15] Ten millions had been paid to the planters since 1833 in the form of a higher price for their produce.[16] Brazilian sugar, sent to Britain to be refined and then exported to the West Indies, could be sold there cheaper than the local article.[17] It was the opinion of shrewd intelligent merchants trading with the West Indies that if Britain had made a present of the goods sold to the West Indies, in return for a free trade with Brazil and Cuba, she would have actually gained.[18]

The proposal for reducing the duties on foreign sugar had first been made by Ewart in 1840. The Government rejected it, pleading that the colonies were still struggling with the end of the apprenticeship system, and drawing a distinction between slave-grown sugar and slave-grown cotton and tobacco, which did not compete with similar articles raised by free labour in the colonies.[19] But in 1841 the Government itself introduced a similar measure, reducing the duties on corn, timber and sugar, ostensibly to find two millions to cover a deficit caused mainly by penny postage.

The protected interests rallied under the more decent cry of free-grown versus slave-grown sugar. All the ancient prejudices against free trade were arrayed under the flag of humanity.[20] It was not slavery but monopoly which

<hr>

12. Ibid., Third Series, Vol. LV, page 79. W. Ewart, June 25, 1840.
13. Ibid., Third Series, Vol. LVIII, pages 648 and 653. May 18, 1841. Palmerston was Foreign Secretary.
14. H. Merivale: *Lectures on Colonization and Colonies, 1839–1841* (London, 1861), page 303.
15. *Parl. Deb.*, Third Series, Vol. LV, page 77. Ewart, June 25, 1840.
16. Ibid., Third Series, Vol. LVIII, page 177. W. E. Gladstone, May 10, 1841.
17. Ibid., page 5. Earl of Mountcashel, May 7, 1841.
18. Ibid., Third Series, Vol. LXIII, page 1173. Cobden, June 3, 1824.
19. Ibid., Third Series, Vol. LV, pages 586 and 588. Mr. Labouchere, June 25, 1840.
20. Ibid., Third Series, Vol. LVIII, page 304. Vernon Smith, Under Secretary of State for the Colonies, May 12, 1841.

was the question at issue. West Indian planters and abolitionists found themselves in the same camp. An East Indian Director wanted to know whether the doctrines of free trade and political economy were paramount to the dictates of humanity and the holiest obligations of religion.[21] The Gladstones had transferred their interests in the West Indies to the East, and the young W. E. Gladstone, forgetting the glass house in which he had until recently lived, began to throw stones. Were they, for small and paltry pecuniary advantages, to consent to forgo the high title and noble character they had earned before the whole world? Were they dragging every inconsistency into the light for the purpose of using it as a plea for further and more monstrous inconsistency, or in order to substitute a uniformity in wrong for an inconsistent acknowledgment of what was right?[22] But what was the world to think of an opposition headed by the member for the greatest mart of slave produce in the world and seconded by an East Indian Director, whose friends spoke of devoting their energies to the abolition of slavery in British India?[23] Those very men who were loudest in their appeals against slave-grown sugar had bonded warehouses in London and Liverpool and sent that sugar to Russia, China, Turkey and Egypt.[24]

The protected interests were at the time too strong. The Government's proposal was rejected and the Government itself defeated at the ensuing election. For the protectionists, however, it was a Pyrrhic victory. Peel repealed the Corn Laws, and in the same year Russell, who replaced him as Prime Minister, introduced a plan for the equalization of the sugar duties in five years. The West Indians, though saying they would ne'er consent, consented, the bribe being East Indian immigration. As well might the Government have repealed the Emancipation Act.[25] When the news reached Havannah, the city was illuminated, and the Brazilian importation of Negroes rose from 20,000, in 1845 to 50,000 in 1846.

The great free trade revolution was complete. Magnanimity in politics was not then the truest wisdom, and a free trade Empire and humanitarian minds went ill together. The stage was set for the still greater inconsistency of 1860, when Lancashire's dependence on the slave-grown cotton of the United States nearly induced Gladstone to recognise the South and led Cobden to regret that the Negro's freedom was to be purchased at the cost of so much white men's blood and women's tears.

---

21. Ibid., page 68, Mr. Hogg, May 7, 1841.
22. Ibid., pages 167 and 169, May 10, 1841.
23. Ibid., page 591. Mr. Villiers, May 18, 1841.
24. *Speeches of Cobden*, page 43. Oct 13, 1843.
25. *Parl. Deb.*, Third Series, Vol. LV, page 95. O'Connell. June 25, 1840.

Appendix One:
The "Influential Men"

Clarkson records two meetings of these "influential men." At the first, at the house of Wilberforce, those present included the Hon. John Villiers, Sir Charles Middleton, Sir Richard Hill, Granville Sharp and Ramsay.[1] At the second meeting, at the house of Bennet Langton, friend of Johnson, the party consisted of Wilberforce, Sir Charles Middleton, Hawkins Browne, Windham, Sir Joshua Reynolds and Boswell.[2]

The books of the East India Company,[3] together with a list of the subscribers to the Abolition Committee,[4] show the following details:—

Sir Charles Middleton—He was the patron of Ramsay.[5] In later years, in the unseemly squabble which arose as to whether Clarkson or Wilberforce deserved the credit of being the first to sponsor the cause of the Africans, Lady Middleton claimed that the credit was due rather to her. Middleton was present at the two meetings recorded by Clarkson. Among the subscribers to the

---

1. *Clarkson; History*, page 159. It was at this meeting that Clarkson introduced the practice of reading papers, and his first paper, according to his own statement, contained "observations as well on the impolicy as on the wickedness of the trade." Ibid., page 159.

2. Ibid., page 160.

3. *East India Company Subscription Journals to £800,000 additional stock*, July 1786; *East India Company Stock Ledgers*, 1783–1791, 1791–1796.

4. *List of the Society established in 1787 for effecting the Abolition of the Slave Trade.*

5. B.T. 6/12. Ramsay's letter to the Committee of Privy Council gave Sir Charles Middleton's address, June 9, 1788. As comptroller of the navy, Middleton gave Clarkson "permission to board every ship of war in ordinary in England." *History*, p. 408.

Abolition Committee was Lady Middleton who subscribed two guineas, and the Committee received, through Lady Middleton, the anonymous gift of £10. Middleton's interest in the Africans was so great that he was a member of the Association formed in 1790 for promoting the discovery of the interior parts of Africa, and was a Director of the Sierra Leone Company. In 1786 he subscribed £1,000 to the vast quantity of stock issued by the East India Company. Purchases at various times gave him a balance in 1791 of £7,500, which was increased by April, 1796 to £9,000.

Hon. John Charles Villiers—At the time when he was present at the meeting at Wilberforce's house, he already owned more than £600 worth of East India stock. The balance to his credit in July, 1791, was £1,230, and heavy buying between 1791 and 1793 gave him in 1796 a balance of £6,995.

Isaac Hawkins Browne—Present at Clarkson's second meeting. At the time when he was subscribing two guineas to further the cause of abolition, he had a balance in the East India Company's ledgers of £800, which remained unchanged up to 1796.

The Thornton Family—The Thorntons formed part of that sect known to history as the "Clapham Sect," famed for its philanthropy. Henry Thornton, one of the substantial bankers of England,[6] gave away before his marriage six-sevenths of his annual profits of about £10,000 a year, and after marriage one-third, and paid a graduated income tax though he was not required to do so.[7] The four Thorntons, John, Samuel, Henry, Robert, all M.P.'s, between them subscribed eleven guineas to the Abolition Committee at its institution. They were all ardent abolitionists. It was Henry Thornton, Chairman of the Sierra Leone Company, whose bill to protect Sierra Leone from the horrors of the slave trade was thrown out in 1799, and who had long ago "called upon all those to whom the character of a British merchant was dear, to come forward and rescue that respectable name from disgrace, by putting an end to a system of barbarity, rapine and murder."[8] Henry Thornton at his death in 1791 left £2,000 worth of stock to each of the others, which gave them all large balances: Henry, £3,000; Robert, £4,000; Samuel, £3,000. By 1796 Robert's balance had decreased to £2,000 and Samuel's to £1,225. One

---

6. *Wilberforce to Hannah More*—"I have a rich banker in London, Mr. H. Thornton, whom I cannot oblige so much as by drawing on him for purposes like these." *Life of Wilberforce*, Vol. I, page 247.

7. *Klingberg, op. cit.*, page 107.

8. *Parl. Hist.*, Vol. XXIX, page 1080. April 2, 1792.

of the Thorntons supported the motion at the East India House debate in 1793 on the cultivation of sugar in the East Indies.

Sir Herbert Mackintosh—Banker to the Abolition Committee, who had subscribed £21 to the Committee, had been one of those to subscribe to the additional stock issued by the East India Company in 1786. He subscribed £500; his balance in 1796 amounted to £1,000.

Paul le Mesurier, M.P., Merchant, Alderman of the City of London—a Member of the Association for discovering the interior parts of Africa, the subscriber of three guineas to the Abolition Committee, he represented that section of the city, which was responsible for that deviation of which Clarkson wrote that "though she was drawn the other way by the cries of commercial interest, (she) made a sacrifice to humanity and justice."[9] A sub-committee of the Abolition Committee, appointed to wait "on Alderman Le Mesurier and other members of that Court and likewise on several of the Common Council," were given "every reasonable encouragement to hope that a petition will be obtained from the City of London."[10] We have already seen Le Mesurier's humble quota in the territories of the East India Company. In 1786 he had subscribed £1,000 to the East India Company's additional issue, and had bought £4,000 on behalf of other people, £2,500 of which was for relatives. The balance to his account in 1796 was £3,500; his relative John had £2,000. Le Mesurier is representative of the London merchant of his age: the commercial orientation of the future was towards the East.

William Wyndham Grenville—As has been stated in another place, Grenville was present on the occasion when Pitt persuaded Wilberforce to introduce a motion against the slave trade. Grenville's elevation to the peerage in 1790 was, as Pitt confessed to Wilberforce, to counteract the influence of the solid anti-abolitionist bloc in the House of Lords.[11] In January, 1791, Grenville made his first purchase of stock which was becoming exceedingly popular, to the amount of £584.7.4. Other purchases in the same year brought his stock by October to over £2,000, but by July, 1792, he began to dispose of his shares and in July, 1795, he sold the remaining £800 he still had.

George Grenville, Marquis of Buckingham—Grenville's brother also began his purchases in 1791, in August. They extended steadily over a long period, up

---

9. *Clarkson: History*, page 282.
10. *Abolition Committee's Proceedings*, Add. Mss, 21254, folio 27. Jan. 15, 1788.
11. *Life of Wilberforce*, Vol. I, pages 284–285.

to November, 1795, and the balance to his credit in April, 1796 amounted to £2,664.11.0d.

It is unnecessary to deal much more in detail with this aspect of the question. For instance, it was not unnatural that Randle Jackson, ardent advocate of the importation of East India sugar, should be found subscribing £500 in 1786, and should have a balance in 1796 of £2,305; that Jackson Barwis, Chairman of that public meeting set up in 1792 to investigate the high price of sugar, who considered the East the natural resource in view of the difficulties of the West, should have £2,000 to his credit in 1796; that the noble Lord Kinnaird, who has already been quoted with reference to the East India House debate of 1793, a balance of £5,000; and that John Prinsep, to whom several tracts on the necessity of importing East India sugar has been attributed, should as early as 1783 be possessed of £3,000 worth of East India stock. Samuel Hoare, Treasurer of the Abolition Committee, was a banker dealing heavily in East India stock; John Harman, merchant of the Old Jewry, who had subscribed two guineas to the Abolition Committee, was also heavily involved in the East India Company; so were Robert Barclay and family, who subscribed generously to the Abolition Committee.

The original twelve members of the Abolition Committee were all merchants. Throughout the abolition movement commercial considerations played their part. One instance will suffice. Clarkson wished to make Wedgwood a proprietor of the Sierra Leone Company. "The obstacle," he wrote, "has been this: The present Proprietors, that is, a majority of them, view the institution in so favourable a light in point of profit, that they wish to keep the whole to themselves. . . . There is no chance whatever . . . that any new member will come in as an additional one for perhaps two years to come for if £100,000 is wanted, the present Proprietors will raise it." Clarkson managed to prevail upon a Mr. Hamilton to transfer his single share to Wedgwood, and Wedgwood, now admitted to the charmed circle, had the option of increasing his share to the maximum permitted, ten.[12] In fairness to Clarkson it must be added that, in his case at least, commercial gain was subordinate to his detestation of the slave trade. In 1795 the drain upon his scanty resources made by his activities on behalf of the Negroes compelled him to sell out some of his shares. He wrote to Wedgwood asking the latter if he knew of any one willing to purchase two shares. He added: "I must beg

---

12. *The Correspondence of Josiah Wedgwood*, pages 167–168. Clarkson to Wedgwood, Aug. 25, 1791.

leave, however, to say that I should not chuse to permit anyone to become a purchaser, who would not be better pleased with the good resulting to Africa than from great commercial profits to himself: not that the latter may not be expected, but in case of a disappointment, I should wish his mind to be made easy by the assurance that he has been instrumental in introducing light and happiness into a country, where the mind was kept in darkness and the body nourished only for European chains."[13]

---

13. Ibid., pages 215–216. June 17, 1793. In Clarkson we see the humanitarianism of the age at its best.

Appendix Two:
Ramsay as an Authority

The authenticity of Ramsay's statements has been called in question. Ramsay himself must have anticipated the charge. "There are few things on which I have more frequently thought," he once confessed.[1] "The reader has here," he wrote in the preface to one of his tracts, "the remarks of about 20 years' experience in the West Indies, and above 14 years' particular application to the subject."[2] He enlarged on this point in a letter to the Privy Council examining the slave trade. "For the period for which I speak, no man has been in equally favorable circumstances with myself for collecting and I trust candidly giving in every possible information respecting the state of slaves in the sugar colonies. I was put early by circumstances on a particular consideration of the subject of slavery, and the opposition I have met with has forced me to sift every circumstance concerning it."[3] In a letter to Wilberforce in 1787, Ramsay wrote, "I am sure of the principles of the business. Nor do I see any possible objection which I have had time to consider. The only use I can be of in the business is as a pioneer to remove obstacles: use me in this way and I shall be happy."[4]

Wilberforce was not satisfied merely with Ramsay's activity and diligence;[5] in a letter to Eden he stated that he had "made inquiries amongst the best

---

1. *Ramsay: Ms. Vol.*, folio I(v) To Jolliffe, Jan. 16, 1785.
2. *Ramsay: Essay on the treatment and conversion of slaves in the British Sugar Colonies*, page vii.
3. B.T. 6/12. June 9, 1788.
4. *Ramsay: Ms. Vol.*, folio 28. Dec. 27, 1787.
5. *Life of Wilberforce*, Vol. I, pages 208–209. "How active and diligent he is!" Diary, March 9, 1789.

informed and most disinterested men respecting the truth of Ramsay's assertions; and they say that his account is substantially true, tho' perhaps some particulars may be a little exaggerated."[6]

Not only contemporaries, even modern historians accept Ramsay. "As a member of the navy," writes an American historian, and as a rector in the islands he had had much practical experience with slavery. He presented nearly all the arguments, used against the slave trade and slavery in 1784 and succeeding years."[7]

Ramsay, in fact, was one of the earliest abolitionists. His arguments are in the main substantiated by other accounts, official and unofficial; and the ruthlessness with which his opponents pursued him—"Ramsay is dead," boasted Molyneux proudly to his natural son, "I have killed him"—is one more proof of the fact that contemporaries are capable judges of their own problems.

---

6. *Auckland Papers*, Add. Mss. 34427, folios 122(v)–123. Nov. 23, 1787.
7. *Klingberg, op. cit.*, pages 60–61.

Appendix Three:
Select Documents Illustrating
the Inter-Colonial Slave Trade

(a) This trade was carried on under the guise of domestic servants in attendance on their masters, and with the connivance of officials and the support of public opinion in the colonies.

C.O. 1111/25. Murray to Bathurst, March 28, 1818.

It was not possible for me to suppose that a violation of the abolition laws could have been countenanced by the acts of all the Governors, Crown Lawyers and Collectors throughout the West Indies or that it could have been so generally practiced and so openly too in the face of the Flag and other officers of His Majesty's squadron in these seas without interruption for so many years.

C.O. 28/102. Extract of a letter to the Secretary of the Anti-Slavery Society, Nov. 30, 1827, and sent by him to Huskisson as "from a person of great respectability."

The removal of the slaves from the island is effected by an evasion, through perjury and fraud, of that provision of the Slave Trade Consolidated Act which allows persons leaving the island to take with them one or more (as it may be) *domestic* slaves for the purpose of attending them on the voyage. Hundreds have been shipped off during the course of the present year; and the trade is rapidly increasing in magnitude. . . . The fact is that our slave population here is, unhappily for the *cause of slavery*, beginning to increase, and this trade is found to be a convenient mode of removing any apprehensions which may be entertained of the consequences of any considerable surplus of slave labour beyond the demand for it.

C.O. 28/103. Att. Gen. to Gov. Lyon, June 25, 1829.

I have always been of opinion that the discretion vested in the Custom House of clearing out slaves as domestics was to be guided, not by any general rule admitting a certain number of domestics to be taken away by each individual applying for leave; but with reference to the circumstance and condition in life, on the state of health of the applicant, and by the sort of service which an applicant might consequently require from domestics. Such could not have been the guide to their discretion used by the Custom House officers; for with such a guide they never could conceive that Mr. Franklyn, a man in very indigent circumstances, or Mr. Franklyn and all his family could require the attendance of fourteen slaves, consisting of five adults, one of whom was a carpenter, and the other nine children, on board a vessel of twenty-two tons, scarcely large enough to carry so many persons as she had on board in comfort and decency.
The extent to which the practice of carrying away slaves from this island to Trinidad has notoriously existed calls for some example to vindicate the laws and shews the necessity of the enquiry which Your Excellency has directed to be made into the present cases.

Plantations, Jamaica, 1829–1830 (Custom House). No.556—Proceedings under the Abolition Laws.
Horace Twiss to Lords Commissioners of Customs, Nov. 20, 1830. (On report from Commissioners of Customs to Lords of Treasury laid before Secretary Sir G. Murray.)

Assuming the fact to be correctly stated, that Mr. James Martin* was in such a state of illness as to have been incapable of acting for himself and that the removal of his slave from Jamaica was not effected by Mr. Martin but by

---

* Martin was Speaker of the House Assembly.

his friends, and that they were ignorant of the law which requires that the certificate of registry shall be on board and the name and occupation of the slave endorsed in the clearance, a case would certainly be made out of great hardship. Still it would remain to enquire whether the master of the vessel laboured under the same ignorance, for if he was acquainted with the law, not only was his own conduct indefensible, but the defence made for the friends of Mr. Martin becomes much more open to suspicion. With respect to the case of Mr. Capon it was merely stated that his slave was taken on board "under similar circumstances, evidently without any improper intention of violating the laws, but merely from ignorance." It is not stated in what respect the circumstances of the two cases were similar. The language of the officers of the customs seems to imply that this gentlemen was at least a voluntary agent in the transaction, and the fact of his having laboured under sickness of any kind is not asserted. . . .

Whatever may be the claims of Messrs. Martin and Capon to an indulgent consideration in this case, Sir G. Murray is of opinion that the utmost relief which can be afforded is to forego any prosecution for the penalties, but in the case of Mr. Capon, Sir G. Murray at present sees no reason even for that lenity, unless it be the fact that he, like Mr. Martin, was disabled by illness from any active interference in the removal of his slave. Mr. Capon is mentioned as a member of the House of Assembly at Jamaica and if a Gentleman in that situation may be relieved from the penalties of the law on the simple ground of ignorance, it is difficult to suppose any case in which the same excuse could be pleaded in vain.

Plantations, Jamaica, 1822–1823 (Custom House). No. 278. Proceedings: "Mary Jane" (Illegal importation of a Negro) Att. Gen. to Commissioners of Customs, Sept. 6, 1823.

In proceedings under the Abolition Laws any relaxation or dispensation by any ordinary authority is so likely to be misunderstood and there are such important public interests at stake in the undeviating strictness with which offences against those laws should be prosecuted by the Colonial authorities that I have ever considered that any partial or personal inconvenience or injury with which a rigorous execution of them might in some few instances operate, was not for a moment to be compared with the great public objects which will be attained by it.

C.O. 28/102. Stephen to Hay (n.d.)

The general rule of law I suppose to be that no person may be removed as a domestic Slave except by his owner,—nor unless he be in attendance upon the owner's person—nor unless the owner be a domiciled inhabitant of the colony from which the removal is to take place—nor unless the real motive of the party effecting the removal be to avail himself of the domestic services of the slave about his own person. Upon the failure of any one of these consideration, as I apprehend, the removal is illegal, and the parties concerned in it are felons. . . .

The fact obviously is that on the present occasion the Custom House Officers are deterred full as much by the unpopularity, as by the inherent difficulty of the task committed to them.

Plantations, Trinidad, 1830–1831 (Custom House). No. 162—Conviction under Abolition Laws. Collector, Port-of-Spain, to Commissioners of Customs, London, March 9, 1831.

Some decisive example should be made at once to put a stop to the practice of bringing slaves here under the character of domestics for the purpose of gain by traffic.

C.O. 295/90. Stephen to Howick, Jan 15, 1831.

The case plainly is, that the execution of the laws for the abolition of the slave trade is so invidious and disagreeable a task that the subordinate officers are constantly seeking assistance, and endeavouring to escape responsibility and reproach by references to their superiors in England. The bounties to be obtained by a successful prosecution do not afford any adequate motive for encountering so much obloquy unless the number of slaves to be condemned is very considerable. Hence it has arisen that the Government have virtually directed almost each prosecution which has taken place, of course making themselves responsible for the expenses. With the resources of the state to defray the costs, the Crown lawyers in the colonies have entered with all imaginable zeal upon these prosecutions, and the charges made by them and by every single person connected with the judicial proceedings have been so extravagant as in many cases to render it necessary to dishonour the bills drawn on account of them. Thus while on the one hand the seizing officers are disinclined to perform their duty, there arises on the other hand a disinclination on the part of His Majesty's Government to enforce its performance on account of the very heavy charge which such prosecutions bring with them.

(See also C.O. 295/81, July 3, 1829, for charges of connivance at violation of the Abolition Laws against the Attorney General and Collector of Customs in Trinidad, made by Mr. Hobson, a Judge and former speaker of the Assembly in Dominica (C.O. 295/86, Stephen to Howick, Dec. 16, 1830—who was prosecuted for the fraudulent importation of nine slaves into Trinidad.)

(b) Specious arguments were used to justify this slave trade. The conditions prevailing in the crown colonies were superior to those in the legislative colonies, and the removal of slaves from the older islands was defended on the ground of humanity and in the interest of the well-being of the Negroes.

C.O. 111/25. Murray to Bathurst, March 28, 1818.

Humanity equity and perhaps policy unite to recommend the transfer of slaves from most of the West India Islands to this fertile and abundant region, happily placed without the track of hurricanes.

C.O. 111/27. Murray to Bathurst, April 27, 1819.

The superiority of the soil in this country, its abundance of animal and vegetable provisions, and the convenience of water communications for conveying the products of the earth to the place of manufacture and thence to that of shipping enables the proprietors to give much higher prices for labourers than can be afforded by those of the other colonies not possessing these advantages—this excited the cupidity of adventurers to carry on a traffic in slaves some by means of licences and regular importations, others possessed of less capital and perhaps less principle masked their minor transactions under the pretended introduction of domestic servants—this practice

was at first easily detected, but the slaves themselves, unless when local at-
tachments interfere, are so desirous of being admitted into the colony that
they soon lent themselves to corroborate any fabricated tale which might
facilitate their introduction, thus rendering the discovery difficult, although
the unfortunate subjects of these speculations were frequently intended for
immediate sale like beasts of burden.

C.O. 111/66. Charles Shand to Huskisson, March 29, 1828.

In transmitting you the memorial of the West India association here relative to the proposed alteration of the duties and bounties on sugar, I avail
myself of the opportunity to endeavour to draw to your consideration, as the
official conservator of the British Colonial interest, the advantage which
would accrue to the negro population themselves, to their owners and also
to the Government by permitting the removal of the greatly redundant negro
population from many of the old islands to Demerary (being the only colony
in the West Indies possessed by Great Britain which can at all cope with the
foreign colonies) which now languishes for want of sufficient population to
bring its capabilities fairly into action, and it seems unreasonable to encourage in the Brazils, by the introduction of *new* Slaves, a cultivation which
could as easily and more profitably for British interests be extended to Demerary by the transfer of negroes, already slaves, and to be benefited by the
transfer, while it is a notorious fact that the French and Dutch planters get
their wants fully supplied by smuggling, at 1/5th in Demerary. . . .

Formerly when the British West India Islands were prosperous, the planters were induced to push their cultivation to the uttermost, the consequence
of which has been that many of them are now greatly overpeopled and overcleared, so much so as to be incapable (even were the whole of the island to
be applied to the raising of food only) to feed their population and are forced
to depend on foreign importations.

This is strongly exemplified in Antigua, where from being overcleared, its
climate has become so arrid that in no year for the last thirty has it produced
a sufficient supply of food for its redundant population . . . and to such distress have the planters often been reduced to obtain provisions, that many of
them have pawned their slaves to raise the means to buy them food, and in
1822 even this expedient failed them and Government was obliged to give
them a loan to save them from starvation, and yet on this occasionally desert

spot the law compel is a greater population to remain than it is capable to support, while their better interests call them elsewhere. These among many other reasons induce me to press most earnestly on your consideration not only the sound policy but also the humanity of permitting the free emigration of the British Negro population from one British colony to another— but if an unrestricted removal cannot be conceded, let a discretionary power be vested in Government to permit it where a clear case of advantage to the Negroes themselves can be made manifest.

C.O. 295/62. Gov. Woodford's views on the removal of slaves to Trinidad, Feb. 7, 1824.

When the advantage of these essential objects which the rich virgin soil lands in Trinidad almost exclusively afford are compared with the drawbacks arising from the sterile and exhausted soil of the Old Islands which daily becomes more and more incapable of bringing to maturity these kinds of food, and therefore oblige the planter to purchase (sometimes at an extravagant price) supplies of dry provisions, viz. flour, cornmeal or beans (the produce of the United States and consequently on that country so far dependent) affording a much less nutritious as well as a less welcome sustenance to the negro than the provisions grown in this country, and occasionally not to be procured at all, the removal of both Proprietor and Slave would appear to be as advantageous to the interest of the one as it is desirable to that comfort which is so fairly due to the other. . . .

It will therefore appear that from local advantages and facility of cultivation the operations of field labor are much lighter to the laborer in Trinidad than they are in the other islands; and the quantity of disposeable land will for very many years to come permit the assignment of a liberal grant to all manumitted slaves to enable them to acquire by honest industry a comfortable livelihood at the same time that the laws do not in any manner restrict the attainment of property by persons whatever may be their condition or origin.

(For similar views see: C.O. 295/65. Woodford to Bathurst, April 22, 1825; C.O. 295/76. Woodford to Horton, July 9, 1827; C.O. 295/78. Farquharson to Bathurst, Oct. 12, 1828; Ibid., Attorney General's views, Oct 12, 1828; Ibid., Protector of Slaves' views, Oct 22, 1828; C.O. 28/102. E. Bowell to Murray, Aug 25, 1828, praying for permission to remove 300 Slaves from

Barbados to Trinidad. See also Ibid., for views of the Council in Barbados on Bowell's application, in Pres. Skeete's of Dec. 2, 1828.)

C.O. 295/78. Att. Gen.'s views on removal of slaves, Oct 12, 1828.

From the objection of the Colonial Legislatures to the introduction of the Trinidad Slave Code it might be further urged in favour of the removal that as the order in council cannot go to the slaves, the slave might be permitted to come to the order in council in Trinidad.

C.O. 295/79. J. Marryat to Murray, Aug. 19, 1828.

Assuming that the provisions of the order in council have the desired effect of meliorating the condition of the slave population and that compulsory manumission enables the slave to accomplish what he finds impracticable in the old colonies, namely to purchase his freedom, it appears inconsistent to oppose the removal of slaves from a colony where these orders are not in force to Trinidad where they are in full operation.

C.O. 295/79. Stephen to Twiss, Oct 17, 1828.

. . . Of 266 domestics imported during the year 1827 from the single island of Barbados, 204 . . . have changed their owners by the end of that year, and 81 . . . within the same short time, have ceased to be domestics. . . .

To my own mind there appears very strong ground for suspecting that the great comparative value of slaves in Trinidad has tempted many persons to make fraudulent importations from Barbados, by attributing the character of domestics to slaves whom it was never intended really to employ in that capacity.

(c) The planters professed their willingness to accede to any conditions which Government chose to insist on, if the removal of slaves were permitted. This benevolence was meant only to hoodwink the public.

C.O. 295/80. Grant to Murray, May 26, 1829.

I may now premise as a natural matter of fact that whatever conditions may be made in favour of the imported slaves the proprietor or other possessor will endeavour to counteract or nullify them by any and every means which may be left in his power. This he will be disposed to do from the impression that every advantage given to the slave will be to him, the proprietor, a proportionable loss, as also from a feeling of jealousy that the slave can be benefited otherwise than through his (the proprietor's) instrumentality; therefore, if progressive freedom is the object it will be necessary to open that sort of path to it which proprietors or other possessors of slaves will not have it in their power to obstruct. If this is done in a decided and incontrovertible manner, the Colonists will cease all attempts to throw obstacles in the way, and as a matter of course, and a matter of interest they will turn their attention to the consideration of the best means how to dispose the minds of persons of African origin to spontaneous and willing habits of industry.

C.O. 295/80. Grant to Murray, June 1, 1829.

. . . It must ever be kept in view that proprietors will never, in sincerity of disposition and feeling give their minds to any measure truly leading to freedom, however confident they might be that the measure would be largely for their advantages, therefore every proposal that may come from any of them, and every act they do or attempt, should be jealously and fastidiously looked into, however feasible and favourable it may at first appear.

C.O. 295/81. Grant to Murray, July 1, 1829.

. . . It might be conditional that all the children of the imported should be free, if born after importation of the mother; on this, which seems to be a general impression, the reasoning and speculative intention appears to be to import only elderly persons and no females but of an age probably past child bearing. I myself heard a principal proprietor here observe that, if Government conditioned that all the children alluded to should be free immediately at their birth, there would comparatively be but few births and of these very few would come to maturity—alluding here to the probability that as the proprietors would have no interest in the progeny, the mothers would not be sufficiently spared. However horrid the idea which this conveys I am most decidedly of opinion that it is sufficiently to be dreaded that it should not be lost sight of.

Bibliography

Primary Sources (Mss.)

A. Public Record Office

Colonial Office Papers: a vast collection of documents which are indispensable for any study of the period. It would have been a herculean task to consult them all, but the Jamaica records for 1787 to 1796 have been consulted not only for the reaction of the most important British colony to the agitation for abolition but for the early ne-gotiations with the St. Domingo planters and the attempted conquest of the island. For Part II of this thesis more than 250 volumes have been consulted, embracing Jamaica and Barbados, the two most important of the older islands, and Trinidad and Demerara, of the newer acquisitions.

Chatham Papers: many letters and documents relating to the British West Indies, St. Domingo, India and France. As Pitt was Prime Minister for all but a brief period from 1784 until his death in 1806 these papers are of cardinal importance.

Foreign Office Papers.

Board of Trade Papers: much scattered information, some of great importance.

Customs Records: vital statistics for a study of the decline of the West Indian colonies and the importance of emancipation to British industrialists.

B. British Museum

Liverpool Papers: a number of very valuable letters and memoranda relating to the British and French colonies, the slave trade, the preliminary negotiations with the

French planters, and Hawkesbury's views on the introduction of West India sugar. Hawkesbury was the most powerful champion of the West Indian interest in Britain, and as President of the Board of Trade wielded great power. The correspondence of the second Earl of Liverpool includes some very valuable letters.

Minute Books of the Committee for the Abolition of the Slave Trade: much valuable information for a study of the abolition movement.

Auckland Papers: five very valuable letters of Wilberforce.

Melville Papers.

Clarkson Papers.

Windham Papers.

Huskisson Papers: a few letters relating to the emancipation movement which are very useful.

C. Miscellaneous
J. Ramsay, Manuscript Volume in his own hand (Rhodes House): many letters and papers of great significance for a study of the abolition movement.

Sugar, Various Mss. (in my possession.)

Stock Ledgers of the East India Company (Bank of England Record Office): these afford incontrovertible proof of some of the interested motives behind the abolition movement.

Custom House Records (Custom House): these comprise a heterogeneous collection of documents which illustrate the Intercolonial Slave Trade.

Primary Sources (Printed)

The Manuscripts of J. B. Fortescue Esq., preserved at Dropmore.

The Manuscripts of Earl Bathurst.

Some Official Correspondence of George Canning.

Despatches, Correspondence and Memoranda of Field Marshal Arthur Duke of Wellington.

Correspondence, Despatches and other Papers of Viscount Castlereagh.

Journal and Correspondence of William, Lord Auckland.

These, representing the correspondence of six of the leading statesmen in the period 1787–1830, Grenville, Auckland, Canning, Bathurst, Castlereagh, Wellington, are very important.

The parliamentary debates are found in the *Parliamentary History* and the *Parliamentary Debates*. They are indispensable.

Secondary Sources

The following parliamentary publications are very important.

(1) *Report of the Lords of the Committee of the Privy Council for all matters relating to Trade and Foreign Plantations, 1788.*

(2) *Report on the Commercial State of the West India Colonies, 1807.*

(3) *Correspondence with British Commissioners and Foreign Powers relative to the Slave Trade, 1823–1825.*

(4) *Statements, Calculations and Explanations submitted to the Board of Trade relating to the Commercial, Financial and Political State of the British West India Colonies, since 19th May 1830.*

(5) *Select Committee appointed to inquire into the Commercial state of the West India Colonies, 1831–1832.*

The contemporary pamphlets are legion. They are scattered in the British Museum, the India Office, the Anti-Slavery Society and Rhodes House, and are of more or less importance.

L. J. Ragatz's monumental Guide for the study of British Caribbean History, 1763–1834, makes a special bibliography unnecessary. But four books deserve to be specially recommended:

(1) *L. J. Ragatz: The Fall of the Planter Class in the British Caribbean* (New York, 1928).

This work is a mine of information. It is also an excellent piece of research, and is easily the best work on the period.

(2) *W. L. Burn: Emancipation and Apprenticeship in the British West Indies* (London, 1937).

The first three chapters of this work deal with emancipation. Before 1833 Burn has made very little use of the manuscript material, but this is none the less a scholarly and valuable work, vastly superior to the mediocre studies of Klingberg and Mathieson.

(3) E. L. Griggs: *Thomas Clarkson, the Friend of Slaves* (London, 1936).

This is another work of great value. It is based on the voluminous Clarkson papers scattered all over the globe.

(4) Dr. *Franz Hochstetter: Die wirtschaftlichen und politischen Motive für die Abschaffung des britischen Sklavenhandels in Jahre 1806–1807.* (Leipzig, 1905).

This little book, though based on secondary authorities, is very well argued and does not merit the neglect which has befallen it. The author has used his authorities well and it deserves to be translated.

Index

Eric Williams was the most prominent intellectual from the English-speaking Caribbean in the twentieth century. He was a leader of West Indian independence and the prime minister of Trinidad and Tobago from 1955 to 1981. His groundbreaking book, *Capitalism and Slavery*, was first published in 1944 and most recently reissued in 1994.

Dale W. Tomich is professor emeritus of sociology at Binghamton University, State University of New York. He is the author of *Through the Prism of Slavery: Labor, Capital, and World Economy* (2004) and numerous articles on Atlantic slavery and on the world economy.

William Darity Jr. is Samuel DuBois Cook Distinguished Professor of Public Policy, professor of African and African American studies, and professor of economics at Duke University.

Made in the USA
Middletown, DE
31 October 2020

23114783R00165